TWENTIETH CENTURY VIEWS

The aim of this series is to present the best in contemporary critical opinion on major authors, providing a twentieth century perspective on their changing status in an era of profound revaluation.

Maynard Mack, *Series Editor*
Yale University

WORDSWORTH

WORDSWORTH

A COLLECTION OF CRITICAL ESSAYS

Edited by
M. H. Abrams

St. Mary Regional High School
Library
310 Augusta Street
South Amboy, New Jersey 08879

Prentice-Hall, Inc.  *Englewood Cliffs, N.J.*

Library of Congress Cataloging in Publication Data

ABRAMS, MEYER HOWARD, comp.
  Wordsworth: a collection of critical essays.

   (Twentieth century views)   (A Spectrum Book)
   Bibliography: p.
   1. Wordsworth, William, 1770–1850. I. Title.
PR5888.A27   821'.7   72-4888
ISBN 0-13-965079-7
ISBN 0-13-965061-X (pbk.)

Quotations from *Coleridge on Imagination*, by I. A. Richards, W. W. Norton & Company, Inc., New York, N.Y., 1950, are reprinted with the permission of the publisher.

© 1972 by Prentice-Hall, Inc., Englewood Cliffs, New Jersey. A SPECTRUM BOOK. All rights reserved. No part of this book may be reproduced in any form or by any means without permission in writing from the publisher. Printed in the United States of America.

10 9 8 7 6 5 4 3 2

PRENTICE-HALL INTERNATIONAL, INC. (*London*)
PRENTICE-HALL OF AUSTRALIA PTY. LTD. (*Sydney*)
PRENTICE-HALL OF CANADA, LTD. (*Toronto*)
PRENTICE-HALL OF INDIA PRIVATE LIMITED (*New Delhi*)
PRENTICE-HALL OF JAPAN, INC. (*Tokyo*)

To Harold Bloom

Contents

Introduction: Two Roads to Wordsworth
by M. H. Abrams ... 1

I. The Poet Wordsworth

Wordsworth
by A. C. Bradley ... 13

Wordsworth and the Revolt against Abstractions
by A. N. Whitehead ... 22

The Isolation of the Human Mind
by David Perkins ... 28

Some Characteristics of Wordsworth's Style
by David Ferry ... 35

Wordsworth and the Iron Time
by Lionel Trilling ... 45

II. *Lyrical Ballads* and Early Poems

The Contemporaneity of the *Lyrical Ballads*
by Robert Mayo ... 67

"The Thorn": Wordsworth's Dramatic Monologue
by Stephen Maxfield Parrish ... 75

"The Idiot Boy": Wordsworth's Narrative and Dramatic Voices
by John F. Danby ... 85

The Myth of Memory and Natural Man
    by Harold Bloom   95

  Wordsworth and the Tears of Adam
    by Neil Hertz   107

  The Ruined Cottage as Tragic Narrative
    by Jonathan Wordsworth   123

III. *The Prelude*

  Intentional Structure of the Romantic Image
    by Paul de Man   133

  The Via Naturaliter Negativa
    by Geoffrey H. Hartman   145

  The Prelude and *The Recluse*: Wordsworth's Long
  Journey Home
    by M. H. Abrams   156

IV. The Later Poems

  Wordsworth and the Paradox of the Imagination
    by Cleanth Brooks   170

  Wordsworth: The Baptised Imagination
    by John Jones   188

  Chronology of Important Dates   205
  Notes on the Editor and Contributors   207
  Selected Bibliography   209
  Index of Titles   213

Introduction:
Two Roads to Wordsworth

by M. H. Abrams

The first critic of Wordsworth's poetry was Wordsworth himself, and in his criticism, as in his poetry, he speaks with two distinct voices. The first voice is that of the "Preface" to *Lyrical Ballads,* in which Wordsworth powerfully applies to his poetry some humanistic values of the European Enlightenment. In his "Preface" the controlling and interrelated norms are the essential, the elementary, the simple, the universal, and the permanent. The great subjects of his poetry, Wordsworth says, are "the essential passions of the heart," "elementary feelings," "the great and simple affections," "the great and universal passions of men," and "characters of which the elements are simple . . . such as exist now, and will probably always exist," as these human qualities interact with "the beautiful and permanent forms of nature." His aim is a poetry written in a "naked and simple" style that is "well adapted to interest mankind permanently." And the poet himself, as "a man speaking to men," both affirms and effects the primal human values: the joy of life, the dignity of life and of its elemental moving force, the pleasure principle, and the primacy of the universal connective, love. The poet "rejoices more than other men in the spirit of life" both within him and without, pays homage "to the grand elementary principle of pleasure, by which he knows, and feels, and lives, and moves," and is "the rock of defense of human nature, carrying everywhere with him relationship and love."

Wordsworth's second critical voice has been far less heeded by his readers. It speaks out in the "Essay, Supplementary to the Preface" of his *Poems* of 1815, and reiterates in sober prose the claims he had made, years before, in the verse "Prospectus" to *The Recluse* (reprinted in his "Preface" to *The Excursion*) and in the opening and closing passages of *The Prelude*: claims that it is his task to confront and find consolation in human suffering—whether the "solitary agonies" of rural life or the "fierce confederate storm / Of sorrow" barricadoed within the walls of cities—since he is a poet who has been singled out "for holy services" in a secular work of man's "redemption." In his "Essay" of 1815, Words-

1

worth addresses himself to explain and justify those aspects of novelty and strangeness in his poetry that have evoked from critics "unremitting hostility, ... slight ..., aversion, ... contempt." He does so by asserting that he, like every "truly original poet," has qualities that are "peculiarly his own," and in specifying his innovations, he does not now take his operative concepts from eighteenth-century humanism, but imports them from theology; that is, he deliberately adapts to poetry the idiom hitherto used by Christian apologists to justify the radical novelty, absurdities, and paradoxes of the Christian mysteries. For Wordsworth claims in this essay that there are "affinities between religion and poetry," "a community of nature," so that poetry shares the distinctive quality of Christianity, which is to confound "the calculating understanding" by its contradictions:

> For when Christianity, the religion of humility, is founded upon the proudest quality of our nature [the imagination], what can be expected but contradictions?

In the "Essay" of 1815, accordingly, Wordsworth does not represent poetry as elemental and simple, but stresses instead its "contradictions" —that is, its radical paradoxicality, its union of antitheses, its fusion of the sensuous and the transcendant, its violation of the customary, and its reversal of status between the highest and lowest. Poetry, for example, imitates the supreme contradiction of the Incarnation itself: it is "etherial and transcendant, yet incapable to sustain her existence without sensuous incarnation." The higher poetry unites the "wisdom of the heart and the grandeur of imagination" and so achieves a "simplicity" that is "Magnificence herself." Wordsworth's own poems manifest "emotions of the pathetic" that are "complex and revolutionary." As for "the sublime"— he is specifically a poet "charged with a new mission to extend its kingdom, and to augment and spread its enjoyments." For as one of the poets who combine the "heroic passions" of pagan antiquity with Christian wisdom he has produced a new synthesis—an "accord of sublimated humanity." And his chief enterprise as a poet is expressed in a Christian paradox—he must cast his readers down in order to raise them up: their spirits "are to be humbled and humanized, in order that they may be purified and exalted."

Wordsworth as primarily the simple, affirmative poet of elementary feelings, essential humanity, and vital joy, and Wordsworth as primarily the complex poet of strangeness, paradox, equivocality, and dark sublimities—these diverse views, adumbrated by Wordsworth himself, were established as persistent alternative ways to the poet by Matthew Arnold and by A. C. Bradley. The cause of Wordsworth's greatness, Arnold said, taking his cue from Wordsworth's "Preface" to *Lyrical Ballads*, "is simple, and may be told quite simply. Wordsworth's poetry is great

Introduction: Two Roads to Wordsworth

because of the extraordinary power" with which he feels and renders and makes us share "the joy offered to us in nature, the joy offered to us in the simple, primary affections and duties." And from the naturalness of his subject and the sincerity of his feeling, his characteristic and matchless style is that of "the most plain, first-hand, almost austere naturalness." [1] Wordsworth's great boon to us in "this iron time," Arnold says in his verses, is that he has restored our lost capacity for spontaneous and uncomplicated responsiveness, "the freshness of the early world." He adds, however, that Wordsworth achieved his "sweet calm" only by the expedient of averting his ken "From half of human fate." [2]

Although Bradley did not publish his great essay on Wordsworth (here reprinted in part) until 1909, thirty years later than Arnold's, he set out explicitly to supplement what he regarded as Arnold's valid but incomplete view of the poet by specifying other qualities without which "Wordsworth is not Wordsworth." His challenge to Arnold's way to Wordsworth is direct and uncompromising: "the road into Wordsworth's mind must be through his strangeness and his paradoxes, and not round them." In pursuing this road Bradley follows the lead, not of Wordsworth's "Preface," but of his vatic poetic pronouncements, which Arnold had noted only to derogate as the style "more properly . . . of eloquent prose." As Bradley's other essays make evident, his critical concepts, and his sensitiveness to negative and paradoxical elements in literature, also owe a great deal to the philosophy of Hegel. As Hegel himself had noted, however, his categories of negation, contradiction, and synthesis are (like Wordsworth's concept of the "contradictions" in the products of the modern poetic imagination) the conceptual equivalents of the paradoxes and the *coincidentia oppositorum* of the Christian mysteries. In the Hegelian cast of his critical concepts, then, Bradley is in broad accord with the spirit of Wordsworth's own "Essay, Supplementary to the Preface" of 1815.

In Bradley's view, that which is most distinctive in Wordsworth's poetry is "peculiar," "audacious," "strange," and Wordsworth's characteristic attitudes are a complex of contraries or contradictions. Although Wordsworth sang of joy and love, "he did not avert his eyes" from anguish or evil, but often represents "a dark world"; and though he undertook to show that suffering and misery can in fact be the conditions of happiness, strength, and glory, he did not pretend that this possibility solved "the riddle of the painful earth"—"the world was to him in the end 'this unintelligible world.'" Wordsworth is "preeminently the poet of solitude," yet "no poet is more emphatically the poet of community."

---

[1] "Wordsworth" (1879), in *Essays in Criticism: Second Series* (London, 1891), pp. 153, 159.
[2] "Memorial Verses" (1850), lines 43, 57; "Stanzas in Memory of the Author of 'Obermann'" (1859), lines 54, 79.

His native bent was not to simplicity, but to "sublimity"; and in this "mystic" or "visionary" strain "there is always traceable a certain hostility to 'sense,'" an intimation of something illimitable, eternal, infinite that is "in some way a denial" of the limited sensible world, "contradicting or abolishing the fixed limits of our habitual view." As Bradley describes the paradoxical qualities of a Wordsworthian spot of time, using a portentous term, "Everything here is natural, but everything is apocalyptic."[3]

Twentieth-century critics of Wordsworth have tended to follow either Arnold's or Bradley's road to the poet, and the diverse approaches have yielded two Wordsworths. One Wordsworth is simple, elemental, forthright, the other is complex, paradoxical, problematic; one is an affirmative poet of life, love, and joy, the other is an equivocal or self-divided poet whose affirmations are implicitly qualified (if not annulled) by a pervasive sense of mortality and an ever-incipient despair of life; one is the great poet of natural man and the world of all of us, the other is a visionary or "mystic" who is ultimately hostile to temporal man and the world of sense and whose profoundest inclinations are toward another world that transcends biological and temporal limitations; one is the Wordsworth of light, the other the Wordsworth of chiaroscuro, or even darkness. Criticism since mid-century continues to manifest, and often to sharpen, this division, although the commentators who take either the one or the other of the old roads to Wordsworth have introduced new critical concepts that make their work seem, in the 1970s, distinctively "modern." I shall try to identify a few of the more conspicuous innovations within both of the traditional perspectives.

I. The Simple Wordsworth

In *The Poet Wordsworth* (1950) Helen Darbishire is an unqualified Arnoldian: Wordsworth is a poet whose motive power was "the depth and force of his feeling for humanity," who vindicated "sense-experience as the foundation of knowledge" and represented "simple men and women who are moved by the great emotions."[4] John F. Danby's poet, in a book published a decade later, is also, as his title asserts, *The Simple Wordsworth*; the innovative element is Danby's view that Wordsworth was an inventive craftsman whose simplicity was an "achieved" simplicity by "an alert and conscious artist," who controls the reader's responses by his management of the narrative personae, "tones of voice," and "masks."

---

[3] "Wordsworth," in *Oxford Lectures on Poetry* (London, 1909), pp. 133, 130–31 (see also footnote, pp. 140–41), 134. (*Note:* in this and the following footnotes, references are given only to passages not included in the essays reprinted in this volume.)

[4] *The Poet Wordsworth* (Oxford, 1950), pp. 26, 161, 172.

Introduction: Two Roads to Wordsworth

Danby's critique of "The Idiot Boy," reprinted here, is a belated recognition that Wordsworth is an accomplished comic poet. Its focus is on the interplay of the narrative voice, the voices of the characters, and the poet's own voice in sustaining the fine balance of humor and human warmth in the evolving story.

Danby expressly opposed his treatment of Wordsworth as intentional artificer to the New Critical approach to a poem as a free-standing and autonomous structure of meanings, to be judged without recourse to the artist or his intention. Cleanth Brooks's essay on Wordsworth's "Intimations Ode" (1947), also included in this volume, demonstrates what can be achieved by such a close reading of the poem "as an independent poetic structure," interrogated for what it "manages to say" entirely "in its own right" as a primarily ironic and paradoxical deployment of thematic imagery. Having assimilated the insights made possible by this strict limitation of perspective in the New Criticism, many critics in the last decade or two have undertaken, like Danby, to rehumanize poetry by viewing the poet, in Wordsworth's phrase in the "Preface," as "a man speaking to men," and by exploiting concepts such as "voice," "persona," "tone," and "point of view," which emphasize the poet's own involvement, as well as his management of the reader's participation, in the fictional process.

Such a revitalized rhetoric of poetry is prominent in many recent writings about Wordsworth. In the third chapter of *The Music of Humanity*, for example, Jonathan Wordsworth demonstrates the essential role, in *The Ruined Cottage*, of the interplay between Wordsworth's two "poetic selves," the Pedlar and the Poet, in effecting the reader's imaginative consent to the author's own attitudes toward the tragic story. In an essay reprinted in this volume that has been much debated, Stephen Parrish reads "The Thorn" not as a quasi-supernatural story, but as an artful dramatic monologue, in which the controlling principle is the revelation of the mental workings of its credulous narrator, the old sea captain. Neil Hertz's essay "Wordsworth and the Tears of Adam"—with a shift of emphasis from Wordsworth's rhetorical artistry to the characteristic disjunction of consciousness in his poetry—discriminates "the transformation of the voice" in a short verse passage, and details the interaction among three "aspects of Wordsworth's self" and a fourth subjectivity, that of the responding reader.

II. The Problematic Wordsworth

In the 1960s there appeared a new mode of criticism in America whose appeal to younger critics presages its growing importance in studies of romantic literature. The primary terms of this criticism are "consciousness" (or "self-consciousness") and the "dialectic" of its dealings with what is not-consciousness, and its characteristic procedure is to find something "problematic" in the surface meaning of single passages and to regard this as a clue to a deep structure manifesting an unspoken preoccupation of the poet. The proximate source of this critical procedure are the diverse movements in European thought loosely classified as "phenomenology," "existentialism," and "structuralism," but its central idiom and concerns derive ultimately from Hegel; so that, when applied to Wordsworth, it can be regarded as a revived form of Bradley's neo-Hegelian approach to that poet. The focus, however, is much sharper than Bradley's, and the chief operative concepts much more restricted. For as Hegel in his *Phenomenology of the Spirit* translated the manifold particularities of human and individual history into diverse moments of the transactions between consciousness and its alienated other, so these critics view the manifold surface particularities of romantic poems as generated primarily by a single submerged plot: the sustained struggle of the poet's consciousness (operating in the mode often called "imagination") to achieve "autonomy," or absolute independence from that adversary which is not itself—namely "nature," the world of sensible objects.

In his influential essay, "Intentional Structure of the Romantic Image," first published in 1960, Paul de Man sets out from the observation that there is a "dialectic" that is "paradoxical"—a "fundamental ambiguity" or "tension" that "never ceases to be problematic"—in romantic attempts to link the polarities of consciousness, or imagination, and nature. De Man's paradigmatic instance is Mallarmé, who is represented as a revealing point of reference because he is a late romantic who took over what had hitherto been an implicit tension of polar attitudes, "the alternating feeling of attraction and repulsion that the romantic poet experiences toward nature," and made it explicit as a "conscious dialectic of a reflective poetic consciousness." Mallarmé, unlike earlier romantic poets, "always remained convinced of the essential priority of the natural object," so that his writings as an extreme "anti-natural poet" are a defiantly hopeless struggle by consciousness (or by the language in which consciousness manifests itself) to annihilate, by reducing to its own self, a nature that Mallarmé knows to be ultimately indefeasible. Wordsworth's poetry, on the other hand, with its "radical contradictions" in the representation of landscape (de Man's example is the passage on crossing the Alps in *The Prelude,* Book 6), puts into question "the ontological priority of the sensory object," by recourse to the faculty he calls "imagination," which "marks . . . a possibility for consciousness to exist entirely by and for itself, independently of all relationship with the outside world."

Geoffrey Hartman also finds that Wordsworth's treatment of nature is "problematic," and that a number of passages in *The Prelude* which "overtly celebrate nature" in fact "share a motif opposed to the overt line of argument." Hartman's repeated reference, however, is not to Mallarmé but to Blake, the extreme representative of a deliberate commitment to a visionary and anti-natural imagination. "Wordsworth," Hartman imagines Blake as saying, "is of his party without knowing it." The difference is that Wordsworth, when he comes face to face with his "autonomous imagination," fears it, shies from it, or veils it. In consequence, his poetry constitutes "a series of evaded recognitions" of imagination and "an avoidance of apocalypse"—where imagination is defined by Hartman as "consciousness of self raised to apocalyptic pitch" and apocalypse signifies "any strong desire to cast out nature and to achieve an unmediated contact with the principle of things," hence as "involving a *death* of nature." It is this "unresolved opposition between Imagination and Nature"—through Wordsworth's "fear of the death of nature"—that "prevents him from becoming a visionary poet." [5]

Two essays in this volume represent another approach to Wordsworth that emphasizes the duplicity and the strain between contradictions in his writings; its major operative concept, however, is not a revived Hegelian opposition between consciousness and an alien other, but the post-Freudian distinction between manifest and latent, conscious and unconscious content. The basic claim is that Wordsworth's overt or surface meaning often overlies a covert countermeaning that expresses what the poet profoundly felt and believed, as against what he rationalized himself into believing.

David Perkins's *Quest for Permanence* undertakes to "go beneath the surface" of Wordsworth's poetry in order to explore the "negative implications" that are sometimes "contrary to his overt intentions and obiter dicta"; for any interpretation that concentrates on Wordsworth's obiter dicta "is not touching what is deepest in him." Under Wordsworth's overt claims that certitude and peace attend upon "the union of mind with nature," Perkins finds a contrary sense that there is a "gulf between human nature . . . and the rest of nature," and that man is doomed to be an isolated being, estranged both from nature and other men. There are symptoms also of "a kind of schizoid retreat" from situations that threaten the poet's composure, which in its extreme form manifests itself in Wordsworth as an attraction to the ultimate security of the grave.[6]

In *The Limits of Mortality*, published in the same year as Perkins's *Quest for Permanence* (1959), David Ferry's aim is to discover in Words-

[5] *Wordsworth's Poetry, 1787–1814* (New Haven, 1964), pp. x, 17–18, 39, 61, 63, 101, 124, 184, 211, 226–27, 233, 338.
[6] *The Quest for Permanence* (Cambridge, Mass., 1959), pp. 24, 30, 40, 45, 47, 48, 50, 55, 89–90.

worth "ideas and feelings which can in some way be related to our own deepest feelings and ideas." Ferry penetrates to this modern element, as he says, by "a special way of reading his poems." This way to Wordsworth is to strike a sharp dichotomy between the " 'surface' of his poems" and the "deeper" and "hidden" meanings which are in "tension" or "conflict" with the surface meanings, and to assert the prepotency of the hidden and antithetic meanings as constituting the "ultimate subject matter" of a poem. As Ferry formulates this semantic peripety:

> [The] apparent subject matter is a kind of cipher or hieroglyph for meanings which reject or devaluate the very experiences which express them. . . . The symbolic meanings of [Wordsworth's] poems tend to reject their sensuous, dramatic surfaces.

Like A. C. Bradley a half-century earlier, Ferry sets out, as he says, to correct Arnold's "tendency to take Wordsworth's vocabulary of feeling at face value," hence to evaluate him as "the poet of the primary affections and simple feelings." By Ferry's interpretative strategy, however, the paradoxical Wordsworth works free from Bradley's careful qualifications to become the polar opposite of Arnold's Wordsworth. The sophisticated modern reader is now enabled to look right through Wordsworth's surface assertions of reverence for a "sacramental" nature, love for elemental man, and esteem for the simple affections and ordinary experience, in order to discern a countermeaning of which the poet himself remained unaware—that is, a "mystical" yearning for an eternal and unchanging realm of being to which nature and man and even the articulations of poetry itself (since all are alike trapped in the conditions of time, space, and vicissitude) are an intolerable obstruction, an offense against the purity of eternity. Hence to the knowing reader Wordsworth's "sacramentalist" poems, far from being simple and natural in style, often turn out to be "contradictions of themselves" and to express a yearning "for their own destruction," and Wordsworth's "mystical imagination" is recognized to be "a hater of temporal nature" and "the enemy of poetry as of all distinctively human experience." Ferry's closing summation of the Wordsworth of the great decade is that "his genius was his enmity to man, which he mistook for love, and his mistake led him into confusions which he could not bear. But when he banished his confusions, he banished his distinctive greatness as well." [7]

Even the confirmed Arnoldian must admit the plausibility of some of the insights achieved by the recent critics who premise their reading of Wordsworth on the paradoxical strains and equivocal attitudes in his poetry. And it is a measure of the range and magnitude of Wordsworth's

[7] *The Limits of Mortality* (Middletown, Conn., 1959), pp. ix, 32–33, 51–53, 160, 173.

Introduction: Two Roads to Wordsworth

the editor to omit many valuable essays. For Wordsworth criticism is in a flourishing condition these days, and its vigorous internal disputes testify to the poet's continuing vitality and pertinence. We are rediscovering what a number of Wordsworth's major contemporaries acknowledged —that he has done what only the greatest poets do. He has transformed the inherited language of poetry into a medium adequate to express new ways of perceiving the world, new modes of experience, and new relations of the individual consciousness to itself, to its past, and to other men. More than all but a very few English writers, Wordsworth has altered not only our poetry, but our sensibility and our culture.

Wordsworth

by A. C. Bradley

There have been greater poets than Wordsworth, but none more original. He saw new things, or he saw things in a new way. Naturally, this would have availed us little if his new things had been private fancies, or if his new perception had been superficial. But that was not so. If it had been, Wordsworth might have won acceptance more quickly, but he would not have gained his lasting hold on poetic minds. As it is, those in whom he creates the taste by which he is relished, those who learn to love him (and in each generation they are not a few), never let him go. Their love for him is of the kind that he himself celebrated, a settled passion, perhaps "slow to begin," but "never ending," and twined around the roots of their being. And the reason is that they find his way of seeing the world, his poetic experience, what Arnold meant by his "criticism of life," to be something deep, and therefore something that will hold. It continues to bring them joy, peace, strength, exaltation. It does not thin out or break beneath them as they grow older and wiser; nor does it fail them, much less repel them, in sadness or even in their sorest need. And yet—to return to our starting-point—it continues to strike them as original, and something more. It is not like Shakespeare's myriad-mindedness; it is, for good or evil or both, peculiar. They can remember, perhaps, the day when first they saw a cloud somewhat as Wordsworth saw it, or first really understood what made him write this poem or that; his unique way of seeing and feeling, though now familiar and beloved, still brings them not only peace, strength, exaltation, but a "shock of mild surprise"; and his paradoxes, long known by heart and found full of truth, still remain paradoxes.

If this is so, the road into Wordsworth's mind must be through his strangeness and his paradoxes, and not round them. I do not mean that they are everywhere in his poetry. Much of it, not to speak of occasional

---

"Wordsworth." From A. C. Bradley, *Oxford Lectures on Poetry*, 2d ed. (London: Macmillan & Co., Ltd., 1950). Copyright © 1909 by Macmillan & Co., Ltd. Reprinted by permission of St. Martin's Press, The Macmillan Company of Canada, and Macmillan London and Basingstoke. Bradley's entire essay incorporates two lectures given at Oxford in 1903. Reprinted here are part 1, a section of part 3, and the concluding pages.

platitudes, is beautiful without being peculiar or difficult; and some of this may be as valuable as that which is audacious or strange. But unless we get hold of that, we remain outside Wordsworth's centre; and, if we have not a most unusual affinity to him, we cannot get hold of that unless we realise its strangeness, and refuse to blunt the sharpness of its edge. Consider, for example, two or three of his statements; the statements of a poet, no doubt, and not of a philosopher, but still evidently statements expressing, intimating, or symbolising, what for him was the most vital truth. He said that the meanest flower that blows could give him thoughts that often lie too deep for tears. He said, in a poem not less solemn, that Nature was the soul of all his moral being; and also that she can so influence us that nothing will be able to disturb our faith that all that we behold is full of blessings. After making his Wanderer tell the heart-rending tale of Margaret, he makes him say that the beauty and tranquillity of her ruined cottage had once so affected him

> That what we feel of sorrow and despair
> From ruin and from change, and all the grief
> The passing shows of Being leave behind,
> Appeared an idle dream, that could not live
> Where meditation was.
> [*The Excursion*, I, 949-53]

He said that this same Wanderer could read in the silent faces of the clouds unutterable love, and that among the mountains all things for him breathed immortality. He said to "Almighty God,"

> But thy most dreaded instrument
> For working out a pure intent
> Is Man arrayed for mutual slaughter;
> Yea, Carnage is thy daughter.
> [*Ode, 1815*, 106-9]

This last, it will be agreed, is a startling statement; but is it a whit more extraordinary than the others? It is so only if we assume that we are familiar with thoughts that lie too deep for tears, or if we translate "the soul of all my moral being" into "somehow concordant with my moral feelings," or convert "all that we behold" into "a good deal that we behold," or transform the Wanderer's reading of the silent faces of the clouds into an argument from "design." But this is the road round Wordsworth's mind, not into it.

Again, with all Wordsworth's best poems, it is essential not to miss the unique tone of his experience. This doubtless holds good of any true poet, but not in the same way. With many poems there is little risk of our failing either to feel what is distinctive of the writer, or to appropriate what he says. What is characteristic, for example, in Byron's lines,

On this day I complete my thirty-sixth year, or in Shelley's *Stanzas written in dejection near Naples,* cannot escape discovery, nor is there any difficulty in understanding the mood expressed. But with Wordsworth, for most readers, this risk is constantly present in some degree. Take, for instance, one of the most popular of his lyrics, the poem about the daffodils by the lake. It is popular partly because it remains a pretty thing even to those who convert it into something quite undistinctive of Wordsworth. And it is comparatively easy, too, to perceive and to reproduce in imagination a good deal that *is* distinctive; for instance, the feeling of the sympathy of the waves and the flowers and the breeze in their glee, and the Wordsworthian "emotion recollected in tranquillity" expressed in the lines (written by his wife),

> They flash upon that inward eye
> Which is the bliss of solitude.

But there remains something still more intimately Wordsworthian:

> I wandered lonely as a Cloud
> That floats on high o'er vales and hills.

It is thrust into the reader's face, for these are the opening lines. But with many readers it passes unheeded, because it is strange and outside their own experience. And yet it is absolutely essential to the effect of the poem.

This poem, however, even when thoroughly conventionalised, would remain, as I said, a pretty thing; and it could scarcely excite derision. Our point is best illustrated from the pieces by which Wordsworth most earned ridicule, the ballad poems. They arose almost always from some incident which, for him, had a novel and arresting character and came on his mind with a certain shock; and if we do not get back to this through the poem, we remain outside it. We may, of course, get back to this and yet consider the poem to be more or less a failure. There is here therefore room for legitimate differences of opinion. Mr. Swinburne sees, no doubt, as clearly as Coleridge did, the intention of *The Idiot Boy* and *The Thorn,* yet he calls them "doleful examples of eccentricity in dullness," while Coleridge's judgement, though he criticised both poems, was very different. I believe (if I may venture into the company of such critics) that I see why Wordsworth wrote *Goody Blake and Harry Gill* and the *Anecdote for Fathers,* and yet I doubt if he has succeeded in either; but a great man, Charles James Fox, selected the former for special praise, and Matthew Arnold included the latter in a selection from which he excluded *The Sailor's Mother.* Indeed, of all the poems at first most ridiculed there is probably not one that has not been praised by some excellent judge. But they were ridiculed by men who judged them without attempting first to get inside them. And this is fatal.

I may bring out the point by referring more fully to one of them. *Alice Fell* was beloved by the best critic of the nineteenth century, Charles Lamb; but the general distaste for it was such that it was excluded "in policy" from edition after edition of Wordsworth's Poems; many still who admire *Lucy Gray* see nothing to admire in *Alice Fell*; and you may still hear the question asked, What could be made of a child crying for the loss of her cloak? And what, I answer, could be made of a man poking his stick into a pond to find leeches? What sense is there in asking questions about the subject of a poem, if you first deprive this subject of all the individuality it possesses in the poem? Let me illustrate this individuality methodically. A child crying for the loss of her cloak is one thing; quite another is a child who has an imagination, and who sees the tattered remnants of her cloak whirling in the wheel-spokes of a post-chaise fiercely driven by strangers on lonesome roads through a night of storm in which the moon is drowned. She was alone, and, having to reach the town she belonged to, she got up behind the chaise, and her cloak was caught in the wheel. And she is fatherless and motherless, and her poverty (the poem is called *Alice Fell, or Poverty*) is so extreme that for the loss of her weather-beaten rag she does not "cry"; she weeps loud and bitterly; weeps as if her innocent heart would break; sits by the stranger who has placed her by his side and is trying to console her, insensible to all relief; sends forth sob after sob as if her grief could never, never have an end; checks herself for a moment to answer a question, and then weeps on as if she had lost her only friend, and the thought would choke her very heart. It was *this* poverty and *this* grief that Wordsworth described with his reiterated hammering blows. Is it not pathetic? And to Wordsworth it was more. To him grief like this is sublime. It is the agony of a soul from which something is torn away that was made one with its very being. What does it matter whether the thing is a woman, or a kingdom, or a tattered cloak? It is the passion that counts. Othello must not agonise for a cloak, but "the little orphan Alice Fell" has nothing else to agonise for. Is all this insignificant? And then—for this poem about a child is right to the last line—next day the storm and the tragedy have vanished, and the new cloak is bought, of duffil grey, as warm a cloak as man can sell; and the child is as pleased as Punch. . . .

Wordsworth's morality is of one piece with his optimism and with his determination to seize and exhibit in everything the element of good. But this is a subject far too large for treatment here, and I can refer to it only in the most summary way. What Arnold precisely meant when he said that Wordsworth "put by" the cloud of human destiny I am not sure. That Wordsworth saw this cloud and looked at it steadily is beyond all question. I am not building on such famous lines as

> The still sad music of humanity,

or

> the fierce confederate storm
> Of sorrow, barricadoed evermore
> Within the walls of cities;

or

> Amid the groves, under the shadowy hills,
> The generations are prepared; the pangs,
> The internal pangs, are ready; the dread strife
> Of poor humanity's afflicted will
> Struggling in vain with ruthless destiny;[1]

for, although such quotations could be multiplied, isolated expressions, even when not dramatic, would prove little. But I repeat the remark already made, that if we review the subjects of many of Wordsworth's famous poems on human life—the subjects, for example, of *The Thorn, The Sailor's Mother, Ruth, The Brothers, Michael, The Affliction of Margaret, The White Doe of Rylstone*, the story of Margaret in *Excursion*, i., half the stories told in *Excursion*, vi. and vii.—we find ourselves in the presence of poverty, crime, insanity, ruined innocence, torturing hopes doomed to extinction, solitary anguish, even despair. Ignore the manner in which Wordsworth treated his subjects, and you will have to say that his world, so far as humanity is concerned, is a dark world—at least as dark as that of Byron. Unquestionably then he saw the cloud of human destiny, and he did not avert his eyes from it. Nor did he pretend to understand its darkness. The world was to him in the end "this unintelligible world," and the only "adequate support for the calamities of mortal life" was faith.[2] But he was profoundly impressed, through the experience of his own years of crisis, alike by the dangers of despondency, and by the superficiality of the views which it engenders. It was for him (and here, as in other points, he shows his natural affinity to Spinoza) a condition in which the soul, concentrated on its own suffering,

---

[1] [The quotations are from "Tintern Abbey"; the "Prospectus" to *The Recluse* (in *Poetical Works*, ed. de Selincourt and Darbishire, vol. 5); *The Excursion*, VI, 553 ff. —ED.]

[2] The second half of this sentence, true of the Wordsworth of the *Excursion*, is perhaps not quite true of his earlier mind.

for that very reason loses hold both of its own being and of the reality of which it forms a part. His experience also made it impossible for him to doubt that what he grasped

> At times when most existence with herself
> Is satisfied,
> [*The Excursion*, IX, 103-4]

—and these are the times when existence is most united in love with other existence—was, in a special sense or degree, the truth, and therefore that the evils which we suffer, deplore, or condemn, cannot really be what they seem to us when we merely suffer, deplore, or condemn them. He set himself to *see* this, as far as he could, and to show it. He sang of pleasure, joy, glee, blitheness, love, wherever in nature or humanity they assert their indisputable power; and turning to pain and wrong, and gazing at them steadfastly, and setting himself to present the facts with a quiet but unsparing truthfulness, he yet endeavoured to show what he had seen, that sometimes pain and wrong are the conditions of a happiness and good which without them could not have been, that no limit can be set to the power of the soul to transmute them into its own substance, and that, in suffering and even in misery, there may still be such a strength as fills us with awe or with glory. He did not pretend, I repeat, that what he saw sufficed to solve the riddle of the painful earth. "Our being rests" on "dark foundations," and "our haughty life is crowned with darkness." [3] But still what he showed was what he *saw*, and he saw it in the cloud of human destiny. We are not here concerned with his faith in the sun behind that cloud; my purpose is only to insist that he "fronted" it "fearlessly." . . .

Partly because he is the poet of mountains he is, even more preeminently, the poet of solitude. For there are tones in the mountain voice scarcely audible except in solitude, and the reader whom Wordsworth's greatest poetry baffles could have no better advice offered him than to do what he has probably never done in his life—to be on a mountain alone. But for Wordsworth not this solitude only, but all solitude and all things solitary had an extraordinary fascination.

> The outward shows of sky and earth,
> Of hill and valley, he has viewed;
> And impulses *of deeper birth*
> Have come to him in solitude.
> ["A Poet's Epitaph"]

The sense of solitude, it will readily be found, is essential to nearly all the poems and passages we have been considering, and to some of quite a

---

[3] [*The Excursion*, IV, 970; "Extempore Effusion upon the death of James Hogg" —Ed.]

different character, such as the Daffodil stanzas. And it is not merely that the poet is alone; what he sees is so too. If the leech-gatherer and the soldier on the moon-lit road had not been solitary figures, they would not have awaked "the visionary power"; and it is scarcely fanciful to add that if the boy who was watching for his father's ponies had had beside him any more than

> The *single* sheep and the *one* blasted tree,
> [*The Prelude* (1850), XII, 319]

the mist would not have advanced along the roads "in such indisputable shapes." With Wordsworth that power seems to have sprung into life at once on the perception of loneliness. What is lonely is a spirit. To call a thing lonely or solitary is, with him, to say that it opens a bright or solemn vista into infinity. He himself "wanders lonely as a cloud": he seeks the "souls of lonely places": he listens in awe to

> One voice, the solitary raven . . .
> An iron knell, with echoes from afar:
> [*The Excursion*, IV, 1178-81]

against the distant sky he descries the shepherd,

> A solitary object and sublime,
> Above all height! like an aerial cross
> Stationed alone upon a spiry rock
> Of the Chartreuse, for worship.
> [*The Prelude* (1850), VIII, 272-75]

But this theme might be pursued for hours, and I will refer only to two poems more. The editor of the *Golden Treasury*, a book never to be thought of without gratitude, changed the title *The Solitary Reaper* into *The Highland Reaper*. He may have had his reasons. Perhaps he had met some one who thought that the Reaper belonged to Surrey. Still the change was a mistake: the "solitary" in Wordsworth's title gave the keynote. The other poem is *Lucy Gray*. "When I was little," a lover of Wordsworth once said, "I could hardly bear to read *Lucy Gray*, it made me feel so lonely." Wordsworth called it *Lucy Gray, or Solitude*, and this young reader understood him. But there is too much reason to fear that for half his readers his "solitary child" is generalised into a mere "little girl," and that they never receive the main impression he wished to produce. Yet his intention is announced in the opening lines, and as clearly shown in the lovely final stanzas, which give even to this ballad the visionary touch which distinguishes it from *Alice Fell*:

> Yet some maintain that to this day
> She is a living child;

> That you may see sweet Lucy Gray
> Upon the lonesome wild.
>
> O'er rough and smooth she trips along,
> And never looks behind;
> And sings a solitary song
> That whistles in the wind.

The solitariness which exerted so potent a spell on Wordsworth had in it nothing "Byronic." He preached in the *Excursion* against the solitude of "self-indulging spleen." He was even aware that he himself, though free from that weakness, had felt

> perhaps too much
> The self-sufficing power of Solitude.
> [*The Prelude* (1850), II, 76–77]

No poet is more emphatically the poet of community. A great part of his verse—a part as characteristic and as precious as the part on which I have been dwelling—is dedicated to the affections of home and neighbourhood and country, and to that soul of joy and love which links together all Nature's children, and "steals from earth to man, from man to earth." And this soul is for him as truly the presence of "the Being that is in the clouds and air" and in the mind of man as are the power, the darkness, the silence, the strange gleams and mysterious visitations which startle and confuse with intimations of infinity. But solitude and solitariness were to him, in the main, one of these intimations. They had not for him merely the "eeriness" which they have at times for everyone, though that was essential to some of the poems we have reviewed. They were the symbol of power to stand alone, to be "self-sufficing," to dispense with custom and surroundings and aid and sympathy—a self-dependence at once the image and the communication of "the soul of all the worlds." Even when they were full of "sounds and sweet airs that give delight and hurt not," the solitude of the Reaper or of Lucy, they so appealed to him. But they appealed also to that austerer strain which led him to love "bare trees and mountains bare," and lonely places, and the bleak music of the old stone wall, and to dwell with awe, and yet with exultation, on the majesty of that "unconquerable mind" which through long years holds its solitary purpose, sustains its solitary passion, feeds upon its solitary anguish. For this mind, as for the blind beggar or the leech-gatherer, the "light of sense" and the sweetness of life have faded or "gone out"; but in it "greatness makes abode," and it "retains its station proud," "by form or image unprofaned." Thus, in whatever guise it might present itself, solitariness "carried far into his heart" the haunting sense of an "invisible world";

of some Life beyond this "transitory being" and "unapproachable by death";

> Of Life continuous, Being unimpaired;
> That hath been, is, and where it was and is
> There shall endure,—existence unexposed
> To the blind walk of mortal accident;
> From diminution safe and weakening age;
> While man grows old, and dwindles, and decays;
> And countless generations of mankind
> Depart; and leave no vestige where they trod.
> [*The Excursion*, IV, 755-62]

For me, I confess, all this is far from being "mere poetry"—partly because I do not believe that any such thing as "mere poetry" exists. But whatever kind or degree of truth we may find in all this, everything in Wordsworth that is sublime or approaches sublimity has, directly or more remotely, to do with it. And without this part of his poetry Wordsworth would be "shorn of his strength," and would no longer stand, as he does stand, nearer than any other poet of the Nineteenth Century to Milton.

Wordsworth and the Revolt against Abstractions

by A. N. Whitehead

So far as concerns English literature we find, as might be anticipated, the most interesting criticism of the thoughts of science among the leaders of the romantic reaction which accompanied and succeeded the epoch of the French Revolution. In English literature, the deepest thinkers of this school were Coleridge, Wordsworth, and Shelley. Keats is an example of literature untouched by science. We may neglect Coleridge's attempt at an explicit philosophical formulation. It was influential in his own generation; but in these lectures it is my object only to mention those elements of the thought of the past which stand for all time. Even with this limitation, only a selection is possible. For our purposes Coleridge is only important by his influence on Wordsworth. Thus Wordsworth and Shelley remain.

Wordsworth was passionately absorbed in nature. It has been said of Spinoza, that he was drunk with God. It is equally true that Wordsworth was drunk with nature. But he was a thoughtful, well-read man, with philosophical interests, and sane even to the point of prosiness. In addition, he was a genius. He weakens his evidence by his dislike of science. We all remember his scorn of the poor man whom he somewhat hastily accuses of peeping and botanising on his mother's grave. Passage after passage could be quoted from him, expressing this repulsion. In this respect, his characteristic thought can be summed up in his phrase, "We murder to dissect."

In this latter passage, he discloses the intellectual basis of his criticism of science. He alleges against science its absorption in abstractions. His consistent theme is that the important facts of nature elude the scientific

"Wordsworth and the Revolt against Abstractions" (editor's title). From Alfred North Whitehead, *Science and the Modern World* (Cambridge: Cambridge University Press, 1926). Copyright © 1925 by The Macmillan Company; copyright renewed 1953 by Evelyn Whitehead. Reprinted by permission of Cambridge University Press and The Macmillan Company. The selection is from chapter 5, "The Romantic Reaction."

method. It is important therefore to ask, what Wordsworth found in nature that failed to receive expression in science. I ask this question in the interest of science itself; for one main position in these lectures is a protest against the idea that the abstractions of science are irreformable and unalterable. Now it is emphatically not the case that Wordsworth hands over inorganic matter to the mercy of science, and concentrates on the faith that in the living organism there is some element that science cannot analyse. Of course he recognises, what no one doubts, that in some sense living things are different from lifeless things. But that is not his main point. It is the brooding presence of the hills which haunts him. His theme is nature *in solido,* that is to say, he dwells on that mysterious presence of surrounding things, which imposes itself on any separate element that we set up as an individual for its own sake. He always grasps the whole of nature as involved in the tonality of the particular instance. That is why he laughs with the daffodils, and finds in the primrose "thoughts too deep for tears."

Wordsworth's greatest poem is, by far, the first book of *The Prelude.* It is pervaded by this sense of the haunting presences of nature. A series of magnificent passages, too long for quotation, express this idea. Of course, Wordsworth is a poet writing a poem, and is not concerned with dry philosophical statements. But it would hardly be possible to express more clearly a feeling for nature, as exhibiting entwined prehensive unities, each suffused with modal presences of others:

> Ye Presences of Nature in the sky
> And on the earth! Ye Visions of the hills!
> And Souls of lonely places! can I think
> A vulgar hope was yours when ye employed
> Such ministry, when ye through many a year
> Haunting me thus among my boyish sports,
> On caves and trees, upon the woods and hills,
> Impressed upon all forms the characters
> Of danger or desire; and thus did make
> The surface of the universal earth
> With triumph and delight, with hope and fear,
> Work like a sea? . . .
> [*The Prelude,* 1850 ed., I. 464–75]

In thus citing Wordsworth, the point which I wish to make is that we forget how strained and paradoxical is the view of nature which modern science imposes on our thoughts. Wordsworth, to the height of genius, expresses the concrete facts of our apprehension, facts which are distorted in the scientific analysis. Is it not possible that the standardised concepts of science are only valid within narrow limitations, perhaps too narrow for science itself?

Shelley's attitude to science was at the opposite pole to that of Wordsworth. He loved it, and is never tired of expressing in poetry the thoughts which it suggests. It symbolises to him joy, and peace, and illumination. What the hills were to the youth of Wordsworth, a chemical laboratory was to Shelley. It is unfortunate that Shelley's literary critics have, in this respect, so little of Shelley in their own mentality. They tend to treat as a casual oddity of Shelley's nature what was, in fact, part of the main structure of his mind, permeating his poetry through and through. If Shelley had been born a hundred years later, the twentieth century would have seen a Newton among chemists.

For the sake of estimating the value of Shelley's evidence it is important to realise this absorption of his mind in scientific ideas. It can be illustrated by lyric after lyric. I will choose one poem only, the fourth act of his *Prometheus Unbound*. The Earth and the Moon converse together in the language of accurate science. Physical experiments guide his imagery. For example, the Earth's exclamation,

> The vaporous exultation not to be confined!

is the poetic transcript of "the expansive force of gases," as it is termed in books on science. Again, take the Earth's stanza,

> I spin beneath my pyramid of night,
> Which points into the heavens,—dreaming delight,
> Murmuring victorious joy in my enchanted sleep;
> As a youth lulled in love-dreams faintly sighing,
> Under the shadow of his beauty lying,
> Which round his rest a watch of light and warmth doth keep.

This stanza could only have been written by someone with a definite geometrical diagram before his inward eye—a diagram which it has often been my business to demonstrate to mathematical classes. As evidence, note especially the last line which gives poetical imagery to the light surrounding night's pyramid. This idea could not occur to anyone without the diagram. But the whole poem and other poems are permeated with touches of this kind.

Now the poet, so sympathetic with science, so absorbed in its ideas, can simply make nothing of the doctrine of secondary qualities which is fundamental to its concepts. For Shelley nature retains its beauty and its colour. Shelley's nature is in its essence a nature of organisms, functioning with the full content of our perceptual experience. We are so used to ignoring the implication of orthodox scientific doctrine, that it is difficult to make evident the criticism upon it which is thereby implied. If anybody could have treated it seriously, Shelley would have done so.

Furthermore Shelley is entirely at one with Wordsworth as to the interfusing of the Presence in nature. Here is the opening stanza of his poem entitled *Mont Blanc*:

> The everlasting universe of Things
> Flows through the Mind, and rolls its rapid waves,
> Now dark—now glittering—now reflecting gloom—
> Now lending splendour, where from secret springs
> The source of human thought its tribute brings
> Of waters,—with a sound but half its own,
> Such as a feeble brook will oft assume
> In the wild woods, among the Mountains lone,
> Where waterfalls around it leap for ever,
> Where woods and winds contend, and a vast river
> Over its rocks ceaselessly bursts and raves.

Shelley has written these lines with explicit reference to some form of idealism, Kantian or Berkeleyan or Platonic. But however you construe him, he is here an emphatic witness to a prehensive unification as constituting the very being of nature.

Berkeley, Wordsworth, Shelley are representative of the intuitive refusal seriously to accept the abstract materialism of science.

There is an interesting difference in the treatment of nature by Wordsworth and by Shelley, which brings forward the exact questions we have got to think about. Shelley thinks of nature as changing, dissolving, transforming as it were at a fairy's touch. The leaves fly before the West Wind

> Like ghosts from an enchanter fleeing.

In his poem *The Cloud* it is the transformations of water which excite his imagination. The subject of the poem is the endless, eternal, elusive change of things:

> I change but I cannot die.

This is one aspect of nature, its elusive change: a change not merely to be expressed by locomotion, but a change of inward character. This is where Shelley places his emphasis, on the change of what cannot die.

Wordsworth was born among hills; hills mostly barren of trees, and thus showing the minimum of change with the seasons. He was haunted by the enormous permanences of nature. For him change is an incident which shoots across a background of endurance,

> Breaking the silence of the seas
> Among the farthest Hebrides.
> ["The Solitary Reaper"]

Every scheme for the analysis of nature has to face these two facts, *change* and *endurance*. There is yet a third fact to be placed by it, *eternality*, I will call it. The mountain endures. But when after ages it has been worn away, it has gone. If a replica arises, it is yet a new mountain. A colour is eternal. It haunts time like a spirit. It comes and it goes. But where it comes, it is the same colour. It neither survives nor does it live. It appears when it is wanted. The mountain has to time and space a different relation from that which colour has. In the previous lecture, I was chiefly considering the relation to space-time of things which, in my sense of the term, are eternal. It was necessary to do so before we can pass to the consideration of the things which endure.

Also we must recollect the basis of our procedure. I hold that philosophy is the critic of abstractions. Its function is the double one, first of harmonising them by assigning to them their right relative status as abstractions, and secondly of completing them by direct comparison with more concrete intuitions of the universe, and thereby promoting the formation of more complete schemes of thought. It is in respect to this comparison that the testimony of great poets is of such importance. Their survival is evidence that they express deep intuitions of mankind penetrating into what is universal in concrete fact. Philosophy is not one among the sciences with its own little scheme of abstractions which it works away at perfecting and improving. It is the survey of sciences, with the special objects of their harmony, and of their completion. It brings to this task, not only the evidence of the separate sciences, but also its own appeal to concrete experience. It confronts the sciences with concrete fact.

The literature of the nineteenth century, especially its English poetic literature, is a witness to the discord between the aesthetic intuitions of mankind and the mechanism of science. Shelley brings vividly before us the elusiveness of the eternal objects of sense as they haunt the change which infects underlying organisms. Wordsworth is the poet of nature as being the field of enduring permanences carrying within themselves a message of tremendous significance. The eternal objects are also there for him,

> The light that never was, on sea or land.
> ["Elegiac Stanzas"]

Both Shelley and Wordsworth emphatically bear witness that nature cannot be divorced from its aesthetic values; and that these values arise from the cumulation, in some sense, of the brooding presence of the whole onto its various parts. Thus we gain from the poets the doctrine that a philosophy of nature must concern itself at least with these five notions: change, value, eternal objects, endurance, organism, interfusion. . . .

. . . But conversely, nothing must be left out. Remembering the poetic rendering of our concrete experience, we see at once that the element of value, of being valuable, of having value, of being an end in itself, of being something which is for its own sake, must not be omitted in any account of an event as the most concrete actual something. "Value" is the word I use for the intrinsic reality of an event. Value is an element which permeates through and through the poetic view of nature. We have only to transfer to the very texture of realisation in itself that value which we recognise so readily in terms of human life. This is the secret of Wordsworth's worship of nature. Realisation therefore is in itself the attainment of value. But there is no such thing as mere value. Value is the outcome of limitation. The definite finite entity is the selected mode which is the shaping of attainment; apart from such shaping into individual matter of fact there is no attainment. The mere fusion of all that there is would be the nonentity of indefiniteness. The salvation of reality is its obstinate, irreducible, matter-of-fact entities, which are limited to be no other than themselves. Neither science, nor art, nor creative action can tear itself away from obstinate, irreducible, limited facts. The endurance of things has its significance in the self-retention of that which imposes itself as a definite attainment for its own sake. That which endures is limited, obstructive, intolerant, infecting its environment with its own aspects. But it is not self-sufficient. The aspects of all things enter into its very nature. It is only itself as drawing together into its own limitation the larger whole in which it finds itself. Conversely it is only itself by lending its aspects to this same environment in which it finds itself. The problem of evolution is the development of enduring harmonies of enduring shapes of value, which merge into higher attainments of things beyond themselves. Aesthetic attainment is interwoven in the texture of realisation. The endurance of an entity represents the attainment of a limited aesthetic success, though if we look beyond it to its external effects, it may represent an aesthetic failure. Even within itself, it may represent the conflict between a lower success and a higher failure. The conflict is the presage of disruption.

The further discussion of the nature of enduring objects and of the conditions they require will be relevant to the consideration of the doctrine of evolution which dominated the latter half of the nineteenth century. The point which . . . I have endeavoured to make clear is that the nature-poetry of the romantic revival was a protest on behalf of the organic view of nature, and also a protest against the exclusion of value from the essence of matter of fact. In this aspect of it, the romantic movement may be conceived as a revival of Berkeley's protest which had been launched a hundred years earlier. The romantic reaction was a protest on behalf of value.

The Isolation of the Human Mind

by David Perkins

What is written largest in Wordsworth as a prototype for modern poetry is not his solution (if it is a solution). Rather it is his sense of the gulf between human nature, with all of its greedy demands, its turbulent assertions, its often chaotic passions, and the rest of nature. Few critics have paid much attention to this side of Wordsworth, for Wordsworth differs from most modern poets in that he does not accept the split as final or necessary. Hence there has been a natural tendency to follow Wordsworth himself, and to stress his hope that the human mind can be formatively infused with the life of nature. But if one asks what motivates and gives urgency to this hope, and if one turns to Wordsworth's poetry without being controlled by his own overt emphasis, one finds that he was seeking to ease a suffocating, almost panicky fear that man is doomed to isolation from the healthful influence of his natural surroundings. In the poetry, this fear expresses itself, first of all, in situations where man is pictured as an actual intruder, whose "restless thoughts" and impulsive actions violate the harmonious "calm of nature."

In one instance the *Prelude* speaks of a "month of calm and glassy days" spent on an island during the war with France. "Each evening, pacing by the still sea-shore," Wordsworth heard the "monitory sound" of the "sunset cannon" (X, 320–325).[1] While the sun

> went down
> In the tranquillity of nature, came
> That voice, ill requiem! seldom heard by me
> Without a spirit overcast by dark
> Imaginations, sense of woes to come,
> Sorrow for human kind, and pain of heart.
> [1850 ed., X, 325–330]

"The Isolation of the Human Mind." From David Perkins, *The Quest for Permanence: The Symbolism of Wordsworth, Shelley and Keats* (Cambridge: Harvard University Press, 1959). Copyright © 1959 by the President and Fellows of Harvard College. Reprinted by permission of the author and the publisher. This essay is part 3 of chapter 1.

[1] [All quotations are from *The Prelude* of 1850. —ED.]

A key word here is the preposition "in." It implies that the sun went down in accordance with the tranquil order of nature proceeding without relation to human activities. But it also suggests that the cannon breaks in upon the "tranquillity of nature," shattering its "glassy" calm, or at least the calm it momentarily imposes on the human observer. The cannon calls to mind the bloody passions associated with war, and the dark imaginations it evokes suggest that the observer himself is all too precarious in his composure. He seems fearfully receptive to the "voice" of the cannon, and as it intrudes it vitiates his response to the natural scene.

Another example would be the poem "Nutting," which describes a boyhood trip to the woods to gather hazelnuts. The child came to a nook which had not previously been visited. Here

> the hazels rose
> Tall and erect, with tempting clusters hung,
> A virgin scene!
> [lines 19-21]

He stood still for a while

> Breathing with such suppression of the heart
> As joy delights in; and with wise restraint
> Voluptuous, fearless of a rival, eyed
> The banquet.
> [lines 22-25]

After dallying beneath the tree, he rose

> And dragged to earth both branch and bough, with crash
> And merciless ravage; and the shady nook
> Of hazels, and the green and mossy bower,
> Deformed and sullied, patiently gave up
> Their quiet being.
> [lines 44-48]

As he turned away from "the mutilated bower," he was "Exulting, rich beyond the wealth of kings"; yet he also "felt a sense of pain when" he "beheld / The silent trees." In this poem, the phrasing carries obvious sexual implications, and the emotions expressed—the joy of anticipated possession, the dallying, the "merciless ravage" and the remorse—affirm the root metaphor. To have felt and described the experience in these terms suggests not only how strongly he was affected but why. For although the remorse, which may be directly related to the patience of nature in enduring the attack, implies some chastening of the child's feelings, the incident revealed a chasm separating nature from the mind and habits of man. The shady nook does not infuse its calm into the human soul. The state of mind in which the grove is entered is the opposite of receptive. Guilty and assertive feeling blots out almost all sensitivity to the scene except the "voluptuous" temptation to take and mar. In other words, we do not discover here an approach to nature with the receptivity Wordsworth would have conceived formative. Instead, it is a misuse, an onslaught; and the place is accordingly left "deformed and sullied."

"Nutting" provides something of a prototype for recurring episodes in the *Prelude*. Among the most marked is the account of stealing out at night, as a child, to snare woodcocks:

> Through half the night,
> Scudding away from snare to snare, I plied
> That anxious visitation;—moon and stars
> Were shining o'er my head. I was alone,
> And seemed to be a trouble to the peace
> [*Prelude*, I, 312–316]

of the surroundings. A passage from an earlier version had related

> How my heart
> Panted among the scattered yew-trees, and the crags
> That look'd upon me, how my bosom beat
> With expectation.

Both versions then relate how "strong desire / O'erpowered" him and he took a bird from someone else's snare:

> and when the deed was done
> I heard among the solitary hills
> Low breathings coming after me, and sounds
> Of undistinguishable motion, steps
> Almost as silent as the turf they trod.
> [*Prelude*, I, 321–325]

As in "Nutting," there is at first a strange, excited expectation. There is also a sense of guilt projected in the "low breathings" and "steps" he hears. But the guilt does not arise primarily from the theft. Significantly, he felt it before he took the bird "Which was the captive of another's toil." As soon as he came among the mountains he felt himself "to be a trouble to the peace / That dwelt among them," and a sense of guilt objectified itself in his consciousness of the "crags / That look'd upon" him. Like Gulliver among the Houyhnhnms, he was the only passionate, desiring intelligence in a harmonious and tranquil world. Similarly, when Wordsworth and his companions came as "plunderers" among the rocks or when he took the boat, "an act of stealth / And troubled pleasure," and rowed swiftly out on the "silent lake," the experience is again construed as guilty desire amid the surrounding tranquillity (I, 326–400).

Boyhood episodes which involve his own personal acts provide particularly clear-cut illustrations of the sense of man as intruder, and the association of this intrusion with guilt. But analogous feelings appear in a reaction to other people—a reaction which may be less immediately vivid but which goes further in explaining the alternating blandness and deep uneasy disturbance with which Wordsworth's poetry treats actual human beings encountered within the setting of nature. Here one must not think of poems with an openly didactic theme, like *Peter Bell,* which is concerned with a human being who is unresponsive to nature, and who is automatically supposed to be guilty. This can be taken for granted. Less obvious, but more general and disturbing, is the feeling that the mere presence of human beings may bring a certain stain, an uneasy ripple, upon the calm surface of nature. A singularly apt example occurs in an episode in the *Prelude* (V, 435 ff.) where the body of a drowned man is recovered from a lake. The setting as a whole is one of complete tranquillity. The man himself, as he rises "bolt upright" with a "ghastly face" is dead. In a real sense, the drowned man has about as much or more repose than human nature would ever wish. But the point is that Wordsworth tacks on to the incident a rather prosaic statement that he was able to tamp down his reaction to it, that it did not unduly affect him. There is surely some significance in this need to reassure himself. It is also suggestive that the actual presentation of the occurrence is far more impressive than the attempt to state that he was capable of taking it in his stride. The "anxious crowd" that huddles in the twilight about the lake, the people in the boat, "sounding with grappling irons," are not themselves an intrusion. They are associations brought in as mere planetary actions gravitating about the rising of the human corpse. What does intrude is the corpse itself, "ghastly" and "bolt upright" in the very midst of the tranquil lake—"mid that beauteous scene / Of trees and hills and water." It is "a spectre shape / Of terror," frightening in itself and possibly the more disturbing because it symbolizes the poet's own fears concerning human nature. And the very violence of these fears may be what compels Wordsworth to assert that the incident could be blunted, the fears managed.

So, in the encounter with the veteran soldier, earlier in the *Prelude* (IV, 353–469), we have a projection of the profound sense of man as alien or intruder, though in this case a temporary or *ad hoc* resolution is found. And the resolution presents, in miniature, what Wordsworth was trying to conceive as a possibility. At the end of the episode, the veteran fades into the context of nature, just as (in a very different way) the dead maiden in "A slumber did my spirit seal" is made one with nature's "diurnal course," caught up in a solemn and inevitable absorption into "rocks, and stones, and trees." In this particular instance, the veteran finally proves, like the leech gatherer, Michael, and other characters who represent Wordsworth's hope for human nature, to have a "demeanour calm," to come close to being "solemn and sublime." In other words, he possesses all the qualities usually located in nature and none that Wordsworth usually associates with man. Hence at the end of the incident the poet finds himself able to continue on his way "with quiet heart."

But the background of the encounter, however it may have been resolved, and the poet's first impressions, are extraordinarily revealing. Wordsworth, to begin with, is returning home, late at night, from a visit with friends. The contrast that this solitary walk presents with the earlier part of the evening is sharp. Certainly there is no conscious intention to refer back to the particular visit or evening-party, but there is still the brooding reflection that we are "parted," as he says, "from our better selves" by

> the hurrying world, and droop,
> Sick of its business, of its pleasures tired.
> [IV, 355-356]

This thought leads immediately to a passage in direct praise of "Solitude" —"How gracious, how benign"—and even of a "mere image of her sway" such as

> a public road,
> When, for the night deserted, it assumes
> A character of quiet more profound
> Than pathless wastes.
> [IV, 367-370]

But Wordsworth also remarks that an image of "Solitude" becomes "Most potent when impressed upon the mind / With an appropriate human centre," a "hermit, / Deep in the bosom of the wilderness," or a "Votary . . . Kneeling at prayers" alone in some "vast cathedral." He goes on to suggest that the lonely veteran standing in the road was also a "human centre" embodying the "soul" of "Solitude." These lines represent Wordsworth's own effort to account for the deep impression made by the encounter. What is striking about them is that the explanation does not seem to accord with the experience, as though Wordsworth himself could not recognize or admit what was involved. At least, when first seen the veteran is felt to be anything but "gracious" or "benign."

Before the encounter, the quiet and calm of the scene is emphasized. Except for the sound of a brook, there is complete silence:

The Isolation of the Human Mind

>No living thing appeared in earth or air,
>And, save the flowing water's peaceful voice,
>Sound there was none.
>
>>[IV, 385-387]

Then suddenly there is the meeting with another person. At once the tranquil peace of the scene, and of Wordsworth's corresponding mood, is shattered. Instead of blending into the natural scene, the man intrudes upon it. He appears as an "uncouth shape," assertively "stiff, lank, and upright" (we may remember that the corpse emerges from the bosom of the lake "bolt upright"). Moreover, this innocent and solitary human being is seen as "ghastly in the moonlight." Even later on, after the meeting, his is a "ghostly figure." Also, when Wordsworth, still unperceived, first notices him,

>From his lips . . .
>Issued low muttered sounds, as if of pain
>Or some uneasy thought.
>
>>[IV, 404-406]

The intrusion, in other words, is more than physical. It involves the presence of human pain and guilt in the natural world. Moreover, the guilt imputed may be something more than what Wordsworth usually associated with human nature. The first reaction may have been to see the man as guilty because he intrudes. Nor do later developments completely belie these impressions. He is, as Wordsworth learns, a veteran soldier, a reminder of the violent emotions unleashed in war. By association, he arouses a disturbing train of images in the poet's mind, yet, at the same time, being solitary and surrounded by the "vast cathedral" of nature, he gradually permits these images and associations to be managed. In fact, as it turns out, he has certain traits of character which offer a kind of catharsis; for when Wordsworth, learning that he is a veteran, is led to broach the subject of

>war, battle, and pestilence,
>Sprinkling this talk with questions, better spared,
>On what he might himself have seen or felt,
>
>>[IV, 437-439]

the veteran answers calmly, with

>a strange half-absence, as of one
>Knowing too well the importance of his theme,
>But feeling it no longer.
>
>>[IV, 443-445]

It is partly this lack of feeling in the veteran which calms and subdues the agitations he had roused. Indeed, this "half-absence" suggests exactly what Wordsworth sought when faced with situations of emotional stress. But however the catharsis or resolution may have been achieved, the poet's immediate reaction may remind us of Robinson Crusoe's sudden fear when, after so many years of solitude, he suddenly discovered a human footprint in the sand.

Some Characteristics of Wordsworth's Style

by David Ferry

It is the main function of the critic of any poet to discover in him ideas and feelings which can in some way be related to our own deepest feelings and ideas, and which are able to make their appeal ultimately outside the limits of their own time. These are the truly formative contents of any good poem, since all its other evidences of unity proceed from them and since all its other, lesser meanings must subsist in them or else be considered irrelevant. Thus, if one should decide that *Lycidas* is merely a poem about the death of Edward King, or merely about the social and spiritual condition of England in Milton's time, then two conclusions are possible—*Lycidas* is minor, or else the critic has not gone far enough to discover its truly formative subject matter, by which alone the poem can be finally judged. Wordsworth says:

> Aristotle, I have been told, has said, that Poetry is the most philosophic of all writing: it is so: its object is truth, not individual and local, but general and operative; not standing upon external testimony, but carried alive into the heart by passion; truth which is its own testimony, which gives competence and confidence to the tribunal to which it appeals, and receives them from the same tribunal.[1]

This kind of truth, as it exists in poetry, is what the critic has to find, and he will know it when he has found it, because it will be its own testimony that he has done so. This kind of truth, I believe, can be found along the line where the critic's insights into content and his insights into style join and become one.

My general conclusion, after an attempt to perform this critical function, is that the ideas and feelings in Wordsworth's best poems are indeed "in some way" related to the ideas and feelings we are accustomed to find

"Some Characteristics of Wordsworth's Style." From David Ferry, *The Limits of Mortality: An Essay on Wordsworth's Major Poems* (Middletown, Conn.: Wesleyan University Press, 1959). Copyright © 1959 by Wesleyan University. Reprinted by permission of Wesleyan University Press and the author. This essay is chapter 1, with the omission of the opening and closing paragraphs.

[1] "Preface to . . . Lyrical Ballads," [in] *Poetical Works*, ed. de Selincourt and Darbishire, II, 394-395.

in a more humane poetry, but related as a great enemy, say, is related to a great hero—as an enemy almost equal in strength to that hero, and loving him almost, but an enemy nevertheless. The ideas and feelings in Wordsworth's most important poems are lovingly hostile to the humane world. I shall try to show how this is true by concentrating on one central subject matter: man's relations to nature with respect to his mortality. For it is the limits of mortality that define man as what he is, individual, idiosyncratic, circumscribed; and it is against the mortal limitations of man that Wordsworth, in my view of him, conceived such a hatred.

To say the very least, this is not the usual view of Wordsworth. That is why I have chosen for the most part to develop my argument through the patient reading of whole poems, rather than more generally and topically and by the quotation of selected passages merely. My case can be argued most effectively by demonstrating how such meanings emerge from their fullest poetic context.

My view of Wordsworth derives from a special way of reading his poems—a way of reading which of course I think is the right one. A poet's style is in the last analysis the habit of reading he trains us in—Wordsworth himself said that an original poet must create "the taste by which he is relished." But Wordsworth has often in the past been read without regard to the special sorts of demands the poems make on us, and this resistance to his training has led to a good deal of distortion. . . . Therefore, I shall try to define some of the special qualities of Wordsworth's style and consequently to describe the habits of reading with which I have read him.

For this purpose it is useful to examine some criticisms Coleridge made of Wordsworth, because in them Coleridge himself (surprisingly enough) demonstrates how the poetry can be misunderstood if it is read with the wrong assumptions in mind. Coleridge, to be sure, thought the criticisms trifling and minor, but I think we will be able to see that their implications are very far from being so.

In the *Biographia Literaria,* Coleridge cites as one of Wordsworth's characteristic defects that of employing "thoughts and images too great for the subject." This, he says,

> . . . is an approximation to what might be called *mental* bombast, as distinguished from verbal: for, as in the latter there is a disproportion of the expressions to the thoughts, so in this there is a disproportion of thought to the circumstances and occasion.

One of his examples of this fault is the poem *Gipsies,* in which

> . . . the poet, having gone out for a day's tour of pleasure, meets early in the morning with a knot of *gipsies,* who had pitched their blanket-tents and straw-beds, together with their children and asses, in some field

by the road-side. At the close of day on his return our tourist found them in the same place. "Twelve hours," says he,

> "Twelve hours, twelve bounteous hours are gone, while I
> Have been a traveller under open sky,
> Much witnessing of change and cheer,
> Yet as I left I find them here."

Whereat the poet, without seeming to reflect that the poor tawny wanderers might probably have been tramping for weeks together through road and lane, over moor and mountain, and consequently must have been right glad to rest themselves, their children and cattle for one whole day; and overlooking the obvious truth, that such repose might be quite as necessary for *them*, as a walk of the same continuance was pleasing or healthful for the more fortunate poet; expresses his indignation in a series of lines, the diction and imagery of which would have been rather above, than below the mark, had they been applied to the immense empire of China improgressive for thirty centuries:

> "The weary SUN betook himself to rest:—
> Outshining, like a visible God,
> The glorious path, in which he trod!
> And now, ascending, after one dark hour,
> And one night's diminution of her power,
> Behold the mighty MOON! this way
> She looks, as if at them—but they
> Regard not her:—oh better wrong and strife,
> Better vain deeds or evil than such life!
> The silent HEAVENS have goings on:
> The STARS have tasks!—but *these* have none!" [2]

This passage calls on us to judge the verses by the touchstone of our most humane and sympathetic reactions to things. For Coleridge the main point is the actual condition of the gipsies themselves, and in order to judge the poem he draws on his own knowledge, as a human being aware of the fortunes of other human beings, of how tired and how glad to rest the gipsies must often be. He accuses the poet of having overlooked an obvious truth about these "poor tawny wanderers" which he should not have overlooked, of having in his own good fortune lorded it over creatures less fortunate than himself. Furthermore, he says that the diction and imagery expended on these objects are too elevated and would have been so even if they had been expended on something far more imposing, say the immense torpid empire of China.

The common-sense foundation of this criticism, the confidence that the gipsies should be "placed" properly in relation to the world around

[2] *Biographia Literaria*, ed. J. Shawcross (2 vols.; London, 1907), II, 109–111.

them, might in a very simple way be called "classicist": the poet's function is to be a more or less disinterested but always humane observer of the world outside himself, whose objects have inherent values from which the poet draws the conclusions which propel and direct his sympathies and antipathies. He looks out on the world, and because his awareness of the human condition is large and sympathetic, he misses no obvious truths which call for his pity and tolerance. But at the same time he is able to see things within the grander frame or structure of values which obtains in the world, and so is never impelled to use impertinent or grandiose language about things whose claims are humble. To such a poet, every object is the meeting ground of two noncontradictory systems of values, those they contain "within themselves" and those they have within the total scheme. It is the poet's duty and special privilege to know both kinds of values and to express their coming together in his language.

Judged by such criteria, it is plain enough that the poem is silly and intolerant, full of a propertied self-content. Gipsies do obviously get tired and need to rest; to cavil at them for it seems mere uninteresting peevishness. And the reader is after all likely to be both puzzled and irritated when the poet calls on sun, moon, and stars to support his caviling. It is shooting a mouse with an elephant gun.

But perhaps such criteria do not really apply. Perhaps it is of the nature of this imagination to overlook "obvious truths" and to treat a band of gipsies like the empire of China. Wordsworth says that the poet is a man "pleased with his own passions and volitions as manifested in the goings-on of the Universe, and habitually impelled to create them where he does not find them." [3] His tenderness is to be lavished on these passions and volitions, not on the outside world, and whatever attention he pays to that world is in the search for versions of those passions and volitions in other things. If the search should fail, the poet is even compelled to make it a success by creating them where he does not find them. Where Coleridge asserts that the poet has obligations to the actual circumstances and conditions of what he sees, that the poet is bound to a sane and just response to what is true of them "in themselves," Wordsworth asserts an extraordinary freedom for the poet from such obligations, the freedom to ignore whatever is irrelevant to his sublime egotism. It is a freedom which upsets the hierarchical system of values within which the empire of China is thought more than a band of gipsies, and which radically alters the way the poet will regard the band of gipsies in itself. The difference is the difference between a poetry which *evaluates* the world according to a reasonable and common-sense set of attitudes, and a poetry which *makes use of* the world for other purposes.

[3] Preface to *Lyrical Ballads, Poetical Works*, II, 393.

We are misled if we understand by "passions and volitions" simply the ordinary complex and multifoliate responses and desires of most men's inner lives. Wordsworth's passions and volitions are specifically religious and metaphysical, and their nature is such as to obliterate all others insofar as possible. Spinoza, whose mind in this respect was very similar to Wordsworth's, provides us with a useful vocabulary here. He says:

> From all this we easily conceive what is the power which clear and distinct knowledge, and especially that . . . kind of knowledge . . . whose foundation is the knowledge itself of God, possesses over the affects; the power, namely, by which it is able, in so far as they are passions, if not actually to destroy them . . . , at least to make them constitute the smallest part of the mind. . . . Moreover, it begets a love towards an immutable and eternal object . . . , of which we are really partakers . . . ; a love which therefore cannot be vitiated by the defects which are in common love, but which can always become greater and greater . . . occupy the largest part of the mind . . . , and thoroughly affect it.

He also says:

> Everything which the mind understands under the form of eternity, it understands not because it conceives the present actual existence of the body, but because it conceives the essence of the body under the form of eternity.

And he explains this further by saying:

> Things are conceived by us as actual in two ways: either in so far as we conceive them to exist with relation to a fixed time and place, or in so far as we conceive them to be contained in God, and to follow from the necessity of the divine nature. But those things which are conceived in this second way as true or real we conceive under the form of eternity, and their ideas involve the eternal and infinite essence of God.[4]

Coleridge's criticism of Wordsworth essentially means, then, that the poet failed to take sufficient account of the gipsies conceived as existing "with relation to a fixed time and place." But if we think of the poet as interested in his own passions and volitions "as manifested in the goings-on of the Universe"—that is, as "contained within God"—we see that he has the authority of Spinoza for reducing to "the smallest part of the mind," for destroying as far as possible, that "common love" which might have seen that the gipsies were tired.

Indeed, Wordsworth would be true to himself if he were to blame the gipsies precisely *because* they are tired, for their weariness is the symptom of their condition with relation to a fixed time and place, the symptom of a stubborn particularity which resists and denies the eternal. Wordsworth blames the gipsies for their mortality, for not participating suffi-

[4] Baruch Spinoza, *Selections*, ed. John Wild (New York, 1930), pp. 383, 387.

ciently in the eternal. He himself participates by imitating the immense courteous interchanges of sun, moon, and stars, emblems of the eternal nature of things, and the tone he takes toward the gipsies is to be thought of not as some glum trivial irritability, but as a sublime arrogance which is almost identified with his joy in the processes of the universe and takes its justification from that joy. And the magnificent imagery with which he bombards the gipsies is not inappropriate, since he is judging them "under the form of eternity" and by contrast to the mighty creatures of the cosmos, sun, moon, and stars. In the freedom of his sublime egotism, the gipsies are a mere convenience for the poet, to express his feelings about eternity. And for this he sacrifices the humane and common-sense considerations which Coleridge has to take into account.

Coleridge also criticized a more famous poem, *I wandered lonely as a cloud*, as exhibiting this same "defect" of "thoughts and images too great for the subject." This poem presents a more intricate problem.

Here again, Coleridge read the poem as if the poet were looking at the daffodils "with relation to a fixed time and place," and of course from one point of view we do respond to it in that way. Coleridge thought Wordsworth had an experience of a particular event, "a vivid image or visual spectrum," and that he had an excessive response to that experience. Daffodils are really too trivial for the attentions of the "inward eye," which might better be reserved for a moral experience of a much higher order, "the joy of retrospection, when the images and virtuous actions of a whole well-spent life, pass before that conscience which is indeed 'the bliss of solitude.'"[5] Even if we grant his assumptions in this case, we do not go along with his strictures quite as readily in this poem as in *Gipsies*. We are all familiar with the pleasures a pretty scene can afford, and the scene of daffodils by a lake is a very pretty one indeed. And we are willing to admit that there are considerable emotional possibilities in such a scene, whose effects are ultimately therapeutic. So Coleridge's demand for a more profound and moral subject matter may perhaps seem captious, too solemn for the charming occasion. But on further reflection there *does* seem to be something more here than the occasion warrants, something which Coleridge's moral vocabulary of "conscience" and of a "well-spent life" cannot tell us much about.

Under the aspect of eternity, daffodils, in their joyous organization, in their dancing, represent as well as anything else the divine organization of things, the "goings-on of the Universe." And it is even a rhetorical advantage to the poet that daffodils, such mere pretty flowers, so humble and modest in the great scheme of things, can represent such grandeur. In the beginning the poet is what the gipsies were, emblem of that which

---

[5] *Biographia Literaria*, II, 109.

does not participate in the eternal. But in his case, by a process of abstraction, by removing himself from the actual scene, and by a process of imagination, by seeing what the daffodils mean as "contained in God," he is able at last to join them, to perceive in them those passions and volitions which in his loneliness he had temporarily lost. And his loneliness has nothing to do with a separation from the world of men. It is a separation from the harmony of things and the aspect of eternity. The whole action of the poem is the symbol of the poet's relation to eternity (and the difficulty of perfecting that relation), of which his experience of daffodils is merely an example.

Certain "obvious truths" about a band of gipsies are ignored in order that they may be used as part of a symbolic design that figures forth the relations of the poet's mind to the universe; a degree of emotion is invested in a field of daffodils which seems excessive if we consider them "with relation to a fixed time and place." The Romantic metaphysical poet of this sort is likely to view nature, then, not as a set of objects, events, conditions which are in themselves his final interest, his final subject matter, but as a *language to be read,* signposts to that metaphysical place to which he wants to go. Insofar as those signposts appear to give him right directions, he will celebrate them, they will seem to him to be holy. And what the objects of physical nature are to the metaphysical nature of which he wants to have experience, the "surface" of his poems—its imagery and its feelings as expressed in tone and attitude—are to its "deeper meanings," its ultimate subject matter, which is the celebration of the metaphysical, the eternal and one. Thus, if we read the poems from a more or less "classicist" and common-sense point of view, as evaluations of this world seen with respect to time and place, we are likely to feel some dissatisfaction, to think that some obvious things about the condition of gipsies have been overlooked or that an excessive response is being made to mere daffodils. But if we read them as symbols of man's relations to the eternal, many of these dissatisfactions disappear. This is the principal habit of reading in which Wordsworth trains us.

But there are further considerations. If the natural world is for such a poet a system of signposts telling him the way to the place he wants to go to, he is likely to feel the sort of impatience with them that we often feel with signposts: if they tell us the way to get there, they also tell us that we have not gotten there yet. They are the sign of the incompleteness of our mission. And if the objects of this world are for Wordsworth signposts to eternity, they are more than that too, they necessarily have particular and individual complexities—he must to some degree see them with relation to a fixed time and place—and this is a cause of impatience too. This impatience is likely to be reflected, for example, in the poet's use of metaphor. The goldenness of the daffodils is first of all a quality which tells us that they are charming, but it is only after the poet has abstracted himself from that golden scene that the physical gold can be converted into a much more valuable gold, "the wealth the show to [him] had brought." In one sense the wealth is the same as the gold he saw in the daffodils at first, but in another it is what that mere physical prettiness had to be *transformed into,* after a rather complex abstractive and imaginative process. If the classical poet is like a miner, sifting through the ore of his experience for its real gold, the Romantic metaphysical poet of this sort is like an alchemist, transforming petty substance into gold. He is unlike most alchemists only in that the gold he achieves may be real gold, but he is like most alchemists in that the splendor of his achievement depends on the pettiness of what he begins with. And the word "show," in the daffodils poem, illustrates this complexity too. The scene was a "show" in the sense that it was the concrete embodiment of the metaphysical joy he was looking for; but it was "only a show" in the sense that the physical scene was the appearance whose reality he was seeking and which he could find only after he had removed himself from that scene. The "inward eye" with which at last he so truly sees is in one sense the outward eye functioning at its most profound, but in another sense it is the opposite of the outward eye and depends on its closing. The "inward eye" sees at that moment when "we are laid asleep / In body, and become a living soul."

Such details illustrate very well the tension and in some respects the hostility between "surface" and "deeper" meanings in Wordsworth's poems, between symbols and what the symbols refer to, even as they illustrate the tension and in some ways the hostility between the physical and the metaphysical natures. An artist can never do entirely without the physical world, and a poet perhaps least of all. It is a condition of language that it involves willy-nilly all sorts of references and appeals not only to particular objects but to highly particularized emotions, and the complex ramifications of these are impossible for the poet utterly to resist. (Music and abstract painting, of course, have this referential quality, this tendency to concreteness, to a far lesser degree.) In later chapters we shall see some larger consequences of this problem for Wordsworth.

Our main point here is the special way in which all these considerations have led us to read the poems. It is often as if the "surface" meanings of the poems were a beautiful and intelligible message, apparent at once, and as if hidden in that message there were clues to a "deeper" meaning, still more beautiful though in some ways at odds with the message one had read at first.

Wordsworth's celebrated sonnet on Westminster Bridge is a marvelous illustration of the sort of poem which has a satisfactory meaning "with relation to a fixed time and place" and an equally wonderful, quite different meaning when understood "under the aspect of eternity":

> Earth has not anything to show more fair:
> Dull would he be of soul who could pass by
> A sight so touching in its majesty:
> This City now doth, like a garment, wear
> The beauty of the morning; silent, bare,
> Ships, towers, domes, theatres, and temples lie
> Open unto the fields, and to the sky;
> All bright and glittering in the smokeless air.
> Never did sun more beautifully steep
> In his first splendour, valley, rock, or hill;
> Ne'er saw I, never felt, a calm so deep!
> The river glideth at his own sweet will:
> Dear God! the very houses seem asleep;
> And all that mighty heart is lying still!

The poem is justly famous. It is a kind of dramatic monologue, in the present tense, and it seems very directly to express immediate pleasure in the eye and ear and to celebrate qualities of a particular, immediate, and personal experience, and to leave it at that, without moralizing or in any way shaking its finger at us. It is solemn without being heavy, and we are at once enchanted by the picture of London in the early morning, with its "ships, towers, domes, theatres, and temples" glittering "in the smokeless air."

The speaker is admiring London at the moment when it is least characteristic of itself, and admiring it because it is at that moment so uncharacteristic of itself. The city wears its beauty "like a garment" which covers its essential, its naked ugliness, as Duessa's ugliness was covered. There is now none of the usual smoke in the air, and the buildings lie open to the fields and sky as if they were ruins of their usual selves. A good deal of the emphasis is given not to what the city looks like but to scenes of an opposite sort, of natural country beauty, "valley, rock, and hill" at sunrise, and of a river uncluttered by the Thames' usual barges. The speaker's attitudes toward country and city, then, are the organizing notions which permit his poem to display its beautiful qualities of pathos and pleasure, the bated breath which characterizes his mood, as if his eye went on tiptoe over the scene, anxious not to awaken the city into the ugliness and confusion he hates. The speaker is a man who likes the calm and quiet of the country and dislikes the bustle of the city. His *opinions* are, in that sense, only the means by which we share his pathos and wonder at this moment, and we do not feel it necessary to agree or disagree with them. The "real subject" of the poem, by this reading, is its qualities of tone and its tactful imagery, the rendering of the particular experience, "conceived as existing with relation to a fixed time and place."

But the poem is queerer than it looks at first, and it expresses doctrines which are the antithesis, in certain ways, of the values of this particularized experience. Read in the context of his poetry as a whole, and with Wordsworth's passion for eternity in mind, the sonnet is a statement about man's essential relations to his experience and to the real, the metaphysical, nature which devaluates his temporal experience. Wordsworth's poems are major documents in the history of symbolism, which is to say that they belong to the history of an art whose "inner" or "final" or "deeper" meanings are not mere extensions or generalizations of the implications of its surface. The surface is an organization of clues to such meanings and is always to a degree depreciated by them, just as a code is in a sense depreciated by its deciphering.

This is not to say that the surface in these poems has no significance in itself. It has the significance that it has. But it is also the means to another end. The dramatic and highly particularized "surface" of the Westminster Bridge sonnet is interesting in itself, but from another point of view it is only a symbol for another set of meanings, which in themselves deny the source of values of the dramatic and the particular. Thus the last line of Wordsworth's sonnet suggests that the city is not merely sleeping but dead, its heart stilled. The poet looks at London and sees it as a sort of corpse and admires it as such, welcomes a death which is the death of what the city has come to stand for in his symbolic world. The city is a collection of men and of all their ordinary experiences, their common loves and attachments, and it therefore represents all the involvements in temporal experience from which the poet would like to escape. London awake would be the rising up of all those passions which Spinoza and Wordsworth would like to destroy or to relegate to "the smallest part of the mind." What is so beautiful to the poet about this moment early in the morning is that these passions seem for the moment to be quieted, even to be expunged. What is so full of pathos, from this point of view, is that it *is* so early in the morning, that London will inevitably awaken, that we are creatures of time, and that we have our pleasures and our pains within the limits of mortality.

The hostility between the dramatic and the symbolic readings of the poem expresses itself here in a curious observation: the "death" the poet is so pleased to witness is the death even of those properties in himself by which he responds so wonderfully to the city at this particular moment. It must always be so in the conflict between the love of eternity and the loves of time, but it is especially poignant that it should be so for a poet. It is especially moving that one of the great representatives of our human powers of articulation should be himself a lover of silence. . . .

Wordsworth and the Iron Time

by Lionel Trilling

Our commemoration of the hundredth anniversary of Wordsworth's death must inevitably be charged with the consciousness that if Wordsworth were not kept in mind by the universities he would scarcely be remembered at all.[1] In our culture it is not the common habit to read the books of a century ago, and very likely all that we can mean when we say that a writer of the past is "alive" in people's minds is that, to those who once read him as a college assignment or who have formed an image of him from what they have heard about him, he exists as an attractive idea, as an intellectual possibility. And if we think of the three poets whom Matthew Arnold celebrated in his "Memorial Verses," we know that Byron is still attractive and possible, and so is Goethe. But Wordsworth is not attractive and not an intellectual possibility. He was once the great, the speaking poet for all who read English. He spoke both to the ordinary reader and to the literary man. But now the literary man outside the university will scarcely think of referring to Wordsworth as one of the important events of modern literature; and to the ordinary reader he is likely to exist as the very type of the poet whom life has passed by, presumably for the good reason that he passed life by.[2]

If we ask why Wordsworth is no longer the loved poet he once was, why, indeed, he is often thought to be rather absurd and even a little despicable, one answer that suggests itself is that for modern taste he is too Christian a poet. He is certainly not to be wholly characterized by the Christian element of his poetry. Nor can we say of him that he is a

"Wordsworth and the Iron Time" by Lionel Trilling. First printed with this title in *Wordsworth: Centenary Studies Presented at Cornell and Princeton Universities* (Princeton: Princeton University Press, 1951). Revised, and printed with the title "Wordsworth and the Rabbis," in Lionel Trilling, *The Opposing Self* (New York: The Viking Press, Inc. 1955). Copyright 1950 by Lionel Trilling. The revised version is reprinted here with a few additions, and with the original title restored, by permission of The Viking Press, Martin Secker & Warburg Ltd., London, and the author.

[1] The Centenary was celebrated in America at Cornell and Princeton Universities on April 21 and 22, 1950.
[2] 1971: Wordsworth's standing as a poet would seem to be considerably higher at the present time than it was when I gave this account of it in 1950.

Christian poet in the same sense that Dante is, or Donne, or Hopkins. With them the specific Christian feeling and doctrine is of the essence of their matter and their conscious intention, as it is not with Wordsworth. Yet at the present time, the doctrinal tendency of the world at large being what it is, that which *is* Christian in Wordsworth may well seem to be more prominent than it ever was before, and more decisive. I have in mind his concern for the life of humbleness and quiet, his search for peace, his sense of the burdens of this life, those which are inherent in the flesh and spirit of man. Then there is his belief that the bonds of society ought to be inner and habitual, not merely external and formal, and that the strengthening of these bonds by the acts and attitudes of charity is a great and charming duty. Christian too seems his responsiveness to the idea that there is virtue in the discharge of duties which are of the great world and therefore dangerous to simple peace—his sense of affinity with Milton was as much with Milton's political as with his poetical career, and the Happy Warrior is the man who has, as it were, sacrificed the virtuous peace of the poet to the necessities of public life. There is his impulse to submit to the conditions of life under a guidance that is at once certain and mysterious; his sense of the possibility and actuality of enlightenment, it need scarcely be said, is one of the characteristic things about him. It was not he who said that the world was a vale of soul-making, but the poet who did make this striking paraphrase of the Christian sentiment could not have uttered it had not Wordsworth made it possible for him to do so.[3] And then, above all, there is his consciousness of the *neighbor*, his impulse to bring into the circle of significant life those of the neighbors who are simple and outside the circle of social pride, and also those who in the judgment of the world are queer and strange and useless: faith and hope were to him very great virtues, but he conceived that they rested upon the still greater virtue, charity.

Certainly what I have called Christian in Wordsworth scarcely approaches, let alone makes up, the sum of Christianity. But then no personal document or canon can do that, not even the work of a poet who is specifically Christian in the way of Dante, or of Donne, or of Hopkins. When we speak of a poet as being of a particular religion, we do not imply in him completeness or orthodoxy, or even explicitness of doctrine, but only that his secular utterance has the decisive mark of the religion upon it. And if a religion is manifold in its aspects and extensive in time, the marks that are to be found on the poets who are in a relation to it will be various in kind. It seems to me that the marks of Christianity on Wordsworth are clear and indelible. It is therefore worth trying the

---

[3] It is of some relevance to our argument that when Keats wrote the famous phrase he believed that he was controverting, not affirming, a tendency of Christian thought.

hypothesis that the world today does not like him because it does not like the Christian quality and virtues.

But the question at once arises whether this hypothesis is actually available to us. Professor Hoxie Neal Fairchild says that it is not. In the chapter on Wordsworth in the third volume of his *Religious Trends in English Poetry,* he tells us that Wordsworth was *not* a Christian poet and goes on to express his doubt that Wordsworth was ever properly to be called a Christian person even when he became a communicant of the Church and its defender. And Professor Fairchild goes so far as to tell us that as a poet Wordsworth is actually dangerous to the Christian faith. He is dangerous in the degree that he may be called religious at all, for his religion is said to be mere religiosity, the religion of nothing more than the religious emotion, beginning and ending in the mere sense of transcendence. Naked of dogma, bare of precise predication of God and the nature of man, this religiosity of Wordsworth's is to be understood as a pretentious and seductive rival of Christianity. It is the more dangerous because it gives license to man's pretensions—Professor Fairchild subscribes to the belief that romanticism must bear a large part of the responsibility for our present ills, especially for those which involve man's direct and conscious inhumanity to man.

We can surely admit the cogency of Professor Fairchild's argument within the terms of its intention. The nineteenth century was in many respects a very Christian century, but in the aspect of it which bulks largest in our minds it developed chiefly the ethical and social aspects of Christian belief, no doubt at the cost of the dogmatic aspect, which had already been weakened by the latitudinarian tendency of the eighteenth century. And it is probably true that when the dogmatic principle in religion is slighted, religion goes along for a while on generalized emotion and ethical intention—"morality touched by emotion"—and then loses the force of its impulse, even the essence of its being. In this sort of attenuation of religion, romanticism in general, and Wordsworth in particular, did indeed play a part by making the sense of transcendence and immanence so real and so attractive. During the most interesting and important period of his career, Wordsworth seems to have been scarcely aware of the doctrines of the Church in which he had been reared. He spoke of faith, hope, and charity without reference to the specifically Christian source and end of these virtues. His sense of the need for salvation did not take the least account of the Christian means of salvation. Of evil in the Christian sense of the word, of sin as an element of the nature of man, he also took no account.

And yet, all this being true, as we look at Wordsworth in the context of his own time and in the context of our time, what may properly be called the Christian element of his poetry can be made to speak to us, as it spoke to so many Christians in the nineteenth century, as it spoke to so many who were not Christians and made them in one degree or another accessible to Christianity.

"Any religious movement," says Christopher Dawson, an orthodox Christian scholar, "which adopts a purely critical and negative attitude to culture is . . . a force of destruction and disintegration which mobilizes against it the healthiest and most constructive elements in society—elements which can by no means be dismissed as worthless from the religious point of view." Romanticism in general was far from worthless to Christianity, far from worthless to that very Anglo-Catholicism which inclines to be so strict with it. And this is true of Wordsworth in particular. He certainly did not in his great period accept as adequate what the Church taught about the nature of man. But he was one of the few poets who really discovered something about the nature of man. What he discovered can perhaps be shown, if the argument be conducted by a comparison of formulas and doctrine, to be at variance with the teachings of Christianity. Yet I think it can also be shown that Wordsworth discovered much that a strong Christianity must take account of, and be easy with, and make use of. It can be shown too, I believe, that the Church has found advantage in what Wordsworth has told us of the nature of man.

Professor Fairchild, I need scarcely say, understands Christianity far better than I do, through his having studied it ever so much more than I have; and of course he understands it far better than I might ever hope to, because he has experienced it as a communicant. He has also, I am sure, tested his conclusions by the whole tendency of the Church to which he gives so strong and thoughtful an allegiance. My own reading of this tendency, at least as it appears in literature and in literary criticism, where it has been so influential, is that it is not inclined to accept Wordsworth as a Christian poet. And still, even against the force of Professor Fairchild's judgment, I cannot help feeling that there is an important element of Christianity with which Wordsworth has a significant affinity, even though this element is not at the present time of chief importance to Christian intellectuals.

But this is not an occasion for anything like contentiousness, and I ought not to seem to be forcing even a great poet into a faith whose members do not want him there. I am not, in any case, so much concerned to prove that Wordsworth is a Christian poet as to account for a certain quality in him which makes him unacceptable to the modern world. And so, without repudiating my first hypothesis, I shall abandon it for this fresh one: that the quality in Wordsworth that now makes him unacceptable is a Judaic quality.

My knowledge of the Jewish tradition is, I fear, all too slight to permit me to hope that I can develop this new hypothesis in any very enlightening way. Yet there is one Jewish work of traditional importance which I happen to know with some intimacy, and it lends a certain color of accuracy to my notion. This is the work called *Pirke Aboth*, that is, the sayings, the *sententiae*, of the Fathers. It was edited in the second century of the present era by the scholar and teacher who bore the magnificent name of Rabbi Jehudah the Prince, and who is traditionally referred to by the even more magnificent name of *Rabbi*—that is to say, *the* rabbi, the master teacher, the greatest of all. In its first intention *Pirke Aboth*, under the name *Aboth*, "Fathers," was one of the tractates of the Mishnah, which is the traditional Jewish doctrine represented chiefly by rabbinical decisions. But *Aboth* itself, the last of the tractates, does not deal with decisions; nor is it what a common English rendering of the longer title, "Ethics of the Fathers," would seem to imply, for it is not a system of ethics at all but simply a collection of maxims and *pensées*, some of them very fine and some of them very dull, which praise the life of study and give advice on how to live it.

In speaking of Wordsworth a recollection of boyhood cannot be amiss— my intimacy with *Pirke Aboth* comes from my having read it many times in boyhood. It certainly is not the kind of book a boy is easily drawn to read, and certainly I did not read it out of piety. On the contrary, indeed: for when I was supposed to be reading my prayers—very long, and in the Hebrew language, which I never mastered—I spent the required time and made it seem that I was doing my duty by reading the English translation of the *Pirke Aboth*, which, although it is not a devotional work, had long ago been thought of as an aid to devotion and included in the prayer book. It was more attractive to me than psalms, meditations, and supplications; it seemed more humane, and the Fathers had a curious substantiality. Just where they lived I did not know, nor just when, and certainly the rule of life they recommended had a very quaint difference from the life I knew, or, indeed, from any life that I wanted to know. Yet they were real, their way of life had the charm of coherence. And when I went back to them, using R. Travers Herford's scholarly edition and translation of their sayings,[4] I could entertain the notion that my early illicit intimacy with them had had its part in preparing the way for my responsiveness to Wordsworth, that between the Rabbis and Wordsworth an affinity existed.

But I must at once admit that a large difficulty stands in the way of the affinity I suggest. The *Aboth* is a collection of the sayings of masters of the written word. The ethical life it recommends has study as both its means and its end, the study of Torah, of the Law, which alone can give

[4] *Pirke Aboth*, edited with introduction, translation and commentary, third edition (New York: 1945). I have also consulted the edition and translation of the Very Rev. Dr. Joseph H. Hertz, Chief Rabbi of the British Empire, and in my quotations I have drawn upon both versions, and sometimes, when it suited my point, I have combined two versions in a single quotation.

blessedness. So that from the start I am at the disadvantage of trying to make a conjunction between scholars living for the perpetual interpretation of a text and a poet for whom the natural world was at the heart of his doctrine and for whom books were barren leaves. The Rabbis expressed a suspiciousness of the natural world which was as extreme as Wordsworth's suspiciousness of study. That the warning was given at all seems to hint that it was possible for the Rabbis to experience the natural world as a charm and a temptation: still, the *Aboth* does warn us that whoever interrupts his study to observe the beauty of a fine tree or a fine meadow is guilty of sin. And yet I think it can be said without more extravagance than marks my whole comparison that it is precisely here, where they seem most to differ, that the Rabbis and Wordsworth are most at one. For between the Law as the Rabbis understood it and Nature as Wordsworth understood that, there is a pregnant similarity.

The Rabbis of the *Aboth* were Pharisees. I shall assume that the long scholarly efforts of Mr. Herford, as well as those of George Foot Moore, have by now made it generally known that the Pharisees were not in actual fact what tradition represents them to have been. They were anything but mere formalists, and of course they were not the hypocrites of popular conception. Here is Mr. Herford's statement of the defining principle of Pharisaism: "The central conception of Pharisaism is Torah, the divine Teaching, the full and inexhaustible revelation which God had made. The knowledge of what was revealed was to be sought, and would be found, in the first instance in the written text of the Pentateuch; but the revelation, the real Torah, was the meaning of what was there written, the meaning as interpreted by all the recognized and accepted methods of the schools, and unfolded in ever greater fullness of detail by successive generations of devoted teachers. The written text of the Pentateuch might be compared to the mouth of a well; the Torah was the water which was drawn from it. He who wished to draw the water must needs go to the well, but there was no limit to the water which was there for him to draw. . . . The study of Torah . . . means therefore much more than the study of the Pentateuch, or even of the whole Scripture, regarded as mere literature, written documents. It means the study of the revelation made through those documents, the divine teaching therein imparted, the divine thought therein disclosed. Apart from the direct intercourse of prayer, the study of Torah was the way of closest approach to God; it might be called the Pharisaic form of the Beatific Vision. To study Torah was, to the devout Pharisee, to 'think God's thoughts after him,' as Kepler said." The Rabbis, that is, found sermons in texts, tongues in the running commentary.

And Mr. Herford goes on to say that it might be observed of the *Aboth* that it makes very few direct references to God. "This is true," he says, "but it is beside the mark. Wherever Torah is mentioned, there God is implied. He is behind the Torah, the Revealer of what is Revealed." What I am trying to suggest is that, different as the immediately present objects were in each case, Torah for the Rabbis, Nature for Wordsworth, there existed for the Rabbis and for Wordsworth a great object, which is from God and might be said to represent Him as a sort of surrogate, a divine object to which one can be in an intimate passionate relationship, an active relationship—for Wordsworth's "wise passiveness" is of course an activity—which one can, as it were, handle, and in a sense create, drawing from it inexhaustible meaning by desire, intuition, and attention.

And when we turn to the particulars of the *Aboth* we see that the affinity continues. In Jewish tradition the great Hillel has a peculiarly Wordsworthian personality, being the type of gentleness and peace, and having about him a kind of *joy* which has always been found wonderfully attractive; and Hillel said—was, indeed, in the habit of saying: he "used to say"—"If I am not for myself, who, then, is for me? And if I am for myself, what then am I?" Mr. Herford implies that this is a difficult utterance. But it is not difficult for the reader of Wordsworth, who finds the Wordsworthian moral essence here, the interplay between individualism and the sense of community, between an awareness of the self that must be saved and developed, and an awareness that the self is yet fulfilled only in community.

Then there is this saying of Akiba's: "All is foreseen, and yet free will is given; and the world is judged by grace, and yet all is according to the work." With how handsome a boldness it handles the problem of fate and free will, or "grace" and "works," handles the problem by stating it as an antinomy, escaping the woeful claustral preoccupation with the alternatives, but not their grandeur. This refusal to be fixed either in fate or in free will, either in grace or in works, and the recognition of both, are characteristic of Wordsworth.

There are other parallels to be drawn. For example, one finds in the *Aboth* certain remarks which have a notable wit and daring because they go against the whole tendency of the work in telling us that the multiplication of words is an occasion for sin, and the chief thing is not study but action. One finds the injunction to the scholar to divide his time between study and a trade, presumably in the interest of humility. And the scholar is warned that the world must not be too much with him, that, getting and spending, he lays waste his powers. There is the concern, so typical of Wordsworth, with the "ages of man," with the right time in the individual's development for each of life's activities. But it is needless to multiply the details of the affinity, which in any case must not be insisted on too far. All that I want to suggest is the community of ideal and sensibility between the *Aboth* and the canon of Wordsworth's work —the passionate contemplation and experience of the great object which is proximate to Deity; then the plain living that goes with the high thinking, the desire for the humble life and the discharge of duty; and last, but not least important, a certain insouciant acquiescence in the anomalies of the moral order of the universe, a respectful indifference to, or graceful surrender before, the mysteries of the moral relation of God to man.

This last element, as it is expressed in the *pensée* of Akiba which I have quoted, has its connection with something in the *Aboth* which for me is definitive of its quality. Actually it is something not in the *Aboth* but left out—we find in the tractate no implication of moral struggle. We find the energy of assiduity but not the energy of resistance. We hear about sin, but we do not hear of the sinful nature of man. Man in the *Aboth* guards against sin but he does not struggle against it, and of evil we hear nothing at all.

When we have observed this, it is natural to observe next that there is no mention in the *Aboth* of courage or heroism. In our culture we connect the notion of courage or heroism with the religious life. We conceive of the perpetual enemy within and the perpetual enemy without, which must be "withstood," "overcome," "conquered"—the language of religion and the language of fighting are in our culture assimilated to each other. Not so in the *Aboth*. The enemy within seems not to be conceived of at all. The enemy without is never mentioned, although the *Aboth* was compiled after the Dispersion, after the Temple and the nation had been destroyed—with what heroism in the face of suffering we know from Josephus. Of the men whose words are cited in the *Aboth*, many met martyrdom for their religion, and the martyrology records their calm and fortitude in torture and death; of Akiba it records his heroic joy. And yet in their maxims they never speak of courage. There is not a word to suggest that the life of virtue and religious devotion requires the heroic quality.

As much as anything else in my boyhood experience of the *Aboth* it was this that fascinated me. It also repelled me. It had this double effect because it went so clearly against the militancy of spirit which in our culture is normally assumed. And even now, as I consider this indifference to heroism of the *Aboth,* I have the old ambiguous response to it, so that I think I can understand the feelings that readers have when they encounter something similar in Wordsworth. It is what Matthew Arnold noted when in the "Memorial Verses" he compared Wordsworth with Byron, who was for Arnold the embodiment of militancy of spirit. Arnold said of Wordsworth that part of his peculiar value to us arose from his indifference to "man's fiery might," to the Byronic courage in fronting human destiny.

> The cloud of mortal destiny,
> Others will front it fearlessly—
> But who, like him, will put it by?

Arnold certainly did not mean that Wordsworth lacked courage or took no account of it. Wordsworth liked nothing better, indeed, than to recite examples of courage, but the Wordsworthian courage is different in kind from the Byronic. For one thing, it is never aware of itself, it is scarcely personal. It is the courage of mute, insensate things, and it is often associated with such things, "with rocks, and stones, and trees," or with stars. Michael on his hilltop, whose character is defined by the light of his cottage, which was called "The Evening Star," and by the stones of his sheepfold; or the Leech Gatherer, who is like some old, great rock; or Margaret, who, like a tree, endured as long as she might after she was blasted—of the Lesser Celandine it is said that its fortitude in meeting the rage of the storm is neither its courage nor its choice but "its necessity in being old," and the same thing is to be said of all Wordsworth's exemplars of courage: they endure because they are what they are, and we might almost say that they survive out of a kind of biological faith, which is not the less human because it is nearly an animal or vegetable faith; and, indeed, as I have suggested, it is sometimes nearly mineral. Even the Happy Warrior, the man in arms, derives his courage not from his militancy of spirit but from his calm submission to the law of things.

In Wordsworth's vision of life, then, the element of quietude approaches passivity, even insentience, and the dizzy raptures of youth have their issue in the elemental existence of which I have spoken. The scholars of the *Aboth* certainly had no such notion; they lived for intellectual sentience. But where the scholars and Wordsworth are at one is in the quietism, which is not in the least a negation of life, but, on the contrary, an affirmation of life so complete that it needed no saying. To the Rabbis, as I read them, there life was, unquestionable because committed to a divine object. There life was—in our view rather stuffy and airless, or circumscribed and thin, but very intense and absolutely and utterly real, not needing to be affirmed by force or assertion, real because the object of its regard was unquestioned, and because the object was unquestionably more important than the individual person who regarded it and lived by it. To Wordsworth, as I read him, a similar thing was true in its own way. Much as he loved to affirm the dizzy raptures of sentience, of the ear and the eye and the mind, he also loved to move down the scale of being, to say that when the sentient spirit was sealed by slumber, when it was without motion and force, when it was like a rock or a stone or a tree, not hearing or seeing, and passive in the cosmic motion—that even then, perhaps especially then, existence was blessed.

Nothing could be further from the tendency of our Western culture, which is committed to an idea of consciousness and activity, of motion and force. With us the basis of spiritual prestige is some form of aggressive action directed outward upon the world, or inward upon ourselves.

During the last century and a half this ideal has been especially strong in literature. If the religious personality of preceding times took to itself certain of the marks of military prestige, the literary personality now takes to itself certain of the marks of religious prestige, in particular the capacity for militant suffering.

A peculiarly relevant example of this lies to hand in T. S. Eliot's explanation of the decline of Wordsworth's genius from its greatness to what Mr. Eliot calls the "still sad music of infirmity." The small joke, so little characteristic of Mr. Eliot's humor, suggests something of the hostile uneasiness that Wordsworth can arouse in us. And Mr. Eliot's theory of the decline suggests the depth of our belief in the value of militancy, of militant suffering, for Mr. Eliot tells us that the trouble with Wordsworth was that he didn't have an eagle: it is that eagle which André Gide's Prometheus said was necessary for success in the spiritual or poetic life—"*Il faut avoir un aigle.*" As an explanation of Wordsworth's poetic career this is, we perceive, merely a change rung on the weary idea that Wordsworth destroyed his poetic genius by reversing his position on the French Revolution or by terminating his connection with Annette Vallon. Wordsworth had no need of an eagle for his greatness, and its presence or absence had nothing to do with the decline of his genius. His pain, when he suffered, was not of the kind that eagles inflict, and his power did not have its source in his pain. But we are disturbed by the absence of the validating, the poetically respectable bird, that *aigle obligatoire*. We like the fiercer animals. Nothing is better established in our literary life than the knowledge that the tigers of wrath are to be preferred to the horses of instruction, a striking remark which is indeed sometimes very true, although not always. We know that we ought to prefer the bulls in the ring to the horses, and when we choose between the two kinds of horses of Plato's chariot we all know that Plato was wrong, that it is the blacks, not the whites, which are to be preferred. We do not, to be sure, live in the fashion of the beasts we admire in our literary lives, but we cherish them as representing something that we all seek. They are the emblems of the *charisma*—to borrow from the sociologists a word they have borrowed from the theologians—which is the hot, direct relationship with Godhead, or with the sources of life, upon which depend our notions of what I have called spiritual prestige.

The predilection for the powerful, the fierce, the assertive, the personally militant, is very strong in our culture. We find it in the liberal-bourgeois admiration of the novels of Thomas Wolfe and Theodore Dreiser. On a lower intellectual level we find it in the long popularity of that curious underground work *The Fountainhead*. On a higher intellectual level we find it in certain aspects of the work of Yeats and Lawrence. We find it too, if not in our religion itself, then at least in one of our dominant conceptions of religion—to many intellectuals the violence of Dostoevski represents the natural form of the religious life, to many gentle spirits the ferocity of Léon Bloy seems quite appropriate to the way of faith; and although some years ago Mr. Eliot reprobated D. H. Lawrence, in the name of religion, for his addiction to this characteristic violence, yet for Mr. Eliot the equally violent Baudelaire is pre-eminently a Christian poet.[5]

I cannot give a better description of the quality of our literature with which I am concerned than by quoting the characterization of it which Richard Chase found occasion to make in the course of a review of a work on the nineteenth century by a notable English scholar, Professor Basil Willey. It is relevant to remark that Professor Willey deals with the nineteenth century from the point of view of the Anglican form of Christianity, and Mr. Chase is commenting on Professor Willey's hostility to a certain Victorian figure who, in any discussion of Wordsworth, must inevitably be in our minds—John Stuart Mill. His name seems very queer and shocking when it is spoken together with the names of the great figures of modern literature. Yet Mr. Chase is right when he says that "among the Victorians, it is Mill who tests the modern mind," and goes on to say that "in relation to him at least two of its weaknesses come quickly to light. The first is its morose desire for dogmatic certainty. The second is its hyperaesthesia: its feeling that no thought is permissible except an extreme thought: that every idea must be directly emblematic of concentration camps, alienation, madness, hell, history, and God; that every word must bristle and explode with the magic potency of our plight."

I must be careful not to seem to speak, as certainly Mr. Chase is not speaking, against the sense of urgency or immediacy, or against power or passion. Nor would I be taken to mean that the Wordsworthian quietism I have described is the whole desideratum of the emotional life. It obviously wasn't that for Wordsworth himself—he may be said to be the first poet who praised movement and speed for their own sakes, and dizziness and danger; he is the poet of rapture. No one can read Book Five of *The Prelude* and remain unaware of Wordsworth's conception of literature as urgency and immediacy, as power and passion. Book Five, which is about literature and the place of reading in our spiritual development, opens with an impressive eschatological vision, a vision of final events—Wordsworth shared in his own way our present sense of the possible end of man and of all the works of man's spirit, and it is important to observe that in the great dream of the Arab who hastens

[5] In his brief introduction to Father Tiverton's *D. H. Lawrence and Human Existence*, Mr. Eliot has indicated that he has changed his mind about Lawrence's relation to the religious life. I think he was right to do so. The revision of his opinion confirms, if anything, what I say of the place of violence in our conception of the religious life.

before the advancing flood to rescue Science and Poetry, represented by the Stone and the Shell he carries, the prophecy of the world destroyed is made to seem the expression of the very essence of literature. It is in this book that Wordsworth defends the violence and fearfulness of literature from the "progressive" ideas of his day; it is here that he speaks of the poet as "crazed / By love and feeling, and internal thought / Protracted among endless solitude," and of the "reason" that lies couched "in the blind and awful lair" of the poet's madness; and it is here that he defends the "maniac's" dedication at the cost of the domestic affections:

> Enow there are on earth to take in charge
> Their wives, their children, and their virgin loves,
> Or whatsoever else the heart holds dear;
> Enow to stir for these. . . .
> [*The Prelude* (1850), V, 153–56]

As we speak of Wordsworth's quietism this opposite element of his poetry must be borne in mind. Then too, if we speak in anything like praise of his quietism, we must be conscious of the connection of his quietism with an aspect of his poetry that we rightly dread. When, in *The Excursion*, the Wanderer and the Poet and the Pastor sit upon the gravestones and tell sad stories of the deaths of other mild old men, for the benefit of the Solitary, who has had his fling at life and is understandably a little bitter, we know that something wrong is being done to us; we long for the winding of a horn or the drawing of a sword; we want someone to dash in on a horse—I think we want exactly a stallion, St. Mawr or another; for there can be no doubt about it, Wordsworth, at the extreme or perversion of himself, carries the element of quietude to the point of the denial of sexuality. And this is what makes the *A both* eventually seem to us quaint and oppressive, what, I suppose, makes a modern reader uneasy under any of the philosophies which urge us to the contemplative accord with a unitary reality and warn us that the accord will infallibly be disturbed and destroyed by the desires. Whether it be the Torah of the Rabbis, or the Cosmos of Marcus Aurelius, or the Nature of Spinoza or of Wordsworth, the accord with the unitary reality seems to depend upon the suppression not only of the sexual emotions but also of the qualities that are associated with sexuality: high-heartedness, wit, creative innovation, will.

But now, when we have touched upon the Wordsworthian quality that is very close to the Stoic *apatheia,* to not-feeling, let us remember what great particular thing Wordsworth is said to have accomplished. Matthew Arnold said that in a wintry clime, in an iron time, Wordsworth taught us to *feel*. This statement, extreme as it is, will be seen to be not inaccurate if we bring to mind the many instances of spiritual and psychological crisis in the nineteenth century in which affectlessness, the loss of the power to feel, played an important part. *Ennui, noia*—how often we meet with them in nineteenth-century biography; and the *acedia* which was once a disorder of the specifically religious life becomes now a commonplace of secular spirituality. Arnold, when he wrote the "Memorial Verses," could not, of course, have read Mill's autobiography, which so specifically and eloquently confirms Arnold's attribution to Wordsworth of a "healing power" through an ability to make us feel. And yet, although Arnold's statement is accurate so far as it goes, and is supported by Wordsworth's own sense of the overarching intention of his poetic enterprise, it does not go far enough. Wordsworth did, or tried to do, more than make us feel: he undertook to teach us how to *be*.

In *The Prelude,* in Book Two, Wordsworth speaks of a particular emotion which he calls "the sentiment of Being." The "sentiment" has been described in this way: "There is, in sanest hours, a consciousness, a thought that rises, independent, lifted out from all else, calm, like the stars, shining eternal. This is the thought of identity—yours for you, whoever you are, as mine for me. Miracle of miracles, beyond statement, most spiritual and vaguest of earth's dreams, yet hardest basic fact, and only entrance to all facts." This, of course, is not Wordsworth, it is Walt Whitman, but I quote Whitman's statement in exposition of Wordsworth's "sentiment of Being" because it is in some respects rather more boldly explicit, although not necessarily better, than anything that Wordsworth himself wrote about the sentiment, and because Whitman goes on to speak of his "hardest basic fact" as a political fact, as the basis, and the criterion, of democracy.

Through all his poetic life Wordsworth was preoccupied by the idea, by the sentiment, by the problem, of being. All experience, all emotions lead to it. He was haunted by the mysterious fact that he existed. He could discover in himself different intensities and qualities of being—"Tintern Abbey" is the attempt to distinguish these intensities and qualities. Being is sometimes animal; sometimes it is an "appetite and a passion"; sometimes it is almost a suspension of the movement of the breath and blood. The *Lyrical Ballads* have many intentions, but one of the chief of them is the investigation of the problems of being. "We are Seven," which is always under the imputation of bathos, is established in its true nature when we read it as an ontological poem; its subject is the question, What does it mean when we say a person *is*? "The Idiot Boy," which I believe to be a great and not a foolish poem, is a kind of comic assertion of the actuality—and, indeed, the peculiar intensity—of being in a person who is outside the range of anything but our merely mechanical understanding. Johnny on the little horse, flourishing his branch of holly under the moon, is a creature of rapture, who, if he is not quite "human," is certainly elemental, magical, perhaps a little divine—"It was Johnny, Johnny everywhere." As much as anyone, and more than many —more than most—he *is,* and feels that he is.

From even the little I have said, it will be seen that as soon as the "sentiment of Being" is named, or represented, there arises a question of its degree of actuality or of its survival. "The glad animal movements" of the boy, the "appetite" and the "passion" of the young man's response to Nature easily confirm the sense of being. So do those experiences which are represented as a "sleep" or "slumber," when the bodily senses are in abeyance. But as the man grows older the stimuli to the experience of the sentiment of being grow fewer or grow less intense—it is this fact rather than any question of poetic creation (such as troubled Coleridge) that makes the matter of the Immortality Ode. Wordsworth, as it were, puts the awareness of being to the test in situations where its presence may perhaps most easily be questioned—in very old people. Other kinds of people also serve for the test, such as idiots, the insane, children, the dead, but I emphasize the very old because Wordsworth gave particular attention to them, and because we can all be aware from our own experience what a strain very old people put upon our powers of attributing to them personal being, "identity." Wordsworth's usual way is to represent the old man as being below the human condition, apparently scarcely able to communicate, and then suddenly, startlingly, in what we have learned to call an "epiphany," to show forth the intensity of his human existence. The old man in "Animal Tranquillity and Decay" is described as being so old and so nearly inanimate that the birds regard him as little as if he were a stone or a tree; for this, indeed, he is admired, and the poem says that his unfelt peace is so perfect that it is envied by the very young. He is questioned about his destination on the road—

> I asked him whither he was bound, and what
> The object of his journey; he replied,
> "Sir! I am going many miles to take
> A last leave of my son, a mariner,
> Who from a sea-fight has been brought to Falmouth,
> And there is dying in an hospital."

The revelation of the actuality of his being, of his humanness, quite dazzles us.[6]

The social and political implication of Wordsworth's preoccupation with ontology is obvious enough. It is not, however, quite what Wordsworth sometimes says it is. The direct political lesson that the poet draws from the Old Cumberland Beggar is interesting, but it is beside his real,

---

[6] The concluding lines of the poem as originally printed in *Lyrical Ballads*, where the poem bears the title "Old Man Travelling," were deleted by Wordsworth in subsequent editions, which is a misfortune.

his essential, point. "Deem not this man useless," he says in his apostrophe to the political theorists who have it in mind to put the Beggar into a workhouse, and he represents the usefulness of the Beggar as consisting in his serving as the object of a habitual charity and thus as a kind of communal institution, a communal bond. But this demonstrated utility of the Beggar is really secondary to the fact that he *is*—he is a person, he takes a pleasure, even though a minimal one, in his being, and therefore he may not in conscience be dealt with as a mere social unit. So with all the dramatis personae of the *Lyrical Ballads*—the intention of the poet is to require us to acknowledge their being and thus to bring them within the range of conscience, and of something more immediate than conscience, natural sympathy. It is an attractive thing about Wordsworth, and it should be a reassuring thing, that his acute sense of the being of others derives from, and serves to affirm and heighten, his acute sense of his own being.

I have spoken of Wordsworth's preoccupation with being as if it were unique, and as if it accounted for, or led to what accounts for, the contemporary alienation from his work and his personality. In some ways his preoccupation *is* unique, and certain aspects of it do lead to the present alienation from him. Yet from what I have said about him, it must be clear that between Wordsworth and the great figures of our literature there is a very close affinity indeed, if only in the one regard of the preoccupation with being. There is scarcely a great writer of our own day who has not addressed himself to the ontological crisis, who has not conceived of life as a struggle to be—not to live, but to be. They do so, to be sure, under a necessity rather different from Wordsworth's, and this necessity makes it seem appropriate that, with Byron, they assert "man's fiery might." (Blake suggests more aptly than Byron the quality of the militancy of most modern writers, but I stay with the terms of the opposition as Arnold gives them to us.) They feel the necessity to affirm the personal qualities that are associated with a former time, presumably a freer and more personally privileged time—they wish, as a character in one of Yeats's plays says, "to bring back the old disturbed exalted life, the old splendor." Their image of freedom and personal privilege is often associated with violence, sometimes of a kind that does not always command the ready assent we are habituated to give to violence when it appears in moral or spiritual contexts. A tenant's sliced-off ear, which is an object of at least momentary pleasure to Yeats, a kick given by an employer to his employee, which wins the approval of Lawrence—these are all too accurately representative of the nature of the political fantasies that Yeats and Lawrence built upon the perception of the loss of freedom and privilege, the loss of the sense of being. Yet we know that this violence stands against an extreme fate of which we are all conscious. We really know in our time what the death of the word can be—for that knowledge we have only to read an account of contemporary Russian literature. We really know what the death of the spirit means—we have seen it overtake whole peoples. Nor do we need to go beyond our own daily lives to become aware, if we dare to, of how we have conspired, in our very virtues, to bring about the devaluation of whatever is bold and assertive and free, replacing it by the bland, the covert, the manipulative. If we wish to understand the violence, the impulse toward charismatic power, of so much of our literature, we have but to consider that we must endure not only the threat to being which comes from without but also the seduction to non-being which establishes itself within. We need, in Coleridge's words, something to "startle this dull pain, and make it move and live." Violence is a means of self-definition; the bad conscience, Nietzsche says, assures us of our existence.

Wordsworth, then, is not separated from us by his preoccupation with being, for it is our preoccupation. Yet he is separated from us. His conception of being seems different from ours.

In Book Five of *The Prelude* Wordsworth gives us a satiric picture of the boy educated according to the "progressive" ideas of his day, and on the whole we follow him readily enough in the objections he makes to these ideas—this can be said even though it often happens that readers, misled by their preconceptions of Wordsworth, take his sarcasm seriously and suppose that he is actually praising "this model of a child." And we follow him when he speaks of the presumptuousness of pedagogical theorists, denouncing them as, in effect, engineers of the spirit: he flatters at least one element of our ambivalence toward the psychological expert. We are responsive to his notion of what a boy should be: "not . . . too good," "not unresentful where self-justified." Possibly we are not in perfect agreement with him on all points—perhaps we will feel that he has dealt rather too harshly with the alert political and social consciousness of the progressive child, or that he goes too far in thinking that a child's imagination should be fed on fanciful books; perhaps, too, the qualities of the boys he really admires would not be precisely the qualities we would specify—"Fierce, moody, patient, venturous, modest, shy." But on the whole his discussion of pedagogics appeals to the enlightened muddled concern with "adjustment" and "aggression" which occupies the P.T.A. segment of our minds, and if we have our reservation about details we can at least, as I say, follow Wordsworth through most of his argument. But I think we cease to follow him when, in the course of the argument, he rises to one of his great poetical moments. This is the passage "There was a Boy. . . ." It was perhaps rather finer when it stood alone as a poem in itself in *Lyrical Ballads,* but it is still very fine in its place in *The Prelude,* where it follows the description of the model child. The Boy is described as having had a trick of imitating the hooting of owls, and at night he would call across Windermere, trying to get the owls to answer; and often they did answer, but sometimes they did not, and then the silence would be strange and significant.

> . . . In that silence, while he hung
> Listening, a gentle shock of mild surprise
> Has carried far into his heart the voice
> Of mountain torrents; or the visible scene
> Would enter unawares into his mind,
> With all its solemn imagery, its rocks,
> Its woods, and that uncertain heaven, received
> Into the bosom of the steady lake.
> [*The Prelude* (1850), V, 381-88]

We may be ready enough to acknowledge the "beauty" of the poem, but the chances are that we will be rather baffled by its intention. We perceive that the Boy is obviously intended to represent something very good and right, meant to be an example of very full being. But what baffles us, what makes us wonder what the poem has to do with education and the development of personality, is that the Boy exercises no will, or at least, when his playful will is frustrated, is at once content with the pleasures that follow upon the suspended will. And as likely as not we will be impelled to refer the poem to that "mysticism" which is supposed to be an element of Wordsworth's mind. Now Wordsworth's mind does have an element of mysticism—it is that "normal mysticism" which, according to a recent writer on the Rabbis, marked the Rabbinical mind.[7] Wordsworth's mysticism, if we wish to call it that, consists of two elements, his conception of the world as being semantic, and his capacity for intense pleasure. When we speak of him as a mystic in any other sense, we are pretty sure to be expressing our incomprehension of the intensity with which he experienced his own being, and our incomprehension of the relation which his sentiment of being bore to his will. Thus, we have no trouble understanding him when, in Book Six of *The Prelude,* in the remarkable episode of the crossing of the Alps, he speaks of the glory of the will.

---

[7] Max Kadushin, *The Rabbinical Mind* (New York: 1951). This impressive work of scholarship has received far less general notice than it deserves. I read it after I had written this essay—read it not only with admiration for its intellectual achievement but also with a peculiar personal pleasure, because its author, in his seminary days, had been one of the long-suffering men who tried to teach me Hebrew, with what success I have indicated; yet he did teach me—it was no small thing for a boy of twelve to be in relation with a serious scholar. Dr. Kadushin has been kind enough to tell me that what I have said about the Rabbis is not wrong. In revising my essay I have not tried to amend my primitive account by what is to be learned from Dr. Kadushin's presentation of the Rabbis in all their great complexity of thought. But the phrase, "normal mysticism," seemed too apt not to quote.

> . . . Whether we be young or old,
> Our destiny, our being's heart and home,
> Is with infinitude, and only there;
> With hope it is, hope that can never die,
> Effort, and expectation, and desire,
> And something evermore about to be.

The note on which the will is affirmed is high, Miltonic—it echoes the accents of Satan's speech in the Council of Hell; and the passage resumes its movement with a line the martial tenor of which we happily respond to: "Under such banners militant, the soul. . . ." But we are checked by what ensues:

> Under such banners militant, the soul
> Seeks for no trophies, struggles for no spoils
> That may attest her prowess, blest in thoughts
> That are their own perfection and reward,
> Strong in herself and in beatitude. . . .
> [*The Prelude* (1850), VI, 603–13]

The soul's energy is directed to the delight of the soul in itself.

Wordsworth is describing the action of what, at a later time, a man of very different mind, Hegel, was to call a new human faculty, the faculty of *Gemüt*. The word, I gather, is not entirely susceptible of translation —"heart," with the implication of responsiveness, and of high-heartedness and large-heartedness, is an approximation. Hegel defines his faculty of *Gemüt* as expressing itself as a desire, a will, which has "no particular aims, such as riches, honors, and the like; in fact, it does not concern itself with any worldly condition of wealth, prestige, etc., but with the entire condition of the soul—a general sense of enjoyment."

Much that I have said about the tendency of our culture would seem to deny the truth of Hegel's statement that *Gemüt* is one of the characteristics of our time, and much more evidence might be adduced to confirm the impression that nothing could be less characteristic of our time than the faculty of *Gemüt*, that we scarcely conceive of it, let alone exercise it. Yet at the same time I think it is true to say that it plays in our culture a covert but very important part.

Of our negative response to *Gemüt*, to the "sentiment of Being," Mr. Eliot provides an instance—again, for it is Mr. Eliot's high gift to be as pertinent when we think him wrong as when we think him right. In *The Cocktail Party* there is a description of the two virtuous ways of life, that of "the common routine" and that of the spiritual heroism of the saint and martyr. The two ways, Mr. Eliot tells us, are of equal value; the way of the saint is not better than that of the householder. Yet when it comes to describing the life of the common routine, Mr. Eliot says of those who elect it that they

> Learn to avoid excessive expectation,
> Become tolerant of themselves and others,
> Giving and taking in the usual actions
> What there is to give and take. They do not repine;
> And are contented with the morning that separates
> And with the evening that brings together
> For casual talk before the fire
> Two people who know that they do not understand each other,
> Breeding children whom they do not understand
> And who will never understand them.

Well, few of us will want to say much for the life of the common routine, and no doubt, under the aspect of modern life with its terrible fatigues, and in the consciousness of its gross threats, the sort of thing that Mr. Eliot says here will be pretty nearly all that any of us will want to say. Yet if we think of the description of the common routine as being not merely the expression of one possible mood among many—and it is not merely that: it is what it says it is, the description of a "way"—we must find it very strange. There is in it no reference to the pain which is an essential and not an accidental part of the life of the common routine. There is no reference to the principles, the ethical discipline, by which the ordinary life is governed—all is habit. There is no reference to the possibility of either joy or glory—I use the Wordsworthian words by intention. The possibility of *Gemüt* does not appear. Mr. Eliot does not say that his couples are in Limbo, that they are in a condition of not-being, which would of course be a true thing to say of many house-holding couples: he is describing the virtuous way of life that is alternative to the way of the saint. This failure to conceive the actuality of the life of common routine is typical of modern literature since, say, Tolstoi. I do not say this in order to suggest that domestic life, the common routine, in itself makes an especially appropriate subject for literature —I don't think it does—but in order to suggest a limitation of our conception of the spiritual life. Mr. Eliot's representation of the two "ways" exemplifies how we are drawn to the violence of extremity. We imagine, with nothing in between, the dull not-being of life, the intense not-being of death; but we do not imagine being—we do not imagine that it can be a joy. We are in love, at least in our literature, with the fantasy of death. Death and suffering, when we read, are our only means of conceiving the actuality of life.

Perhaps this is not new and we but intensify what is indigenous in our culture. Perhaps this is in the nature of life as Western culture has long been fated to see it. Perhaps it is inescapable for us that the word "tragic" should be used as an ultimate recommendation of a sense of life. Yet we, when we use the word, do not really mean it in its old, complex, mysterious sense—we mean something like "violent" or "conclusive": we mean death. And just here lies a paradox and our point. For it is precisely what Wordsworth implies by his passionate insistence on being, even at a very low level of consciousness, pride, and assertiveness, as well as at the highest level of quasi-mystic intensity, that validates a conception of tragedy, and a conception of heroism. The saintly martyrdom which Mr. Eliot represents in his play is of course not intended to be taken as tragic: the idea of martyrdom precludes the idea of tragedy. But if we ask why the martyrdom seems as factitious as it does, must we not answer that this is because it is presented in a system of feeling which sets very little store by—which, indeed, denies the possibility of—the "beatitude" which Wordsworth thought was the birthright of every human soul? And this seems to be borne out by the emphasis which Mr. Eliot puts on the peculiar horror of the mode of the martyr's death, as if only by an extremity of pain could we be made to realize that a *being* was actually involved, that a life has been sacrificed—or, indeed, has been lived.

Wordsworth's incapacity for tragedy has often been remarked on, and accurately enough. Yet we cannot conclude that Wordsworth's relation to tragedy is wholly negative. The possibility of tragic art depends primarily upon the worth we ascribe not to dying but to living, and to living in "the common routine." The power of the Homeric tragedy, for example, derives from the pathos, which the poet is at pains to bring before us repeatedly, of young men dying, of not seeing ever again the trees of their native farmsteads, of their parents never again admiring and indulging them, of the cessation of their being in the common routine. The tragic hero, Achilles, becomes a tragic hero exactly because he has made choice to give up the life of the common routine, which all his comrades desire, in favor of a briefer but more intense quality of being of transcendent glory. The pathos of his particular situation becomes the great thing it is because of the respondent pathos of Hector and Priam, which is the pathos of the family and the common routine, which we understand less and less and find ourselves more and more uncomfortable with. And I think it can be shown that every tragic literature owes its power to the high esteem in which it holds the common routine, and the sentiment of being which arises from it, the elemental *given* of biology. And that is what Wordsworth had in mind when, in the "Preface" of 1800, defending the idea that poetry should give "immediate pleasure," he said that this idea was "a homage paid to the native and naked dignity of man, to the grand elementary principle of pleasure, by which he knows, and feels, and lives, and moves."

Yet if we are aware of the tendency of our literature I have exemplified by the passage from Mr. Eliot's play, we must at the same time be aware of the equally strong counter-tendency. In speaking of our alienation from Wordsworth, it has not been my intention to make a separation between Wordsworth and the literature of our time. The separation cannot be made. Wordsworth and the great writers of our time stand, as I have said, on the common ground of the concern with being and its problems —Wordsworth, indeed, may be said to have discovered and first explored the ground upon which our literature has established itself. Our hyperaesthesia, our preference for the apocalyptic subject and the charismatic style, do indeed constitute a taste which alienates many readers from Wordsworth, and no doubt the more if we believe, as some do, that it is a taste wholly appropriate to the actualities of our historical situation. Yet we can without too much difficulty become aware of how much of the Wordsworthian "mildness," which so readily irritates us, and how much of the Wordsworthian quietism (as I have called it), which dismays us, are in the grain of our literature, expressed through the very intensities which seem to deny them. Thus, to bring Wordsworth and James Joyce into conjunction might at first seem a joke or a paradox, or an excess of historicism, at best a mere device of criticism. We will at once be conscious of the calculated hauteur of Joyce's implied personality, the elaborations of his irony, the uncompromising challenge of his style and his manner, and by the association of contrast we will remember that horrendous moment in *The Prelude* when Wordsworth says, "My drift I fear / Is scarcely obvious." How can we fail to think only of the abysses of personality, theory, and culture that separate the two men? And yet when we have become acclimated to Joyce, when the charismatic legend becomes with familiarity not so fierce and the vatic paraphernalia of the style and method less intimidating, do we not find that we are involved in a conception of life that reiterates, in however different a tonality, the Wordsworthian vision? [8] One of the striking things about *Ulysses* (to speak only of that work) is that the idea of evil plays so small a part in it. One hears a good deal about the essential Christian orthodoxy of Joyce, and perhaps this is an accurate opinion, but his orthodoxy, if he has it, takes no account of the evil which is so commonly affirmed by the literary expressions of orthodoxy; the conception of sin has but a tangential relevance to the book. The element of sexuality which plays so large a part in the story does not raise considerations of sin and evil; it is dealt with in the way of poetic naturalism. The character of Leopold Bloom, who figures in the life of Joyce's Poet much as the old men in Wordsworth

---

[8] 1971: At this date the conjunction of Wordsworth and Joyce will probably not seem at all bizarre, especially in view of what we now know of Joyce's admiration for Wordsworth. In a letter of 1905 to his brother Stanislaus, Joyce said, "I think Wordsworth of all English men of letters best deserves your word 'genius.'" (*Letters of James Joyce*, ed. Richard Ellmann [London, 1957–66], II, 91.)

figure in his life—met by chance and giving help of some transcendent yet essentially human kind—is conceived in Wordsworthian terms: in terms, that is, of his humbleness of spirit. If we speak of Wordsworth in reference to the Rabbis and their non-militancy, their indifference to the idea of evil, their acceptance of cosmic contradiction, are we not to say that Bloom is a Rabbinical character? It is exactly his non-militancy that makes him the object of general contempt and, on one occasion, of rage. It is just this that has captivated his author, as the contrast with the armed pride, the jealousy and desire for prestige, the bitter militancy of Stephen Dedalus. Leopold Bloom is deprived of every shred of dignity except the dignity of that innocence which for Joyce, as for Wordsworth, goes with the "sentiment of Being."

Again and again in our literature, at its most apocalyptic and intense, we find the impulse to create figures who are intended to suggest that life is justified in its elemental biological simplicity, and, in the manner of Wordsworth, these figures are conceived of as being of humble status and humble heart: Lawrence's simpler people or primitive people whose pride is only that of plants or animals; Dreiser's Jennie Gerhardt and Mrs. Griffiths, who stand as oases in the wide waste of their creator's dull representation of energy; Hemingway's waiters with their curious silent dignity; Faulkner's Negroes, of whom it is said, as so often it is said in effect of Wordsworth's people, *they endured;* and Faulkner's idiot boys, of whom it is to be said, *they are*—the list could be extended to suggest how great is the affinity of our literature with Wordsworth. And these figures express an intention which is to be discerned through all our literature—the intention to imagine, and to reach, a condition of the soul in which the will is freed from "particular aims," in which it is "strong in itself and in beatitude." At least as early as Balzac our literature has shown the will seeking its own negation—or, rather, seeking its own affirmation by its rejection of the aims which the world sets before it and by turning its energies upon itself in self-realization. Of this particular affirmation of the will Wordsworth is the proponent and the poet.

The Contemporaneity of the *Lyrical Ballads*

by Robert Mayo

A fruitful but unfrequented approach to the *Lyrical Ballads* is through the poetry of the magazines. The volume unquestionably belongs to 1798, and seen in relation to the popular verse of that day, its contemporaneous features are very striking. We have been asked to consider too exclusively the revolutionary aspects of the *Lyrical Ballads*. Revolutionary they unquestionably were, but not in every respect. Except that they were much better than other poems published in 1798, the *Ballads* were not such a "complete change" as some writers would have us believe.[1] Even their eccentricity has been exaggerated. Actually, there is a conventional side to the *Lyrical Ballads*, although it is usually overlooked. It is by way of the general taste for poetry in the 1790's that this essay will approach the poems, and it will attempt to show that they not only conformed in numerous ways to the modes of 1798, and reflected popular tastes and attitudes, but enjoyed a certain popularity in the magazines themselves.

The general interest in poetry during the last decades of the eighteenth century, also, is a phenomenon which is largely ignored, although it is relevant in a number of ways to the new poetry of Southey, Coleridge, Wordsworth, Byron, and Scott. Something is known of the popularity of

---

"The Contemporaneity of the *Lyrical Ballads*" by Robert Mayo. From *PMLA*, 69 (1954). Copyright © 1954 by The Modern Language Association of America. Reprinted by permission of PMLA and the author. A middle section of the essay has been omitted.

[1] "The volume [of 1798] undoubtedly was a puzzle, for it marked a complete change from anything that had appeared before" (Elsie Smith, *An Estimate of William Wordsworth by His Contemporaries*, Oxford, 1932, p. 33). The phrase is T. J. Wise's: ". . . the *Ballads* marked a complete change from the style and character of poetical composition then regarded as classic" (*A Bibliography of the Writings in Prose and Verse of William Wordsworth*, London, 1916, p. 31). But the opinion has been widely expressed. Cf. Oliver Elton: "They [the *Ballads*] are mostly reflective narratives, of a great variety of forms. . . . There had been nothing of the sort before; the very faults were new" (*A Survey of English Literature, 1780–1830*, 4th imp., London, 1933, II, 64). Also Littledale: "The Volume of *Lyrical Ballads* made its appeal in 1798 to a small and unprepared public; it had to create the taste by which it was enjoyed" (*Wordsworth and Coleridge, Lyrical Ballads, 1798*, ed. H. Littledale, London: Oxford University Press, 1931, p. vii).

such writers as Helen Maria Williams, Anna Seward, Erasmus Darwin, W. L. Bowles, "Peter Pindar," Charlotte Smith, Henry James Pye, Mary Robinson, and Mrs. West; but except for Bowles they are usually dealt with summarily as a deservedly forgotten generation. For most historians they are the "modern writers" whose "gaudiness and inane phraseology" were repudiated by the Advertisement and the Preface of the *Lyrical Ballads*. But critical as Wordsworth was of his contemporaries, he cannot be completely dissociated from them. He belonged to their generation, and he addressed himself to their audience. Moreover, he was not insensitive to popular favor. He repeatedly asserted in 1798-99 that he had published the *Lyrical Ballads* to make money; *The Ancient Mariner*, with its "old words" and "strangeness," had hurt the sale of the volume, and in the second edition he "would put in its place some little things which would be more likely to suit the common taste."[2] This is a fairly appropriate description of some of the contents of the second edition.

The student who wishes to consider the coinage of "the common taste" will find in the magazines of the late eighteenth century the richest and most accessible repository. There poetry enjoyed a more honored place than any other form of imaginative writing, and poetry departments were an inevitable feature of such serials as the *Gentleman's Magazine*, the *Monthly Magazine*, the *Scot's Magazine*, the *European Magazine*, and the *Lady's Magazine*—to name only a few of the more popular. Together these five magazines alone published about five hundred poems a year; and their total monthly circulation in 1798 must have exceeded 25,000. At the same time a great number of lesser miscellanies in London, Edinburgh, Glasgow, Dublin, and the provincial towns, sought to satisfy in the same way the general taste for verse. It was, in more than one sense, a period of poetic inflation. Seemingly, anything was acceptable for publication, provided it was not too long, and did not offend the proprieties. The average poetry department was a hodgepodge, which by and large provides a very effective measure of popular taste. Its effectiveness is owing to several factors: the great abundance and immediacy of the poetry printed; the flexible combination of both new and reprinted verse; and the prevailing reader-writer situation, in which amateurs wrote the kind of "original" verse in which they were interested.

As a result of the accepted interpretation of the Parliamentary Act of 1710, magazines lay outside the usual restrictions of the copyright laws, and the poetry departments of most miscellanies like the *Lady's Magazine* and the *Universal Magazine* are therefore likely to contain a large number of reprinted poems, collected from new books of verse, reviews of such volumes, newspapers, poetical miscellanies, and other magazines. Such

---

[2] *The Early Letters of William and Dorothy Wordsworth, 1787-1805*, ed. Ernest de Selincourt (Oxford, 1935), pp. 225-227.

poems were read by—or at least exposed to—thousands of readers, and their influence should be measured accordingly. Pieces like Bürger's *Lenore* and M. G. Lewis' *Alonzo the Brave* enjoyed a tremendous popularity in the magazine world, being caught up and carried from miscellany to miscellany until their total circulation must have reached many thousands. "Because of the trash which infests the magazines," Wordsworth proposed that *The Philanthropist* (The "Monthly Miscellany" which he projected in 1794) offer *reprinted* poetry exclusively, "from new poetical publications of merit, and such *old* ones as are not generally known."[3] The *Lyrical Ballads*, we shall find, were promptly raided in this manner by half a dozen magazines, so that the general acquaintance with *Goody Blake, We are Seven,* and other poems in the volume cannot be gauged by the number of copies of the original publication in circulation.

At the same time that they helped themselves from outside sources, the magazines also printed quantities of what was termed "original poetry"—that is, new poems written by the editor or his acquaintances, by readers, or by professionals. Some of the more substantial miscellanies like the *Gentleman's Magazine,* the *European Magazine,* and the *Monthly Magazine,* published "original poetry" almost exclusively, and were willing to pay for it. *The Ancient Mariner,* for example, was first planned by the two poets as a joint contribution to the new *Monthly Magazine,* for which it was hoped that five pounds might be obtained. But many miscellanies were unwilling to remunerate writers, and sought rather to obtain contributions gratis from their army of readers. The number of amateur scribblers in the 1790's is legion, and they are mostly anonymous. They are also inveterate plagiarists, so that the first appearance of any poem in the magazines, no matter how it is signed, is always a matter of conjecture. The distinction between "original," adapted, and reprinted verses is never sure. The only certainty is that there is a confused and eddying flood of popular poetry flowing through the magazines from the middle of one century to the next—some old, some new, some written by hacks, much more written by amateurs, who endlessly copied the accepted masterpieces of the past and rang changes on the approved models of the day. The vast proportion of this verse literature is hopelessly mediocre, and deservedly forgotten, except that it provides the best available chart for the shifting currents of popular taste. Through it we can partly understand the ground swell of popular favor which helped to raise the *Lyrical Ballads* to eminence in spite of hostile criticism from the Edinburgh reviewer and others.

The student who approaches the *Lyrical Ballads* by way of the magazines may be struck first by differences rather than by resemblances. To

[3] Ibid., p. 122.

most of the verse of the poetry departments the *Ballads* seem to have little relation, except to represent a kind of recoil. It is easy to see what the poets were reacting against in the Advertisement. The "common taste" of the miscellanies not only approved the "gaudy" and "inane"; it was in most respects extremely conservative, if not antique. There is in much of the magazine verse of the 1790's a literary lag of at least half a century. In his attacks on Pope, Gray, Prior, and Dr. Johnson in the 1802 Appendix Wordsworth was not exactly beating dead horses. These poets, together with Gay, Parnell, Thomson, Akenside, and Thomas Warton, were still the accepted masters for many verse-writers, amateur and professional alike; and most of the hackneyed elegies, odes, occasional poems, and so on which flooded the poetry departments of the miscellanies can only be described as the backwash of the Augustan era.

The insipidity of magazine poetry, however, is deceptive. It is not uniformly antique, and it is far from being homogeneous. Not all of the verses in the magazines are imitations of Gray's *Elegy*, Pope's *Pastorals*, and *The Pleasures of Melancholy*. A persistent minority—original and reprinted alike—are occupied with new subjects of poetry and written in the new modes of the late eighteenth century. The *Monthly Magazine* in particular, after 1796, was the resort of many of the new poets, but actually their writings, and imitations of them, are likely to be encountered anywhere. With the poems of this minority the *Lyrical Ballads* have a great deal in common, and although the resemblances are often superficial, they are numerous enough to show that Wordsworth and Coleridge were not out of touch with contemporary modes. A great deal of effort has been admirably expended in the last twenty years in developing the background of the poets' thought, and in showing the organic relation of the ideas and attitudes expressed in the *Lyrical Ballads* to the larger movements of eighteenth-century thought and taste. It remains still to suggest the many ways in which they also conform to the literary fashions of the 1790's. These we may attempt to describe roughly with respect first to "content," and second, to "form," although such a separation, of course, is quite artificial.

There are twenty-three poems in the first edition, and viewed in the light of what we now know of their authorship and composition, the volume no doubt seems, as Legouis says, "a somewhat random and incongruous assemblage." [4] But the incongruities were certainly less likely to "puzzle and disconcert" contemporaries than they do modern histo-

---

[4] Emile Legouis, "Some Remarks on the Composition of the *Lyrical Ballads* of 1798," *Wordsworth and Coleridge: Studies in Honor of George McLean Harper* (Princeton, 1939), pp. 3, 7. Cf. also C. H. Herford: "So singular a medley, touching, sometimes on adjoining pages, the grotesque and the exquisite, the pathetic and the sublime, was likely to divide or bewilder criticism when it came to be seriously judged at all" (*Wordsworth*, London: Routledge, 1930, p. 100).

rians. None of the writers of the notices for the 1798 edition, at least, was sufficiently struck with this feature of the volume to remark upon it. They all presumed, without any visible effort, that the poems were of single authorship, and by and large seemed to feel that the collection was not greatly out of line with contemporary practice. It was a period of feverish poetical activity and mawkish experimentalism, and a good deal of the lack of unity which Legouis and others have found in the *Lyrical Ballads* is obviously the heterogeneity of the literary fashion. In fact, compared with Southey's *Poems* of 1797, the *Ballads* are anything but extraordinary in unevenness of style and miscellaneousness of contents. Southey's volume moves with amateurish abruptness from one manner and one subject to another, whereas the movement of the *Lyrical Ballads*, on the surface at least, is fairly simple. Once the Ancient Mariner has gone his way, the other verses in the volume follow a more or less familiar course for 1798. In general, the drift is in several directions only—towards "nature" and "simplicity," and towards humanitarianism and sentimental morality. Without discriminating too precisely between these categories, the reader of that day would tend to construe most of the contents of the *Lyrical Ballads* in terms of these modes of popular poetry, with which he was already familiar.

He would, for example, if the poetry departments of the magazines are any index, regard as perfectly normal a miscellany of ballads on pastoral subjects (treated both sentimentally and jocularly), moral and philosophic poems inspired by physical nature, and lyrical pieces in a variety of kinds describing rural scenes, the pleasures of the seasons, flora and fauna, and a simple life in the out-of-doors. Subjects drawn from "nature," including both landscape and rural life, as many writers have pointed out, were commonplace in the minor verse of the last years of the eighteenth century. Viewed in relation to this considerable body of writing, poems like *Lines Written in Early Spring, Lines Left upon a Seat in a Yew-tree, Lines Written near Richmond,* and *The Nightingale* are obviously not experimental in subject; nor in *form* either, as a matter of fact. Considered as a species of poetry, the "nature" poems of the *Lyrical Ballads* were anything but surprising in 1798.[5] Novelty, of course,

---

[5] A representative list of "Wordsworthian" titles from the magazines of 1788–98 is as follows: *The Delights of a Still Evening, Stanzas on a Withered Leaf, A Thought on the Vicissitudes of the Seasons, On the Singing of a Red-Breast Late in Autumn, Inscription for a Rural Arbour, Sonnet to the River Arun, Inscription for a Coppice near Elsfield, Sonnet Written during a Morning's Walk, To a Tuft of Violets, On the Month of May, On the Return to the Country, An Autumn Thought, The Lake of Wyndemere, Description of a Morning in May, Contemplation by Moonlight, To the Daisy, To the Primrose, Ode to the Cuckoo.* The exact citations will not be given, since there are literally hundreds of such poems. Underneath many of the "nature" poems of the magazines is the familiar conviction that nature is beautiful and full of joy; that man is corrupted by civilization; that God may be found in nature; and

is a very complex and ephemeral quality in any poem or collection of poems, extremely difficult to isolate. It depends upon a thousand particulars, now vanished, which were once an unmistakable part of the literary climate. But the more one reads the popular poetry of the last quarter of the eighteenth century, the more he is likely to feel that the really surprising feature of these poems in the *Lyrical Ballads* (as well as of many of the others)—apart from sheer literary excellence—is their intense fulfillment of an already stale convention, and not their discovery of an interest in rivers, valleys, groves, lakes, and mountains, flowers and budding trees, the changing seasons, sunsets, the freshness of the morning, and the songs of birds. This fact is a commonplace. Yet it is astonishing how often responsible Wordsworthians go astray in this respect, and tend to view Wordsworth and Coleridge as reacting with a kind of totality against contemporary fashions in verse. The question is not whether the *Ballads* were altogether conventional, which no one would attempt to affirm, but whether they were completely out of touch with popular taste. This was certainly the nineteenth-century conception of Wordsworth, who was viewed as a kind of prophet writing in the wilderness; and it is evidently still the view of some present-day critics and historians, who, struck by the phenomenal literary quality of the *Ballads*, tend to confuse one kind of change with another.[6] They have perhaps been misled by the ambiguities of the Advertisement of 1798, which seems to claim more than it actually does.[7] . . .

---

that the study of nature not only brings pleasure, therefore, but generates moral goodness. The nature poetry of the *Christian's Magazine* (1760-67), for example, has numerous "Wordsworthian" features.

[6] Cf. Catherine M. Maclean: "[Wordsworth] created new interests. But some of these have now become so much part and parcel of most people's mentality that they have ceased to interest. These too have become hackneyed. Appreciation of the externals of Nature is now a commonplace" (*Dorothy and William Wordsworth*, Cambridge, 1927, p. 118). J. R. Sutherland: "[Wordsworth] himself 'created the taste by which he is to be enjoyed.' But I am not sure that he has not induced some of his disciples to lose their sense of proportion about Nature, and he is largely responsible, along with his fellow romantics, for that dreariest of all cults, the cult of scenery" ("Wordsworth and Pope," *Proc. Brit. Acad.*, xxx [1944], 49). Derek Patmore: "Readers still under the influence of the eighteenth-century tradition and its stiff formality are not ready for Wordsworth with his cult of Nature and his poems about the humble of this world" ("Wordsworth and His Contemporaries," *Tribute to Wordsworth*, London, 1950, p. 229). George Mallaby: "It is . . . a plain fact that in the world of literature Wordsworth ignored the fashion of the age and marched boldly forward along his own chosen path amongst the jeers of the idle and ignorant scoffers, until he had succeeded in creating the taste by which he desired to be judged. It is evident enough that the objects of his poetry . . . and the style . . . do not belong to the eighteenth century . . ." (*Wordsworth, a Tribute*, Oxford, 1950, pp. 27-28).

[7] How much is embraced by the "experiments" of the *Lyrical Ballads*? Is it the *language* alone? Or the *style* in a larger sense? Or does it involve also the *materials* of poetry—"human passions, human characters, and human incidents"? In Hazlitt's

The Contemporaneity of the Lyrical Ballads

It is well to observe, in terminating this study, that those commentators who have emphasized the "originality" of the *Lyrical Ballads* to the exclusion of their many signs of contemporaneity, or who see the volume as a daring "manifesto" in total defiance of the general taste, overlook Coleridge's explicit statements to the contrary in the *Biographia Literaria*. Writing in 1815–16, at a time removed yet close enough to the event itself, he denied categorically that the *Lyrical Ballads* were "the original occasion of this fiction of a new school of poetry," or even that he and Southey had been the initiators of a tendency which extended back at least to Bowles and Cowper, among modern poets "the first who reconciled the heart with the head." In fact, he appears to support the literary orthodoxy of the *Ballads* in both subject and manner by insisting upon their overwhelming acceptability to the reading public of their time, saying that in his studied opinion at least two-thirds of the poems would have pleased the average reader, and that "the omission of less than a hundred lines [from the 437 pages of the 1800 edition] would have precluded nine-tenths of the criticism on this work"—supposing, of course, "that the reader has taken it up, *as he would have done any other collection of poems* [italics ours] purporting to derive their subjects or interests from the incidents of domestic or ordinary life, intermingled with higher strains of meditation which the poet utters in his own person and character." It was not the subjects or the manner which offended in the volume, according to Coleridge, but "the critical remarks" which were "prefixed and annexed" to it—remarks which were in part erroneous, which were greatly misunderstood, and which invited by their "supposed heresy" attacks from readers who otherwise would have accepted without question the greater part of the work itself.

Viewed casually, in other words, the *Lyrical Ballads* would tend to merge with familiar features of the literary landscape; read carefully, they would give suddenly a tremendous impression of clarity, freshness, and depth. Wordsworth's true genius was "the original gift of spreading the tone, the atmosphere, and with it the depth and height of the ideal world around forms, incidents, and situations, of which, for the common view, custom had bedimmed all the lustre, had dried up the sparkle and the dewdrops." Coleridge is probably speaking here of the "forms, incidents, and situations" of *real* life, rather than of literature; but not necessarily so. It could be both. Certainly the poetry of the magazines was lusterless and stale. The "modifying colors" of Wordsworth's "imagination" could play over the "forms, incidents, and situations" reflected in contemporary verse, as well as those in the life behind it, and the record

---

account (in "My first Acquaintance with Poets") the *Lyrical Ballads* are explicitly described as an experiment in language alone; and this is the burden of the *Biographia* as well.

shows that they unquestionably did. Wordsworth's forte was not producing novelties, but operating in a new dimension where "original" combinations of "fixities and definites" were largely irrelevant. To claim more for his poetry, as some have done, would be for Coleridge to claim less. It would be to throw emphasis upon the *subjects* of his poetry, rather than its *substance*. It would be to confuse the "drapery" of poetic genius with its "soul." It would be to confound the superior powers of imagination with the inferior powers of the fancy.

"The Thorn": Wordsworth's Dramatic Monologue

by Stephen Maxfield Parrish

In Dorothy Wordsworth's Alfoxden journal the entry for March 19, 1798, opens: "Wm. and Basil [Montagu] and I walked to the hill-tops, a very cold bleak day. We were met on our return by a severe hailstorm." The scenes of this walk were familiar, but during the storm Wordsworth's eye was caught and his poetic imagination fired by a solitary, aged tree. Dorothy marked the event by noting laconically as she closed the day's entry: "William wrote some lines describing a stunted thorn." Forty-five years later William corroborated her account of the genesis of one of his "lyrical ballads." "The Thorn," he told Isabella Fenwick, "arose out of my observing, on the ridge of Quantock Hill, on a stormy day, a thorn which I had often passed in calm and bright weather without noticing it. I said to myself, 'Cannot I by some invention do as much to make this Thorn permanently an impressive object as the storm has made it to my eyes at this moment?'"

The lines in which Wordsworth tried to make impressive his vision of a tree in a hailstorm have excited a good deal of critical attention. De Selincourt summed up majority opinion when he called them "the extreme example of W.'s experiment 'to ascertain how far the language of conversation in the middle and lower classes of society is adapted to the purposes of poetic pleasure'" (*Poetical Works*, II, 513). The poem was experimental, but the nature of the experiment has, I believe, been misunderstood, and the poem almost universally misread. Of the dozens of critics who have commented on "The Thorn," hardly one appears to have discerned who the central character is and what the poem is about. The readings fall, roughly, into two traditions. One holds that the narrator mars the poem: "The Thorn" would have been more satisfying had Wordsworth spoken it in his own voice. The other overlooks the narra-

---

"'The Thorn': Wordsworth's Dramatic Monologue" by Stephen Maxfield Parrish. First printed in *ELH*, 24, no. 2 (1957), 153-63. Copyright © 1957 by The Johns Hopkins Press. The essay has been revised by the author, and is printed by his permission and that of *ELH*.

tor, focusing on the story he tells, the tragedy of Martha Ray: "The Thorn" is a haunting and powerful study in social morality. In the one view, "The Thorn" is a bad poem because of the narrator, in the other, a good poem in spite of the narrator.

It would be hard to decide which view is the more misleading, for what neither recognizes is that the narrator is not only the central figure but, in a sense, the subject of the poem. As its author conceived it, "The Thorn" is not a poem about an abandoned mother and her murdered infant, as nearly all critics have supposed, nor a poem about the maternal passion. It would be more accurate to call it a poem, first, about a tree, and second, about a man. It was intended to be a psychological study, a poem about the way the mind works. The mind whose workings are revealed is that of the narrator, and the poem is, in effect, a dramatic monologue.[1]

That Wordsworth's design should have been lost sight of seems astonishing, for he took unusual pains to make it clear. In the "Advertisement" to the first edition of *Lyrical Ballads* he singled out five poems for comment. Besides touching on the sources of three and on the style of another, he had remarked meaningfully: "The poem of the Thorn, as the reader will soon discover, is not supposed to be spoken in the author's own person: the character of the loquacious narrator will sufficiently shew itself in the course of the story." In 1800, after the narrator's character had totally failed to show itself, Wordsworth attached a lengthy note telling precisely what he had intended to do in "The Thorn." He began by confessing that "this Poem ought to have been preceded by an introductory Poem," implying that he would have sketched there the history of "The Thorn's" narrator, then went on to supply the information that poem might have contained. He asked the reader to visualize "a man, a Captain of a small trading vessel, for example, who being past the middle age of life, had retired . . . to some village or country town of which he was not a native." Why a man of this sort? Because, the poet explained, reaching his point deliberately and then summing it up: "Such men, having little to do, become credulous and talkative from indolence; and from the same cause, and other predisposing causes . . . they are prone to superstition. On which account it appeared to me proper to select a character like this to exhibit some of the general laws by which superstition acts upon the mind."

Could any statement of poetic intent be plainer? As Wordsworth conceived it, "The Thorn" is a portrayal of the superstitious imagination. More literally than any other poem, it carries out the principal object of

---

[1] That is, loosely, a poem in which the events related are meaningful not in themselves but as they reveal the character of the person who relates them. Actually, "The Thorn" is a dialogue, but the second voice enters only to ask questions in language that echoes the narrator's, giving the effect (probably intentional) of a ballad refrain.

Lyrical Ballads: to trace in situations of common life "the primary laws of our nature," chiefly "as regards the manner in which we associate ideas in a state of excitement." For the manner in which the narrator associates ideas is precisely what "The Thorn" is about. The ideas themselves—that is, the "events" of the poem—are unimportant except as they reflect the working of the narrator's imagination. In fact, the point of the poem may very well be that its central "event" has no existence outside of the narrator's imagination—that there is no Martha Ray sitting in a scarlet cloak behind a crag on the mountain top, that the narrator has neither seen her nor heard her, that what he has seen is a gnarled old tree in a blinding storm, that what he has heard (besides the creaking of the branches, or the whistling of the mountain wind) is village superstition about a woman wronged years ago.

This reading of "The Thorn," differing sharply from any traditional reading, alters the poem radically. It becomes not a poem about a woman but a poem about a man (and a tree); not a tale of horror but a psychological study; not a ballad but a dramatic monologue. Based as the reading is on Wordsworth's statements of intent, the question it may seem to raise is whether the poem Wordsworth meant to write resembles the poem he did write. To take the question seriously is to show a singular skepticism about Wordsworth's understanding of his own craft (his careful statements of intent were written after the poem, not before). Yet once raised it must be answered. If we look closely at the poem Wordsworth did write in 1798, we shall find, I think, that it does correspond to the poem he later told us he had meant to write.

The design of "The Thorn" is revealed in the order in which the narrator associates ideas—the order, that is, in which the poem's "events" pass through his mind. The poem begins, as it began in Wordsworth's mind, with the tree.

> There is a thorn; it looks so old,
> In truth you'd find it hard to say,
> How it could ever have been young,
> It looks so old and grey.

As the narrator's imagination begins to work (Stanza 2), he sees the old tree, "hung with heavy tufts of moss," engaged in a drama of nature:

> Up from the earth these mosses creep,
> And this poor thorn they clasp it round
> So close, you'd say that they were bent
> With plain and manifest intent,
> To drag it to the ground. . . .

After this brief flight the narrator drops to prosaic detail, describing the thorn's location, the "little muddy pond," and the hill of moss "like an infant's grave in size." Not until Stanza 6 does he mention "a woman in a scarlet cloak," and when his listener asks why the unhappy creature sits by the thorn crying her doleful cry, the flat answer is (Stanza 9):

> I cannot tell; I wish I could;
> For the true reason no one knows. . . .

But two stanzas later it turns out that the narrator can tell what everyone does know—and the story of Martha Ray begins slowly to unfold. His imagination warming, the old mariner relates what he has learned about the incidents that took place "some two and twenty" years ago (long before he came to the village): Martha's abandonment, her pregnancy, and her madness. But again he breaks off abruptly (Stanza 15):

> No more I know, I wish I did,
> And I would tell it all to you;
> For what became of this poor child
> There's none that ever knew:
> And if a child was born or no,
> There's no one that could ever tell;
> And if 'twas born alive or dead,
> There's no one knows, as I have said. . . .

Again, the professions of ignorance prove not to be serious, for we learn at once that Martha was seen that summer on the mountain, and that cries were later heard there, some "plainly living voices," others, it was believed, "voices of the dead" (Stanza 16). Here the narrator exhibits a nice skepticism.

> I cannot think, whate'er they say,
> They had to do with Martha Ray.

To this point, the pattern of the poem has been consistent: as the narrator's loquacity ebbs and flows he retails, piece by piece, village recollection and superstition about Martha Ray. With Stanza 17, however (some two-thirds of the way through the poem), he suddenly offers first-hand testimony. He claims actually to have seen the woman by the tree. His testimony is highly important because he had already suggested that no one else has seen her there. Inviting his listener (Stanza 9) to view the spot, he had cautioned him to make sure first that Martha was in her hut ("Pass by her door—'tis seldom shut"), adding meaningfully:

> I never heard of such as dare
> Approach the spot when she is there.

He would not, we gather, now venture to approach it himself; he had stumbled on it unknowingly (Stanza 17),

> When to this country first I came
> Ere I had heard of Martha's name. . . .

On that occasion, the narrator and the poet now take impressive pains to point out (Stanzas 17 and 18), the visibility was wretched:

> A storm came on, and I could see
> No object higher than my knee.
> 'Twas mist and rain, and storm and rain,
> No screen, no fence could I discover,
> And then the wind! in faith, it was
> A wind full ten times over.
> I looked around, I thought I saw
> A jutting crag, and off I ran,
> Head-foremost, through the driving rain. . . .

But instead of a crag he saw, he thinks, "A woman seated on the ground." After a glimpse of her face through the rain he "turned about," then, above the wind, heard her cry, "O misery! O misery!"

Encouraged, perhaps, by the sound of his own testimony, and with his imagination now glowing hot, the narrator lets fall (Stanzas 20 to 22) the terrible superstitions he has been holding back: some say that Martha hanged her child, some that she drowned it, but all agree that it lies buried in the little mound; some say that the moss is red with blood, some that the infant's face can be seen on the pond, and some that the ground shook when the little tomb was threatened. After these revelations the narrator subsides abruptly, returning in the final stanza to the tree with which he had begun and the testimony he has offered:

> I cannot tell how this may be,
> But plain it is, the thorn is bound
> With heavy tufts of moss, that strive
> To drag it to the ground.
> And this I know, full many a time,
> When she was on the mountain high,
> By day, and in the silent night,
> When all the stars shone clear and bright,
> That I have heard her cry,
> "O misery! O misery!
> "O woe is me! oh misery!"

From this review of its "events" the design of the poem should be clear. Stimulated by his memory of a tree, the narrator begins to relate village gossip about a woman. Some of it is factual, some not. Martha Ray and her lover did evidently exist twenty years ago, and the tree, the pond, the mound, and a "hut" nearby with a woman in it evidently exist now.

On the other hand (Wordsworth was not, it is agreed, a poet of the supernatural), the ghostly voices from the mountain head, the shaking grass and the stirring moss, the "shadow of a babe" on the pond, are superstitions, products of the villagers' imaginations. But as the narrator retails these superstitions, his own imagination is roused to activity, and he proceeds to show how superstition acts upon his mind. By the end of the poem he clings to two ideas: that the moss on the tree is struggling to drag it down, and that near the spot he has heard the woman's cry. Both ideas are colored with imagination—"by which word I mean the faculty," said Wordsworth in his note, "which produces impressive effects out of simple elements." They may, moreover, be closely related, the first showing how the narrator first saw the tree, the second suggesting how he saw it later, under the influence of village superstition—and that is perhaps why they fall together in the last lines of a poem designed to make a tree "impressive."

For consider the second idea in its context. After indicating that no one else could have seen the woman under the thorn, the narrator claims (but only after working deep into his story) to have glimpsed her once himself, at the height of a blinding storm. Wordsworth left ambiguities in the poem, but to leave one here—to suggest that Martha Ray was really on view by the tree in storms some twenty years after—would have been to throw away his best opportunity both of making the tree "impressive" and of exhibiting the "laws by which superstition acts upon the mind." For Martha's presence in the poem surely illustrates one law: that when a credulous old seaman catches sight in a storm of a suggestively-shaped tree hung with moss and later crams his head with village gossip, then his imagination can turn the tree into a woman, the brightly-colored moss into her scarlet cloak, and the creaking of the branches into her plaintive cry, "O misery! O misery!"

The same effect was evidently created on March 19, 1798, by the imagination of a poet who had already crammed his head with German or Scottish ballads and tragedies of real life. One feature of the poem that has been called "inexplicable" might, on this assumption, be quite simply explained: this is the naming of Martha Ray after the grandmother of little Basil Montagu. When we remember that the boy went along on the walk past Quantock Hill we may conceivably have a revelation of the way the tree looked to Wordsworth during the hailstorm. By giving the creature in the poem the name of the creature who flashed before his eyes, Wordsworth may have been obeying a law of association, even one of the "laws by which superstition acts upon the mind."

For the growth of the poem in the mind of its author almost certainly parallels the growth of the story on the mind of its narrator. In this connection, the sources of "The Thorn" have been as widely misunderstood as its subject. Most critics have attached heavy importance to parallel

"The Thorn": Wordsworth's Dramatic Monologue

recitals of the poem's "events." But these are superficial analogies, and they throw little light on the genesis of "The Thorn." Far more important than any literary parallels are the scenes in nature that haunted Wordsworth's imagination, often seeming to come alive and take on human shape or significance: the rock in the shape of an old woman seated on Helm Crag, the "Stone-Man" on the top of a hill at Grasmere, the lonely whistling hawthorns and ghostly yews in Somerset and the Lakes, "The single sheep, and the one blasted tree" of the *Prelude* (XI, 379), the single "Tree, of many, one, / A single Field which I have looked upon" of the "Intimations" Ode. The way in which such materials could work on a youthful poet's imagination is told in the *Prelude*, not only in the "spots of time" passages, but more explicitly where Wordsworth speaks of certain habits of his early fancy (VIII, 510–540). For a time, before he outgrew it,

> From touch of this new power
> Nothing was safe: the Elder-tree that grew
> Beside the well-known Charnel-house had then
> A dismal look; the Yew-tree had its Ghost,
> That took its station there for ornament.

No common sight, no common event could escape exaggeration. If a widow were seen to visit her husband's grave once or twice,

> The fact was caught at greedily, and there
> She was a visitant the whole year through,
> Wetting the turf with never-ending tears
> And all the storms of Heaven must beat on her

—just as they beat on Martha Ray, in the old Captain's superstitious imagination.

Whatever the case, it may be helpful here to turn for a moment to *Peter Bell*, composed at about the same time as "The Thorn," a time when Wordsworth was preoccupied with the power of the human imagination.[2] Addressing the "Spirits of the Mind" who seize control of men's faculties, "Disordering colour form and stature" (l. 813), the poet testifies (ll. 826–830):

> Your presence I have often felt
> In darkness and the stormy night;

---

[2] In the letter to Southey, April 7, 1819, prefaced to *Peter Bell*, Wordsworth touched on a central belief which had governed that poem's composition and probably also "The Thorn's," "a belief that the Imagination not only does not require for its exercise the intervention of supernatural agency, but that, though such agency be excluded, the faculty may be called forth as imperiously, and for kindred results of pleasure, by incidents within the compass of poetic probability, in the humblest departments of daily life." *Poetical Works*, II, 331.

> And well I know, if need there be,
> Ye can put forth your agency
> When earth is calm, and heaven is bright.

A few stanzas later, the vision that Peter sees under the Spirits' influence, when "Distraction reigns in soul and sense" (l. 968), strikingly resembles the vision that haunted "The Thorn's" narrator. Peter's vision begins with a shrub—not a thorn, but a "flowering furze"—and features an abandoned female wailing a rhythmic lament (ll. 976–980):

> And stretch'd beneath the furze he sees
> The Highland girl—it is no other;
> And hears her crying, as she cried
> The very moment that she died,
> "My mother! oh my mother!"

Wordsworth left fewer ambiguities in *Peter Bell* than in "The Thorn" (perhaps because while still working on it he had the instructive experience of seeing "The Thorn" misread), but he must have felt that even in "The Thorn" he was planting ample evidence that the narrator's vision was the handiwork of "Spirits of the Mind," called up not by guilt but by superstition.

That evidence is complemented by one fact of the poem's later history: Wordsworth did not, it soon became clear, consider "The Thorn" to be essentially a poem about the maternal passion. The title alone might suggest this fact, but plainer suggestions lie in the way the piece was classified. In the letter to Coleridge of May, 1809, in which Wordsworth first spoke of collecting his poems, he designated as a separate class "those relating to Maternal feeling, connubial or parental," and named as examples "The Sailor's Mother," "The Emigrant Mother," "The Affliction of Margaret ——," "The Mad Mother," and "The Idiot Boy." In the collected edition of 1815 all these pieces, together with "The Complaint of a Forsaken Indian Woman," and others, turned up as "Poems founded on the Affections."

But not "The Thorn." It was never linked with any of these titles. In 1809 Wordsworth placed it in a class of poems "relating to human life." His account of the class is somewhat diffuse, but a meaningful distinction does emerge, a distinction between the "affections" and the imagination, and as might be expected "The Thorn" turned up in 1815 among "Poems of the Imagination," where it remained in later editions.

If "The Thorn's" classification was fixed by 1815, however, its form was not. The event that led to its alteration was the appearance of *Biographia Literaria,* in which "The Thorn" was given more critical attention than any other single poem. Coleridge, who had remained perversely insensitive to his partner's experimental study of the superstitious imagination, used it to point up his dissent from the theories about rustic characters and the language of common life set forth in the preface to *Lyrical Ballads*. Maintaining (Chapter 17) that "it is not possible to imitate truly a dull and garrulous discourser, without repeating the effects of dullness and garrulity," Coleridge suggested that "The Thorn's" best passages were those "which might as well or still better have proceeded from the poet's own imagination, and have been spoken in his own character," while the worst were those "exclusively appropriate to the supposed narrator." His dissent stood even more sharply revealed toward the close of Chaper 17, which ended with a quotation from Wordsworth's "Thorn" note of 1800. Wordsworth had explained: "It was my wish in this poem to show the manner in which such men [as the narrator] cleave to the same ideas; and to follow the turns of passion, always different, yet not palpably different, by which their conversation is swayed." Hence the narrator wanders from one superstitious idea to another, repeats himself, strains for precision on unimportant details (as in the line measuring the pond—" 'Tis three feet long, and two feet wide"), alternately pleads ignorance and floods his listener with facts, as he proceeds to make the tree "impressive" (both to his listener and to the reader) by communicating casually yet inexorably and always with passion, his vision of horror. This technique Coleridge pointedly condemned (II, 42–43): "It is indeed very possible to adopt in a poem the unmeaning repetitions, habitual phrases, and other blank counters, which an unfurnished or confused understanding interposes at short intervals, in order to keep hold of his subject, which is still slipping from him, and to give him time for recollection; or in mere aid of vacancy. . . . But what assistance to the poet, or ornament to the poem, these can supply, I am at a loss to conjecture."

These remarks indicate that Coleridge had no sympathy with Wordsworth's immediate aim in "The Thorn"—to show how superstition works upon the mind—and little understanding of Wordsworth's ultimate aim —to make a tree "impressive." It is one thing to say that Wordsworth lacked dramatic skill, or that he chose his narrator unwisely. It is quite another to suggest that he should have dispensed with the narrator and related the "events" of the poem himself. Coleridge appears never to have accepted the idea that the "events" might be a product of the narrator's imagination, that "The Thorn" was not a ballad but a dramatic monologue.

The profound disagreement between the partners in *Lyrical Ballads* which comes into focus in Coleridge's remarks—a disagreement, essentially, about dramatic method—is a highly important one, but it was over by the time the remarks were published. Wordsworth, who had defended "The Thorn" for years, was now ready to abandon the struggle: he revised the poem extensively for the edition of 1820. The revisions had a single end, to elevate the language, making it less dramatic and more "poetic." Ironically, by yielding to the first of Coleridge's somewhat contradictory charges against the poem—that the narrator's language was homely—Wordsworth laid himself more open to the second, which was more substantial—that the dramatic illusion was not sustained. However, the revisions hardly changed the poem. Their importance is that they marked a retreat on Wordsworth's part from a daring and skillful experiment in a new genre. They have also, unfortunately, done their share to keep generations of readers and critics from appreciating the nature of that experiment, or its meaning, or its success.

"The Idiot Boy": Wordsworth's Narrative and Dramatic Voices

by John F. Danby

Wordsworth seems to have had an exceptional ear for tones of voice. "The Waggoner" (1802) is evidence of his ventriloquism. There the narrator's voice is replaced naturally by the Cumberland tones of the Waggoner himself or of an understanding Cumberland neighbour. We are constantly aware of the two levels. Wordsworth obtains his effect by modulating neither into dialect syntax nor vocabulary, but by reproducing the much subtler thing only a native ear could recognize—the vowel harmonies of the northern rhymes and word-sequences:

> The rain rushed down—the road was battered,
> As with the force of billows shattered;
> The horses are dismayed, nor know
> Whether they should stand or go;
> And Benjamin is groping near them,
> Sees nothing, and can scarcely hear them.
> He is astounded,—wonder not,—
> With such a charge in such a spot;
> Astounded in the mountain gap
> With thunder peals, clap after clap,
> Close-treading on the silent flashes—
> And somewhere, as he thinks, by crashes
> Among the rocks; with weight of rain,
> And sullen motions long and slow,
> That to a dreary distance go—
> Till, breaking in upon the dying strain,
> A rending o'er his head begins the fray again.
> [ll. 188–304]

" 'The Idiot Boy': Wordsworth's Narrative and Dramatic Voices" (editor's title). From John F. Danby, *The Simple Wordsworth: Studies in the Poems, 1797–1807* (London: Routledge & Kegan Paul, 1960). Copyright © 1960 by John F. Danby. Reprinted by permission of Routledge & Kegan Paul Ltd., Barnes & Noble, and the author. This selection is part of chapter 2.

All poets need to find their voice, or voices. Wordsworth began, as most do, with a voice not his own but belonging to the eighteenth century. *The Borderers* which followed closely on the early period may have opened out the possibilities of dramatic projection. In *Lyrical Ballads,* at any rate, Wordsworth has discovered his vehicle—the voice of the "Statesman," or peasant small-holder, the voice of the retired sea-captain or West-country balladist; a literary personality that had not been used for serious purposes in this way before.

The mixed mode of the dramatic-narrative poem allows for a range of voices, and each voice for an ironic shift in point of view. It is unfortunate that Wordsworth's irony has not been much remarked. If irony, however, can mean perspective and the co-presence of alternatives, the refusal to impose on the reader a predigested life-view, the insistence on the contrary that the reader should enter, himself, as full partner in the final judgement on the facts set before him—then Wordsworth is a superb ironist in *Lyrical Ballads*. In the mixed mode of the poems the poet can take up and lay down his masks. And with each assumption or discard a new, sometimes excitingly dramatic, shift of standpoint is possible. The narrator, the characters involved in the story, the poet himself as the finally responsible assembler—these are the three main levels at which the voices work. By changing the voice one can step from one frame to another and back again. Stepping apparently out of the frame of mere "literature" altogether and into the reader's own reality (his reality of experience and of judgement), confronting the reader with the need to be aware of what he is judging with as well as what he is judging —this is, above all, the Wordsworthian trick in *Lyrical Ballads*. . . .

Apart from Hutchinson and Dowden few people have thought of Wordsworth as a comic poet. Yet it is clear that in *Lyrical Ballads* Wordsworth, in some of his most successful poems, is writing in a humorous vein. Hutchinson's note is fairly dismissive:

> The humour and pathos of *The Idiot Boy* are sadly marred by his clumsy attempts at mirth. Hazlitt, in his pen-portrait of Wordsworth, speaks of a certain "convulsive inclination to laughter about the mouth, a good deal at variance with the solemn, stately expression of the rest of his face." Not less awkward and incongruous, surely, are the heavy pleasantries in which the poet of *Peter Bell* and *The Idiot Boy* seeks an occasional vent for his exuberant cheerfulness. "At rare times in his poetry Wordsworth shows an inclination for frolic: it is the frolic of good spirits in the habitually grave, and he cannot caper lightly and gracefully."

One has to bear in mind, of course, that for the nineteenth-century critic serious poetry could not be both serious and comic at the same time. One has also to bear in mind, in justice to the commentators, that on

"The Idiot Boy": Wordsworth's Narrative and Dramatic Voices 87

the whole serious Wordsworthian comedy is rare. There is, however, the testimony of *Lyrical Ballads,* and the undeniable evidence of the introduction to "Peter Bell," which belongs to the same period.

"The Thorn" and "The Idiot Boy" were Wordsworth's own favourites in the *Lyrical Ballads* volume. And Wordsworth may have been right. He was a mature twenty-seven, the volume was a sophisticated experiment as well as a revolutionary manifesto, and the poet had clear ideas as to what he was doing.

From the start of the poem we are aware of the distinctive narrating voice, and of the narrator's power to merge his own voice in that of the actors in the story, as well as of his capacity to re-emerge when necessary and regain his commenting distinctness. The story-teller is near enough in social status to Betty Foy to have ready and sympathetic insight into the working of her mind. At the same time he is not in her shoes. He does not share either her concern or her simple-mindedness. He is, however, in every sense, a good neighbour. The mergence of his voice with his neighbours is all the easier because he has the same village language, and the outlook that goes with it:

> 'Tis eight o'clock—a clear March night,
> The moon is up—the sky is blue,
> The owlet in the moonlight air,
> He shouts from nobody knows where;
> He lengthens out his lonely shout,
> Halloo! halloo! a long halloo!
>
> —Why bustle thus about your door,
> What means this bustle, Betty Foy?
> Why are you in this mighty fret?
> And why on horseback have you set
> Him whom you love, your idiot boy?
>
> Beneath the moon that shines so bright,
> Till she is tired, let Betty Foy
> With girth and stirrup fiddle-faddle;
> But wherefore set upon a saddle
> Him whom she loves, her idiot boy?

The voice expresses surprise, impatience, and some disapproval. The observer is neither an idiot, nor a silly woman: "fiddle-faddle" carries its own comment on the fussy confusion of Betty's muddledness and misplaced pride, and on the womanish clumsiness with "girth and stirrup" —those traditionally masculine implements of management and control.

But, once the silliness might really lead to serious consequences, the observer can easily slip into Betty's and Susan's situation:

> Poor Susan moans, poor Susan groans,
> "As sure as there's a moon in heaven,"
> Cries Betty, "he'll be back again;
> They'll both be here, 'tis almost ten,
> They'll both be here before eleven!"

He can even assume the point of view of the pony, which is included in the same comprehensive sentence, and awarded in the poem a wisdom and dignity of its own:

> But then he is a horse that thinks!
> But when he thinks his pace is slack;
> Now, though he knows poor Johnny well,
> Yet for his life he cannot tell
> What he has got upon his back.

The tone is beautifully mock-solemn and yet indulgently ready with its sympathy. We are encouraged to take the other's point of view, but not allowed to forget the observer's. It is not a dismissive fun, nor the detachment of aloofness. The superiority is also a magnanimity. We are called on for tenderness rather than condescension: but not to surrender our own identity. Wordsworth's peculiar achievement is an irony of detachment and loving-kindness.

It is Wordsworth himself, of course, who is the narrator, and he makes us aware of his masks. Dropping the rôle of merged narrator he steps in front of the curtain when Betty's anxiety has reached its climax. The timing is perfect—and so is the surprise: the irony that is now turned on the reader himself:

> Oh reader! now that I might tell
> What Johnny and his horse are doing!
> What they've been doing all this time,
> Oh could I put it into rhyme,
> A most delightful tale pursuing!

> Perhaps, and no unlikely thought!
> He with his pony now doth roam
> The cliffs and peaks so high that are,
> To lay his hands upon a star,
> And in his pocket bring it home.

> Perhaps he's turned himself about,
> His face unto his horse's tail,
> And still and mute, in wonder lost,

> All like a silent horseman-ghost,
> He travels on along the vale.
>
> And now, perhaps, he's hunting sheep,
> A fierce and dreadful hunter he!
> Yon valley, that's so trim and green,
> In five months' time, should he be seen,
> A desert wilderness will be.
>
> Perhaps, with head and heels on fire,
> And like the very soul of evil,
> He's galloping away, away,
> And so he'll gallop on for aye,
> The bane of all that dread the devil.
>
> I to the Muses have been bound,
> These fourteen years, by strong indentures;
> Oh gentle muses! let me tell
> But half of what to him befel,
> For sure he met with strange adventures.
>
> Oh gentle Muses! is this kind?
> Why will ye thus my suit repel?
> Why of your further aid bereave me?
> And can ye thus unfriended leave me?
> Ye muses! whom I love so well.

The irony turns against the reader. The reader wants marvels? Wordsworth will hold up a screen on which he can project his own. They are terribly stale literary stock—the sublimely whimsical, the Monk Lewis, the Quixotic; mad Ajaxes and romantic wild-men. Wordsworth conjures up the fancies in order to indulge so many reading-public weaknesses, and, again, detach himself from them. But as he can tolerate the silliness he can cater for the vacuity. The equable rebuke, however, or warning, is implicit in his manner all the time. The simpleton-narrator uses his folly as a stalking horse. This is the point in the poem (a point occurring, too, in "Simon Lee" and "The Thorn") of the defecation of the "literary." Betty finds Johnny safe. On their return home Susan is better. When Johnny is asked how he spent his time, his reply is the idiotic verse which set Wordsworth off writing the poem:

> "The cocks did crow to-whoo, to-whoo,
> And the sun did shine so cold."
> —Thus answered Johnny in his glory,
> And that was all his travel's story.

"The Idiot Boy" is a comedy, though admittedly a Wordsworthian comedy. The story has mock-epic features: a life-and-death issue; the last chance of success depending on the last person likely to succeed; mental conflict between mother-love and good-neighbourliness; the anguished search and rescue of the rescuer; finally, the happy issue out of everyone's afflictions, Susan's included. At times Wordsworth's management of stanza and rhyme can remind us of the professional humourist:

> Long Susan lay deep lost in thought,
> And many dreadful fears beset her,
> Both for her messenger and nurse;
> And as her mind grew worse and worse,
> Her body it grew better.

That is at least as good as Tom Hood, but instead of the merely local pun on a word there is a kind of story-pun: Betty having gone off after Johnny, Susan catches a cumulative anxiety for them both. There is also the sane psychology as well as the joke, and the moral implied: Susan is cured of her psychological bed-riddenness by an honest and maybe unwonted care for others. Generosity rallies to the aid of generosity. The fun never falls outside Wordsworth's major convictions concerning what being human entails.

Wordsworth is capable also however of a comic vision that points more to his eighteenth-century origin than to his mid-Victorian destination. There is, for example, the encounter with the Doctor:

> And now she's at the doctor's door,
> She lifts the knocker, rap, rap, rap;
> The doctor at the casement shews
> His glimmering eyes that peep and doze;
> And one hand rubs his old night-cap.
>
> "Oh Doctor! Doctor! where's my Johnny?"
> "I'm here, what is't you want with me?"
> "Oh Sir! you know I'm Betty Foy,
> "And I have lost my poor dear boy,
> "You know him—him you often see;
>
> "He's not so wise as some folk be."
> "The devil take his wisdom!" said
> The Doctor, looking somewhat grim,
> "What, woman! should I know of him?"
> And, grumbling, he went back to bed.

There is nothing here of the clumsy frolic Dowden objected to. The social observation is swift and accurate. The rattling comic tempo is perfectly maintained. Everything happens in character, and the best joke is one that Wordsworth doesn't labour:

> "Oh Doctor! Doctor! where's my Johnny?"
> "I'm here, what is't you want with me?"

Wordsworth displays great tact in not underlining his jokes. It is obvious, for example, that Betty should have carried Johnny's message to the Doctor: that she forgot is part of the comedy. Wordsworth, however, at this point, is willing to let the joke look after itself. He is more concerned to preserve the proportion between joke and seriousness that his poem requires. With all the comedy we are reminded that Betty is genuinely upset, and that Wordsworth has a sincere regard for her capacity to care.

It is most important to remember the seriousness that embraces the comic in Wordsworth's achievement. Wordsworth's irony, we have said, is an irony of detachment and loving-kindness. His comedy, too, requires us to overcome the taboo on tenderness. From Jonson onwards literary laughter had had to be punitive and corrective. Wordsworth asks us to understand (which implies detachment) and to forgive (which implies engagement). He neither scorns nor sentimentalizes the actors in his story. And, in fact, none of the emotions woven into the plot are mean or reprehensible. Susan is a neighbour really in distress. Betty Foy is a mother and a neighbour really attempting something noble whichever way the situation throws her. Her fiddle-faddle and infatuation may be both silly and risky, but neither is contemptible. Her anguished anxiety also is only laughable if our laughter has the Wordsworthian correlative: if we would be as ready to relieve it as to point out its (eventually to be made apparent) unnecessariness.

There is an essential poignancy and idiocy in emotion itself. Only the final upshot can decide which aspect will come uppermost. The great comedy of "The Idiot Boy," quite apart from its surface jokes, has to do with this: it is a comedy of the passions. Far from being another Man of Feeling Wordsworth, in this poem, is the satirist of feeling. Betty's access of concern for Susan makes her send Johnny off on the errand. Fatuously she sees her idiot son as public hero. When he does not return, fear for his safety brings her back to the facts, and dispels neighbourly concern—and so on. And, as we have already hinted, the pattern is repeated in Susan, too. Her mysterious illness vanishes as she frets more and more about the others. Finally she is cured of imaginary illness by real emotional distress. Passions spin the plot—but arbitrarily. The idiocy of passion can precipitate its puppets into irrational misery or unpredictable joy. It all depends, but the dependence is not on the actors in the story as prudent agents. Man, as mere man of feeling, sits on a crazy seesaw.

The Idiot Boy himself, of course, gives still another dimension. The Idiot is not on the see-saw of passion. This means, from one point of view, he will escape its particular kinds of silliness. Wordsworth is fully aware of the Divine Fool archetype he is using. In his letter to Wilson (1802) he wrote

> *I have often applied to idiots, in my own mind, that sublime expression of Scripture that Their Life is Hidden with God.* They are worshipped, probably from a feeling of this sort, in several parts of the East. . . . I have, indeed, often looked upon the conduct of parents, in the lower ranks of society, toward idiots as a great triumph of the human heart. *It is there that we see the strength, disinterestedness, and grandeur of love;* nor have I ever been able to contemplate an object that calls out so many excellent and virtuous sentiments without finding it hallowed thereby, and having something in one which bears down before it like a deluge every feeble sensation of disgust and aversion.

The primitive force of the symbol exerts itself throughout the poem. Johnny has a dual rôle. He cannot be responsible for his actions, and it is his failure to fetch the doctor that is more effective than his mother's concern for her neighbour. That is the comic side. The divine is suggested not only through "the strength, the disinterestedness, and the grandeur of love" he evokes in Betty and Susan (though not in the doctor), but also in the invulnerability of the joy that goes with him, an inaccessible but real emotion, the incomprehensible but mysteriously meaningful dialogue in which he takes part:

> Burr, burr—now Johnny's lips they burr,
> As loud as any mill, or near it,
> Meek as a lamb the pony moves,
> And Johnny makes the noise he loves,
> And Betty listens, glad to hear it.
>
> Away she hies to Susan Gale:
> And Johnny's in a merry tune,
> The owlets hoot, the owlets curr,
> And Johnny's lips they burr, burr, burr,
> And on he goes beneath the moon.

It would be easy to exaggerate this side of the Idiot in the poem. He is there, certainly, however, as an indication of the possibility of other dimensions, worlds unrealized that may be realizable. But Wordsworth does not make him more than a token of the possibilities. More important for the Wordsworthian seriousness of the tale is the Wordsworthian background into which Johnny is merged: the pony "meek as

"The Idiot Boy": Wordsworth's Narrative and Dramatic Voices

a lamb," the moon, the river and waterfall, the whole natural universe that comes to life at the moments of greatest human stress or distraction:

> She listens, but she cannot hear
> The foot of horse, the voice of man;
> The streams with softest sound are flowing,
> The grass you almost hear it growing,
> You hear it now if e'er you can.
>
> The owlets through the long blue night
> Are shouting to each other still:
> Fond lovers, yet not quite hob nob,
> They lengthen out the tremulous sob,
> That echoes far from hill to hill.

It is the background which incarnates all the values the human world does not; energy and calm, permanence and process, spontaneity and order, ranging from the stars in the sky to the nearby birds:

> By this the stars were almost gone,
> The moon was setting on the hill,
> So pale you hardly looked at her:
> The little birds began to stir,
> Though yet their tongues were still.

Johnny is shut out from the various harmony of this order as inevitably as he is excluded from the confusions of the human order. Where the Idiot is concerned, Wordsworth is a realist:

> Of moon or stars he takes no heed:
> Of such we in romances read.

That is why we are left with Johnny's mad remark at the end:

> "The cocks did crow to-whoo, to-whoo,
> And the sun did shine so cold."

The Idiot has an insulated joy; Betty and Susan the confined, pitiful vulnerability of conflicting compassions; the Doctor sullenly slams the window on both. Nowhere in the human sphere is there the massive and potent integration of force, serenity, and tenderness, we find in the world of the waterfall, moon, and owls. The comedy, then, has its sombre side.

The especially poignant thing about the happy ending is its chance-givenness. Wordsworth will need, ultimately a third position beyond the dilemma which both "The Thorn" and "The Idiot Boy" leave him with. For Martha Ray and the Idiot Boy are the two horns of a dilemma. In spite of their surface differences in mood and in conclusion, the two poems agree that feeling, as feeling, is a kind of unhingement. The alienation of the normal which we see in "The Idiot Boy" might be an even more pessimistic vision than that of "The Thorn": for Martha's tragedy can be regarded, mitigably, as exceptional and personal. Betty's and Susan's, and the Doctor's, on the other hand is the alienation of the everyday and general. From this, complete idiocy is the only escape, unless an ultimate marriage of human mind and natural order might somehow and somewhere be possible.

The Myth of Memory and Natural Man

by Harold Bloom

I. Tintern Abbey

Tintern Abbey (July 1798) is a miniature of the long poem Wordsworth never quite wrote, the philosophical and autobiographical epic of which *The Prelude*, the *Recluse* fragment, and *The Excursion* would have been only parts. As such, *Tintern Abbey* is a history in little of Wordsworth's imagination. The procedure and kind of the poem are both determined by Coleridge's influence, for *The Eolian Harp* (1795) and *Frost at Midnight* (February 1798) are its immediate ancestors, with the eighteenth-century sublime ode in the farther background. Yet we speak justly of the form of *Tintern Abbey* as being Wordsworth's, for he turns this kind of poem to its destined theme, the nature of a poet's imagination and that imagination's relation to external Nature. Coleridge begins the theme in his "conversation poems," but allows himself to be distracted from it by theological misgivings and self-abnegation. *Tintern Abbey*, and not *The Eolian Harp*, is the father of Shelley's *Mont Blanc* and Keats's *Sleep and Poetry*.

In the renewed presence of a remembered scene, Wordsworth comes to a full understanding of his poetic self. This revelation, though it touches on infinity, is extraordinarily simple. All that Wordsworth learns by it is a principle of reciprocity between the external world and his own mind, but the story of that reciprocity becomes the central story of Wordsworth's best poetry. The poet loves Nature for its own sake alone, and the presences of Nature give beauty to the poet's mind, again only for that mind's sake. Even the initiative is mutual; neither Nature nor poet gives in hope of recompense, but out of this mutual generosity an identity is established between one giver's love and the other's beauty. The process of reciprocity is like a conversation that never stops, and cannot therefore be summed up discursively or analyzed into static elements. The most im-

---

"The Myth of Memory and Natural Man" (editor's title). From Harold Bloom, *The Visionary Company: A Reading of English Romantic Poetry* (Ithaca, N.Y.: Cornell University Press, 1971). Copyright © 1961 by Harold Bloom; copyright © 1971 by Cornell University. Reprinted by permission of the publisher and the author. This selection consists of two parts from chapter 2, "William Wordsworth."

mediate consequence of this process is a certain "wide quietness," as Keats was to call it in his *Ode to Psyche.* As the dialogue of love and beauty ensues, love does not try to find an object, nor beauty an expression in direct emotion, but a likeness between man and Nature is suggested. The suggestion is made through an intensification of the dominant aspect of the given landscape, its seclusion, which implies also a deepening of the mood of seclusion in the poet's mind:

>   —Once again
> Do I behold these steep and lofty cliffs,
> That on a wild secluded scene impress
> Thoughts of more deep seclusion; and connect
> The landscape with the quiet of the sky.

The further connection is with the quiet of Wordsworth's mind, for the thoughts of more deep seclusion are impressed simultaneously on the landscape and on its human perceiver.

We murder to dissect, Wordsworth wrote in another context, and to dissect the renewed relationship between the poet and this particular landscape ought not to be our concern. Wordsworth wants to understand the interplay between Mind and Nature without asking *how* such dialogue can be, and this deliberate refusal to seek explanation is itself part of the meaning of *Tintern Abbey.* The poet has reached a point where the thing seen

> yields to a clarity and we observe,
>
> And observing is completing and we are content,
> In a world that shrinks to an immediate whole,
>
> That we do not need to understand, complete
> Without secret arrangements of it in the mind.

This is Wallace Stevens, in *Description without Place,* a poem that tries to suggest that to seem is to be, so that seeming, as well as everything we say of the past, is description without place, "a cast of the imagination." Until *Peele Castle,* natural seeming and reality are one for Wordsworth, and so his theory of poetry is a theory of description also. The language of description is employed by him both for the external world and for himself; if he will not analyze Nature, still less will he care to analyze man. The peculiar *nakedness* of Wordsworth's poetry, its strong sense of being alone with the visible universe, with no myth or figure to mediate between ego and phenomena, is to a surprisingly large extent not so much a result of history as it is of Wordsworth's personal faith in the reality of the body of Nature.

Away from the landscape he now rejoins, the poet had not forgotten it, but indeed had owed to memories of it sensations sweet, felt in hours

The Myth of Memory and Natural Man

of urban weariness, and therapeutic of the lonely ills he has experienced. Such tranquil restoration is only one gift of memory. Another is of more sublime aspect:

> that blessed mood,
> In which the burthen of the mystery,
> In which the heavy and the weary weight
> Of all this unintelligible world,
> Is lightened:—that serene and blessed mood,
> In which the affections gently lead us on,—
> Until, the breath of this corporeal frame
> And even the motion of our human blood
> Almost suspended, we are laid asleep
> In body, and become a living soul:
> While with an eye made quiet by the power
> Of harmony, and the deep power of joy,
> We see into the life of things.

This is not mysticism but, rather, a state of aesthetic contemplation. All contemplation of objects except the aesthetic is essentially practical, and so directed toward personal ends. The poet's genius frees contemplation from the drive of the will, and consequently the poet is able to see with a quiet eye. To see into the life of things is to see things for themselves and not their potential use. The poet attains to this state through memories of Nature's presence, which give a quietness that is a blessed mood, one in which the object world becomes near and familiar, and ceases to be a burden. The best analogue is the difference we feel in the presence of a stranger or a good friend. From this serenity the affections lead us on to the highest kind of naturalistic contemplation, when we cease to *have* our bodies, but *are* our bodies, and so are "laid asleep / In body, and become a living soul."

Having made this declaration, Wordsworth gives his first intimation of doubt as to the efficacy of Nature's presences:

> And now, with gleams of half-extinguished thought,
> With many recognitions dim and faint,
> And somewhat of a sad perplexity,
> The picture of the mind revives again.

The "sad perplexity" concerns the future and the enigma of the imagination when transposed from past to future time. In this moment of renewed covenant with a remembered and beloved landscape, is there indeed life and food for future years?

> And so I dare to hope,
> Though changed, no doubt, from what I was when first
> I came among these hills.

The process of change is what troubles Wordsworth. He speaks of three stages of development already accomplished, and fears the onset of a fourth. The "glad animal movements" of his boyish days preceded any awareness of nature. Then came the time when his perception of natural objects brought an immediate joy, so that he speaks of the simultaneity of vision and emotion as

> An appetite; a feeling and a love,
> That had no need of a remoter charm,
> By thought supplied, nor any interest
> Unborrowed from the eye.

That time is past, and Wordsworth has lost its "aching joys" and "dizzy raptures." He has entered into a third time, and other gifts have recompensed him for such loss. In this mature stage he *looks* on Nature, and *hears* in it

> The still, sad music of humanity,
> Nor harsh nor grating, though of ample power
> To chasten and subdue.

The dialectic of the senses here is vital in Wordsworth. The young child has an organic sense that combines seeing and hearing. The older child, awakening to the phenomenal world, sees a gleam in it that the mature man cannot see again. But the man gains an intimation of immortality, of his renewed continuity with the young child, by hearing a still, sad music *as* he sees a soberer coloring in Nature. Here in *Tintern Abbey*, eight years before the completion of the Great Ode, Wordsworth anticipates the totality of its myth. As he listens to the sad music ("still" because it pipes to the spirit, not to the sensual ear of man) he hears evidence not only of man's mortality but of man's inseparable bond with Nature. But perception and response are no longer simultaneous, and it is an act of meditation that must bring the riven halves together. This meditation does not start in the mind, but is first felt as a presence that disturbs the mind with the joy of elevated thoughts:

> a sense sublime
> Of something far more deeply interfused,
> Whose dwelling is the light of setting suns,
> And the round ocean and the living air,
> And the blue sky, and in the mind of man:
> A motion and a spirit, that impels
> All thinking things, all objects of all thought
> And rolls through all things.

This is parallel to Coleridge's *The Eolian Harp*:

> O! the one Life within us and abroad,
> Which meets all motion and becomes its soul,
> A light in sound, a sound-like power in light,
> Rhythm in all thought, and joyance every where.

As a consecration or sacramental vision this becomes the main burden of Wordsworth's song, until in *Peele Castle* it is exposed as only a dream, and the great light pervading it is deprecated as "the light that never was, on sea or land." When Wordsworth still believed in that light, as in this crucial passage from *Tintern Abbey*, he was able to see and hear a primal unity manifested simultaneously in all subjects and all objects. Again, it is a laziness of our imaginations that tempts us to call this vision mystical, for the mystical is finally incommunicable and Wordsworth desires to be a man talking to men about matters of common experience. The emphasis in *Tintern Abbey* is on things seen and things remembered, on the light of sense, not on the invisible world. The presence of outer Nature disturbs the mind, sets it into motion, until it realizes that Nature and itself are not utterly distinct, that they are mixed together, interfused. They are more interfused than the reciprocal relation between the outer presence and the mind's inner elevation in response would seem to indicate, for in speaking of that relation the poet still uses the vocabulary of definiteness and fixity. But the imagination dissolves such separateness. Within both Nature and Wordsworth is something that moves and breathes, and that blends subject and object as it animates them. *Therefore* the poet, though he has lost the aching joy that is Nature's direct gift, still loves Nature as he can apprehend it by eye and ear:

> —both what they half create,
> And what perceive; well pleased to recognise
> In nature and the language of the sense
> The anchor of my purest thoughts, the nurse,
> The guide, the guardian of my heart, and soul
> Of all my moral being.

But why "half create"? Though the boundaries between man and Nature have wavered, Wordsworth wishes to avoid the suggestion of a total absorption of Nature into man. Man is almost totally absorbed in Nature in his childhood, and again in extreme old age, as in *The Old Cumberland Beggar* and the Leech Gatherer of *Resolution and Independence*. But for the mature man, outward Nature must be recognized as external. That is his freedom and his grief. His consolation is that he half creates as well as perceives "outward" Nature, for what is outward comes to him only through the gates of his own perception, and whatever cannot come to him is not relevant to his condition. Eyes and ears, the gates of perception, are not passive but selective. He cannot create the phenomena that present themselves to him; they are given. But his choice among them is a kind of creation, and his choice is guided by memory. Memory is the mother of poetry for Wordsworth because the poem's half of the act of creation cannot proceed without the catalyst of recollecting the poet's response to an earlier version of the outward presence of Nature. Nature's half of the act is mysterious, except that Wordsworth insists that it cannot proceed without the initiating expression of man's love for what is outside himself.

This mature love for Nature leads to love for other men, to hearing the still, sad music of *humanity*. The soul of a man's moral being, its inwardness, *is* Nature once the earlier relation between man and Nature, where no meditation was necessary between perception of natural beauty and the deep joy of the perceiver's response, is in the past. The meditation of the later stage, the time of mature imagination, brings vision and joy together again by linking both with the heart's generosity toward our fellow men.

This is the teaching that preserves Wordsworth's "genial spirits" from decay, but the teacher himself is uncertain of the efficacy of his doctrine in the fourth stage that is to come, when natural decay may dull his responsiveness to the presences of beauty. He turns therefore to his sister Dorothy as an incarnation of his earlier self, as one who still feels the dizzy joys of natural communion that he himself can only recollect. The curious element in this ritualistic substitution is that the poet is only twenty-eight, and his sister just a year younger. Wordsworth's troubled forebodings were nevertheless justified; his imagination aged very quickly, and Dorothy's remained young and perpetually receptive to the beauty of the natural world:

> and in thy voice I catch
> The language of my former heart, and read
> My former pleasures in the shooting lights
> Of thy wild eyes. Oh! yet a little while
> May I behold in thee what I was once,
> My dear, dear Sister!

There is an urgency in the tone of this which deepens almost to a desperation:

> and this prayer I make,
> Knowing that Nature never did betray
> The heart that loved her.

The prayer thus heralded is never quite expressed in the remainder of the poem. Its burden is more life, survival, imaginative immortality. More directly, it is a desire to be free of the fear that enters so early into

The Myth of Memory and Natural Man

the poet's life and his poem. When he bounded like a roe over the mountains, and followed wherever Nature led, he was

> more like a man
> Flying from something that he dreads than one
> Who sought the thing he loved.

He sped as if to out-distance time, and sought an immediacy he was doomed to lose. Only Nature has the privilege of leading us from joy to joy; we have to wait upon her, brood on past joys, and have faith that she will not abandon hearts that have loved her. Wordsworth uses the strong word "betray" with its sexual implications, which are certainly present in the opening lines of the poem, where the poet's renewed passion is a lover's return. The lover returns, not to the wild ecstasy he had known, but to the sober pleasure of a marriage with Nature.

The most beautiful lines in *Tintern Abbey* invoke the possibility of perpetual renewal for Dorothy:

> Therefore let the moon
> Shine on thee in thy solitary walk;
> And let the misty mountain-winds be free
> To blow against thee.

As in *Michael* and *The Prelude*, the freedom of mountain mist and wind, sudden in their comings and goings, is a natural type of the wild freedom of ecstatic human imagination, the deep joy of that time when Nature for us is all in all.

Wordsworth looks forward to Dorothy's return to the beloved landscape, and prophesies the healing power memories of it will have for her. The fear of mortality, which has been haunting the poem, finally becomes overt:

> Nor, perchance—
> If I should be where I no more can hear
> Thy voice, nor catch from thy wild eyes these gleams
> Of past existence—wilt thou then forget
> That on the banks of this delightful stream
> We stood together.

In her wild eyes he sees the gleam that he can no longer see in Nature, but that once he did see, so that he almost literally reads his former pleasures in the eyes of another. His survival will be in those eyes, even as his earlier self has already survived there. He will live in her memory, and his faith will have its historical record:

> and that I, so long
> A worshipper of Nature, hither came

> Unwearied in that service: rather say
> With warmer love—oh! with far deeper zeal
> Of holier love.

This is the vocabulary of religious devotion, displaced into a naturalistic mode. Certainly he protests too much; we feel a desperation in his insistence, another presage of waning faith, or faith affirmed more vehemently even as it ebbs. We begin to understand the prayer he intends but does not make explicit. It is "Do not forget, or the life in me, the creative joy, will die." The closing lines, with their immense music, are not complete:

> Nor wilt thou then forget
> That after many wanderings, many years
> Of absence, these steep woods and lofty cliffs,
> And this green pastoral landscape, were to me
> More dear, both for themselves and for thy sake!

He leaves out "for my sake," but the poem has made clear that his salvation, as man and poet, is dependent upon the renovation he celebrates. The parallels of *Tintern Abbey* exist in many kinds of experience, including sexual and religious, but we do best to hold to the poem's own central story, its account of aesthetic contemplation and its personal myth of memory as salvation.

The misgivings and the ultimate fear of mortality are part of the poem because of Wordsworth's insistence upon autobiographical honesty. They help to make *Tintern Abbey* the major testament it is, for through them the poem convinces us it has earned the heights upon which it moves. The consoling story of a natural growth that tests the soul, teaches it generosity, and accepts its love becomes finally what Wallace Stevens in *The Rock* calls "a cure of the ground and of ourselves, in the predicate that there is nothing else." This predicate of nakedness is a sublime act of honesty, and prepares us for the Wordsworth who is the first poet ever to present our human condition in its naturalistic truth, vulnerable and dignified, and irreducible, not to be explained away in any terms, theological or analytical, but to be accepted as what it is. The mind, knowing only itself and Nature, but remembering a time when Nature gave it direct joy, and having remoter memories of an earlier time when it knew itself only in union with Nature, is able to turn back through memory for a faith that at last gives courage and a love for others. Blake did not believe in the goodness of the natural heart, and Coleridge could neither believe in nor deny it, but Wordsworth brings its possibility as truth alive into our hearts, as he did into the heart of Keats. There are greater Romantic poems than *Tintern Abbey*, but they surpass it as vision or rhetoric, not as consolation. No poem, unless it be *The Old Cumberland Beggar*, humanizes us more.

II. The Old Cumberland Beggar

The Old Cumberland Beggar (1797) is Wordsworth's finest vision of the irreducible natural man, the human stripped to the nakedness of primordial condition and exposed as still powerful in dignity, still infinite in value. The Beggar reminds us of the beggars, solitaries, wanderers throughout Wordsworth's poetry, particularly in *The Prelude* and *Resolution and Independence*. He differs from them in that he is not the agency of a revelation; he is not responsible for a sudden release of Wordsworth's imagination. He is not even of visionary utility; he is something finer, beyond use, a vision of reality in himself. I am not suggesting that *The Old Cumberland Beggar* is the best of Wordsworth's poems outside *The Prelude*; it is not in the sublime mode, as are *Tintern Abbey*, the Great Ode, *Resolution and Independence*. But it is the most Wordsworthian of poems, and profoundly moving.

Nothing could be simpler than the poem's opening: "I saw an aged Beggar in my walk." The Old Man (the capitalization is the poet's) has put down his staff, and takes his scraps and fragments out of a flour bag, one by one. He scans them, fixedly and seriously. The plain beginning yields to a music of love, the beauty of the real:

> In the sun,
> Upon the second step of that small pile,
> Surrounded by those wild unpeopled hills,
> He sat, and ate his food in solitude:
> And ever, scattered from his palsied hand,
> That, still attempting to prevent the waste,
> Was baffled still, the crumbs in little showers
> Fell on the ground; and the small mountain birds,
> Not venturing yet to peck their destined meal,
> Approached within the length of half his staff.

It is difficult to describe *how* this is beautiful, but we can make a start by observing that it is beautiful both because it is so matter of fact, and because the fact is itself a transfiguration. The Old Man is in his own state, and he is radically innocent. The "wild unpeopled hills" complement his own solitude; he is a phenomenon of their kind. And he is no more sentimentalized than they are. His lot is not even miserable; he is too absorbed into Nature for that, as absorbed as he can be and still retain human identity.

He is even past further aging. The poet has known him since his childhood, and even then "he was so old, he seems not older now." The Old Man is so helpless in appearance that everyone—sauntering horseman or toll-gate keeper or post boy—makes way for him, taking special care to keep him from harm. For he cannot be diverted, but moves on like a natural process. "He travels on, a solitary Man," Wordsworth says, and then repeats it, making a refrain for that incessant movement whose only meaning is that it remains human though at the edge of our condition:

> He travels on, a solitary Man;
> His age has no companion. On the ground
> His eyes are turned, and, as he moves along,
> They move along the ground; and, evermore,
> Instead of common and habitual sight
> Of fields with rural works, of hill and dale,
> And the blue sky, one little span of earth
> Is all his prospect.

He is bent double, like the Leech Gatherer, and his vision of one little span of earth recalls the wandering old man of Chaucer's *Pardoner's Tale*. But Chaucer's solitary longed for death, and on the ground he called his mother's gate he knocked often with his staff, crying, "Dear mother, let me in." Wordsworth's Old Man sees only the ground, but he is tenaciously alive, and is beyond desire, even that of death. He sees, and yet hardly sees. He moves constantly, but is so still in look and motion that he can hardly be seen to move. He is all process, hardly character, and yet almost stasis.

It is so extreme a picture that we can be tempted to ask, "Is this life? Where is its use?" The temptation dehumanizes us, Wordsworth would have it, and the two questions are radically dissimilar, but his answer to the first is vehemently affirmative and to the second an absolute moral passion. There is

> a spirit and pulse of good,
> A life and soul, to every mode of being
> Inseparably linked.

The Old Man performs many functions. The most important is that of a binding agent for the memories of good impulses in all around him. Wherever he goes,

> The mild necessity of use compels
> To acts of love.

These acts of love, added one to another, at last insensibly dispose their performers to virtue and true goodness. We need to be careful in our reaction to this. Wordsworth is not preaching the vicious and mad doc-

The Myth of Memory and Natural Man

trine that beggary is good because it makes charity possible. That would properly invoke Blake's blistering reply in *The Human Abstract*:

> Pity would be no more
> If we did not make somebody Poor;
> And Mercy no more could be
> If all were as happy as we.

Wordsworth has no reaction to the Old Man which we can categorize. He does not think of him in social or economic terms, but only as a human life, which necessarily has affected other lives, and always for the better. In particular, the Old Man has given occasions for kindness to the very poorest, who give to him from their scant store, and are the kinder for it. Again, you must read this in its own context. Wordsworth's best poetry has nothing directly to do with social justice, as Blake's or Shelley's frequently does. The old beggar is a free man, at home in the heart of the solitudes he wanders, and he does not intend the humanizing good he passively causes. Nor is his social aspect at the poem's vital center; only his freedom is:

> —Then let him pass, a blessing on his head!
> And, long as he can wander, let him breathe
> The freshness of the valleys; let his blood
> Struggle with frosty air and winter snows;
> And let the chartered wind that sweeps the heath
> Beat his grey locks against his withered face.

Pity for him is inappropriate; he is pathetic only if shut up. He is a "figure of capable imagination," in Stevens' phrase, a Man perfectly complete in Nature, reciprocating its gifts by being himself, a being at one with it:

> Let him be free of mountain solitudes;
> And have around him, whether heard or not,
> The pleasant melody of woodland birds.

Mountain solitudes and sudden winds are what suit him, whether he reacts to them or not. The failure of his senses does not cut him off from Nature; it does not matter whether he can hear the birds, but it is fitting that he have them around him. He has become utterly passive toward Nature. Let it be free, then, to come in upon him:

> if his eyes have now
> Been doomed so long to settle upon earth
> That not without some effort they behold
> The countenance of the horizontal sun,
> Rising or setting, let the light at least
> Find a free entrance to their languid orbs.

The Old Man is approaching that identity with Nature that the infant at first knows, when an organic continuity seems to exist between Nature and consciousness. Being so naturalized, he must die in the eye of Nature, that he may be absorbed again:

> And let him, *where* and *when* he will, sit down
> Beneath the trees, or on a grassy bank
> Of highway side, and with the little birds
> Share his chance-gathered meal; and, finally,
> As in the eye of Nature he has lived,
> So in the eye of Nature let him die!

The poem abounds in a temper of spirit that Wordsworth shares with Tolstoy, a reverence for the simplicities of *caritas,* the Christian love that is so allied to and yet is not pity. But Tolstoy might have shown the Old Cumberland Beggar as a sufferer; in Wordsworth he bears the mark of "animal tranquillity and decay," the title given by Wordsworth to a fragment closely connected to the longer poem. In the fragment the Old Man travels on and moves not with pain, but with thought:

> He is insensibly subdued
> To settled quiet . . .
> He is by nature led
> To peace so perfect that the young behold
> With envy, what the Old Man hardly feels.

We know today, better than his contemporaries could, what led Wordsworth to the subject of human decay, to depictions of idiocy, desertion, beggars, homeless wanderers. He sought images of alienated life, as we might judge them, which he could see and present as images of natural communion. The natural man, free of consciousness in any of our senses, yet demonstrates a mode of consciousness which both intends Nature for its object and at length blends into that object. The hiding places of man's power are in his past, in childhood. Only memory can take him there, but even memory fades, and at length fades away. The poet of naturalism, separated by organic growth from his own past, looks around him and sees the moving emblems of a childlike consciousness in the mad, the outcast, and the dreadfully old. From them he takes his most desperate consolation, intimations of a mortality that almost ceases to afflict.

Wordsworth and the Tears of Adam

by Neil Hertz

This essay on literary influence grew out of my bewilderment with one of the better-documented relationships in English poetry, that of Wordsworth to Milton. How was one to understand this case of influence? It was not just a theoretical problem but a puzzle, line by line, to the practical critic. Anyone who has tried to draw the lines of force between two poets, one in the more distant, one in the more recent past, will know what I mean: a reader quickly finds himself perplexed, conscious not only of the movement of the texts relative to each other, but of the shifting, contingent quality of his own relation to either poet's work. Of course this may be the case with any interpretive effort, but the study of influence has a way of bringing the point home with particular force. For what one finds, again and again, is that one's most interesting perceptions seem suspiciously anachronistic—as if it were really Wordsworth who was influencing Milton—or subjective—as if it were merely one's own interpretive acts that had become a source of fascination, a distracting influence from still another direction.

Yet it may be that both a sense of anachronism and of a certain kind of subjectivity are not only unavoidable in such studies, but often signs that one is on the right track; for they may mean that the reader is moving into that order of time in which works of literature have their existence and in which the significant encounters between writers take place. In the pages that follow, since I would like to show what can be gained by ignoring chronology, I shall begin by looking at a poem of Wordsworth's, then, with that in mind, turn to look backwards towards a passage in *Paradise Lost,* then finally move forward again to consider "The Ruined Cottage." Fortunately, we are dealing with two writers who would find this approach congenial. Their works have traditionally raised questions about the nature of poetic subjectivity, and they are poets for whom anachronism held no terrors, to whom phrases like "the child is father of the man" or "Adam the goodliest man of men since born his sons" were both meaningful and peculiarly satisfying. As such,

"Wordsworth and the Tears of Adam" by Neil Hertz. From *Studies in Romanticism,* 7 (1967). Copyright © 1967 by Boston University. Reprinted, with revisions by the author, by his permission and that of *Studies in Romanticism.*

it will not only be in their relation to one another, but in the encounters that take place within their individual works, that Milton and Wordsworth can help us to understand the encounter of poet with poet.

I

Here, first, is a text in many ways typical of Wordsworth: the experience it records is a characteristic one, and Wordsworth rightly considered his rendering of it an example of his best blank verse. But there are two things that are unusual about it which make it, from my point of view, particularly interesting. We most frequently find Wordsworth, in his major poems, writing in the first person and engaged in the imaginative retrieval of events in the more or less distant past. He is, we know, the poet of the egotistical sublime, and he is the poet who, in his own words, was "unused to make a present joy the matter of a song." But here we shall find him offering a third-person account of an experience which we know from his note to have been his own, and which he turned into poetry almost immediately after it had occurred. What is surprising is how little these differences seem to matter: the poem remains perfectly illustrative of Wordsworth's recurrent concerns. To understand how this can be so is to learn something about the quality of Wordsworthian subjectivity and of Wordsworth's interest in the past. The poem is "A Night-Piece" (1798):

>   —The sky is overcast
> With a continuous cloud of texture close,
> Heavy and wan, all whitened by the Moon,
> Which through that veil is indistinctly seen,
> A dull, contracted circle, yielding light
> So feebly spread, that not a shadow falls,
> Chequering the ground—from rock, plant, tree, or tower.
> At length a pleasant instantaneous gleam
> Startles the pensive traveller while he treads
> His lonesome path, with unobserving eye
> Bent earthwards; he looks up—the clouds are split
> Asunder,—and above his head he sees
> The clear Moon, and the glory of the heavens.
> There, in a black-blue vault she sails along,
> Followed by multitudes of stars, that, small
> And sharp, and bright, along the dark abyss
> Drive as she drives: how fast they wheel away,
> Yet vanish not! the wind is in the tree,
> But they are silent;—still they roll along
> Immeasurably distant; and the vault,

> Built round by those white clouds, enormous clouds,
> Still deepens its unfathomable depth.
> At length the Vision closes; and the mind,
> Not undisturbed by the *delight* it feels,
> Which slowly settles into peaceful calm,
> Is left to muse upon the solemn scene.[1]

The poem traces the movement of a mind imaginatively engaged with the external world, a movement that could be charted in a number of ways. For example, we might notice how the moon is gradually realized as a powerful presence. At first totally denaturalized ("a dull, contracted circle"), then "the clear Moon," she finally emerges, fully personified, in line 14. When that happens, the visible world is transformed: it no longer makes up a field for empirical observation. Instead it is reconstituted, under the presiding light of the moon, as a "Vision," a "solemn scene" which bears musing on, because it is now emblematic.[2]

Inseparable from this process is another, involving the transformation of the voice we hear telling the story. The speaker of the opening lines is calmly and rather distantly observing the scene: his language, in its neutral, faintly scientific accuracy ("continuous cloud," "texture," "contracted circle"), corresponds in want of feeling to the "dull" quality of the scene itself. Whoever this spectator may be, he is certainly *ab extra*: the "pensive traveller" only appears in the ninth line, and his "unobserving eye / Bent earthwards" is presumably not the eye that so carefully registered details of cloud and moonlight earlier. But as the moon is revealed, and the power and significance of the scene take possession of the traveller, the narrative voice is itself changed, moving from the (still uninvolved) notation of emotional response ("a pleasant . . . gleam / Startles the pensive traveller") to conventional hyperbole ("the glory of the heavens"), then to a more excited participation: "how fast they wheel away / Yet vanish not!"

In that exclamation, the speaker's response is indistinguishable from the traveller's. Both seem to have been brought alive by this silent and powerful manifestation. We can speak of their state as one of heightened subjectivity, but here we must note that characteristically in Wordsworth such heightening creates not a more highly individualized subject, but a more impersonal and generalized one. So it is here: speaker and traveller no longer occupy distinct points of view, and it is because of this coalescence that the poem can end as it does, now no longer referring

---

[1] Quotations in this paper are from *The Poetical Works of William Wordsworth*, ed. E. de Selincourt (Oxford, 1940–49); and *The Poetical Works of John Milton*, ed. Helen Darbishire (Oxford Univ. Press, 1958).

[2] On the transformation of the scene, see David Ferry, *The Limits of Mortality* (Middletown, Conn., 1959), pp. 30–31; and James Kissane, "'A Night-Piece': Wordsworth's Emblem of the Mind," *MLN*, LXXI (1956), 183–186.

either to a pensive traveller or an anonymous observer or even to a poet recollecting emotion in tranquillity, but inclusively to "the mind." Indeed, one measure of the poem's success is that the encompassing gesture implicit in saying "the mind" embraces the reader as well, for he too, as the last lines settle into a calm regularity of cadence, is made to participate in the mind that muses on the solemn scene.

Wordsworth's note to the poem[3] confirms what we may have suspected anyway, that the observer, the pensive traveller and the writer of the poem were really one and the same; they are simply aspects of Wordsworth's self following one upon the other in time. But the poem Wordsworth chose to write does not take that continuity for granted: rather, he seems in this case to have gone out of his way, by writing in the third person, to insist on the disjunctive nature of the self. The note suggests why this maneuver may have seemed necessary to him. If the poem was, in fact, composed extempore, the entire experience—the visual revelation and its verbal repetition—would have had about it a specious feeling of personal continuity. The man who works into blank verse the exclamation "How fast they wheel away . . . !" at, say, 9:35 p.m. is very obviously—too obviously, for Wordsworth's purposes—the same man who, at 9:30, had initially exclaimed those words. No great effort of the imagination would seem necessary in order to recapture sensations so recently experienced. By writing in the third person, Wordsworth deliberately introduces into this apparently seamless experience a gap, a vacancy between aspects of the self that makes his account of this "present joy" identical in structure to the more familiar poetry of childhood remembered. Here are some lines from the Second Book of *The Prelude* (1805):

> A tranquillizing spirit presses now
> On my corporeal frame: so wide appears
> The vacancy between me and those days,
> Which yet have such self-presence in my mind
> That, sometimes, when I think of them, I seem
> Two consciousnesses, conscious of myself
> And of some other Being. (ll. 27–33)

These are the circumstances in which Wordsworth's finest poetry is written, and what "A Night-Piece" makes clear is how necessary it was for him to experience this doubling of consciousness. It was a state of mind that would come more or less naturally when he was musing on the almost-forgotten past, but here we find him obliged to induce it quite

---

[3] "Composed on the road between Nether Stowey and Alfoxden, extempore. I distinctly recollect the very moment when I was struck, as described,—'He looks up at the clouds, etc.'" *The Poetical Works,* II, 503.

deliberately, by manipulating the dramatic structure of his account. The result is to split the self into a poet existing in the present and "some other Being" who acts as a mediating figure—often a childhood self, but in this case the mature man seen as "pensive traveller." But this mediator is also involved in another powerfully resonant relation, usually with a natural object—as the pensive traveller is, here, with the moon—and it is precisely this relational moment that Wordsworth seeks to bring into connection with his present poetic activity. What he thus succeeds in creating is a chain of successive and analogous relations: the moon is to the pensive traveller as the pensive traveller is to the poet as the poet is to the reader; or, to schematize the more frequently encountered sequence, Nature : child :: child : poet :: poet : reader. The intention of Wordsworth's major poetry is never essentially the recreation of the past. When his imagination turns backward towards the original experience, it is in search of that "other Being"—neither poet nor reader—who will, when paired with the poet, occupy the central position in the chain of relations I have just described.

I want to linger on this metaphor of a chain because I believe it will make it easier to bring into connection a number of aspects of Wordsworth's thought. For one thing, it suggests why a critic's interest in Wordsworthian rhetoric (that is, the relation of reader to poet) is inseparable from an interest in Wordsworthian memory (the relation of poet to child) and in Wordsworthian metaphysics (the relation of child to Nature). Secondly, it can give us an insight into the peculiar quality of time encountered in Wordsworth's poetry, and into the connection between that time and the kind of human consciousness—autonomous, subjective, and impersonal—that comes into existence at certain moments in his poetry, moments like the one we have observed towards the end of "A Night-Piece." There we noticed that the center of subjectivity, "the mind," was inclusively that of the traveller, the poet, and the reader. Yet Wordsworth was insisting that there was a gap between poet and traveller of the same sort that exists between poet and reader, and that that gap may be bridged but is not thereby removed. As a result, the poem testifies to a remarkable generosity, a willingness on Wordsworth's part to confer autonomy on prior moments in his own existence and on the consciousness of his reader as well. But the order of time in which this autonomous subjectivity is constituted, in which the chain of relations is created, is not ordinary historical time. If we ask when the exclamation "How fast they wheel away!" takes place, we cannot locate it exclusively at the moment of the traveller's original experience, nor can we place it at the moment at which the poet repeats the words, nor yet at the moment the reader encounters them. The chain exists in a mode of present time—call it the narrative present—which is a creation of the language of the poem, of the telling of the story, and in which traveller and poet and reader mutually participate. Finally, the metaphor of a chain will be helpful when we turn to examine another relation, that of poet to poet, of Wordsworth to Milton, for it suggests that there might be a way of thinking about literary influence that honors the autonomy of both poets involved.

II

We can begin by raising the question of Milton's subjectivity, that is, of the quality of his presence in his work. That question no longer engages our attention as it once did that of the Romantics, probably because the whole issue was so badly confused during the nineteen-thirties. Then too much of the wrong sort of attention was paid to the ways Milton's personality made itself heard in *Paradise Lost,* usually on the part of critics who found him personally offensive and who were bothered by any signs of his intrusion. Attacks on his personality generally were accompanied by attacks on his idiosyncrasies as a stylist or as a thinker; so, in reply, recent students of *Paradise Lost* have taken pains to show that particular aspects of Milton's poetry are neither as strange nor as peculiar to him as they were once held to be. These later studies have generally been convincing, and working together they have produced a more sophisticated sense of Milton's location in history. But one consequence of this emphasis has been a relative lack of interest in what Coleridge spoke of as the "subjectivity of the poet, as of Milton, who is himself before himself in every thing he writes."[4] The lines of Wordsworth's we have just considered can suggest the variety of ways in which a poet can be "before himself" as he writes, as well as the impersonal quality of the highest reach of poetic subjectivity; as such they can serve as a guide to a still-disputed and interesting section of *Paradise Lost.*

In the Eleventh Book, the Archangel Michael, sent to expel Adam from the Garden, first offers him a prophetic account of history, that is, of the long-range consequences of his fall. The prophecy takes the form of a series of visions, each of which provokes a response from Adam—usually one of grief or dismay, for the scenes Adam is shown are almost universally grim. Each of Adam's responses, in turn, elicits an explanation from Michael, and the tone of these explanations in general matches the visions, and sometimes even surpasses them, in grimness. Commenting on a group of sinners who appear to be enjoying

[4] In *Table Talk,* May 12, 1830; reprinted in *Coleridge on the Seventeenth Century,* ed. Roberta Florence Brinkley (Durham, N.C., 1955), p. 587.

themselves, Michael is made to say, with the air of a man clearly enjoying *him*self, that they

> now swim in joy,
> (Erelong to swim at large) and laugh; for which
> The World erelong a world of tears must weepe. (XI, 625–627)

Critics have fastened on lines such as these as proof that there was something immoderately sour about Milton's view of history, imputing the edge in Michael's tone either to the personal bitterness the poet may be imagined to have felt after the Restoration or, in less flatly *ad hominem* terms, to the rigors of his later theology. "In this portion of the poem," one writer complains, "Milton's imagination seems to take wing only in delineating scenes of destruction."[5]

I have seen no defense of the Eleventh Book that directly confronts these *ad hominem* complaints. Instead, admirers of this section of the poem argue their case in more objective terms, locating Milton's imaginative investment either in his reworking a vein of Christian historiography that goes back to St. Paul, or in his careful plotting of the drama of Adam's education.[6] Both these interpretations are valid, although, like much educational dialogue, the exchanges of Adam and Michael constitute a rather lumbering "drama." But there is another dramatic movement discernible in Book XI, one which involves Milton more directly in the fabric of his poem, and one which our Wordsworthian model puts us in a position to appreciate.

Late in the Book, Milton's own voice interrupts the dialogue of Adam and the Angel; the poet breaks off his account of Noah's Flood in order to address his sympathy directly to Adam:

> How didst thou grieve then, *Adam,* to behold
> The end of all thy Ofspring, end so sad,
> Depopulation; thee another Floud,
> Of tears and sorrow a Floud thee also drownd,
> And sunk thee as thy Sons; till gently reard
> By th' Angel, on thy feet thou stoodst at last,
> Though comfortless, as when a Father mourns
> His Children, all in view destroyd at once. (XI, 754–761)

---

[5] Louis L. Martz, *The Paradise Within* (New Haven, 1964), p. 153.
[6] A brief summary of critical opinion on Books XI and XII followed by a perceptive and informed account of their significance can be found in Barbara Keifer Lewalski, "Structure and the Symbolism of Vision in Michael's Prophecy, *Paradise Lost,* Books XI–XII," *PQ,* XLII (1963), 25–35. See also George Williamson, "The Education of Adam," and Lawrence A. Sasek, "The Drama of Paradise Lost, Books XI and XII," both articles available in Arthur E. Barker's anthology, *Milton: Modern Essays in Criticism* (New York, 1965).

This far along in the poem, we have become accustomed to the constant and often subtle pressure Milton exercises to shape his reader's response to the story he is telling; and we are also accustomed to his sometimes turning away from his readers entirely, in prayer or invocation. What is rare—I count only three instances throughout the poem[7]—is for the poet to thus address himself to a character. Even more surprising is the quality of this address: the tenderness implicit in the repeated use of *thee* and *thou* and *thy*, and the powerful sense of loss these lines communicate. Tenderness, we know, has not been the dominant note of Book XI, nor have we been led to expect Milton to grieve at the thought of sinners being swept away. Yet here it seems as if the act of imagining the Flood, far from providing a source of grim pleasure to Milton, has liberated in him a flow of compassion: "thee another Floud, / Of tears and sorrow a Floud thee also drown'd."

"In the Paradise Lost," wrote Coleridge, "the sublimest parts are the revelations of Milton's own mind, producing itself and evolving its own greatness."[8] He was thinking of the Invocation to Light in Book III when he wrote this, but signs of the same evolution may be observed in the Eleventh Book: it is possible to read this section as a dramatic development of the poet's consciousness, analogous to the movement of mind recorded in Wordsworth's "Night-Piece," and tending toward the address to Adam. To read the passage in this way is to accept the imputations of *ad hominem* critics, to agree that Milton's personal resentment (along with other less damaging sentiments) may be heard in the voice of the Archangel; but it is also to carry the tonal analysis one step further, and to insist that the accents of personal resentment that we may catch in Michael's speech are no longer audible when Milton himself addresses Adam. Paradoxically, that moment when Milton speaks out in his own voice is among the least personal in the poem. It is worth considering how this might have come about, and what its implications are for a reading of the rest of *Paradise Lost*.

A good place to begin is with one of the lessons that Michael's account of history seems intended to teach: where there are multitudes, there is sin. Adam's fall has put God's command to increase and multiply in a new and ironic light. The sequence of visions Adam is shown brings home the lesson, as each new scene is enlarged in scope and more confusingly populous. Counterpointing this association of sin with human multitudes is an increasing stress on the unique and isolated figure of the righteous man. This is less obvious in the opening vision

---

[7] The other moments occur when Milton addresses Adam and Eve at IV, 773 ("Sleep on, / Blest pair . . ."), and Eve at IX, 404 ("O much deceived, much failing, hapless *Eve* . . .").

[8] In *The Literary Remains of Samuel Taylor Coleridge* (London, 1836–39), I, 172 f.; reprinted in Brinkley, p. 578.

of Cain and Abel, although Michael makes the point when he comments that "th'unjust the just hath slain" (XI, 455); but in the later visions of Enoch ("The onely righteous in a World perverse" [XI, 701]) and of Noah ("The one just Man alive" [XI, 818]) this Old Testament motif that had so long and so deeply engaged Milton's imagination is made quite explicit.

If we set out—as *ad hominem* critics do—to ground this dialectic in the actualities of Milton's life, it is easy enough to see how, in the 1660s, the figures of the citizen as the One Just Man or the poet as the severe but truth-telling Archangel would have been appealing images to Milton, stirring in him the bitter satisfactions of self-righteousness. Something of this sort is undoubtedly going on in Book XI; but it soon becomes clear that the demands of Milton's imagination are not fully met by these mediators, and that his mind is moving beyond them toward a confrontation with what Wordsworth would call "some other Being," a figure who will mediate to him a truer sense of his poetic identity. That figure is Adam, not Adam seen as an archetype of innocence, but Adam after the Fall, surviving but mortal, and listening in tears to the sad tale of loss.

The turning point is the story of the Flood, which begins with an account of Noah testifying against the ways of the multitude and preaching "Conversion and Repentance":

> But all in vain: which when he saw, he ceas'd
> Contending, and remov'd his Tents farr off;
> Then from the Mountain hewing Timber tall,
> Began to build a Vessel of huge bulk.   (XI, 726–729)

This is the One Just Man in his finest hour, aloof but irreproachably so. But now the mood of the poem changes as Milton turns for his text from the account in *Genesis* to the stranger poetry of Deucalion's flood in Ovid:

> Meanwhile the Southwind rose, and with black-wings
> Wide hovering, all the Clouds together drove
> From under Heav'n; the Hills to their supplie
> Vapour, and Exhalation dusk and moist,
> Sent up amain; and now the thick'nd Skie
> Like a dark Ceeling stood; down rushd the Rain
> Impetuous, and continu'd till the Earth
> No more was seen; the floating Vessel swum
> Uplifted; and secure with beaked prow
> Rode tilting o'er the Waves, all dwellings else
> Flood overwhelm'd, and them with all thir pomp
> Deep under water rould; Sea coverd Sea,

> Sea without shour; and in thir Palaces
> Where luxurie late reignd, Sea-monsters whelpd
> And stabl'd.   (XI, 738–752)

This is certainly Ovid moralized; the grotesque underwater details illustrate the wages of sin, for Milton is still concerned with "*thir* pomp," "*thir* Palaces / Where luxurie late reignd." But the metamorphic power of these images and cadences, the sense of sea-change familiar to readers of "Lycidas," reaches out beyond the sinful multitudes—those others—to involve the consciousness of the righteous poet as well. As the scene is radically diminished in scope, the pathos of loss is suddenly the dominant feeling, mingled with a sense of how fragile is the vessel in which righteousness survives: "of Mankind, so numerous late, / All left, in one small bottom swum imbarkt" (XI, 752–753). With this the transformation of the poet's voice is completed, and he can turn, in sympathy and in the recognition of kinship, to Adam.

But what are the grounds of this kinship? Adam's response to the vision turns out to be characteristically generous but, as usual, exaggerated, for it is based on a misapprehension. Moved by the scope of the disaster and ignorant of its outcome, he naturally assumes that all mankind did indeed perish, including Noah and his family, whom he imagines finally dying of "Famine and anguish . . . Wandring that watrie Desert" (XI, 778–779). Later, when Michael enlightens him and goes on to describe the receding of the waters and the renewal of the Covenant, Adam joyfully brings his feelings into line with his new understanding of the event:

> Farr less I now lament for one whole World
> Of wicked Sons destroyd, then I rejoyce
> For one Man found so perfet and so just.   (XI, 874–876)

Adam's self-correction has about it some of the same harsh zest with which Milton, in a more famous passage in the poem—the description of Mulciber's fall—suddenly reins in his own erring imagination. The comparison is worth considering, for just as there Milton had allowed his verse to affectionately linger over the story as the Greeks told it before pulling himself up short to insist on its falsity, so in directly addressing himself to Adam, in taking Adam's interpretation of the scene so readily for granted, he has lent himself to this error. To break into the texture of the poem at this point is to imaginatively assume the burden of Adam's ignorance and of his innocence of Christian doctrine. It is as if Milton had been moved by the compelling poetry of the Flood to momentarily suspend his sense of the certainties of his faith—moved back beyond doctrine, beyond the hope of redemption, to an encounter with Adam in the heart of loss.

This interpretation needn't obscure the Christian intention of *Paradise Lost* or the presence of a redemptive pattern as a structural element in the last two books. The poetry of the Flood takes its place in that pattern, of course, for Michael's prophecy is intended to serve as an object lesson for Adam in Pauline faith, in "the substance of things unseen." So the lines that unfold the dimensions of Adam's loss may be read as part of his education, a negative experience designed to detach his hopes from the wrong objects so that they may fix themselves on the promised end. We have seen what Adam learns from the first account of the Flood: it is to "renounce a World of wicked Sons," to temper his hopes that blood lineage can provide an alternative to the permanence he has forfeited at the Fall. Later, there is another passage intended to teach him a related lesson, to purge him of any false hopes about the permanence of his dwelling place. It comes from Michael's speech after the vision of the Flood, and it is unusual in one respect: for it has not been Michael's practice, when commenting on the visions he produces, to get so caught up in their detail. Yet here he begins by interpreting the Flood and ends by vividly retelling the story. He has come to the point where Noah is commanded to "save himself and houshold from amidst / A World devote to universal rack":

> No sooner hee with them of Man and Beast
> Select for life shall in the Ark be lodg'd,
> And shelterd round, but all the Cataracts
> Of Heav'n set op'n on the Earth shall powre
> Raine day and night, all fountains of the Deep
> Broke up, shall heave the Ocean to usurp
> Beyond all bounds, till inundation rise
> Above the highest Hills: then shall this Mount
> Of Paradise by might of Waves be moovd
> Out of his place, pusht by the horned floud,
> With all his verdure spoild, and Trees adrift
> Down the great River to the op'ning Gulf,
> And there take root an Iland salt and bare,
> The haunt of Seales and Orcs, and Sea-mews' clang:
> To teach thee that God attributes to place
> No sanctitie, if none be thither brought
> By Men who there frequent, or therein dwell. (XI, 822–838)

The moral is clear and relevant, but it is not at all adequate to the full suggestiveness of this poetry. Nor can we really account for the length of this reprise or for its appearance at this point in the poem by reflecting on Michael's motives as a prophet or as a teacher. It is certainly Milton whose imagination is caught up in the story, and to understand the fascination that the Flood held for him, I think that, instead of looking further along in the poem for signs of the redemptive pattern, we should turn back to the poet's address to Adam.

I have suggested that Milton, in addressing Adam, has achieved the same quality of impersonality that can be heard in Wordsworth's voice in the climactic lines of "A Night-Piece": there are still other analogies between the two texts which I would like to pursue. Consider what it means for Milton to break into his narrative and speak to a character: it involves an odd—and, for the surprised reader, a very exciting—leap of the imagination in time. For if we ask when this address takes place, we must say it occurs neither in Adam's ordinary time—sometime between the Fall and the Expulsion—nor in Milton's—sometime in the 1660s. Chronology becomes misleading and we must locate this point of imaginative contact in another order of time. This is the same situation we found ourselves in when we were considering "A Night-Piece," and asking when the exclamation "How fast they wheel away . . . !" occurs. In the case of Wordsworth's poetry, I have called that order of time the narrative present, and noted that it was a creation of the language of the poem, brought into being by the telling of a story, and hence available for the participation of the reader or the hearer of the tale. And that too may be said of this moment in *Paradise Lost*. For what moves Adam to tears is not an event in his immediate experience but the image of one that has not yet taken place, as it is summoned up for him, in a prospective vision, by the angelic narrator; and what moves Milton to compassion is not his witnessing the Flood itself, but his imaginative participation in Adam's subjective response to it. For an instant, Adam and Milton meet, not as eye-witnesses to a disaster, but as members of Michael's audience, and much of the poignancy of their encounter is due to this. Like Milton's own audience they are, in effect, listening to a story, one which will be perpetuated by successive retellings—Michael to Adam, Moses to the children of Israel, and so on. In fact, what Milton's audience is listening to is simultaneously both the earliest and the most recent telling of the tale; for Adam was the first to hear it, and its latest rehearsal is here and now, as a story within the story of *Paradise Lost*.

This, of course, is true of the entire prophecy in Books XI and XII. But within that structure the story of the Flood is unique, not only because of its length or the generally high quality of its verse, but because so many elements in that section of the poem are brought into tight and resonant interrelation. The lines describing the drowning of the sinful are also the occasion of a symbolic drowning or transformation of the poet's voice, a movement from a self-righteous identification with the One Jûst Man, through a moment of self-loss, toward a compassionate identification with Adam fallen, who is now recognizable as a fellow-survivor, someone who has himself experienced, as he weeps for his descendants, a death-by-water. Finally these multiplied and interinvolved instances of loss are related to the most formal element in the encounter of Milton and Adam, the fact that it takes place through the mediation of a prospective vision or story. For listening to a story, regardless of its theme, is also an experience of self-loss, of the suspension of one's commitments in ordinary time in favor of an alternative sequence of events in narrative time. Yet here formal and thematic elements are inseparable: Milton's moving out of self-righteousness is concurrent with his moving through the poetry of the Flood into the story, into the time in which he can confront Adam. When that encounter takes place, a chain of relations is established similar to that created in Wordsworth's poem, for not only Adam and Milton, but Milton's reader as well has been brought into the narrative continuum: if we are moved by what we hear in these lines, then we find ourselves in a relation to the voice of their poet that is not identical with but analogous to the relation he is in to Adam, and that Adam bears to Michael's vision of his drowning sons.

What I would like to suggest is that this perpetuation of the story of the Flood provides Milton with an emblem of continuity which is as compelling to his imagination as is the perpetuation of faith in the redemptive process. For it is through the rehearsal of the story that the encounter with Adam is brought about, and the poet led to an insight into the nature of loss and the nature of human subjectivity and the relation between the two. It is the firm—although fleeting—possession of that insight which underwrites the new note of generosity that can be heard in Milton's voice, a compassion that embraces, in Adam, mankind at large, the sinful and the righteous alike. For Milton to have arrived at that height of address is a sign that he has, in one sense, gone as far as he can go: the transformed voice no longer sounds in need of redemption. Perhaps this can help to explain the rather perfunctory treatment which the Redemption receives in Book XII, as well as the relative inertness of the verse there when compared with these passages on the Flood.

There are other points in *Paradise Lost* where an analysis of the play of personal and impersonal accents in the poet's voice would produce very different conclusions: in the great invocations, for example, the means by which the voice arrives at its authority are quite consciously and traditionally Christian. But the poetry of the Flood both participates in the central Christian intention of the poem and enacts other Miltonic intentions which are, at best, tangential to Christian thought. This situation is not unique in Milton's poetry. The last eight lines of "Lycidas," for example, come as a surprise, after the totally convincing language of Christian apotheosis, by introducing a new speaker, one who detaches himself from the body of the poem and contemplates it at a distance. His doing so is not at all felt to be ironically destructive of the religious concerns of the poem, yet this movement of the imagination does not seem to have grown out of those concerns, nor does the cool, impersonal but highly subjective voice to be heard in those last lines seem to draw its authority from Milton's faith. If it is possible to discriminate such distinct intentions in "Lycidas" or in *Paradise Lost* it is chiefly because the achievement of poets like Wordsworth has set the body of Miltonic poetry in a new light. I would like now to turn to a final Wordsworthian text, a poem which is at once an indication of his achievement and an illustration of what is most Miltonic about his imagination.

III

"The Ruined Cottage" was more or less completed in 1798, not long after Wordsworth composed "A Night-Piece," but it was not immediately published. It was put aside for a few years, taken up and revised during the winter of 1801–02, then finally printed as the first book of *The Excursion* in 1814. There it serves as an introduction to the character Wordsworth calls "the Wanderer," who functions as the poet's hero and spokesman throughout that long work. In its final form, "The Ruined Cottage" begins with the poet moving "across a bare wide Common," toward a prearranged meeting with the Wanderer, a rendezvous set in a shady grove surrounding an abandoned and dilapidated cottage. Wordsworth comes in sight of the grove, but postpones his account of their meeting until he has described at length how the Wanderer had come to be as he is, an exemplary Wordsworthian man, aged, wisely passive, profoundly and serenely in touch with Nature. The description of the Wanderer's childhood could have been composed for the opening books of *The Prelude,* but Wordsworth avoids insisting on his likeness to the older man. Rather he admiringly sets the Wanderer off at a distance, in a realm of calm self-possession that the poet himself has yet to attain. This distancing provides Wordsworth with a principle of dramatic structure for the rest of the poem, which falls quite naturally into two roughly equal sections. The first describes the Wanderer's education, a model of the gentle and molding power of Nature; the second half of the poem obliquely echoes this process, for it is concerned with what is really an incident in the poet's education, although this time it is not Nature but the Wanderer's words that exercise the benign influence. Like Adam listening to Michael, Wordsworth is gradually led toward the truth, and toward the appropriate response to the truth, as he listens to the Wanderer tell a sad story, the history of the last occupants of the now-ruined cottage.

Characteristically the Wanderer insists that what he is telling is only "a common tale, / An ordinary sorrow of man's life" (ll. 636–637), but the accents in which he begins his story mark his intention as prophetic:

> Thus did he speak. "I see around me here
> Things which you cannot see: we die, my Friend,
> Nor we alone, but that which each man loved
> And prized in his peculiar nook of earth
> Dies with him, or is changed; and very soon
> Even of the good is no memorial left. (ll. 469–474)

And that is the burden of the story which follows. A family disintegrates; the wife, Margaret, abandoned by her husband, gradually loses hope of his return, allows one of her children to leave her for a distant farm, the other to fall ill and die. She herself finally dies, and her cottage and its garden are now to be seen caught in the slow process of wasting back into the landscape. Like Milton's story of the Flood, the story of Margaret may be taken as an object lesson: the dead child, the overgrown garden, the ruined cottage speak of the same losses that Adam is made to feel as he learns that the Flood will sweep away his descendants and his dwelling-place; and the play of Wordsworth's curiosity and grief against the wiser but not entirely impassive understanding of the Wanderer recapitulates the dialogue of Adam and the Archangel. There is even a Wordsworthian analogue of the redemptive process, for it is suggested that Nature herself, the Nature that ministered to the Wanderer as a child, is providentially overseeing this episode in human history. But it is chiefly in the telling of the tale, in the rehearsal in words of the truth of loss, that the poem asserts a saving continuity; the pathos of Margaret's history is given additional depth and poignancy because it comes to us as a story within a story, and, just as in *Paradise Lost*, a chain of mediations is established that brings the reader into the continuum, into the repetitive process by which reality is turned into truth.[9]

These structural and thematic resemblances would, in themselves, make us suspect that Wordsworth had meditated on Milton's story of the Flood. But they also can tell us more than that, for they point beyond the similarities of these particular texts towards a clue to Milton's influence on Wordsworth and, possibly to the general nature of literary influence. In this particular case, influence is best understood not by picking up the echoes of specific bits of Milton's language or the reappearance of Miltonic themes, but by noticing the interrelation of theme and structure, of the theme of loss and the structure of narrative. The loss of human continuities is the burden of ordinary historical time; the creation of another order of time, in which that loss is confronted and

---

[9] I am indebted to Geoffrey Hartman's discussion of "The Ruined Cottage" in *Wordsworth's Poetry 1787–1814* (New Haven, 1964), pp. 135–140, 302–306, and to his remark *à propos* of "Michael" that "the poet is Michael's true heir" (p. 266). I should also record the degree to which Hartman's article "Milton's Counterplot," *ELH*, xxv (1958), 1–12, has encouraged me to read *Paradise Lost* xi as I do.

acknowledged, is the achievement of narrative. Taken singly, both the poetry of the Flood and "The Ruined Cottage" embody these truths; taken together, they exemplify the kind of continuity with which each is concerned. For the encounter of poet with poet is analogous to that of Michael with Adam, or of Milton with Adam, or of Wordsworth with the Wanderer.

I would like to close with one more quotation, this time not from the poetry but from Dorothy Wordsworth's *Journal*. It is intended to illustrate once again the nature of the influence we have been considering, by bringing the relation of poet to poet more closely in line with that of reader to poet. In the early months of 1802, Wordsworth was at work revising "The Ruined Cottage," which by that time he had taken to calling "The Pedlar." Here is part of Dorothy's entry for Tuesday, February 2nd:

> The sun shone but it was cold. After dinner William worked at *The Pedlar*. After tea I read aloud from the eleventh book of *Paradise Lost*. We were much impressed, and also melted into tears.[10]

For a moment, the two orders of time we have been considering—historical time and the narrative present—meet here as Wordsworth listens to *Paradise Lost*: the tears he wept that afternoon are the same tears that Adam weeps in Milton's poem.

[10] *Journals of Dorothy Wordsworth*, ed. E. de Selincourt (New York, 1941), I, 106.

The Ruined Cottage as Tragic Narrative

by Jonathan Wordsworth

The Ruined Cottage and *Michael* are both about the refusal to admit despair, but there is the important difference that positive hope is possible in the one and not the other. Michael's refusal shows itself in an acceptance of the hopelessness of his position, and an unrelenting continuation of the life he has always lived. Margaret, by contrast, increasingly lacks the will to keep up the routine of life, but never ceases to hope that Robert will return. It is in the moment of apparently total despair that one becomes aware of the greatness of Margaret's hope:

> Margaret stood near, her infant in her arms,
> And, seeing that my eye was on the tree,
> She said, "I fear it will be dead and gone
> Ere Robert come again."
>   Towards the house
> Together we returned, and she inquired
> If I had any hope. But for her Babe,
> And for her little friendless Boy, she said,
> She had no wish to live—that she must die
> Of sorrow. Yet I saw the idle loom
> Still in its place. His sunday garments hung
> Upon the self-same nail, his very staff
> Stood undisturbed behind the door.   (ll. 423–34)

As before, there is the balancing of appearance and reality, but the positions are reversed. Where Margaret's state had been shown on the evidence of her garden to be worse than it seemed, now she herself appears utterly despairing, but the house belies her words. She may say that she is living only for the child, but her husband's things are still

---

"*The Ruined Cottage* as Tragic Narrative" (editor's title). From Jonathan Wordsworth, *The Music of Humanity: A Critical Study of Wordsworth's "Ruined Cottage"* (London: Thomas Nelson and Sons, 1969). Copyright © 1969 by Jonathan Wordsworth. Reprinted by permission of A. D. Peters and Company, Harper & Row, Publishers, and the author. This selection is part 1, chapter 6.

where he would expect to find them. The point is reinforced by the speed with which Wordsworth moves on to

> And when
> I passed this way beaten by Autumn winds,
> She told me that her little babe was dead
> And she was left alone.   (ll. 434–7)

The brief reference to autumn winds is the only reminder of the elaborate transitions used to separate the Pedlar's earlier visits. The manuscript in fact reads straight on with no more than a comma to divide the two ideas, and mark the six months' gap:

> his very staff
> Stood undisturbed behind the door, and when
> I passed this way. . . .

The child for whom alone she wished to live is dead, and she lives on, still hoping for Robert's return:

> That very time,
> I yet remember, through the miry lane
> She walked with me a mile, when the bare trees
> Trickled with foggy damps, and in such sort
> That any heart had ached to hear her, begged
> That wheresoe'er I went I still would ask
> For him whom she had lost.   (ll. 437–43)

The pace of the narrative has quickened. It is not only that there is no longer time for the leisurely building up towards successive climaxes: the garden-descriptions which formed the lulls between moments of dialogue are actually incompatible with the hope that Wordsworth now wishes to stress. The garden at the beginning of the poem is gloomy—"Within that cheerless spot . . ."—and as long as Margaret's story is considered in purely human terms, its return to wildness can only record the progress towards gloom.

The Ruined Cottage as a whole is remarkable for the extent to which Wordsworth has visualized the movements and positions of his characters. Again and again a brief reference to the setting intensifies one's response:

> Margaret looked at me
> A little while, then turned her head away
> Speechless, and *sitting down upon a chair*
> Wept bitterly.   (ll. 247–50)

> "I perceive
> You look at me, and you have cause. . . ."   (ll. 347–8)

The last part of Margaret's story particularly depends on this technique. Up to this point Wordsworth has recorded the stages of her decline, but now his precise time-sequence is abandoned, and he talks instead of "*the warm summer*," "*the* long winter."[1] Five tedious years are evoked in a series of moving individual scenes: Margaret on her bench, her eye

> busy in the distance, shaping things
> Which made her heart beat quick.　(ll. 456–7)

Margaret spinning hemp, but stopping to ask soldiers and crippled sailors about Robert; Margaret standing to open the gate for horsemen so that she may ask "the same sad question"—if she dares; Margaret, "Last human tenant" of walls already ruined. She dies, still hoping, of sickness brought on by the decay of her cottage. On a conscious level she has "no wish to live," and though kept alive by torturing hope she cannot keep up the routine of survival, symbolized in Robert's closing up of chinks "At the first nippings of October frost." There is no question of despair, but hope is no longer the resilient optimism which enabled her to take up Robert's tools at the end of the Pedlar's first visit:

> And so she lived
> Through the long winter, reckless and alone,
> Till this reft house, by frost, and thaw, and rain,
> Was sapped; and when she slept, the nightly damps
> Did chill her breast, and in the stormy day
> Her tattered clothes were ruffled by the wind
> Even at the side of her own fire. Yet still
> She loved this wretched spot, nor would for worlds
> Have parted hence; and still that length of road,
> And this rude bench, one torturing hope endeared,
> Fast rooted at her heart. And here, my friend,
> In sickness she remained; and here she died,
> Last human tenant of these ruined walls.　(ll. 480–92)

It has been suggested that *The Ruined Cottage* ceases to be tragic when an optimistic conclusion is added. Lindenberger, for instance, compares it to Tate's version of *King Lear*:

> The additional lines, especially the image of the spear-grass and mist, are lovely in themselves and provide a cool, elegiac close to the stark tale narrated earlier; but we must also recognize that they (plus other additions to the pedlar's role) have created a new poem altogether and, above all, a poem of an entirely different genre, as different from the poem which

---

[1] There is bound to be awkwardness in referring to the narrative sequence of a poem where the end was written before the middle.

Coleridge first read in 1797 as the *King Lear* of Nahum Tate is from Shakespeare's tragedy.[2]

But it would be more to the point to say that Wordsworth first ended his *Lear*,

> "Why should a Dog, a Horse, a Rat have life,
> And thou no breath at all?"

then made it tolerable—though not retrospectively less terrible—by making Lear's heart "burst smilingly" ("She sleeps in the calm earth, and peace is here"), and settling the business of a return to normality (the Pedlar and Poet's exit to a rustic inn).

The whole question of Wordsworth's attitude to suffering at this period has recently been brought up by Cleanth Brooks, who cites as examples first *The Old Cumberland Beggar* and then *The Ruined Cottage*. But the two cases are radically different. Of the Cumberland Beggar's usefulness he writes:

> carrying out this function costs the old man something. The beggar serves, but he suffers in the process. How justify, for example, letting an old man walk the roads in all weathers? Here Wordsworth has been shockingly candid. In the very act of breathing a blessing on the beggar's head, the poet rather goes out of his way to express a wish that the beggar's blood should "Struggle with frosty air and winter snows," and adds:
>
>> let the chartered wind that sweeps the heath
>> Beat his gray locks against his withered face.[3]

In Wordsworthian terms the beggar does not suffer. His life may or may not seem attractive to modern readers, but the wind that sweeps the heath is "chartered" because it too is breathing a blessing on the old man's head. Wordsworth no more wishes suffering on him than he wishes it on his sister—"let the misty mountain-winds be free / To blow against thee . . ."—at the end of *Tintern Abbey*.[4]

The Ruined Cottage is very different. Margaret *does* suffer, and her suffering is presented as almost without relief. She too lives "in the eye

---

[2] *On Wordsworth's "Prelude,"* pp. 228–9. Cf. Edward E. Bostetter: "In affixing such a conclusion, Wordsworth has in effect repudiated the story as he has told it, denied the truth of his artistic experience." *The Romantic Ventriloquists* (Seattle, 1963), p. 65.

[3] "Wordsworth and Human Suffering: Notes on Two Early Poems," *From Sensibility to Romanticism, Essays Presented to Frederick A. Pottle*, ed. Frederick W. Hilles and Harold Bloom (New York, 1965), p. 377.

[4] Bostetter, *op. cit.*, p. 55, concedes Wordsworth's good intentions, but is indignant that "The beggar himself is not consulted or thought of as a man." Wordsworth is not interested as he should be in the social injustice of beggary, and his blessing on the old man is "a chilling prayer," "an illuminating example of selfish projection." But, like Brooks, he is surely upset by a suffering that is no part of the poem.

The Ruined Cottage as Tragic Narrative

of Nature," but it is no comfort to her. Brooks puts the relevant questions:

> Is Wordsworth saying here that, seen in the full perspective of nature, seen as a portion of nature's beautiful and unwearied immortality, Margaret with her sorrows is simply one detail of an all-encompassing and harmonious pattern? One can, for example, look at the rabbit torn by the owl in something like this fashion, and the rabbit's agony, no longer isolated and dwelt upon in itself, may cease to trouble us when understood as a necessary part of a total pattern, rich and various and finally harmonious, in which even the rabbit's pain becomes not a meaningless horror since it partakes of the beauty of the whole.

Or does *The Ruined Cottage* anticipate

> what might be called the reconciliation of suffering in the aesthetic vision. . . . Man is so various, so wonderful, capable of so much triumph and agony, suffering and joy, malice and goodness, that if one can take his stance far enough away from the individual case to allow him to see life in its wholeness, with all its rich variety—if one can do that, he can accept not only suffering but active wickedness as an inevitable and necessary part of the human drama, and can even rejoice in it as a testimony to the depths of man's feeling and his power to experience and endure.[5]

The first position Brooks is unwilling to accept—"One shrinks from concluding that such an interpretation as this is Wordsworth's own; and I do not mean to do so"—but, attractive or otherwise, it must be largely right. To some extent the second point of view is implied in all tragic writing, and it is the basis of one's attitude during the main part of *The Ruined Cottage*; but the consolation offered at the end of the poem is clearly that Margaret is now part of a total pattern. It is not just that she is no longer "stretched" on the rack of this tough world: where Lear in conventional terms was "better" dead, she is positively *happier*.

Several things contribute to make this position tolerable. Perkins has written:

> as the narrator looks raptly at the grass, in the close of this story, the pathetic history of Margaret's life appears to him only as an "idle dream." The reader is supposed to quit the poem not with vibrant feelings of grief or protest, but with "meditative sympathies." . . .[6]

Perhaps this may be so. By the same token we are supposed to leave *The Mayor of Casterbridge* wondering with Elizabeth-Jane

> at the persistence of the unforeseen, when the one to whom such unbroken tranquillity had been accorded in the adult stage was she whose

---
[5] *Op. cit.* pp. 385–6.
[6] David Perkins, *Wordsworth and the Poetry of Sincerity* (Cambridge, Mass., 1964), p. 116.

youth had seemed to teach that happiness was but the occasional episode in a general drama of pain.[7]

But we don't. If it was Wordsworth's intention to show Margaret's life as in retrospect an "idle dream" he was fortunately very undogmatic about it. It is presented as the Pedlar's view—and one takes comfort from the fact that Margaret's pain *can* be so generalized—but the Poet, who has throughout been identified with the reader, does not specifically accept it. His acceptance is implied in the "slant and mellow radiance" which replaces the "thirsty heat" of the opening lines, just as peace is implied in the changing roles of the speargrass, but in neither case is a message forced on one. Nor are Brooks' analogies entirely justified. Margaret is not the rabbit harmoniously torn by the owl. In death she becomes, or can be seen as being, part of a total pattern; but her suffering is not retrospectively explained or condoned. Wordsworth does not suggest that the rabbit's pain is needful or meaningful. He offers a comforting personal view of death, or rather of the state of being dead. It is the mood which Dorothy Wordsworth describes in her *Journal* of April 1802:

> We then went to John's grove, sate a while at first. Afterwards William lay, and I lay, in the trench under the fence—he with his eyes shut, and listening to the waterfalls and the Birds. . . . William heard me breathing and rustling now and then, but we both lay still, and unseen by one another; he thought that it would be as sweet thus to lie so in the grave, to hear the *peaceful* sounds of the earth, and just to know that our dear friends were near.
>
> (*Journals*, p. 152—Dorothy's italics)

Margaret "sleeps" in the calm earth. The word is undeniably euphemism, and perhaps self-deception too on the part of the poet; but it is not felt to be either. The valid comparison in this case is *Lycidas*. Presumably few readers would take literally the thought of saints singing to Edward King, and drying his eyes for him—

> There entertain him all the Saints above,
> In solemn troops, and sweet societies,
> That sing, and singing in their glory move,
> And wipe the tears forever from his eyes.

—and yet the beauty of the lines is not diminished. One can if one chooses reduce them to the prose statement, "Edward King is in heaven"

---

[7] Cf. Edgar's fatuous final comment in *King Lear*:
> The oldest hath borne most, we that are young,
> Shall never see so much, nor live so long.

The tendency of tragic writers to stand back at the end and generalize in fact makes very little difference to the total effect of their work.

and say that one doubts it, or that it is no sufficient consolation for his friends; but to do so has no more relevance than Dr. Johnson's famous literal-minded remark: "We know that they never drove a field, and that they had no flocks to batten . . . ." The lines work within the context of the poem. And similarly in *The Ruined Cottage* one is *imaginatively* convinced that Margaret is at peace because she is part of a world whose beauty is the outward sign of its beneficence. It is an idea that has, as Wordsworth put it, "sufficient foundation in humanity." [8] That it is "untrue" has no importance unless it is felt to be so, and the power of the poetry ensures that it is not:

> She sleeps in the calm earth, and peace is here.
> I well remember that those very plumes,
> Those weeds, and the high spear-grass on that wall,
> By mist and silent rain-drops silvered o'er,
> As once I passed, did to my mind convey
> So still an image of tranquility,
> So calm and still, and looked so beautiful
> Amid the uneasy thoughts that filled my mind,
> That what we feel of sorrow and despair
> From ruin and from change, and all the grief
> The passing shews of being leave behind,
> Appeared an idle dream that could not live
> Where meditation was. I turned away
> And walked along my road in happiness.   (ll. 512-25)

The consolation that Wordsworth asks his readers to accept is not in fact on a very different level from the rest of the poem. The "retreat from 'uneasy thoughts,'" as Perkins points out, is achieved largely by "converting the events of Margaret's life into abstractions" ("sorrow and despair / From ruin and from change . . .").[9] These generalize, but they do not falsify, the story that has been told. Nor is Margaret herself depersonalized in a way that does violence to the earlier descriptions. Previously she has been seen as the rose that is pulled down, the apple-tree whose tender stem is nibbled round by truant sheep: now she becomes by implication the speargrass "silvered o'er" with mist and—in a curiously peaceful, evocative phrase—"*silent* raindrops." The full force of "passing *shews* of being" is certainly hard to accept, but the Pedlar's words are offered as personal experience, the description of a single occasion and a particular mood: "As *once* I passed did to my mind con-

---

[8] "I took hold of the notion of pre-existence as having sufficient foundation in humanity for authorising me to make for my purpose the best use of it I could as a Poet." (Note on the *Intimations Ode, Poetical Works*, ed. de Selincourt, IV, 464.)

[9] [*The Poetry of Sincerity*, p. 116—ED.]

vey . . . ." Their effect is to distance Margaret's suffering, making bearable a story which in its original conclusion was too painful, too abrupt.

But the poem does not end here. There is the last section, in which *Lycidas* becomes not a parallel, but a positive influence:

> Thus sang the uncouth swain to th'oaks and rills,
> While the still morn went out with sandals gray;
> He touched the tender stops of various quills,
> With eager thought warbling his Doric lay:
> And now the sun had stretched out all the hills,
> And now was dropped into the western bay;
> At last he rose, and twitched his mantle blue:
> Tomorrow to fresh woods, and pastures new. (ll. 186–993)

> He ceased. By this the sun declining shot
> A slant and mellow radiance, which began
> To fall upon us where beneath the trees
> We sate on that low bench. And now we felt,
> Admonished thus, the sweet hour coming on:
> A linnet warbled from those lofty elms,
> A thrush sang loud, and other melodies
> At distance heard, peopled the milder air.
> The old man rose and hoisted up his load,
> Together casting then a farewell look
> Upon those silent walls, we left the shade;
> And, ere the stars were visible, attained
> A rustic inn, our evening resting-place. (ll. 526–38)

"The old man rose and hoisted up his load" sounds like parody when placed too close to "At last he rose, and twitched his mantle blue," but the correspondence between the two passages goes beyond mere verbal echo. Wordsworth was reminded of *Lycidas* by the need to round his poem off, and by genuine likeness of situation. His ending too says in effect, "Tomorrow to fresh woods, and pastures new." In *Lycidas*, however, the final passage stands outside the dramatic framework of the poem—it is the only place where the writer speaks in his own voice—whereas the last lines of *The Ruined Cottage* are a culmination of what has gone before. At the beginning of the poem the Poet and Pedlar enter separately, with their separate attitudes: at the end they go off together, their differences resolved through their shared response to the story that is told. At the beginning of the poem the Poet toils through the sun "with thirsty heat oppressed," the Pedlar sleeps contentedly his face dappled by shadows from the "breezy elms above": at the end both equally are *admonished* by the "slant and mellow radiance." The word is important. In the central stanza of *The Leech Gatherer* the old man is said to be "like a man from some far region sent" to give the poet "human strength *by apt admonishment*," but in *The Ruined Cottage* strength comes from being in harmony with one's surroundings, not from quasi-supernatural interventions. At the end of the poem the Poet and Pedlar are at peace with the world into which Margaret has been absorbed. The pattern is complete.

There seem to be two forms of tragedy—or at least two extremes—the fight against odds (*The Agamemnon, Beowulf,* perhaps *The Mayor of Casterbridge*) and the tragedy of waste (*Othello, Lear, Clarissa, Tess of the D'Urbervilles*). The first is moving because despite human dignity happiness is known to be impossible, the second precisely because one feels that happiness *was* possible, though in fact prevented by circumstance. In a curious way *The Ruined Cottage* unites the two. Margaret's story opens with her death, is told among the ruins where she died. She herself doesn't know that Robert will not return, but the reader does. Her suffering from the first is known to be pointless, her courage futile; and this constant awareness creates much that is beautiful in the poem. But fated tragedy is the lesser form, and Margaret's hope is moving not merely in its emptiness. In it one sees the power of her love. *The Ruined Cottage* shows a relationship pointlessly destroyed, a relationship which one is convinced could have made for great happiness. Angel Clare sleepwalks with Tess in his arms because he cannot accept her awake, Desdemona dies trying to shield Othello—

Emilia
Oh who hath done this deed?

Desdemona
No body: I my selfe, farewell:
Commend me to my kinde Lord:

—Lovelace rides impotently by the house where Clarissa is dying: Margaret's love is less dramatic, but the force which makes her go on living, go on hoping as she grows weaker and more and more intellectually certain that Robert will not return, is no less tragic.

In the last resort literary criticism is personal: one has to fall back on "This moves me," "This doesn't." [10] Coleridge said that he had never read *The Brothers* with "an unclouded eye," but described *The Ruined Cottage* as "the finest poem in our language, comparing it with any of the same or similar *length*." Myself I find *The Brothers* deeply moving, *Michael* much more so, while *The Ruined Cottage* moves me as I am

---

[10] "I may be wrong, but I speak as I felt, and the most profitable criticism is the record of sensations. . . ." Wordsworth to J. H. Reynolds, November 1816 ([*Letters: The Middle Years*], p. 759). For a more fashionable view, see W. K. Wimsatt Jr., "The Affective Fallacy," *The Verbal Icon* (Lexington, 1954).

moved by only one other poem, the medieval Scottish *Testament of Cresseid,* by two plays (*Lear* and *Othello*), and by a handful of novels. F. R. Leavis has stated categorically that it is Wordsworth's finest poem; but it is difficult to find standards of comparison. Perhaps one has to fall back on saying that in its idiom it is as great as are *The Prelude* and the *Ode* in theirs. It shows in Wordsworth a humanity, an insight into emotions not his own, that is wholly convincing—places him, perhaps unexpectedly, among the very few great English tragic writers.

Intentional Structure of the Romantic Image

by Paul de Man

In the history of Western literature, the importance of the image as a dimension of poetic language does not remain constant. One could conceive of an organization of this history in terms of the relative prominence and the changing structure of metaphor. French poetry of the sixteenth century is obviously richer and more varied in images than that of the seventeenth, and medieval poetry of the fifteenth century has a different kind of imagery than that of the thirteenth. The most recent change remote enough to be part of history takes place towards the end of the eighteenth century and coincides with the advent of romanticism. In a statement of which equivalences can be found in all European literatures, Wordsworth reproaches Pope for having abandoned the imaginative use of figural diction in favor of a merely decorative allegorization. Meanwhile the term *imagination* steadily grows in importance and complexity, in the critical as well as in the poetic texts of the period. This evolution in poetic terminology—of which parallel instances could easily be found in France and in Germany—corresponds to a profound change in the texture of poetic diction. The change often takes the form of a return to a greater concreteness, a proliferation of natural objects that restores to the language the material substantially which had been partially lost. At the same time, in accordance with a dialectic that is more paradoxical than may appear at first sight, the structure of the language becomes increasingly metaphorical and the image—be it under the name of symbol or even of myth—comes to be considered as the most prominent dimension of the style. This tendency is still prevalent today, among poets as well as among critics. We find it quite natural that theoretical studies such as, for example, those of Gaston Bachelard in France, of Northrop Frye in America, or of William Empson in England should take the metaphor as their starting point for an investigation of literature in gen-

"Intentional Structure of the Romantic Image" by Paul de Man. First printed, with the title "Structure intentionelle de l'image romantique," in *Revue internationale de philosophie*, 51 (1960). Reprinted slightly revised, and in a translation by the author, in Harold Bloom, ed., *Romanticism and Consciousness: Essays in Criticism* (New York: W. W. Norton & Company, Inc., 1970). Copyright © 1968 by Paul de Man. Reprinted by permission of the author.

eral—an approach that would have been inconceivable for Boileau, for Pope, and even still for Diderot.

An abundant imagery coinciding with an equally abundant quantity of natural objects, the theme of imagination linked closely to the theme of nature, such is the fundamental ambiguity that characterizes the poetics of romanticism. The tension between the two polarities never ceases to be problematic. We shall try to illustrate the structure of this latent tension as it appears in some selected poetic passages.

In a famous poem, Hölderlin speaks of a time at which "the gods" will again be an actual presence to man:

> . . . nun aber nennt er sein Liebstes
> Nun, nun müssen dafür Worte, wie Blumen entstehn.
> ("Brot und Wein," stanza 5)

Taken by itself, this passage is not necessarily a statement about the image: Hölderlin merely speaks of words (*"Worte"*), not of images (*"Bilder"*). But the lines themselves contain the image of the flower in the simplest and most explicit of all metaphorical structures, as a straightforward simile introduced by the conjunction *wie*. That the words referred to are not those of ordinary speech is clear from the verb: to originate ("entstehn"). In everyday use words are exchanges and put to a variety of tasks, but they are not supposed to originate anew; on the contrary, one wants them to be as well known, as "common" as possible, to make certain that they will obtain for us what we want to obtain. They are used as established signs to confirm that something is recognized as being the same as before; and re-cognition excludes pure origination. But in poetic language words are not used as signs, not even as names, but in order *to name:* "Donner un sens plus pur aux mots de la tribu" (Mallarmé) or "erfand er für die Dinge eigene Nahmen" (Stefan George): poets know of the act of naming—"nun aber *nennt* er sein Liebstes"— as implying a return to the source, to the pure motion of experience at its beginning.

The word "entstehn" establishes another fundamental distinction. The two terms of the simile are not said to be identical with one another (the word = the flower), nor analogous in their general mode of being (the word is like the flower), but specifically in the way they originate (the word originates like the flower).[1] The similarity between the two terms does not reside in their essence (identity), or in their appearance (anal-

---

[1] The line is ambiguous, depending on whether one gives the verb "entstehn" a single or a double subject. It can mean: words will originate that are like flowers ("Worte, die wie Blumen sind, müssen dafür entstehn"). But the meaning is much richer if one reads it: words will have to originate in the same way that flowers originate ("Worte müssen dafür entstehn wie Blumen entstehn"). Syntax and punctuation allow for both readings.

Intentional Structure of the Romantic Image 135

ogy), but in the manner in which both originate. And Hölderlin is not speaking of any poetic word taken at random, but of an authentic word that fulfills its highest function in naming being as a presence. We could infer, then, that the fundamental intent of the poetic word is to originate in the same manner as what Hölderlin here calls "flowers." The image is essentially a kinetic process: it does not dwell in a static state where the two terms could be separated and reunited by analysis; the first term of the simile (here, "words") has no independent existence, poetically speaking, prior to the metaphorical statement. It originates with the statement, in the manner suggested by the flower-image, and its way of being is determined by the manner in which it originates. The metaphor requires that we begin by forgetting all we have previously known about "words"—"donner un sens plus pur aux mots de la tribu"—and then informing the term with a dynamic existence similar to that which animates the "flowers." The metaphor is not a combination of two entities or experiences more or less deliberately linked together, but one single and particular experience: that of origination.

How do flowers originate? They rise out of the earth without the assistance of imitation or analogy. They do not follow a model other than themselves which they copy or from which they derive the pattern of their growth. By calling them *natural* objects, we mean that their origin is determined by nothing but their own being. Their becoming coincides at all times with the mode of their origination: it is as flowers that their history is what it is, totally defined by their identity. There is no wavering in the status of their existence: existence and essence coincide in them at all times. Unlike words, which originate like something else ("like flowers"), flowers originate like themselves: they are literally what they are, definable without the assistance of metaphor. It would follow then, since the intent of the poetic word is to originate like the flower, that it strives to banish all metaphor, to become entirely literal.

We can understand origin only in terms of difference: the source springs up because of the need to be somewhere or something else than what is now here. The word "entstehn," with its distancing prefix, equates origin with negation and difference. But the natural object, safe in its immediate being, seems to have no beginning and no end. Its permanence is carried by the stability of its being, whereas a beginning implies a negation of permanence, the discontinuity of a death in which an entity relinquishes its specificity and leaves it behind, like an empty shell. Entities engendered by consciousness originate in this fashion, but for natural entities like the flower, the process is entirely different. They originate out of a being which does not differ from them in essence but contains the totality of their individual manifestations within itself. All particular flowers can at all times establish an immediate identity with an original Flower, of which they are as many particular emanations.

The original entity, which has to contain an infinity of manifestations of a common essence, in an infinity of places and at an infinity of moments, is necessarily transcendental. Trying to conceive of the natural object in terms of origin leads to a transcendental concept of the Idea: the quest for the Idea that takes the natural object for its starting-point begins with the incarnated "minute particular" and works its way upwards to a transcendental essence. Beyond the Idea, it searches for Being as the category which contains essences in the same manner that the Idea contains particulars. Because they are natural objects, flowers originate as incarnations of a transcendental principle. "Wie Blumen entstehn" is to become present as a natural emanation of a transcendental principle, as an epiphany.

Strictly speaking, an epiphany cannot be a beginning, since it reveals and unveils what, by definition, could never have ceased to be there. Rather, it is the rediscovery of a permanent presence which has chosen to hide itself from us—unless it is we who have the power to hide from it:

> So ist der Mensch; wenn da ist das Gut und es sorget mitgaben
> Selber ein Gott für ihn, kennet und sieht er es nicht.
> ("Brot und Wein," stanza 5)

Since the presence of a transcendental principle, in fact conceived as omnipresence (parousia), can be hidden from man by man's own volition, the epiphany appears in the guise of a beginning rather than a discovery. Hölderlin's phrase: "Wie Blumen entstehn" is in fact a paradox, since origination is inconceivable on the ontological level; the ease with which we nevertheless accept it is indicative of our desire to forget. Our eagerness to accept the statement, the "beauty" of the line, stems from the fact that it combines the poetic seduction of beginnings contained in the word "entstehn" with the ontological stability of the natural object—but this combination is made possible only by a deliberate forgetting of the transcendental nature of the source.

That this forgetting, this ignorance, is also painful becomes apparent from the strategic choice of the word "flower," an object that seems intrinsically desirable. The effect of the line would have been thoroughly modified if Hölderlin had written, for instance, "Steinen" instead of "Blumen," although the relevance of the comparison would have remained intact as long as human language was being compared to a natural thing. The obviously desirable sensory aspects of the flower express the ambivalent aspiration towards a forgotten presence that gave rise to the image, for it is in experiencing the material presence of the particular flower that the desire arises to be reborn in the manner of a natural creation. The image is inspired by a nostalgia for the natural object, expanding to become nostalgia for the origin of this object. Such a nostalgia can only exist when the transcendental presence is forgotten, as in the "dürftiger Zeit" of Hölderlin's poem which we are all too eager to circumscribe as if it were a specific historical "time" and not Time in general. The existence of the poetic image is itself a sign of divine absence, and the conscious use of poetic imagery an admission of this absence.

It is clear that, in Hölderlin's own line, the words do *not* originate like flowers. They need to find the mode of their beginning in another entity; they originate out of nothing, in an attempt to be the first words that will arise as if they were natural objects, and, as such, they remain essentially distinct from natural entities. Hölderlin's statement is a perfect definition of what we call a natural image: the word that designates a desire for an epiphany but necessarily fails to be an epiphany, because it is pure origination. For it is in the essence of language to be capable of origination, but of never achieving the absolute identity with itself that exists in the natural object. Poetic language can do nothing but originate anew over and over again: it is always constitutive, able to posit regardless of presence but, by the same token, unable to give a foundation to what it posits except as an intent of consciousness. The word is always a free presence to the mind, the means by which the permanence of natural entities can be put into question and thus negated, time and again, in the endlessly widening spiral of the dialectic.

An image of this type is indeed the simplest and most fundamental we can conceive of, the metaphorical expression most apt to gain our immediate acquiescence. During the long development that takes place in the nineteenth century, the poetic image remains predominantly of the same kind that in the Hölderlin passage we took for our starting-point—and which, be it said in passing, far from exhausts Hölderlin's own conception of the poetic image. This type of imagery is grounded in the intrinsic ontological primacy of the natural object. Poetic language seems to originate in the desire to draw closer and closer to the ontological status of the object, and its growth and development are determined by this inclination. We saw that this movement is essentially paradoxical and condemned in advance to failure. There can be flowers that "are" and poetic words that "originate," but no poetic words that "originate" as if they "were."

Nineteenth century poetry reexperiences and represents the adventure of this failure in an infinite variety of forms and versions. It selects, for example, a variety of archetypal myths to serve as the dramatic pattern for the narration of this failure; a useful study could be made of the romantic and post-romantic versions of Hellenic myths such as the stories of Narcissus, of Prometheus, of the War of the Titans, of Adonis, Eros and Psyche, Proserpine, and many others; in each case, the tension and duality inherent in the mythological situation would be found to reflect the inherent tension that resides in the metaphorical language itself. At times, romantic thought and romantic poetry seem to come so close to giving in completely to the nostalgia for the object that it becomes difficult to distinguish between object and image, between imagination and perception, between an expressive or constitutive and a mimetic or literal language. This may well be the case in some passages of Wordsworth and Goethe, of Baudelaire and Rimbaud, where the vision almost seems to become a real landscape. Poetics of "unmediated vision," such as those implicit in Bergson and explicit in Bachelard, fuse matter and imagination by amalgamating perception and reverie, sacrificing, in fact, the demands of consciousness to the realities of the object. Critics who speak of a "happy relationship" between matter and consciousness fail to realize that the very fact that the relationship has to be established within the medium of language indicates that it does not exist in actuality.

At other times, the poet's loyalty towards his language appears so strongly that the object nearly vanishes under the impact of his words, in what Mallarmé called "sa presque disparition vibratoire." But even in as extreme a case as Mallarmé's, it would be a mistake to assume that the ontological priority of the object is being challenged. Mallarmé may well be the nineteenth century poet who went further than any other in sacrificing the stability of the object to the demands of a lucid poetic awareness. Even some of his own disciples felt they had to react against him by reasserting the positivity of live and material substances against the annihilating power of his thought. Believing themselves to be in a situation where they had to begin their work at the point where Mallarmé had finished his, they took, like Claudel, the precise counterpart of his attitudes or, like Valéry, reversed systematically the meaning of some of his key-images. Yet Mallarmé himself had always remained convinced of the essential priority of the natural object. The final image of his work, in *Un Coup de Dés*, is that of the poet drowned in the ubiquitous "sea" of natural substances against which his mind can only wage a meaningless battle, "tenter une chance oiseuse." It is true that, in Mallarmé's thought, the value-emphasis of this priority has been reversed and the triumph of nature is being presented as the downfall of poetic defiance. But this does not alter the fundamental situation. The alternating feeling of attraction and repulsion that the romantic poet experiences towards nature becomes in Mallarmé the conscious dialectic of a reflective poetic consciousness. This dialectic, far from challenging the supremacy of the order of nature, in fact reasserts it at all times. "Nous savons, victimes d'une formule absolue, que certes n'est que ce qui est," writes Mallarmé, and this absolute identity is rooted, for him, in "la première en date, la nature. Idée tangible pour intimer quelque réalité aux sens frustes. . . ."

Mallarmé's conception and use of imagery is entirely in agreement with this principle. His key-symbols—sea, winged bird, night, the sun, constellations, and many others—are not primarily literary emblems but are taken, as he says, "au répertoire de la nature"; they receive their meaning and function from the fact that they belong initially to the natural world. In the poetry, they may seem disincarnate to the point of abstraction, generalized to the point of becoming pure ideas, yet they never entirely lose contact with the concrete reality from which they spring. The sea, the bird, and the constellation act and seduce in Mallarmé's poetry, like any earthly sea, bird, or star in nature; even the Platonic "oiseau qu'on n'ouit jamais" still has about it some of the warmth of the nest in which it was born. Mallarmé does not linger over the concrete and material details of his images, but he never ceases to interrogate, by means of a conscious poetic language, the natural world of which they are originally a part—while knowing that he could never reduce any part of this world to his own, conscious mode of being. If this is true of Mallarmé, the most self-conscious and anti-natural poet of the nineteenth century, it seems safe to assert that the priority of the natural object remains unchallenged among the inheritors of romanticism. The detailed study of Mallarmé bears this out; the same is true, with various nuances and reservations, of most Victorian and post-Victorian poets. For most of them, as for Mallarmé, the priority of nature is experienced as a feeling of failure and sterility, but nevertheless asserted. A similar feeling of threatening paralysis prevails among our own contemporaries and seems to grow with the depth of their poetic commitment. It may be that this threat could only be overcome when the status of poetic language or, more restrictively, of the poetic image, is again brought into question.

The direction that such a reconsideration might take can better be anticipated by a reading of the precursors of romanticism than by the study of its inheritors. Assumptions that are irrevocably taken for granted in the course of the nineteenth century still appear, at an earlier date, as one among several alternative roads. This is why an effort to understand the present predicament of the poetic imagination takes us back to writers that belong to the earlier phases of romanticism such as, for example, Rousseau. The affinity of later poets with Rousseau—which can well be considered to be a valid definition of romanticism as a whole—can, in turn, be best understood in terms of their use and underlying conception of imagery. The juxtaposition of three famous passages can serve as an illustration of this point and suggest further developments.

The three passages we have selected each represent a moment of spiritual revelation; the use of semi-religious, "sacred," or outspokenly sublime language in all three makes this unquestionably clear. Rousseau is probably the only one to have some awareness of the literary tradition that stands behind the topos: his reference to Petrarch (*La Nouvelle Héloise*, Part I, XXIII) suggests the all-important link with the Augustinian lesson contained in Petrarch's letter narrating his ascent of Mont Ventoux. A similar experience, in a more Northern Alpine setting, is related in the three passages. The Rousseau text is taken from the letter in *La Nouvelle Héloïse* in which Saint-Preux reports on his sojourn in the Valais:

> Ce n'était pas seulement le travail des hommes qui rendait ces pays étranges si bizarrement contrastés; la nature semblait encore prendre plaisir à s'y mettre en opposition avec elle-même, tant on la trouvait différente en un même lieu sous divers aspects. Au levant les fleurs du printemps, au midi les fruits de l'automne, au nord les glaces de l'hiver: elle réunissait toutes les saisons dans le même instant, tous les climats dans le même lieu, des terrains contraires sur le même sol, et formait l'accord inconnu partout ailleurs des productions des plaines et de celles des Alpes. . . . J'arrivai ce jour là sur des montagnes les moins élevées, et, parcourant ensuite leurs inégalités, sur celles des plus hautes qui étaient à ma portée. Après m'être promené dans les nuages, j'atteignis un séjour plus serein, d'ou l'on voit dans la saison le tonerre et l'orage se former au-dessous de soi; image trop vaine de l'âme du sage, dont l'exemple n'exista jamais, ou n'existe qu'aux mêmes lieux d'où l'on en a tiré l'emblême.
>
> Ce fut là que je démêlai sensiblement dans la pureté de l'air où je me trouvais la véritable cause du changement de mon humeur, et du retour de cette paix intérieure que j'avais perdue depuis si longtemps. En effet, c'est une impression générale qu'éprouvent tous les hommes, quoiqu'ils ne l'observent pas tous, que sur les hautes montagnes, où l'air est pur et subtil, on se sent plus de facilité dans la respiration, plus de légèreté dans le corps, plus de sérénité dans l'esprit; les plaisirs y sont moins ardents, les passions plus modérées. Les méditations y prennent je ne sais quel caractère grand et sublime, proportionné aux objets qui nous frappent, je ne sais quelle volupté tranquille qui n'a rien d'âcre et de sensuel. Il semble qu'en s'élévant au-dessus du séjour des hommes on y laisse des sentiments bas et terrestres, et qu'à mesure qu'on approche des régions éthérées, l'âme contracte quelquechose de leur inaltérable pureté. On y est grave sans mélancolie, paisible sans indolence, content d'être et de penser. . . . Imaginez la variété, la grandeur, la beauté de mille étonnants spectacles; le plaisir de ne voir autour de soi que des objets tout nouveaux, des oiseaux étranges, des plantes bizarres et inconnues, d'observer en quelque sorte une autre nature, et de se trouver dans un nouveau monde. Tout cela fait aux yeux un mélange inexprimable, dont le charme augmente encore par la subtilité de l'air qui rend les couleurs plus vives, les traits plus marqués, rapproche tous les points de vue; les distances paraissent moindres que dans les plaines, où l'épaisseur de l'air couvre la terre d'un voile, l'horizon présente aux yeux plus d'objets qu'il semble n'en pouvoir contenir: enfin le spectacle a je ne sais quoi de magique, de surnaturel, qui ravit l'esprit et les sens; on oublie tout, on s'oublie soi-même, on ne sait plus où l'on est. . . .

Wordsworth's text is taken from Book VI of *The Prelude* and describes the poet's impressions in crossing the Alps, after having taken

Intentional Structure of the Romantic Image

part in one of the celebrations that mark the triumph of the French Revolution. Wordsworth begins by praying for the safeguard of the Convent of the Grande Chartreuse, threatened with destruction at the hands of the insurrection; his prayer is first aimed at God, then "for humbler claim" at nature:

> . . . and for humbler claim
> Of that imaginative impulse sent
> From these majestic floods, yon shining cliffs,
> The untransmuted shapes of many worlds,
> Cerulean ether's pure inhabitants,
> These forests unapproachable by death,
> That shall endure as long as man endures,
> To think, to hope, to worship, and to feel,
> To struggle, to be lost within himself
> In trepidation, from the blank abyss
> To look with bodily eyes, and be consoled.
> (*The Prelude*, 1850 ed., VI, 461-471)

Somewhat later in the same section, Wordsworth describes the descent of the Simplon pass:

> . . . The immeasurable height
> Of woods decaying, never to be decayed,
> The stationary blasts of waterfalls,
> And in the narrow rent at every turn
> Winds thwarting winds, bewildered and forlorn,
> The torrents shooting from the clear blue sky,
> The rocks that muttered close upon our ears,
> Black drizzling crags that spake by the way-side
> As if a voice were in them, the sick sight
> And giddy prospect of the raving stream,
> The unfettered clouds and region of the Heavens,
> Tumult and peace, the darkness and the light—
> Were all like workings of one mind, the features
> Of the same face, blossoms upon one tree;
> Characters of the great Apocalypse,
> The types and symbols of Eternity,
> Of first, and last, and midst, and without end.
> (*The Prelude*, VI, 624-640)

Hölderlin's poem "Heimkunft" begins by the description of a sunrise in the mountains, observed by the poet on his return from Switzerland to his native Swabia:

> Drin in den Alpen ists noch helle Nacht und die Wolke,
> Freudiges dichtend, sie deckt drinnen das gähnende Tal.

Dahin, dorthin toset und stürzt die scherzende Bergluft,
Schroff durch Tannen herab glänzet und schwindet ein Strahl.
Langsam eilt und kämpft das freudigschauernde Chaos,
Jung an Gestalt, doch stark, feiert es liebenden Streit
Unter den Felsen, es gärt und wankt in den ewigen Schranken,
Denn bacchantischer zieht drinnen der Morgen herauf.
Denn es wächst unendlicher dort das Jahr und die heilgen
Stunden, die Tage, sie sind kühner geordenet, gemischt.
Dennoch merket die Zeit der Gewittervogel und zwischen
Bergen, hoch in der Luft weilt er und rufet den Tag.
. . . .
Ruhig glänzen indes die silbernen Höhen draüber,
Voll mit Rosen ist schon droben der leuchtende Schnee.
Und noch höher hinauf wohnt über dem Lichte der reine
Selige Gott vom Speil heiliger Strahlen erfreut.
Stille wohnt er allein, und hell erscheinet sein Antlitz,
Der ätherische scheint Leben zu geben geneigt. . . .

("Heimkunft," st. I and II)

Each of these texts describes the passage from a certain type of nature, earthly and material, to another nature which could be called mental and celestial, although the "Heaven" referred to is devoid of specific theological connotations. The common characteristic that concerns us most becomes apparent in the mixed, transitional type of landscape from which the three poets start out. The setting of each scene is located somewhere between the inaccessible mountain peaks and the humanized world of the plains; it is a deeply divided and paradoxical nature that, in Rousseau's terms, "seems to take pleasure in self-opposition." Radical contradictions abound in each of the passages. Rousseau deliberately mixes and blurs the order of the seasons and the laws of geography. The more condensed, less narrative diction of Wordsworth transposes similar contradictions into the complexity of a language that unites irreconcilable opposites; he creates a disorder so far-reaching that the respective position of heaven and earth are reversed: ". . . woods decaying, never to be decayed . . . ," ". . . torrents shooting from the sky . . . ," ". . . the stationary blasts of waterfalls. . . ." Hölderlin's text also is particularly rich in oxymorons; every word-combination, every motion expresses a contradiction: "helle Nacht," "langsam eilt," "liebende Streit," "toset und stürzt," "geordnet, gemischt," "freudigschauernd," etc. One feels everywhere the pressure of an inner tension at the core of all earthly objects, powerful enough to bring them to explosion.

The violence of this turmoil is finally appeased by the ascending movement recorded in each of the texts, the movement by means of which the poetic imagination tears itself away, as it were, from a terrestrial nature

Intentional Structure of the Romantic Image

and moves towards this "other nature" mentioned by Rousseau, associated with the diaphanous, limpid and immaterial quality of a light that dwells nearer to the skies. Gaston Bachelard has described similar images of levitation very well, but he may not have stressed sufficiently that these rêveries of flight not only express a desire to escape from earthbound matter, to be relieved for a moment from the weight of gravity, but that they uncover a fundamentally new kind of relationship between nature and consciousness; it is significant, in this respect, that Bachelard classifies images of repose with earth and not with air, contrary to what happens in the three selected texts. The transparency of air represents the perfect fluidity of a mode of being that has moved beyond the power of earthly things and now dwells, like the God in Hölderlin's "Heimkunft," higher even than light ("über dem Lichte"). Like the clouds described by Wordsworth, the poets become "Cerulean ether's pure inhabitants." Unlike Mallarmé's "azur" or even the constellation at the end of *Un Coup de Dés* which are always seen from the point of view of the earth by a man about to sink away, their language has itself become a celestial entity, an inhabitant of the sky. Instead of being, like the "flower" in Hölderlin's "Brot und Wein," the fruit of the earth, the poetic word has become an offspring of the sky. The ontological priority, housed at first in the earthly and pastoral "flower," has been transposed into an entity that could still, if one wishes, be called "nature," but could no longer be equated with matter, objects, earth, stones, or flowers. The nostalgia for the object has become a nostalgia for an entity that could never, by its very nature, become a particularized presence.

The passages describe the ascent of a consciousness trapped within the contradictions of a half-earthly, half-heavenly nature "qui semblait prendre plaisir à (se) mettre en opposition avec elle-même," towards another level of consciousness, that has recovered "cette paix intérieure . . . perdue depuis si longtemps." (It goes without saying that the sequel of the three works from which the passages have been taken indicate that this tranquillity is far from having been definitively reconquered. Yet the existence of this moment of peace in *La Nouvelle Héloïse,* in *The Prelude,* and in the poem "Heimkunft"—"*Ruhig* glänzen indes die silbernen Höhen darüber . . ."—determines the fate of the respective authors and marks it as being an essentially poetic destiny.) In the course of this movement, in a passage that comes between the two descriptions we have cited, Wordsworth praises the faculty that gives him access to this new insight, and he calls this faculty "Imagination":

> Imagination! lifting up itself
> Before the eye and progress of my Song
> Like an unfather'd vapour; . . .
>   . . . in such strength

>   Of usurpation, in such visitings
>   Of awful promise, when the light of sense
>   Goes out in flashes that have shewn to us
>   The invisible world, doth Greatness make abode,
>   . . . .
>   The mind beneath such banners militant
>   Thinks not of spoils or trophies, nor of aught
>   That may attest its prowess, blest in thoughts
>   That are their own perfection and reward,
>   Strong in itself, and in the access of joy
>   Which hides it like the overflowing Nile.
>   (*The Prelude,* 1805 ed., VI, 525–548)

But this "imagination" has little in common with the faculty that produces natural images born "as flowers originate." It marks instead a possibility for consciousness to exist entirely by and for itself, independently of all relationship with the outside world, without being moved by an intent aimed at a part of this world. Rousseau stressed that there was nothing sensuous ("rien d'âcre et de sensuel") in Saint-Preux's moment of illumination; Wordsworth, who goes so far as to designate the earth by the astonishing periphrase of "blank abyss," insists that the imagination can only come into full play when "the light of sense goes out" and when thought reaches a point at which it is "its own perfection and reward"—as when Rousseau, in the Fifth *Rêverie,* declares himself "content d'être" and "ne jouissant de rien d'extérieur à soi, de rien sinon de soi-même et de sa propre existence."

We know very little about the kind of images that such an imagination would produce, except that they would have little in common with what we have come to expect from familiar metaphorical figures. The works of the early romantics give us no actual examples, for they are, at most, *underway* towards renewed insights and inhabit the mixed and self-contradictory regions that we encountered in the three passages. Nor has their attempt been rightly interpreted by those who came after them, for literary history has generally labeled "primitivist," "naturalistic," or even pantheistic the first modern writers to have put into question, in the language of poetry, the ontological priority of the sensory object. We are only beginning to understand how this oscillation in the status of the image is linked to the crisis that leaves the poetry of today under a steady threat of extinction, although, on the other hand, it remains the depository of hopes that no other activity of the mind seems able to offer.

The Via Naturaliter Negativa

by Geoffrey H. Hartman

Many readers have felt that Wordsworth's poetry honors and even worships nature. In this they have the support of Blake, a man so sensitive to any trace of "Natural Religion" that he is said to have blamed some verses of Wordsworth's for a bowel complaint which almost killed him.[1] Scholarship, luckily, tempers the affections, and the majority of readers have emphasized the poet's progression from nature worship or even pantheism to a highly qualified form of natural religion, with increasing awareness of the "ennobling interchange" between mind and nature and a late yielding of primacy to the activity of the mind or the idealizing power of imagination. A very small group, finally, has pointed to the deeply paradoxical character of Wordsworth's dealings with nature and suggested that what he calls imagination may be *intrinsically* opposed to nature. This last and rarest position seems to me closest to the truth, yet I do not feel it conflicts totally with more traditional readings stressing the poet's adherence to nature. It can be shown, via several important episodes of *The Prelude,* that Wordsworth thought nature itself led him beyond nature; and, since this movement of transcendence, related to what mystics have called the negative way, is inherent in life and achieved without violent or ascetic discipline, one can think of it as the progress of a soul which is *naturaliter negativa*.

I

The Prelude opens with a success immediately followed by a failure. Released from the "vast city" and anticipating a new freedom, the poet pours out a rush of fifty lines: "poetic numbers came / Spontaneously

---

"The Via Naturaliter Negativa." From Geoffrey Hartman, *Wordsworth's Poetry, 1787–1814* (New Haven: Yale University Press, 1964). Copyright © 1964 by Yale University. Reprinted by permission of the publisher and the author. This selection is chapter 2, sections 1–3.

[1] See *Blake, Coleridge, Wordsworth, Lamb, etc., Being Selections from the Remains of Henry Crabb Robinson,* ed. E. J. Morley (Manchester, 1932), pp. 5 and 15.

to clothe in priestly robe / A renovated spirit" (I.51–53).[2] Here is the consecration, the promise of poetry as a sacrament, a gift efficacious beyond the moment. Why should a chance inspiration assume such significance? The reason is that Wordsworth was not used to make "A present joy the matter of a song"; yet here, apparently, is evidence that he may soon become self-creative, or need no more than a "gentle breeze" (the untraditional muse of the epic's opening) to produce a tempest of poetry. "Matins and vespers of harmonious verse!" is the hope held out to him, and having punctually performed matins the poet is content to slacken, to be gradually calmed by the clear autumn afternoon.

He meditates beneath a tree on a great poetic work soon to be begun. The sun sets, and city smoke is "ruralised" by distance. He starts to continue his journey, but now it is clearly time for vespers:

> It was a splendid evening, and my soul
> Once more made trial of her strength, nor lacked
> Aeolian visitations.   (I.94–96)

An outside splendor challenges the creative mind. Is the poet strong enough to answer it spontaneously, as if he needed only a suggestion, the first chord?

>   but the harp
> Was soon defrauded, and the banded host
> Of harmony dispersed in straggling sounds,
> And lastly utter silence! "Be it so;
> Why think of any thing but present good?"   (I.96–100)

Wordsworth once again sees present good, like present joy, strangely opposed to the quickening of verse. The poetic outburst which he had considered a religious thing ("punctual service high . . . holy services") is now disdained as profane and *servile:*

> So, like a home-bound labourer I pursued
> My way beneath the mellowing sun, that shed
> Mild influence; nor left in me one wish
> Again to bend the Sabbath of that time
> To a servile yoke.   (I.101–05)

His reversal of mood is surprisingly complete. One who, at the impassioned outset of his reflections, had been so sure of the freely creative, autonomous nature of his poetic soul that famous passages on the eman-

---

[2] . . . Quotations from *The Prelude* . . . are from the 1850 text. . . .

cipated spirit—from *Paradise Lost* and Exodus[3]—swell the current of his verse, while he thinks to possess total freedom of choice,

> now free,
> Free as a bird to settle where I will   (I.8–9)

that same person now writes of himself, with a slight echo of Gray's *Elegy:*

> So, like a home-bound labourer I pursued
> My way.

The meaning of the reversal is not immediately clear. It does not deject the poet; it endows him, on the contrary, with a Chaucerian kind of cheer and leisure:

> What need of many words?
> A pleasant loitering journey, through three days
> Continued, brought me to my hermitage.
> I spare to tell of what ensued, the life
> In common things—the endless store of things.   (I.105–09)

The form of the reversal is that of a return to nature, at least to its rhythm. For the moment no haste remains, no tempest, no impatience of spirit. It is the mood of the hawthorn shade, of a portion of Wordsworth's Cambridge days, when he laughed with Chaucer and heard him, while birds sang, tell tales of love (III.278–81).

In the exultant first lines of *The Prelude,* Wordsworth had foreseen the spirit's power to become self-creative. Though fostered by nature it eventually outgrows its dependence, sings and storms at will (I.33–38). The poet's anticipation of autonomy is probably less a matter of pride than of necessity: he will steal the initiative from nature so as to freely serve or sustain the natural world should its hold on the affections slacken. His poetic power, though admittedly in nature's gift, must perpetuate, like consecration, vital if transitory feelings. Without poetry the supreme moment is nothing.

> Dear Liberty! Yet what would it avail
> But for a gift that consecrates the joy?   (I.31–32)

But he is taught that the desire for immediate consecrations is a wrong form of worship. The world demands a devotion less external and willful, a wise passiveness which the creative will may profane. The tempest "vexing its own creation" is replaced by a "mellowing sun, that shed / Mild influence." Nature keeps the initiative. The mind at its most free is still part of a deep mood of weathers.

Wordsworth's failure to consecrate, through verse, the splendid evening is only the last event in this reversal. It begins with the poet placing

[3] Emancipated—but through exile. For the allusions to *Paradise Lost* and Exodus, see *Prelude* I.14 and 16–18.

(so to say) the cart before the horse, Poetry before Nature: "To the open fields I told / A prophecy: poetic numbers came . . ." (I.50 ff.). He never, of course, forgets the double agency of inward and outward which informs every act of poetry. So his heart's frost is said to be broken by both outer and inner winds (I.38 ff.).[4] Such reciprocity is at the heart of all his poems. Yet he continually anticipates a movement of transcendence: Nature proposes but the Poet disposes. Just as the breeze engendered in the mind a self-quickening tempest, so poetry, the voice from that tempest, re-echoing in the mind whence it came, seems to increase there its perfection (I.55 ff.). The origin of the whole moves farther from its starting point in the external world. A *personal* agent replaces that of nature: "I paced on . . . down I sate . . . slackening my thoughts by choice" (I.60 ff.). There is a world of difference between this subtle bravado and the ascendancy of *impersonal* constructions in the final episode: "Be it so; / Why think of any thing but . . . What need of many words? . . . I pursued / My way . . . A pleasant loitering journey . . . brought me to my hermitage."

This change, admittedly, is almost too fine for common language. Syntax becomes a major device but not a consistent one. In the 1850 text, while the poet muses in the green, shady place, certain neoclassical patterns, such as the noble passive combined with synecdoche, create an atmosphere in which personal and impersonal, active and passive, blend strongly:

> Many were the thoughts
> Encouraged and dismissed, till choice was made
> Of a known Vale, whither my feet should turn. (I.70–72)

Devices still more subtle come into play. In the passage immediately preceding, Wordsworth describes the quiet autumn afternoon:

> a day
> With silver clouds, and sunshine on the grass,
> And in the sheltered and the sheltering grove
> A perfect stillness. (I.67–70)

"Sheltered and sheltering"—typical Wordsworthian verbosity? The redundance, however, does suggest that whatever is happening here happens in more than one place; compare "silver clouds, and sunshine on the grass." The locus doubles, redoubles: that twofold agency which seems to center on the poet is active all around to the same incremental effect. The grove, sheltered, shelters in turn, and makes "A perfect stillness." The poet, in a sense, is only a single focus to something universally active.

---

[4] Cf. M. H. Abrams, "The Correspondent Breeze: A Romantic Metaphor," in *English Romantic Poets,* ed. Abrams (Galaxy paperback, New York, 1960), pp. 37–54.

The Via Naturaliter Negativa

He muses on this intensifying stillness, and within him rises a picture, gazing on which with *growing* love "a higher power / Than Fancy" enters to affirm his musings. The reciprocal and incremental movement, mentioned explicitly in I.31 ff., occurs this time quite unself-consciously, clearly within the setting and through the general influences of Nature.

No wonder, then, that the city, which the poet still strove to shake off in the first lines, appears now not only distant but also "ruralised," taking on the colors of nature, as inclosed by it as the poet's own thought. The last act of the reversal is the episode of the splendid sunset. Wordsworth not only cannot, he *need* not steal the initiative from nature. Her locus is universal, not individual; she acts by expedients deeper than will or thought. Wordsworth's failure intensifies his sense of a principle of generosity in nature. That initial cry of faith, "I cannot miss my way" (I.18), becomes true, but not because of his own power. The song loses its way.

Wordsworth's first experience is symptomatic of his creative difficulties. One impulse vexes the creative spirit into self-dependence, the other exhibits nature as that spirit's highest object. The poet is driven at the same time from and toward the external world. No sooner has he begun to enjoy his Chaucerian leisure than restiveness breaks in. The "pilgrim," despite "the life / In common things—the endless store of things," cannot rest content with his hermitage's sabbath. Higher hopes, "airy phantasies," clamor for life (I.114 ff.). The poet's account of his creative difficulties (I.146-269) documents in full his vacillation between a natural and a more than natural theme, between a Romantic tale and one of "natural heroes," or "a tale from my own heart" and "some philosophic song"—but he adds, swinging back to the more humble, "Of Truth that cherishes our daily life." Is this indeterminacy the end at which nature aims, this curious and never fully clarified restlessness the ultimate confession of his poetry?

It would be hard, in that case, to think of *The Prelude* as describing the "growth of a poet's mind"; for what the first part of Book I records is, primarily, Wordsworth's failure to be a visionary or epic poet in the tradition of Spenser and Milton. No poem of epic length or ambition ever started like his. The epic poet begins confidently by stating his subject, boasts a little about the valor of his attempt, and calls on the Muse to help him. Yet Wordsworth's confident opening is deceptive. He starts indeed with a rush of verses which are in fact a kind of self-quotation, because his subject is poetry or the mind which has separated from nature and here celebrates its coming-of-age by generously returning to it. After this one moment of confidence, all is problematic. The song loses its way, the proud opening is followed by an experience of aphasia, and Wordsworth begins the story of the growth of his mind to prove, at least to himself, that nature had intended him to be a poet.

Was it for this, he asks, for this timidity or indecision, that nature spent all her care (I.269 ff.)? Did not nature, by a process of both accommodation and weaning, foster the spirit's autonomy from childhood on? Yet when the spirit tries to seize the initiative, to quicken of itself like Ezekiel's chariot, either nature humbles it or Wordsworth humbles himself before her. "Thus my days," says Wordsworth sadly, "are past / In contradiction; with no skill to part / Vague longing, haply bred by want of power, / From paramount impulse not to be withstood, / A timorous capacity from prudence, / From circumspection, infinite delay" (I.237–42).

Wordsworth never achieved his philosophic song. *Prelude* and *Excursion* are no more than "ante-chapels" to the "gothic church" of his unfinished work. An unresolved opposition between Imagination and Nature prevents him from becoming a visionary poet. It is a paradox, though not an unfruitful one, that he should scrupulously record nature's workmanship, which prepares the soul for its independence from sense-experience, yet refrain to use that independence out of respect of nature. His greatest verse *still takes its origin* in the memory of given experiences to which he is often pedantically faithful. He adheres, apparently against nature, to natural fact.

II

There are many who feel that Wordsworth could have been as great a poet as Milton but for this return to nature, this shrinking from visionary subjects. Is Wordsworth afraid of his own imagination? Now we have, in *The Prelude,* an exceptional incident in which the poet comes, as it were, face to face with his imagination. This incident has many points in common with the opening event of *The Prelude;* it also, for example, tells the story of a failure of the mind vis-à-vis the external world. I refer to the poet's crossing of the Alps, in which his adventurous spirit is again rebuffed by nature, though by its strong absence rather than presence. His mind, desperately and unself-knowingly in search of a nature adequate to deep childhood impressions, finds instead *itself,* and has to acknowledge that nature is no longer its proper subject or home. Despite this recognition, Wordsworth continues to bend back the energy of his mind and of his poem to nature, but not before we have learned the secret behind his fidelity.

Having finished his third year of studies at Cambridge, Wordsworth goes on a walking tour of France and Switzerland. It is the summer of 1790, the French Revolution has achieved its greatest success and acts as a subtle, though, in the following books, increasingly human background to his concern with nature. Setting out to cross the Alps by way of the Simplon Pass, he and a friend are separated from their companions and try to ascend by themselves. After climbing some time and not overtaking anyone, they meet a peasant who tells them they must return to their starting point and follow a stream down instead of further ascending, i.e. they had already, and without knowing it, crossed the Alps. Disappointed, "For still we had hopes that pointed to the clouds," they start downward beset by a "melancholy slackening," which, however, is soon dislodged (VI.557–91, 616 ff.).

This naive event stands, however, within a larger, interdependent series of happenings: an unexpected revelation comes almost immediately (624–40), and the sequence is preceded by a parallel disappointment with the natural world followed by a compensatory vision (523 ff.). In addition to this pattern of blankness and revelation, of the soulless image and the sudden renewed immediacy of nature, we find a strange instance of the past flowing into the present. Wordsworth, after telling the story of his disappointment, is suddenly, in the very moment of composition, overpowered by a feeling of glory to which he gives expression in rapturous, almost self-obscuring lines (VI.592 ff.). Not until the moment of composition, some fourteen years after the event,[5] does the real reason behind his upward climb and subsequent melancholy slackening strike home; and it strikes so hard that he gives to the power in him, revealed by the extinction of the immediate external motive (his desire to cross the Alps) and by the abyss of intervening years, the explicit name Imagination:

> Imagination—here the Power so called
> Through sad incompetence of human speech,
> That awful Power rose from the mind's abyss
> Like an unfathered vapour that enwraps,
> At once, some lonely traveller. I was lost;
> Halted without an effort to break through;
> But to my conscious soul I now can say—
> "I recognise thy glory."   (VI.592–99)

Thus Wordsworth's failure vis-à-vis nature (or its failure vis-à-vis him) is doubly redeemed. After descending, and passing through a gloomy strait (621 ff.), he encounters a magnificent view. And crossing, one might say, the gloomy gulf of time, his disappointment becomes retrospectively a prophetic instance of that blindness to the external world which is the tragic, pervasive, and necessary condition of the mature poet. His failure of 1790 taught him gently what now (1804) literally *blinds* him: the independence of imagination from nature.

I cannot miss my way, the poet exults in the opening verses of *The Prelude*. And he cannot, as long as he respects the guidance of nature, which leads him along a gradual via negativa to make his soul more than

---

[5] That the rising up of imagination occurred as Wordsworth was remembering his disappointment rather than immediately after it (i.e., in 1804, not in 1790) was first pointed out by W. G. Fraser in the *Times Literary Supplement* (April 4, 1929), p. 276.

"a mere pensioner / On outward forms" (VI.737 f.). It is not easy, however, to "follow Nature." The path, in fact, becomes so circuitous that a poet follows least when he thinks he follows most. For he must cross a strait where the external image is lost yet suddenly revived with more than original immediacy. Thus a gentle breeze, in the first book, calls forth a tempest of verse, but a splendid evening wanes into silence. A magnificent hope, in the sixth book, dies for lack of sensuous food, but fourteen years later the simple memory of failure calls up that hope in a magnificent tempest of verse. When the external stimulus is too clearly present the poet falls mute and corroborates Blake's strongest objection: "Natural Objects always did and now do weaken, deaden, and obliterate Imagination in Me."[6] The poet is forced to discover the autonomy of his imagination, its independence from present joy, from strong outward stimuli—but this discovery, which means a passing of the initiative from nature to imagination, is brought on gradually, mercifully.

Wordsworth does not sustain the encounter with Imagination. His direct cry is broken off, replaced by an impersonal construction—"here the Power." It is not Imagination but his "conscious soul" he addresses directly in the lines that follow. What, in any case, is the soul to do with its extreme recognition? It has glimpsed the height of its freedom. At the end of his apostrophe to Imagination, Wordsworth repeats the idea that the soul is halted by its discovery, as a traveler by a sudden bank of mist. But the simile this time suggests not only a divorce from but also (proleptically) a return to nature on the part of the soul,

> Strong in herself and in beatitude
> That hides her, like the mighty flood of Nile
> Poured from his fount of Abyssinian clouds
> To fertilise the whole Egyptian plain. (VI.613–16)

III

It follows that nature, for Wordsworth, is not an "object" but a presence and a power; a motion and a spirit; not something to be worshiped and consumed, but always a guide leading beyond itself. This guidance starts in earliest childhood. The boy of *Prelude* I is fostered alike by beauty and by fear. Through beauty, nature often makes the boy feel at home, for, as in the Great Ode, his soul is alien to this world. But through fear, nature reminds the boy from where he came, and prepares him, having lost heaven, also to lose nature. The boy of *Prelude*

---

[6] Marginalia to Volume I of Wordsworth's *Poems* of 1815. I may venture the opinion that Wordsworth, at the beginning of *The Prelude*, goes back to nature not to increase his chances of sensation but rather to emancipate his mind from immediate external excitements, the "gross and violent stimulants" (1800 Preface to *Lyrical Ballads*) of the city he leaves behind him.

The Via Naturaliter Negativa

I, who does not yet know he must suffer this loss as well, is warned by nature itself of the solitude to come.

I have suggested elsewhere how the fine skating scene of the first book (425-63), though painted for its own sake, to capture the animal spirits of children spurred by a clear and frosty night, moves from vivid images of immediate life to an absolute calm which foreshadows a deeper and more hidden life.[7] The Negative Way is a gradual one, and the child is weaned by a premonitory game of hide-and-seek in which nature changes its shape from familiar to unfamiliar, or even fails the child. There is a great fear, either in Wordsworth or in nature, of traumatic breaks: *Natura non facit saltus.*

If the child is led by nature to a more deeply meditated understanding of nature, the mature singer who composes *The Prelude* begins with that understanding or even beyond it—with the spontaneously creative spirit. Wordsworth plunges into *medias res*, where the *res* is Poetry, or Nature only insofar as it has guided him to a height whence he must find his own way. But Book VI, with which we are immediately concerned, records what is chronologically an intermediate period, in which the first term is neither Nature nor Poetry. It is Imagination in embryo: the mind muted yet also strengthened by the external world's opacities. Though imagination is with Wordsworth on the journey of 1790, nature seems particularly elusive. He goes out to a nature which seems to hide as in the crossing of the Alps.

The first part of this episode is told to illustrate a curious melancholy related to the "presence" of imagination and the "absence" of nature. Like the young Apollo in Keats' *Hyperion*, Wordsworth is strangely dissatisfied with the riches before him, and compelled to seek some other region:

> Where is power?
> Whose hand, whose essence, what divinity
> Makes this alarum in the elements,
> While I here idle listen on the shores
> In fearless yet in aching ignorance?[8]

To this soft or "luxurious" sadness, a more masculine kind is added, which results from a "stern mood" or "underthirst of vigor"; and it is in order to throw light on this further melancholy that Wordsworth tells the incident of his crossing the Alps.

The stern mood to which Wordsworth refers can only be his premonition of spiritual autonomy, of an independence from sense-experience foreshadowed by nature since earliest childhood. It is the "underground"

---

[7] *The Unmediated Vision* (New Haven, 1954), pp. 17-20.
[8] *Hyperion* III.103-07.

form of imagination, and *Prelude* II.315 ff. describes it as "an obscure sense / Of possible sublimity," for which the soul, remembering *how* it felt in exalted moments, but no longer *what* it felt, continually strives to find a new content. The element of obscurity, related to nature's self-concealment, is necessary to the soul's capacity for growth, for it vexes the latter toward self-dependence. Childhood pastures become viewless; the soul cannot easily find the source from which it used to drink the visionary power; and while dim memories of a passionate commerce with external things drive it more than ever to the world, this world makes itself more than ever inscrutable.[9] The travelers' separation from their guides, then that of the road from the stream (VI.568), and finally their trouble with the peasant's words that have to be "translated," express subtly the soul's desire for a *beyond*. Yet only when poet, brook, and road are once again "fellow-travellers" (VI.622), and Wordsworth holds to Nature, does that reveal—a Proteus in the grasp of the hero—its prophecy.

This prophecy was originally the second part of the adventure, the delayed vision which compensates for his disappointment (the "Characters of the great Apocalypse," VI.617-40). In its original sequence, therefore, the episode has only two parts: the first term or moment of natural immediacy is omitted, and we go straight to the second term, the inscrutability of an external image, which leads via the gloomy strait to its renewal. Yet, as if this pattern demanded a substitute third term, Wordsworth's tribute to "Imagination" severs the original temporal sequence, and forestalls nature's renewal of the bodily eye with ecstatic praise of the inner eye.

The apocalypse of the gloomy strait loses by this the character of a *terminal* experience. Nature is again surpassed, for the poet's imagination is called forth, at the time of writing, by the barely scrutable, not by the splendid emotion; by the disappointment, not the fulfillment. This (momentary) displacement of emphasis is the more effective in that the style of VI.617 ff., and the very characters of the apocalypse, suggest that the hiding places of power cannot be localized in nature.[10] Though the apostrophe to Imagination—the special insight that comes to Words-

[9] Cf. the Intimations Ode; also *Prelude* I.597 ff.

[10] Of the four sentences which comprise lines 617-40, the first three alternate the themes of eager and of restrained movement ("melancholy slackening . . . Downwards we hurried fast . . . at a slow pace"); and the fourth sentence, without explicit transition, commencing in mid-verse (line 624), rises very gradually and firmly into a development of sixteen lines. These depend on a single verb, an unemphatic "were," held back till the beginning of line 636; the verb thus acts as a pivot that introduces, without shock or simply as the other side of the coin, the falling and interpretative movement. This structure, combined with a skillful interchange throughout of asyndetic and conjunctive phrases, always avoids the sentiment of abrupt illumination for that of a majestic swell fed by innumerable sustaining events, and thereby strengthens our feeling that the vision, though climactic, is neither terminal nor discontinuous.

The Via Naturaliter Negativa

worth in 1804—is a real peripety, reversing a meaning already established, it is not unprepared. But it takes the poet many years to realize that nature's "end" is to lead to something "without end," to teach the travelers to transcend nature.

The three parts of this episode, therefore, can help us understand the mind's growth toward independence of immediate external stimuli. The measure of that independence is Imagination, and carries with it a precarious self-consciousness. We see that the mind must pass through a stage where it experiences Imagination as a power separate from Nature, that the poet must come to think and feel as if by his own choice, or from the structure of his mind.[11]

VI-a (557–91) shows the young poet still dependent on the immediacy of the external world. Imagination frustrates that dependence secretly, yet its blindness toward nature is accompanied by a blindness toward itself. It is only a "mute Influence of the soul, / An Element of nature's inner self" (1805, VIII.512–13).

VI-b (592–616) gives an example of thought or feeling that came from the poet's mind without immediate external excitement. There remains, of course, the memory of VI-a (the disappointment), but this is an internal feeling, not an external image. The poet recognizes at last that the power he has looked for in the outside world is really within and frustrating his search. A shock of recognition then feeds the very blindness toward the external world which helped to produce that shock.

In VI-c (617–40) the landscape is again an immediate external object of experience. The mind cannot separate in it what it desires to know and what it actually knows. It is a moment of revelation, in which the poet sees not as in a glass, darkly, but face to face. VI-c clarifies, therefore, certain details of VI-a and *seems* to actualize figurative details of VI-b.[12] The matter-of-fact interplay of quick and lingering movement, of up-and-down perplexities in the ascent (VI.567 ff.), reappears in larger letters; while the interchanges of light and darkness, of cloud and cloudlessness, of rising like a vapor from the abyss and pouring like a flood from heaven have entered the landscape bodily. The gloomy strait also participates in this actualization. It is revealed as the secret middle term which leads from the barely scrutable presence of nature to its resurrected image. The travelers who move freely with or against the terrain, hurrying upward, pacing downward, perplexed at crossings, are now led narrowly by the pass as if it were their rediscovered guide.

[11] Cf. Preface (1802) to *Lyrical Ballads:* [The poet] has acquired a greater readiness and power in expressing . . . especially those thoughts and feelings which, by his own choice, or from the structure of his own mind, arise in him without immediate external excitement."

[12] VI-c was composed before VI-b, so while the transference of images goes structurally from VI-b to VI-c, *chronologically* the order is reversed.

The Prelude and *The Recluse:*
Wordsworth's Long Journey Home

by M. H. Abrams

In the "Prospectus" to his intended masterwork, *The Recluse*, Wordsworth announces that his "high argument" will be the capacity of the mind of man, "When wedded to this goodly universe / In love and holy passion," to transform the world into a paradise which will be "A simple produce of the common day." [1] He then goes on to pray to the "prophetic Spirit" that

> if with this
> I mix more lowly matter; with the thing
> Contemplated, describe the Mind and Man
> Contemplating; and who, and what he was—
> The transitory Being that beheld
> This Vision; when and where, and how he lived;—
> Be not this labour useless.

In this way Wordsworth designated and justified the personal narrative which makes up the opening book of *The Recluse* he called *Home at Grasmere*, as well as the entire poem that his wife later named *The Prelude*. Wordsworth described the latter work as a "tributary" and also "as a sort of portico to the Recluse, part of the same building." [2] The

---

"*The Prelude* and *The Recluse:* Wordsworth's Long Journey Home." From M. H. Abrams, *Natural Supernaturalism: Tradition and Revolution in Romantic Literature* (New York; W. W. Norton & Company, 1971). Copyright © 1971 by W. W. Norton and Company, Inc., and Oxford University Press. Reprinted by permission of the publishers. This essay incorporates a revised version of chapter 2, section 1, and chapter 5, section 2.

[1] Wordsworth excerpted the verse passage that he called "a kind of Prospectus of the design and scope" of *The Recluse* from the conclusion to *Home at Grasmere* and printed it in his Preface to *The Excursion* (1814). For the manuscript drafts, composed probably between 1800 and 1806, see M. H. Abrams, *Natural Supernaturalism* (New York, 1971), Appendix.

[2] To DeQuincey, 6 March 1804, *Letters: The Early Years* (2d ed.; Oxford, 1967), p. 454; to Beaumont, 3 June 1805, *ibid.*, p. 594.

time taken to compose *The Prelude* straddled the writing of the Prospectus, and the completed work was conceived as an integral part of the overall structure whose "design and scope" Wordsworth specified in that poetic manifesto. "The Poem on the growth of your own mind," as Coleridge recalled the plan in 1815, "was as the ground-plat and the Roots, out of which the Recluse was to have sprung up as the Tree"— two distinct works, but forming "one compleat Whole."[3] The role of *The Prelude*, as Wordsworth himself describes his grand design, is to recount the circumstances and mental growth of a "transitory Being," culminating in his achievement of a "Vision" and in the recognition that his mission is to impart the vision in the public and enduring form of an unprecedented kind of poem:

> Possessions have I that are solely mine,
> Something within which yet is shared by none . . .
> I would impart it, I would spread it wide,
> Immortal in the world which is to come.[4]

The Idea of The Prelude

In this era of constant and drastic experimentation with literary materials and forms, it is easy to overlook the radical novelty of *The Prelude* when it was completed in 1805. The poem amply justified Wordsworth's claim to have demonstrated original genius, which he defined as "the introduction of a new element into the intellectual universe" of which the "infallible sign is the widening the sphere of human sensibility."[5]

The Prelude is a fully developed poetic equivalent of two portentous innovations in prose fiction, of which the earliest examples had appeared in Germany only a decade or so before Wordsworth began writing his poem: the *Bildungsroman* (Wordsworth called *The Prelude* a poem on "the growth of my own mind") and the *Künstlerroman* (Wordsworth also spoke of it as "a poem on my own poetical education," and it far surpassed all German examples in the detail with which his "history," as he said, was specifically "of a *Poet's* mind").[6] The whole poem is written as a sustained address to Coleridge—"I speak bare truth / As if alone to thee in private talk" (X, 372-3); Coleridge, however, is an auditor *in absentia*, and the solitary author often supplements this form with an interior monologue, or else carries on an extended colloquy with the landscape in which the interlocutors are "my mind" and "the speaking

[3] To Wordsworth, 30 May 1815, *Collected Letters* (Oxford, 1956-9), IV, 573.
[4] *Home at Grasmere*, ll. 686-91, preceding the Prospectus.
[5] "Essay, Supplementary to the Preface of 1815."
[6] *Letters: The Early Years*, p. 518, Isabella Fenwick note to "There Was a Boy," and *The Prelude*, XIII, 408. (All references are to *The Prelude* of 1805, unless indicated by the date "1850.")

face of earth and heaven" (V, 11–12). The construction of *The Prelude* is radically achronological, starting not at the beginning, but at the end—during Wordsworth's walk to "the Vale that I had chosen" (I, 100), which telescopes the circumstances of two or more occasions but refers primarily to his walk to the Vale of Grasmere, that "hermitage" (I, 115) where he has taken up residence at that stage of his life with which the poem concludes.[7] During this walk an outer breeze, "the sweet breath of Heaven," evokes within the poet, "a corresponding mild creative breeze," a prophetic *spiritus* or inspiration which assures him of his poetic mission and, though it is fitful, eventually leads to his undertaking *The Prelude* itself; in the course of the poem, at times of imaginative dryness, the revivifying wind recurs in the role of a poetic leitmotif.[8]

Wordsworth does not tell his life as a simple narrative in past time but as the present remembrance of things past, in which forms and sensations "throw back our life" (I, 660–1) and evoke the former self which coexists with the altered present self in a multiple awareness that Wordsworth calls "two consciousnesses." There is a wide "vacancy" between the I now and the I then,

> Which yet have such self-presence in my mind
> That, sometimes, when I think of them, I seem
> Two consciousnesses, conscious of myself
> And of some other Being. (II, 27–33)

The poet is aware of the near impossibility of disengaging "the naked recollection of that time" from the intrusions of "after-meditation" (III, 644–8). In a fine and subtle figure for the interdiffusion of the two consciousnesses (IV, 247–64), he describes himself as one bending from a drifting boat on a still water, perplexed to distinguish actual objects at the bottom of the lake from surface reflections of the environing scene, from the tricks and refractions of the water currents, and from his own intrusive but inescapable image (that is, his present awareness). Thus "incumbent o'er the surface of past time" the poet, seeking the elements of continuity between his two disparate selves, conducts a persistent exploration of the nature and significance of memory, of his power to sustain freshness of sensation and his "first creative sensibility" against the deadening effect of habit and analysis, and of manifestations of the enduring and the eternal within the realm of change and time. Only intermittently does the narrative order coincide with the order of actual oc-

---

[7] For convincing evidence that the chief prototype of the walk described in the "preamble" to *The Prelude* was Wordsworth's walk to Grasmere, see John Finch, "Wordsworth's Two-Handed Engine," *Bicentenary Wordsworth Studies*, ed. Jonathan Wordsworth (Ithaca, N.Y., 1970). But Wordsworth probably telescoped events from several walks in real life, to make the "preamble" to *The Prelude* a typological change of venue, signifying a new stage in his spiritual history.

[8] E.g., VII, 1–56; XI, 1–12.

currence. Instead Wordsworth proceeds by sometimes bewildering ellipses, fusions, and as he says, "motions retrograde" in time (IX, 8).

Scholars have long been aware that it is perilous to rely on the factual validity of *The Prelude*, and in consequence Wordsworth has been charged with intellectual uncertainty, artistic ineptitude, bad memory, or even bad faith. The poem has suffered because we know so much about the process of its composition between 1798 and 1805—its evolution from a constituent part to a "tail-piece" to a "portico" of *The Recluse*, and Wordsworth's late decision to add to the beginning and end of the poem the excluded middle: his experiences in London and in France. A work is to be judged, however, as a finished and free-standing product; and in *The Prelude* as it emerged after six years of working and reworking, the major alterations and dislocations of the events of Wordsworth's life are imposed deliberately, in order that the design inherent in that life, which has become apparent only to his mature awareness, may stand revealed as a principle which was invisibly operative from the beginning. A supervising idea, in other words, controls Wordsworth's account and shapes it into a structure in which the protagonist is put forward as one who has been elected to play a special role in a providential plot. As Wordsworth said in the opening passage, which represents him after he has reached maturity: in response to the quickening outer breeze

> to the open fields I told
> A prophecy: poetic numbers came
> Spontaneously, and cloth'd in priestly robe
> My spirit, thus singled out, as it might seem,
> For holy services.   (I, 59–63)

Hence in this history of a poet's mind the poet is indeed the "transitory Being," William Wordsworth, but he is also the exemplary poet-prophet who has been singled out, in a time "of hopes o'erthrown . . . of dereliction and dismay" (II, 448–57), to bring mankind tidings of comfort and joy; as Wordsworth put it in one version of the Prospectus,

> that my verse may live and be
> Even as a light hung up in heaven to chear
> Mankind in times to come.

The spaciousness of his chosen form allows Wordsworth to introduce some of the clutter and contingency of ordinary experience. In accordance with his controlling idea, however, he selects for extended treatment only those of his actions and experiences which are significant for his evolution toward an inherent end, and organizes his life around an event which he regards as the spiritual crisis not of himself only, but of his generation: that shattering of the fierce loyalties and inordinate hopes for mankind which the liberal English—and European—intellectuals had invested in the French Revolution.

> Not in my single self alone I found,
> But in the minds of all ingenuous Youth,
> Change and subversion from this hour.
>
> (X, 232-4)

The Prelude, correspondingly, is ordered in three stages. There is a process of unified mental development which, although at times suspended, remains a continuum; this process is shattered by a crisis of apathy and despair; but the mind then recovers an integrity which, despite admitted losses, is represented as a level higher than the initial unity, in that the mature mind possesses powers, together with an added range, depth, and sensitivity of awareness, which are the products of the critical experiences it has undergone. The discovery of this fact resolves a central problem which has been implicit throughout *The Prelude*—the problem of how to justify the human experience of pain and loss and suffering; he is now able to recognize that his life is "in the end / All gratulant if rightly understood" (XIII, 384-5).

The narrative is punctuated with recurrent illuminations, or "spots of time," and is climaxed by two major revelations. The first of these is Wordsworth's discovery of precisely what he has been born to be and to do. At Cambridge he had reached a stage of life, "an eminence," in which he had felt that he was "a chosen Son" (III, 82 ff., 169), and on a walk home from a dance during a summer dawn he had experienced an illumination that he should be, "else sinning greatly, / A dedicated Spirit" (IV, 343-4); but for what chosen, or to what dedicated, had not been specified. Now, however, the recovery from the crisis of despair after his commitment to the French Revolution comprises the insight that his destiny is not one of engagement with what is blazoned "with the pompous names / Of power and action" in "the stir / And tumult of the world," but one of withdrawal from the world of action so that he may meditate in solitude: his role in life requires not involvement, but detachment.[9] And that role is to be one of the "Poets, even as Prophets," each of whom is endowed with the power "to perceive / Something unseen before," and so to write a new kind of poetry in a new poetic style. "Of these, said I, shall be my Song; of these . . . / Will I record the praises": the ordinary world of lowly, suffering men and of commonplace or trivial things transformed into "a new world . . . fit / To be transmitted," of dignity, love, and heroic grandeur (XII, 220-379). Wordsworth's crisis, then, involved what we now call a crisis of identity, which was resolved in the discovery of "my office upon earth" (X, 921).

[9] *The Prelude,* XII, 44-76, 112-16. Cf. *Home at Grasmere,* ll. 664-752.

And since the specification of this office entails the definition, in the twelfth book, of the particular innovations in poetic subjects, style, and values toward which his life had been implicitly oriented, *The Prelude* is a poem which incorporates the discovery of its own *ars poetica*.

His second revelation he achieves on a mountain top. The occasion is the ascent of Mount Snowdon, which Wordsworth, in accordance with his controlling idea, excerpts from its chronological position in his life in 1791, before the crucial experience of France, and describes in the concluding book of *The Prelude*. As he breaks through the cover of clouds the light of the moon "upon the turf / Fell like a flash," and he sees the total scene as "the perfect image of a mighty Mind" in its free and continuously creative reciprocity with its milieu, "Willing to work and to be wrought upon" and so to "create / A like existence" (XIII, 36–119). What has been revealed to Wordsworth in this symbolic landscape is the grand locus of *The Recluse* which he announced in the Prospectus, "The Mind of Man— / My haunt, and the main region of my song," as well as the "high argument" of that poem, the union between the mind and the external world and the resulting "creation . . . which they with blended might / Accomplish." The event which Wordsworth selects for the climactic revelation in *The Prelude,* then, is precisely the moment of the achievement of "this Vision" by "the transitory Being" whose life he had, in the Prospectus, undertaken to describe as an integral part of *The Recluse*.

In the course of *The Prelude* Wordsworth repeatedly drops the clue that his work has been designed to round back to its point of departure. "Not with these began / Our Song, and not with these our Song must end," he had cried after the crisis of France, invoking the "breezes and soft airs" that had blown in the "glad preamble" to his poem (XI, 1 ff. and VII, 1 ff.). As he nears the end of the song, he says that his self-discovery constitutes a religious conclusion ("The rapture of the Hallelujah sent / From all that breathes and is") which is at the same time, as he had planned from the outset, an artistic beginning:

> And now, O Friend; this history is brought
> To its appointed close: the discipline
> And consummation of the Poet's mind.
>   . . . we have reach'd
> The time (which was our object from the first)
> When we may, not presumptuously, I hope,
> Suppose my powers so far confirmed, and such
> My knowledge, as to make me capable
> Of building up a work that should endure.
>   (XIII, 261–78)

That work, of course, is *The Recluse,* for which *The Prelude* was designed to serve as "portico . . . part of the same building." *The Prelude*, then, is an involuted poem which is about its own genesis—a prelude to itself. Its structural end is its own beginning; and its temporal beginning, as I have pointed out, is Wordsworth's entrance upon the stage of his life at which it ends. The conclusion goes on to specify the circular shape of the whole. Wordsworth there asks Coleridge to "Call back to mind / The mood in which this Poem was begun." At that time,

> I rose
> As if on wings, and saw beneath me stretch'd
> Vast prospect of the world which I had been
> And was; and hence this Song, which like a lark
> I have protracted. . . .   (XIII, 370–81)

This song, describing the prospect of his life which had been made visible to him at the opening of *The Prelude*, is *The Prelude* whose composition he is even now concluding. . . .

The Circuitous Journey

It is time to notice that Wordsworth's account of unity achieved, lost, and regained is held together, as various critics have remarked, by the recurrent image of a journey: like a number of works by his contemporaries, Wordsworth's "poem on my own poetical education" converts the wayfaring Christian of the Augustinian spiritual journey into the self-formative traveler of the Romantic educational journey. The poem in fact opens, as Elizabeth Sewell has said, "with the poet in a prospect of wide landscape and open sky," on a literal walk which serves as "the great over-all poetic figure or trope of a journey which he is about to undertake." [10] In the course of this episode the aimless wanderer becomes "as a Pilgrim resolute" who takes "the road that pointed toward the chosen Vale," and at the end of the first book the road translates itself into the metaphorical way of his life's pilgrimage:

> Forthwith shall be brought down
> Through later years the story of my life.
> The road lies plain before me. . . .
> (1850; I, 91–3, 638–40)

The Prelude is replete with "the Wanderers of the Earth" (XII, 156), and after the period of childhood, its chief episodes are Wordsworth's own wanderings through the English countryside, the Alps, Italy, France, and Wales—literal journeys through actual places which modulate easily into symbolic landscapes traversed by a metaphorical wayfarer. This or-

---

[10] *The Orphic Voice: Poetry and Natural History* (New Haven, 1960), pp. 338–9.

ganizing figure works in two dimensions. In one of these, *The Prelude* represents the life which the poet narrates as a self-educative journey, "from stage to stage / Advancing," in which his early development had been "progress on the self-same path," the crisis following the French Revolution had been "a stride at once / Into another region," and the terminus was his achievement of maturity in "the discipline / And consummation of the Poet's mind." [11] In the second application, the poet repeatedly figures his own imaginative enterprise, the act of composing *The Prelude* itself, as a perilous quest through the uncharted regions of his own mind.

At times the vehicle for this latter poetic journey is a voyage at sea, connoting the wanderings of Odysseus in his search for home:

> What avail'd,
> When Spells forbade the Voyager to land,
> The fragrance which did ever and anon
> Give notice of the Shore? . . .
> My business was upon the barren sea,
> My errand was to sail to other coasts.
>   (XI, 48–56; see I, 35–8)

Elsewhere Wordsworth's implied parallel is to Dante, who "Nell mezzo del cammin di nostra vita" had been granted a visionary journey, with a relay of guides, through hell and the earthly paradise to heaven:

> A Traveller I am,
> And all my Tale is of myself; even so,
> So be it, if the pure in heart delight
> To follow me; and Thou, O honor'd Friend!
> Who in my thoughts art ever at my side,
> Uphold, as heretofore, my fainting steps.
>   (III, 196–201)

At the beginning of the ninth book, "as a traveller, who has gained the brow / Of some aerial Down" and "is tempted to review / The region left behind him," Wordsworth turns back to his earlier youth, before he moves reluctantly on into the discordant "argument" that begins with his residence in France—"Oh, how much unlike the past!" (1850: IX, 1–22). The eleventh book, narrating the process of Wordsworth's recovery, opens in a parallel to Milton's description of his epic journey back from hell to the realms of light (XI, 1–7; see *Paradise Lost,* III, 13–20). And through all these regions the imagined presence of Coleridge serves both as auditor and guide, heartening the exhausted poet in his pilgrimage and quest:

[11] *The Prelude,* XI, 43–4; X, 239–42; XIII, 270–1.

> Thou wilt not languish here, O Friend, for whom
> I travel in these dim uncertain ways
> Thou wilt assist me as a Pilgrim gone
> In quest of highest truth. (XI, 390–3)

The last book of *The Prelude,* in symmetry with its first book, also opens with a literal walk which translates itself into a metaphor for the climactic stage both of the journey of life and of the imaginative journey which is the poem itself. This time the walk is not a movement along an open plain but the ascent of a mountain, the traditional place for definitive visions since Moses had climbed Mount Sinai. As in Hegel's contemporary *Phenomenology* the spirit, at the close of its educational journey, recognizes itself in its other, so Wordsworth's mind, confronting nature, discovers itself in its own perfected powers:

> A meditation rose in me that night
> Upon the lonely Mountain . . .
>   and it appear'd to me
> The perfect image of a mighty Mind.

In the earliest stage of its development Wordsworth's "Babe, / Nurs'd in his Mother's arms" had not only acquired "The gravitation and the filial bond . . . that connect him with the world," but had also, as "inmate of this *active* universe," established the beginnings of the reciprocative power by which

>   his mind . . .
> Creates, creator and receiver both,
> Working but in alliance with the works
> Which it beholds.—Such, verily, is the first
> Poetic spirit of our human life.
>
> (II, 265–76)

On Mount Snowdon, in an evident parallel and complement to this early passage, his mind recognizes, in that image of itself "which Nature thus / Thrusts forth upon the senses," the same power, which has now developed into "the fulness of its strength." As mist and moonlight transform the natural scene, so higher minds by a similar "Power"

>   can send abroad
> Like transformation, for themselves create
> A like existence, and, whene'er it is
> Created for them, catch it by an instinct . . .
> Willing to work and to be wrought upon

by the works which they behold. An essential alteration, however, is that the mature poetic mind, whose infant perception had been a state of undifferentiated consciousness, has acquired self-consciousness, and is able to sustain the sense of its own identity as an individuation-in-unison with the objects it perceives. In Wordsworth's terse rendering,

> hence the highest bliss
> That can be known is theirs, the consciousness
> Of whom they are habitually infused
> Through every image, and through every thought,
> And all impressions.   (XIII, 84–111)

I have remarked that *The Prelude* has a circular organization. This circularity of its form, we now see, reflects the circularity of its subject matter. In the opening passage of *The Prelude* the narrator is confirmed in his vocation as a poet-prophet and, in response to an impulse from the autumnal wood, chooses as his goal "a known Vale, whither my feet should turn," in the assurance "of some work of glory there forthwith to be begun." "Keen as a Truant or a Fugitive, / But as a Pilgrim resolute," and also (in a complementary pedestrian metaphor) "like a home-bound labourer," he then pursued his way until a three days' walk "brought me to my hermitage" (1850; I, 71–80, 90–107). At the end of *The Prelude* Wordsworth, having taken up his "permanent abode" (XIII, 338) in this hermitage, calls "back to mind" the occasion of its beginning. But *The Prelude* has a complex function, for it is designed not only as a poem in itself, but also as a "portico" to *The Recluse*. The spiritual journey thus circles back at its conclusion to the literal journey with which it had originated; but this beginning at once turns over into the opening book of Wordsworth's "work of glory," *The Recluse* proper, which describes his way of life in the chosen vale.[12] Only now does he identify the aspect of the vale which had all along made it the goal of his tortuous literal, spiritual, and poetic journey. That goal, as in all the ancient genre of the circuitous pilgrimage of life, is home—*Home at Grasmere*.

The initial passage of *Home at Grasmere* makes it clear that the place to which the poet has returned is not his literal home but one which, on his first overview of the "Vale below" when, solitary, he had chanced across it as "a roving School-boy," he had recognized to be his spiritual home. "Perfect was the Spot . . . stirring to the Spirit"; and he had immediately felt that "here / Must be his Home, this Valley be his World." Throughout his youth the vale had lingered in memory, "shedding upon joy / A brighter joy," and now the home of his imagining has become his actual home (the word reverberates through the opening passage):

---

[12] As de Selincourt points out (*Wordsworth's Poetical Works*, V, 365), the opening book of *The Recluse* "is in fact a continuation of his poetical autobiography from the place where *The Prelude* leaves off." This place, as we have seen, is also the place from which *The Prelude* has set out.

> And now 'tis mine, perchance for life, dear Vale,
> Beloved Grasmere (let the Wandering Streams
> Take up, the cloud-capt hills repeat, the Name),
> One of thy lowly Dwellings is my Home.
>
> (1-59)

The place in which, "on Nature's invitation" (line 71), Wordsworth's literal and metaphoric wanderings have terminated is identified, after the venerable formula of the Christian quest, as a home which is also a recovered paradise. In his Pisgah-sight of it as a schoolboy he had looked upon it as a "paradise before him" (line 14); and it remains, after he takes up his abode in it, an "earthly counterpart" of heaven (line 642), which he describes in terms echoing Milton's description of the Garden of Eden, and in which Wordsworth and Dorothy, "A solitary pair" (line 255) are somewhat incongruously the Adam and Eve. The journey to this ultimate stage has taken him through "the realities of life so cold," but this had been a fortunate fall into experience, for "the cost" of what he has lost from the earlier stage of his life is greatly outweighed by "what I keep, have gain'd / Shall gain," so that

> in my day of Childhood I was less
> The mind of Nature, less, take all in all,
> Whatever may be lost, than I am now.

For him, man's ancient dream of felicity has been brought down from a transcendent heaven and located in this very world—

> the distant thought
> Is fetch'd out of the heaven in which it was.
> The unappropriated bliss hath found
> An owner, and that owner I am he.
> The Lord of this enjoyment is on Earth
> And in my breast.[13]

Here he dwells, therefore, as a second and more fortunate Adam, because unlike his predecessor he possesses an Eden which has been gained:

> The boon is absolute; surpassing grace
> To me hath been vouchsafed; among the bowers
> Of blissful Eden this was neither given,
> Nor could be given, possession of the good
> Which had been sighed for, ancient thought fulfilled

---

[13] Lines 60 ff., MS variant, *Poetical Works*, V, 315-16.

And dear Imaginations realized
Up to their highest measure, yea and more.[14]

As in comparable passages in Hölderlin and Novalis (in Blake the parallel is more with Beulah than with the New Jerusalem), all the natural scene becomes alive, human, and feminine, and encloses the poet in an embrace of love:

Embrace me then, ye Hills, and close me in. . . .
But I would call thee beautiful, for mild
And soft, and gay, and beautiful thou art,
Dear Valley, having in thy face a smile
Though peaceful, full of gladness.

(lines 110–7)

And when the solitary pair had first entered this valley together in the winter season, its elements had addressed them as fellow beings:

"What would ye," said the shower,
"Wild Wanderers, whither through my dark domain?"
The sunbeam said, "be happy." When this Vale
We entered, bright and solemn was the sky
That faced us with a passionate welcoming,
And led us to our threshold

—a threshold which in an earlier version of the text had been that of "a home / Within a home, which was to be" (lines 168–73, and footnote). This terminus of all the poet's journeyings is not only home and paradise, but also a recovered unity and wholeness which he had experienced nowhere else except "as it found its way into my heart / In childhood"; for this "blended holiness of earth and sky" is

A termination, and a last retreat,
A Centre, come from wheresoe'er you will,
A Whole without dependence or defect,
Made for itself; and happy in itself,
Perfect Contentment, Unity entire.

(lines 135–51)

[14] Lines 103–9. As late as in a poem of 1811 Wordsworth parallels his "Departure from the Vale of Grasmere" to that of a tenant of "Elysian plains" or of "celestial Paradise," whom it might please to absent himself from felicity long enough to take a round trip to a lower realm.

O pleasant transit, Grasmere! to resign
Such happy fields, abodes so calm as thine. . . .
Ne'er can the way be irksome or forlorn
That winds into itself for sweet return.

(*Poetical Works*, III, 64)

And only here does he find a human community. Man "truly is alone" only in the "vast Metropolis," where he is "doomed / To hold a vacant commerce . . . / With objects wanting life, repelling love," and where "neighbourhood serves rather to divide / Than to unite." In this rural place, however, all is on a human scale, a multeity-in-unity in which individuality is preserved in a society which is a family writ large, and which finds itself thoroughly at home in its natural milieu.

> Society is here
> A true Community, a genuine frame
> Of many into one incorporate. . . .
> One household, under God, for high and low,
> One family, and one mansion, . . .
>   possessors undisturbed
> Of this Recess. . . . their glorious Dwelling-place.
>   (lines 592–624)

The poet's spiritual home, however, remains ineluctably a paradise of this earth, for in the vale man differs "but little from the Man elsewhere" and exhibits the common qualities of "selfishness, and envy, and revenge, . . . / Flattery and double-dealing, strife and wrong" (lines 347–57). But, he asks, is there not a strain of words that shall be "the acknowledged voice of life," and so speak "of solid good / And real evil" in a higher poetic harmony than that of the unalloyed pastoral fantasy—

> More grateful, more harmonious than the breath,
> The idle breath of softest pipe attuned
> To pastoral fancies?   (lines 401–9)

For this poetry of real life he dismisses the poetry of wish-fulfillment, "All Arcadian dreams / All golden fancies of the golden Age" engendered by man's "wish to part / With all remembrance of a jarring world" (lines 625–32). Confident of "an internal brightness," he assumes "his office" as a mature artist and announces his manifesto: in this "peaceful Vale . . . / A Voice shall speak, and what will be the Theme?" (lines 660–90, 751–3).

Home at Grasmere concludes with the answer to this question, in the passage Wordsworth later excerpted to serve as the Prospectus to the subject and argument of *The Recluse* and all its related poems. This statement in fact epitomizes, and proclaims as valid for other men, what the poet himself has learned from the long and arduous journey of his life that has just terminated in Grasmere Vale. The subject, he tells us, will incorporate the poetic narrative of that life itself, in the account of "the transitory Being" who had beheld the "Vision" which constituted his poetic credential, and which it was his unique mission to impart. This vision is of "the Mind of Man," through which he will undertake a poetic journey that must ascend higher than Milton's heaven and sink deeper than Milton's hell. Of this audacious poetic enterprise it will be the high argument that we can re-create the experienced world, and that this new world, despite the inescapable fact of evil and anguish—no less evident in the solitude of "fields and groves" than when they are "barricadoed . . . / Within the walls of cities"—will provide a sufficient paradise to which we have immediate access. Here we return to Wordsworth's figure for an imaginative apocalypse that will restore paradise, taken from the vision of the marriage of the Lamb in the biblical Apocalypse and adapted to his naturalistic premises of mind and its relations to nature. Only let a man succeed in restoring his lost integrity, by consummating a marital union between his mind and a nature which, to the sensual in their sleep of death, has become a severed and alien reality, and he shall find "Paradise, and groves Elysian, . . . A simple produce of the common day."

Wordsworth and the Paradox of the Imagination

by Cleanth Brooks

Wordsworth's great "Intimations" ode has been for so long intimately connected with Wordsworth's own autobiography, and indeed, Wordsworth's poems in general have been so consistently interpreted as documents pertaining to that autobiography, that to consider one of his larger poems as an object in itself may actually seem impertinent. Yet to do so for once at least is not to condemn the usual mode of procedure and it may, in fact, have positive advantages.

Wordsworth's spiritual history is admittedly important: it is just possible that it is ultimately the important thing about Wordsworth. And yet the poems are structures in their own right; and, finally, I suppose, Wordsworth's spiritual biography has come to have the importance which it has for us because he is a poet.

At any rate, it may be interesting to see what happens when one considers the "Ode" as a poem, as an independent poetic structure, even to the point of forfeiting the light which his letters, his notes, and his other poems throw on difficult points. (That forfeiture, one may hasten to advise the cautious reader, need not, of course, be permanent.) But to enforce it for the moment will certainly avoid confusion between what the poem "says" and what Wordsworth in general may have meant; and it may actually surprise some readers to see how much the poem, strictly considered in its own right, manages to say, as well as precisely what it says.

If we consider the "Ode" in these terms, several observations emerge. For one thing, the poem will be seen to make more use of paradox than is commonly supposed. Of some of these paradoxes, Wordsworth himself must obviously have been aware; but he was probably not aware, the reader will conjecture, of the extent to which he was employing paradox.

"Wordsworth and the Paradox of the Imagination." From Cleanth Brooks, *The Well Wrought Urn* (New York: Harcourt Brace Jovanovich, Inc., 1947). Copyright © 1947 by Cleanth Brooks. Reprinted by permission of Harcourt Brace Jovanovich, Inc., Dennis Dobson Ltd., and the author.

Wordsworth and the Paradox of the Imagination

The poem, furthermore, displays a rather consistent symbolism. This may be thought hardly astonishing. What may be more surprising is the fact that the symbols reveal so many ambiguities. In a few cases, this ambiguity, of which Wordsworth, again, was apparently only partially aware, breaks down into outright confusion. Yet much of the ambiguity is rich and meaningful in an Empsonian sense, and it is in terms of this ambiguity that many of the finest effects of the poem are achieved.

There are to be found in the "Ode" several varieties of irony; and some of the themes which Wordsworth treats in the poem are to be successfully related only through irony. Yet the principal defect of the "Ode" results from the fact that Wordsworth will not always accept the full consequences of some of his ironical passages.

Lastly, as may be surmised from what has already been remarked, the "Ode" for all its fine passages, is not entirely successful as a poem. Yet, we shall be able to make our best defense of it in proportion as we recognize and value its use of ambiguous symbol and paradoxical statement. Indeed, it might be maintained that, failing to do this, we shall miss much of its power as poetry and even some of its accuracy of statement.

It is tempting to interpret these propositions as proof of the fact that Wordsworth wrote the "Ode" with the "dark" side of his mind—that the poem welled up from his unconscious and that his conscious tinkering with it which was calculated to blunt and coarsen some of the finest effects was, in this case, held to a minimum. But it hardly becomes a critic who has just proposed to treat the poem strictly as a poem, apart from its reflections of Wordsworth's biography, to rush back into biographical speculation. It is far more important to see whether the generalizations proposed about the nature of the poem are really borne out by the poem itself. This is all the more true when one reflects that to propose to find in the poem ambiguities, ironies, and paradoxes will seem to many a reader an attempt to fit the poem to a Procrustean bed—in fine, the bed in which John Donne slept comfortably enough but in which a Romantic poet can hardly be supposed to find any ease.

In reading the poem, I shall emphasize the imagery primarily, and the success or relative failure with which Wordsworth meets in trying to make his images carry and develop his thought. It is only fair to myself to say that I am also interested in many other things, the metrical pattern, for example, though I shall necessarily have to omit detailed consideration of this and many other matters.

In the "Ode" the poet begins by saying that he has lost something. What is it precisely that he has lost? What does the poem itself say? It says that things uncelestial, the earth and every common sight, once seemed apparelled in celestial light. The word "apparelled" seems to me important. The light was like a garment. It could be taken off. It was not natural to the earth; it *has* been taken off. And if the celestial light is a garment, the earth must have been clad with the garment by someone (the garment motif, by the way, is to appear later with regard to the child: "trailing clouds of glory do we come").

The earth, which has had to be apparelled in the garment of light, is counterbalanced by the celestial bodies like the sun, moon, and stars of the next stanza. These are lightbearers capable of trailing clouds of glory themselves, and they clothe the earth in light of various sorts. One is tempted here to say that the poles of the basic comparison are already revealed in these first two stanzas: the common earth on which the glory has to be conferred, and the sun or moon, which confers glory. We can even anticipate the crux of the poem in these terms: has the child been clothed with light? Or does he himself clothe the world about him in light? But more of this later.

This celestial apparel, the garment of light, had, the speaker says, the glory and the freshness of a dream. A dream has an extraordinary kind of vividness often associated with strong emotional coloring. It frequently represents familiar objects, even homely ones, but with the familiarity gone and the objects endowed with strangeness. But the dream is elusive, it cannot be dissected and analyzed. (Even if Wordsworth could have been confronted with Dr. Freud, he would, we may surmise, have hardly missed seeing that Freud's brilliant accounts of dreams resemble science less than they do poems—"Odes on the Intimations of all too human humanity from unconscious recollections of early childhood.") Moreover, the phrase, taken as a whole, suggests that the glory has the unsubstantial quality of a dream. Perhaps this is to overload an otherwise innocent phrase. But I should like to point out as some warrant for this suggestion of unsubstantiality that "dream" is rhymed emphatically with "To me did *seem*," and that it is immediately followed by "It is not now as it hath been of yore." The dream quality, it seems to me, is linked definitely with the transience of the experience. Later in the poem, the dream is to be connected with "visionary gleam," is to be qualified by the adjective "fugitive," and finally is to be associated with "Those shadowy recollections."

The ambiguous character of the child's vision as remembered by the man is implicit, therefore, in the first stanza of the poem. What the speaker has lost, it is suggested, is something which is fleeting, shadowy, and strange, but something which possesses a quality of insight and wholeness which no amount of other perception—least of all patient analysis—will duplicate. It is *visionary;* that is, like a vision, a revelation. But visionary perhaps also suggests something impractical, not completely real. Perhaps most interesting of all, the speaker, a little later in the "Ode," has it fade into the light of common day, which is inimical to both its freshness and its glory. The vision which has been lost is at once more intense and less intense than common daylight.

The second stanza, I think, is very important in defining further the relation of the visionary gleam to the man and to the earth. Ostensibly, this second stanza simply goes on to define further the nature of the thing lost: it is not mere beauty; nature is still beautiful, but a special quality has been lost. Yet the imagery seems to me to be doing something else beneath this surface statement, and something which is very important. In contrast to the earth, we have the rainbow, the moon, the stars, and the sun—all examples of celestial light; and to these we may add the rose by the sort of extension, not too difficult to be sure, by which Cowley treats it as light in his "Hymn to Light." Wordsworth says that the rainbow and the rose are beautiful. We expect him to go on to say the same of the moon. But here, with one of the nicest touches in the poem, he reverses the pattern to say, "The moon doth with delight / Look round her when the heavens are bare." The moon is treated as if she were the speaker himself in his childhood, seeing the visionary gleam as she looks round her with joy. The poet cannot see the gleam, but he implies that the moon can see it, and suggests how she can: she sheds the gleam herself; she lights up and thus creates her world. This seems to me a hint which Wordsworth is to develop later more explicitly, that it is the child, looking round him with joy, who is at once both the source and the recipient of the vision. In this stanza even the sunshine (though as the source of common day it is to be used later in the poem as the antithesis of the visionary gleam) participates in the glory—"The sunshine is a glorious birth." The word *birth,* by the way, suggests that it is a dawn scene: it is the childhood of the sun's course, not the maturity. Like the moon, the sun joyfully creates its world. The poet is giving us here, it seems to me, some very important preparation for Stanza V, in which he is to say "Our birth is but a sleep and a forgetting: / The Soul that rises with us, our life's Star, / Hath had elsewhere its setting. . . ." Surely, it is perfectly clear here that the child, coming upon the world, trailing his clouds of glory, is like the sun or moon which brings its radiance with it, moonlight or starlight or dawn light.

I shall not try to prove here that Wordsworth consciously built up the imagery of Stanza II as preparation for Stanza V. In one sense I think the question of whether or not Wordsworth did this consciously is irrelevant. What I am certain of is this: that the lines

> The Moon doth with delight
> Look round her. . . .

strike any sensitive reader as fine to a degree which their value as decoration will not account for. Certainly it is a testimony of many readers that the famous passage "Our birth is but a sleep, etc." has registered with a special impact, with more impact than the mere "beauty" of the images will account for. The relation of both passages to the theme, and their mutual interrelations seem to me one way of accounting for their special force.

This relation of both passages to the theme is so important, however, that I should like for the moment to pass over consideration of Stanzas III and IV in order to pursue further the central symbolism of light as treated in Stanza V. The basic metaphor from line sixty-seven onward has to do with the child's moving away from heaven, his home—the shades of the prison house closing about him—the youth's progress further and further from the day-spring in the east. We should, however, if the figure were worked out with thorough consistency, expect him to arrive at darkness or near darkness, the shades of the prison house having closed round the boy all but completely—the youth having traveled into some darkened and dismal west. Yet the tantalizing ambiguity in the symbol which we have noticed earlier, continues. The climax of the process is not darkness but full daylight: "At length the Man perceives it die away, / And fade into the light of common day." We have a contrast, then, between prosaic daylight and starlight or dawn light—a contrast between kinds of light, not between light and darkness. There is a further difficulty in the symbolism: the sunlight, which in Stanza II was a glorious birth, has here become the symbol for the prosaic and the common and the mortal.

I point out the ambiguities, not to convict the poet of confusion, but to praise him for his subtlety and accuracy. I suggest that the implied comparison of the child to the sun or the moon is still active here, and that Wordsworth is leaning on his earlier figure more heavily than most of his critics have pointed out, or than, perhaps, he himself realized. If the sun, at his glorious birth, lights up a world with the glory and freshness of a dream, with a light which persists even after he has begun to ascend the sky, yet the sun gradually becomes the destroyer of his earlier world and becomes his own prisoner. Indeed it is very easy to read the whole stanza as based on a submerged metaphor of the sun's progress: the soul is like our life's star, the sun, which has had elsewhere its setting. It rises upon its world, not in utter nakedness. The trailing clouds of glory suggest the sunrise. The youth is like the sun, which, as it travels farther from the east, leaves the glory more and more behind it, and approaches prosaic daylight. But it is the sun itself which projects the prosaic daylight, just as the man projects the common day which surrounds him, and upon which he now looks without joy.

I do not insist that we have to read the stanza as a consistent parallelism between the growing boy and the rising sun. Certainly other metaphors intrude: that of the darkening prison house, for example. But whether or not we bring the dominant symbolism to the surface, there is no question, I think, that it is at work within the stanza. And it *is* a symbolism: we are not permitted to pick up the metaphors when we please and drop them when we please. Light plays throughout the poem, and the "Ode," one must remember, closes with another scene in which sunlight again figures prominently:

> The Clouds that gather round the setting sun
> Do take a sober colouring from an eye
> That hath kept watch o'er man's mortality. . . .

Here, by the way, the hint that it is the child who confers the "gleam" upon the world becomes explicit. The clouds take their sober coloring from the eye. Even if we make "eye" refer to the sun as the eye of day, we have but brought the basic metaphors into closer relationship. If the sun, the eye of heaven, after it has watched over mortality, is sobered, so is the eye of the man who has kept the same watch. The parallel between the sun and the developing child which we noticed in Stanza V is completed.

To some readers, however, the occurrence of the word "shades" may still render such an interpretation bizarre. But such a reader will have to prepare himself to face another even more startling ambiguity in the central symbol. Blindness and darkness in this poem are not the easy and expected antitheses to vision and light. The climax of man's falling away from his source is, as we have seen, not the settling down of complete darkness, but of common day. In Stanza IX when the poet pays his debt of gratitude to the childhood vision he actually associates it with blindness and darkness:

> But for those obstinate questionings
> Of sense and outward things,
> Fallings from us, vanishings;
> Blank misgivings. . . .
>
> But for those first affections,
> Those shadowy recollections,
>   Which, be they what they may,
> Are yet the fountain light of all our day,
> Are yet a master light of all our seeing. . . .

The supernal light, the master-light of all our seeing, is here made to flow from the shadowy recollections. Even if we argue that "shadowy" means merely "fitful," "fugitive," we shall still find it difficult to discount some connection of the word with shades and darkness. And if we consider the changing points of view in the "Ode," we shall see that it is inevitable that light should shift into dark and dark into light. For the man who has become immersed in the hard, white light of common day, the recollections of childhood are shadowy; just as from the standpoint of the poet, such a man, preoccupied with his analysis and dissection, must appear merely blind.

As a matter of fact, I think we shall have to agree that there is method in Wordsworth's paradoxes: he is trying to state with some sensitiveness the relation between the two modes of perception, that of the analytic reason and that of the synthesizing imagination. They do have their relationships; they are both ways of seeing. The ambiguities which light and darkness take on in this poem are, therefore, not confusions, as it seems to me, but necessary paradoxes.

A further treatment of the relationship in which Wordsworth is certainly making a conscious use of paradox seems to clinch the interpretation given. I refer to the passage in which the child is addressed as

> Thou best Philosopher, who yet dost keep
> Thy heritage, thou Eye among the blind,
> That, deaf and silent, read'st the eternal deep. . . .
>
> Why with such earnest pains dost thou provoke
> The years to bring the inevitable yoke,
> Thus blindly with thy blessedness at strife?

The child who sees, does not know that he sees, and is not even aware that others are blind. Indeed, he is trying his best (or soon will try his best) to become blind like the others. Yet, in this most extravagant passage in the poem, Wordsworth keeps the balance. In the child we are dealing with the isolated fact of vision.[1] The eye, taken as an organ of sense, is naturally deaf and silent. The child cannot tell what he reads in the eternal deep, nor can he hear the poet's warning that he is actually trying to cast away his vision. If the passage seems the high point of extravagance, it is also the high point of ironic qualification. How blind is he who, possessed of rare sight, *blindly* strives to forfeit it and become blind!

In pursuing the implications of the light-darkness symbolism, however, I do not mean to lose sight of the "Ode" as a rhetorical structure. To this matter—the alternation of mood, the balance of stanza against stanza, the metrical devices by which the poet attempts to point up these contrasts—to this matter, I shall be able to give very little attention. But I do not mean to desert altogether the line of development of the poem. It is high time to turn back to Stanzas III and IV.

With Stanza III the emphasis is shifted from sight to sound. It is a

---

[1] Cf. I. A. Richards' discussion of this passage in *Coleridge on Imagination* (London, 1934), pp. 133 ff. [Quotations in this essay from *Coleridge on Imagination* are reprinted by permission of W. W. Norton & Company, Inc., New York.]

very cunning touch. The poet has lamented the passing of a glory from the earth. But he can, he suggests, at least *hear* the mirth of the blessed creatures for whom the earth still wears that glory. Stanza III is dominated by sound: the birds' songs, the trumpets of the cataracts, echoes, the winds—presumably their sound—one can't *see* them. Even the gamboling of the lambs is associated with a strong auditory image—"As to the tabor's sound." Hearing these sounds, the poet tries to enter into the gaiety of the season. He asks the shepherd boy to shout, and he goes on to say in Stanza IV,

> Ye blessed Creatures, I have heard the call
> Ye to each other make. . . .

The effect is that of a blind man trying to enter the joyful dawn world. He can hear the blessed creatures as they rejoice in the world, but he himself is shut out from it. If one argues against this as oversubtle—and perhaps it is—and points out that after the poet says,

> . . . I have heard the call
> Ye to each other make

he goes on immediately to say

> I *see*
> The heavens laugh with you in your jubilee,

we are not left entirely without a rejoinder. One can point out that at this point another strong auditory image intervenes again to make sound the dominant sense, not sight. One sees a smile, but laughter is vocal. The heavens are laughing with the children. The poet does in a sense enter into the scene; certainly he is trying very hard to enter into it. But what I notice is that the poet seems to be straining to work up a gaiety that isn't there. If his heart is at the children's festival, it is their festival, after all, not his. I hasten to add that this sense of a somewhat frenetically whipped-up enthusiasm is dramatically quite appropriate. (The metrical situation of the stanza, by the way, would seem to support the view that the strained effect is intentional.) The poet under the influence of the morning scene, feeling the winds that blow "from the fields of sleep," tries to relive the dream. He fails.

But to return to the contrast between sight and sound, the poet should be saying at the climax of his ecstasy,

> I *see*, I *see*, with joy I *see!*

not,

> I hear, I hear, with joy I hear!

Consequently, we are not surprised that the sudden collapse of his afflatus occurs in the very next line, and occurs with the first particular object which is concretely visualized in this stanza:

> —But there's a Tree, of many, one,
> A single Field which I have looked upon. . . .

The influences of the May morning will no longer work.

I have already discussed the manner in which the first two stanzas of the "Ode" charge the imagery of the famous fifth stanza. I should like to take a moment to glance at another aspect of this stanza. The poet, in "explaining" the loss of vision, says,

> Our birth is but a sleep and a forgetting. . . .

The connection with

> The glory and the freshness of a dream

of Stanza I is obvious, but I think few have noticed that the expected relation between the two is neatly reversed. Our life's star is rising: it is dawn. We expect the poet to say that the child, in being born, is waking up, deserting sleep and the realm of dream. But instead, our birth, he says, is a sleep and a forgetting. Reality and unreality, learning and forgetting, ironically change places.

Parallel ambiguities are involved in the use of "earth." In general, earth is made to serve as a foil for the celestial light. For example, when the poet writes,

> . . . when meadow, grove, and stream,
> The earth and every common sight,

it is almost as if he had said "even the earth," and this is the implication of "While earth *herself* is adorning," in Stanza IV. Yet, logically and grammatically, we can look back and connect "earth" with "meadow, grove, and stream"—all of which are aspects of earth—just as properly as we can look forward to connect "earth" with "every common sight." The poet himself is willing at times in the poem to treat the earth as the aggregate of all the special aspects of nature, at least of terrestrial nature. This surely is the sense of such a line as

> . . . there hath passed away a glory from the earth

where the emphasis suggests some such statement as: the whole world has lost its glory.

But these somewhat contradictory aspects of the word "earth" overlay a far more fundamental paradox: in general, we think of this poem as a celebration of the influence of nature on the developing mind, and surely, to a large degree, this is true. The poem is filled with references to valleys, mountains, streams, cataracts, meadows, the sea. Yet, though these aspects are so thoroughly interwoven with the spontaneous joy of the child which the poet has himself lost, it is the earth which is responsible for the loss. Stanza VI is concerned with this paradox:

> Earth fills her lap with pleasures of her own. . . .

What are these pleasures? They would seem to be suspiciously like the pleasures which engage the children on this May morning and in which the speaker of the poem regrets that he cannot fully indulge. It is true that the next stanza of the "Ode" does emphasize the fact that the world of human affairs, as the stanza makes clear, is seized upon by the child with joy, and that this is a process which is eminently "natural":

> Fretted by sallies of his mother's kisses,
> With light upon him from his father's eyes!

Earth, "even with something of a Mother's mind," "fills her lap with pleasures."

> Yearnings she hath in her own natural kind.

What are these yearnings but yearnings to involve the child with herself? We can translate "in her own natural kind" as "pertaining to her," "proper to the earth"; yet there is more than a hint that "natural" means "pertaining to nature," and are not the yearnings proper to the earth, *natural* in this sense, anyway?

In trying to make the child forget the unearthly or supernatural glory, the Earth is acting out of kindness. The poet cannot find it in him to blame her. She wants the child to be at home. Here we come close upon a Wordsworthian pun, though doubtless an unpremeditated pun. In calling the Earth "the homely Nurse" there seems a flicker of this suggestion: that Earth wants the child to be at home. Yet "homely" must surely mean also "unattractive, plain." [2] She is the drudging common earth after all, homely, perhaps a little stupid, but sympathetic, and kind. Yet it is precisely this Earth which was once glorious to the poet, "Apparelled in celestial light."

This stanza, though not one of the celebrated stanzas of the poem, is one of the most finely ironical. Its structural significance too is of first importance, and has perhaps in the past been given too little weight. Two of its implications I should like to emphasize. First, the stanza definitely insists that the human soul is not merely natural. We do not of course, as Wordsworth himself suggested, have to take literally the doctrine about

---

[2] It has been objected that "homely" in British English does not have this sense. Perhaps it does not today, but see Milton's *Comus*:

> It is for homely features to keep home,
> They had their name thence. . . .

pre-existence; but the stanza makes it quite clear, I think, that man's soul brings an alien element into nature, a supernatural element. The child is of royal birth—"that imperial palace whence he came"—the Earth, for all her motherly affection, is only his foster-mother after all. The submerged metaphor at work here is really that of the foundling prince reared by the peasants, though the phrase, "her Inmate Man," suggests an even more sinister relation: "Inmate" can only mean inmate of the prison-house of the preceding stanza.

The second implication is this: since the Earth is really homely, the stanza underlies what has been hinted at earlier: namely, that it is the child himself who confers the radiance on the morning world upon which he looks with delight. The irony is that if the child looks long enough at that world, becomes deeply enough involved in its beauties, the celestial radiance itself disappears.

In some respects, it is a pity that Wordsworth was not content to rely upon this imagery to make his point and that he felt it necessary to include the weak Stanza VII. Presumably, he thought the reader required a more explicit account. Moreover, Wordsworth is obviously trying to establish his own attitude toward the child's insight. In the earlier stanzas, he has attempted to define the quality of the visionary gleam, and to account for its inevitable loss. Now he attempts to establish more definitely his attitude toward the whole experience. One finds him here, as a consequence, no longer trying to recapture the childhood joy or lamenting its loss, but withdrawing to a more objective and neutral position. The function of establishing this attitude is assigned to Stanza VII. The poet's treatment of the child here is tender, but with a hint of amused patronage in the tenderness. There is even a rather timid attempt at humor. But even if we grant Wordsworth's intention, the stanza must still be accounted very weak, and some of the lines are very flat indeed. Moreover, the amused tenderness is pretty thoroughly overbalanced by the great stanza that follows. I am not sure that the poem would not be improved if Stanza VII were omitted.

If Stanza VII patronizes the child, Stanza VIII apparently exalts him. What is the poet's attitude here? Our decision as to what it is—that is, our decision as to what the poem is actually saying here—is crucial for our interpretation of the poem as a whole. For this reason I believe that it is worth going back over some of the ground already traversed.

Coleridge, one remembers, found the paradoxes which Wordsworth uses in Stanza VIII too startling. Several years ago, in his *Coleridge on Imagination*, I. A. Richards answered Coleridge's strictures. He replies to one of Coleridge's objections as follows:

> The syntax is "faulty" only in that the reader may be required to reflect. He may have to notice that *eye* is metaphorical already for *philosopher*—that the two conjointly then have a meaning that neither

would have apart. "An idea in the mind is to a Natural Law as the power of seeing is to light," said Coleridge himself. As an eye, the philosopher is free from the need to do anything but respond to the laws of his being. *Deaf* and *silent* extend the metaphor by perfectly consentaneous movements. . . . The child will not hear (cannot understand) our words; and he will tell us nothing. That which Wordsworth would derive from him he cannot give; his silence (as we take it through step after step of interpretation, up to the point at which it negates the whole *overt* implication of the rest of Wordsworth's treatment) can become the most important point in the poem. We might look to Lao Tzu to support this: "Who knows speaks not; who speaks knows not." But it is enough to quote, from Coleridge himself, "the words with which Plotinus supposes NATURE to answer a similar difficulty. 'Should anyone interrogate her, how she works, if graciously she vouchsafe to listen and speak, she will reply, it behoves thee not to disquiet me with interrogatories, but to understand in silence even as I am silent, and work without words.'"

Before going further with Richards, however, the reader may wonder how far Wordsworth would be prepared to accept this defense of the lines, particularly in view of Richards' statement that the child's silence "*can* become the most important point in the poem." *Did* it become the most important part for Wordsworth? And regardless of how we answer that question, *does* it become such for us? How is it that the child is an eye among the blind?

Because he "yet [doth] keep / [His] heritage"; because he still dreams and remembers, for all that birth is a sleep and a forgetting; because he is still near to God, who is our home. This, I take it, is what Richards calls the "*overt* implication of . . . Wordsworth's treatment." But it is not so simple as this in Wordsworth's poem. We have seen the hints of another interpretation: the suggestion that the child is like the moon which "with delight / Look[s] round her," and the association of the joyous vision of the child with the child's own joyous activity, and further, with the joyous activity of the birds and the lambs. Is the poem theistic or pantheistic? Coleridge was certainly alive to the difficulties here. He went on to question:

> . . . In what sense can the magnificent attributes, above quoted, be appropriated to a *child*, which would not make them equally suitable to a *bee*, or a *dog*, or a *field of corn;* or even to a ship, or to the wind and waves that propel it?

Richards' answer is forthright:

> . . . why should Wordsworth deny that, in a much less degree, these attributes are equally suitable to a bee, or a dog, or a field of corn? What else had he been saying with his
>
>> And let the young lambs bound
>> As to the tabor's sound!

And what else is Coleridge himself to say in Appendix B of his *Statesman's Manual?* "Never can I look and meditate on the vegetable creation without a feeling similar to that with which we gaze at a beautiful infant. . . ."

Whatever Coleridge was to say later, there can be little doubt as to what Wordsworth's poem says. The lambs and birds are undoubtedly included, along with the children, in the apostrophe, "Ye blessed Creatures." It will be difficult, furthermore, to argue that the poet means to exclude the moon, the stars, and the sun. (If Wordsworth would have excluded the bee and the dog, the exclusion, we may be sure, would have been made on other grounds—not philosophical but poetic.) The matter of importance for the development of the poem is, of course, that the child is father to the man, to the man Wordsworth, for example, as the birds, the lamb, and the moon are not. But it is also a point of first importance for the poem that the child, whatever he is to develop into later, possesses the harmony and apparent joy of all these blessed creatures. It may not be amiss here to remind ourselves of Coleridge's definition of joy with which Wordsworth himself must have been familiar: ". . . a consciousness of entire and therefore well being, when the emotional and intellectual faculties are in equipoise."

Consider, in this general connection, one further item from the poem itself, the last lines from the famous recovery stanza, Stanza IX:

> Nor all that is at enmity with joy,
> Can utterly abolish or destroy!
> Hence in a season of calm weather
>   Though inland far we be,
> Our Souls have sight of that immortal sea
>   Which brought us hither,
>   Can in a moment travel thither,
> And see the Children sport upon the shore,
> And hear the mighty waters rolling evermore.

Wordsworth has said that the child as the best philosopher "read'st the eternal deep," and here for the first time in the poem we have the children brought into explicit juxtaposition with the deep. And how, according to the poem, are these best philosophers reading it? By sporting on the shore. They are playing with their little spades and sand-buckets along the beach on which the waves break. This is the only explicit exhibit of their "reading" which the poem gives. It seems to corroborate Richards' interpretation perfectly.

In writing this, I am not trying to provoke a smile at Wordsworth's expense. Far from it. The lines are great poetry. They are great poetry because, although the sea is the sea of eternity, and the mighty waters are rolling evermore, the children are not terrified—are at home—are filled with innocent joy. The children exemplify the attitude toward eternity which the other philosopher, the mature philosopher, wins to with difficulty, if he wins to it at all. For the children are those

> On whom these truths do rest,
> Which we are toiling all our lives to find.

The passage carries with it an ironic shock—the associations of innocence and joy contrasted with the associations of grandeur and terror—but it is the kind of shock which, one is tempted to say, is almost normal in the greatest poetry.

I asked a few moments ago how the child was an "Eye among the blind." The poem seems to imply two different, and perhaps hostile, answers: because the child is from God and still is close to the source of supernal light; *and,* because the child is still close to, and like, the harmonious aspects of nature, just as are the lamb or the bee or the dog. According to the first view, the child is an eye among the blind because his soul is filled with the divine; according to the second, because he is utterly natural. Can these two views be reconciled? And are they reconciled in the poem?

Obviously, the question of whether "divine" and "natural" can be reconciled in the child depends on the senses in which we apply them to the child. What the poem is saying, I take it, is that the child, because he is close to the divine, is utterly natural—natural in the sense that he has the harmony of being, the innocence, and the joy which we associate with the harmonious forms of nature. Undoubtedly Wordsworth found a symbol of divinity in such "beauteous forms" of nature; but the poem rests on something wider than the general context of Wordsworth's poetry: throughout the entire Christian tradition, the lamb, the lilies of the field, etc., have been used as such symbols.

But we may protest further and say that such a reading of "nature" represents a selection, and a loaded selection at that, one which has been made by Wordsworth himself—that there are other accounts of nature which will yield "naturalism" which is hostile to the claims to the divine. It is profitable to raise this question, because an attempt to answer it may provide the most fundamental explanation of all for the ambiguities and paradoxes which fill the "Ode."

Richards says that from "Imagination as a 'fact of mind'" there are "two doctrines which Coleridge (and Wordsworth) at times drew from it as to a life in or behind Nature." The two doctrines he states as follows:

> 1. The mind of the poet at moments, penetrating "the film of familiarity and selfish solicitude," gains an insight into reality, reads Nature as a symbol of something behind or within Nature not ordinarily perceived.

[In the "Ode," the child, untarnished by "the film of familiarity and selfish solicitude," sees nature clad in a *celestial* light.]

2. The mind of the poet creates a Nature into which his own feelings, his aspirations and apprehensions, are projected. [In the "Ode," the child projects his own joy over nature as the moon projects its light over the bare heavens.]

In the first doctrine man, through Nature, is linked with something other than himself which he perceives through her. In the second, he makes of her, as with a mirror, a transformed image of his own being.

But Richards interrupts the process of determining which of these doctrines Coleridge held and which, Wordsworth, to raise two questions which he suggests have a prior status: the questions are, namely, "(1) Are these doctrines necessarily in opposition to one another? (2) What is the relation of any such doctrine to the fact of mind from which it derives?" And Richards goes on to argue:

The Imagination projects the life of the mind not upon Nature . . . [in the sense of the whole] field of the influences from without to which we are subject, but upon a Nature that is already a projection of our sensibility. The deadest Nature that we can conceive is already a Nature of our making. It is a Nature shaped by certain of our needs, and when we "lend to it a life drawn from the human spirit" it is reshaped in accordance with our other needs. [We may interrupt Richards to use Wordsworth's own phrasing from "Tintern Abbey": ". . . all this mighty world / Of eye, and ear,—both what they half create, / And what perceive. . . ."] But our needs do not originate in us. They come from our relations to Nature . . . [as the whole field of influences from without]. We do not create the food that we eat, or the air that we breathe, or the other people we talk to; we do create, from our relations to them, every image we have "of" them. *Image* here is a betraying and unsatisfactory word; it suggests that these images, with which all that we can know is composed, are in some way insubstantial or unreal, mere copies of actualities other than themselves—figments. But *figment* and *real* and *substantial* are themselves words with no meaning that is not drawn from our experience. To say of anything that it is a figment seems to presuppose things more real than itself; but there is nothing within our knowledge more real than these images. To say that anything is an image suggests that there is something else to which it corresponds; but here all correspondence is between images. In short, the notion of reality derives from comparison between images, and to apply it as between images and things that are not images is an illegitimate extension which makes nonsense of it.

This deceiving practice is an example of that process of abstraction which makes it almost inevitable that the two doctrines . . .—the projective and the realist doctrines of the life in Nature—should be conceived as contradictory. "If projected, not real; if real, not projected," we shall say, unless we are careful to recall that the meanings of *real* and *projected* derive from the imaginative fact of mind, and that when they are thus put in opposition they are products of abstraction and are useful only for other purposes than the comprehension of the fact of mind.

This is all very well, I can hear someone say; but even if we grant that the realist and projective doctrines are not necessarily in opposition, what warrant have we for believing that *Wordsworth* believed they were not in opposition? In trying to answer this objection, I should agree that merely to point out that both realist and projective doctrines seem to *occur* in the "Ode" is not to give an answer. We can argue for the reconciliation of these doctrines only if we can find where these doctrines impinge upon each other. Where do they meet? That is to say, where is the real center of the poem? What is the poem essentially about?

The poem is about the human heart—its growth, its nature, its development. The poem finds its center in what Richards has called the "fact of imagination." Theology, ethics, education are touched upon. But the emphasis is not upon these: Wordsworth's rather awkward note in which he repudiates any notion of trying to inculcate a belief in preexistence would support this view. The greatness of the "Ode" lies in the fact that Wordsworth is about the poet's business here, and is not trying to inculcate anything. Instead, he is trying to dramatize the changing interrelations which determine the major imagery. And it is with this theme that the poem closes. Thanks are given, not to God—at least in this poem, not to God—but to

. . . the human heart by which we live,
Thanks to its tenderness, its joys, and fears. . . .

It is because of the nature of the human heart that the meanest flower can give, if not the joy of the celestial light, something which the poet says is not sorrow and which he implies is deeper than joy: "Thoughts that do often lie too deep for tears."

If the poem is about the synthesizing imagination, that faculty by which, as a later poet puts it,

Man makes a superhuman
Mirror-resembling dream

the reason for the major ambiguities is revealed. These basic ambiguities, by the way, assert themselves as the poem ends. Just before he renders thanks to the human heart, you will remember, the poet says that the clouds do not give *to,* but take *from,* the eye their sober coloring. But in the last two lines of the stanza, the flower does not take *from,* but gives *to,* the heart. We can have it either way. Indeed, the poem implies that we must have it *both* ways. And we are dealing with more than optics. What the clouds take from the eye is more than a sober coloring—the soberness is from the mind and heart. By the same token, the flower, though it gives a color—gives more, it gives thought and emotion.

It has not been my purpose to present this statement of the theme as a discovery; it is anything but that. Rather, I have tried to show how the imagery of the poem is functionally related to a theme—not vaguely and loosely related to it—and how it therefore renders that theme powerfully, and even exactly, defining and refining it. But I can make no such claim for such precision in Wordsworth's treatment of the "resolution," the recovery. In a general sense we know what Wordsworth is doing here: the childhood vision is only one aspect of the "primal sympathy"; this vision has been lost—is, as the earlier stanzas show, inevitably lost—but the primal sympathy remains. It is the faculty by which we live. The continuity between child and man is actually unbroken.

But I must confess that I feel the solution is asserted rather than dramatized. Undoubtedly, we can reconstruct from Wordsworth's other writings the relationship between the primal sympathy and the joy, the "High instincts" and the "soothing thoughts," but the relationship is hardly digested into poetry in the "Ode." And some of the difficulties with which we meet in the last stanzas appear to be not enriching ambiguities but distracting confusions: e.g., the years bring the philosophical mind, but the child over which the years are to pass is already the best philosopher. There is "something" that remains alive in our embers, but it is difficult for the reader to define it in relation to what has been lost. If we make a desperate effort to extend the implied metaphor—if we say that the celestial light is the flame which is beautiful but which must inevitably burn itself out—the primal sympathy is the still-glowing coal—we are forced to realize that such extension is overingenious. The metaphor was not meant to bear so much weight. With regard to this matter of imagery, it would be interesting to compare with the "Ode" several poems by Vaughan which embody a theme very closely related to that of the "Ode." And lest this remark seem to hint at an inveterate prejudice in favor of the metaphysicals, I propose another comparison: a comparison with several of Yeats's poems which deal with still another related theme: unity of being and the unifying power of the imagination. Such comparisons, I believe, would illuminate Wordsworth's difficulties and account for some of the "Ode's" defects. Yet, in closing this account of the "Ode," I want to repudiate a possible misapprehension. I do not mean to say that the general drift of the poem does not come through. It does. I do not mean that there is not much greatness in the poem. There is. But there is some vagueness—which is not the same thing as the rich multiplicity of the greatest poetry; and there are some loose ends, and there is at least one rather woeful anticlimax.

But if the type of analysis to which we have subjected the "Ode" is calculated to indicate such deficiencies by demanding a great deal of the imagery, it is only fair to remind the reader that it focuses attention on the brilliance and power of the imagery, a power which is sustained almost throughout the poem, and with which Wordsworth has hardly been sufficiently credited in the past. Even the insistence on paradox does not create the defects in the "Ode"—the defects have been pointed out before—but it may help account for them. Indeed, one can argue that we can perhaps best understand the virtues and the weaknesses of the "Ode" if we see that what Wordsworth wanted to say demanded his use of paradox, that it could only be said powerfully through paradox, and if we remember in what suspicion Wordsworth held this kind of poetic strategy.

Wordsworth: The Baptized Imagination

by John Jones

What is new and Christian in *The Excursion* is not always ineffectual. Wordsworth can still write persuasively of things that he has seen, though his gaze is now heavenward:

> homeward the shepherds moved
> Through the dull mist, I following—when a step,
> A single step that freed me from the skirts
> Of the blind vapour, opened to my view
> Glory beyond all glory ever seen
> By waking sense or by the dreaming soul!
> The appearance, instantaneously disclosed,
> Was of a mighty city—boldly say
> A wilderness of building, sinking far
> And self-withdrawn into a boundless depth,
> Far sinking into splendour—without end!
> Fabric it seemed of diamond and of gold,
> With alabaster domes, and silver spires,
> And blazing terrace upon terrace. . . .   [II, 828 ff.]

And while his eyes are raised to the Kingdom of Heaven, he still stands on earth; so that there is fugue-like movement of finite and infinite through the passage. The immediate occasion of the experience is clearly stated:

> By earthly nature had the effect been wrought
> Upon the dark materials of the storm
> Now pacified. . . .

But no less clear, as he returns to it, is the sight of

"Wordsworth: The Baptized Imagination." From John Jones, *The Egotistical Sublime: A History of Wordsworth's Imagination* (London: Chatto and Windus Ltd., 1954). Copyright © 1954 by Chatto and Windus Ltd. Reprinted by permission of the publisher and the author. This selection includes all except the opening section of chapter 4.

> that marvellous array
> Of temple, palace, citadel, and huge
> Fantastic pomp of structure without name. . . .

Finally, the contrast of familiar valley and city that has suddenly usurped it, becomes explicit:

> This little Vale, a dwelling-place of Man,
> Lay low beneath my feet; 'twas visible—
> I saw not, but I felt that it was there.
> That which I *saw* was the revealed abode
> Of Spirits in beatitude. . . .
> . . . there I stood and gazed:
> The apparition faded not away,
> And I descended.

Wordsworth sees Paradise as a jewelled and holy city, as the New Jerusalem of Revelation. That the city should play this part is at once remarkable, since it has hitherto been very unimportant to him. The city of social and satirical poetry appears scarcely at all, because he was not this kind of poet. The city has no place within the greater landscape: if it has any poetic function, it is the negative one of circumscribing the unmanageable. This is not to say that all Wordsworth's poetry of the city is bad: sometimes, as in *The Prelude's* description of the "anarchy and din" of St. Bartholomew's Fair, the countryman's wide-eyed stare, his fearful amazement, his almost unwilling fascination, are vividly conveyed. And once or twice, as when he saw London from Westminster Bridge "all bright and glittering" in the dress of early morning, or, in a fine poem which he left unpublished,

> white with winter's purest white, as fair,
> As fresh and spotless as he ever sheds
> On field or mountain,[1]

the city is suddenly transmuted, and one can just understand how he came to see that other that has no need of sun or moon to shine upon it.

Even so, the *Excursion* city is a new thing—Paradise in an exact Christian and literary sense. It would be a tidy thesis that followed Wordsworth's imaginative course from the Garden of Eden in his greater landscape to the New Jerusalem in his late poetry. But it would not be true. The landscape is paradisal only in that difficult sense in which Wordsworth's early poetry is optimistic. Neither is it Christian nor is it the Never Never Land of Classical and Rousseauite myth: it is northern

---

[1] ["St. Paul's," in *Poetical Works*, ed. de Selincourt and Darbishire, vol. 4, 374–75 —Ed.]

and severe, with a terrible simplicity that the pastoral Wordsworth of Arnold's tradition could not have compassed. And Wordsworth did not see his landscape as he now sees the holy city. Then, the point of his vision was the literalness that enabled him, as he insisted in a hundred different ways, to see things as they are. Now there is a duality which he openly admits. The valley "was visible," yet he did not see it. What he saw—and he italicizes the word so that there shall be no mistake—was "*the revealed abode*" of the blessed. "Revealed" emphasizes the divine gift of second-sight. We must believe that Wordsworth was in the spirit when he beheld this vision.

Nor does Wordsworth's spiritual eye report anything grey or ghostly: the picture is as brilliant and as substantial as that described in Revelation. This directness of visual appeal owes much to the philosophical innocence that allowed Wordsworth to write about the Kingdom of Heaven unalarmed by the huge difficulties at least as old as Plato's *Parmenides*, that attend belief in a transcendent order of reality. In this *Excursion* passage he is entirely concerned, like Blake, to report what he saw, in the faith that visions justify themselves; and, like Blake, he sees his problem as one of adequate description. Sustained prophetic frenzy is very rare in Wordsworth, but he is clearly attracted to the lunatic state, as to childhood, for its privileged access to the supernatural. A late poem about a woman driven mad by the pain of bereavement ends thus:

> Nor of those maniacs is she one that kiss
> The air or laugh upon a precipice;
> No, passing through strange sufferings towards the tomb,
> She smiles as if a martyr's crown were won:
> Oft, when light breaks through clouds or waving trees,
> With outspread arms and fallen upon her knees
> The Mother hails in her descending Son
> An Angel, and in earthly ecstasies
> Her own angelic glory seems begun.[a]

The Christianity of this poetry is very unlike that which inspired the almost incredible final couplet of his *Address to a Skylark*:

> I, with my fate contented, will plod on,
> And hope for higher raptures, when life's day is done.

Anything but mean and pinched, its nature is already being unfolded in the architecture and jewelry of the holy city, and in the ceremonious action of lunacy—demoniac with those that "laugh upon a precipice" and adoring with the woman "fallen upon her knees": for art and sym-

---

[a] *The Widow on Windermere Side*.

bolic action and eternity precious and unbreathing are the subject of his late poetry.

The Immortality Ode once more proves a turning-point. Arnold, and many since Arnold, have been offended by what they take for an unwordsworthian element in the ode's imagery and diction. The child comes earthward from an "imperial palace." The lambs that "bound As to the tabor's sound" discover the rhythm of their game in the Old Testament. The ode is suggestive of ritual form in "jubilee," "festival," "wedding," "funeral"; in "my head hath its coronal," in "the gladness of the May," in "other palms are won." Critics are right to complain, but wrong to take no further interest in these discordancies.

The same thing happens in *The Prelude*, and is partly responsible for the discreteness of the later version.

> Witness, ye Solitudes! where I received
> My earliest visitations   [XIII, 123–24]

in the 1805 text becomes in 1850

> compassed round by mountain solitudes,
> Within whose solemn temple I received
> My earliest visitations. . . .   [1850 ed., XIV, 139–41]

Wordsworth is not simply indulging his taste for circumlocution. The God-graven temple of earth is one of the most persistent images in his late poetry, and one aspect of his changed attitude to the entire natural order. The ̶̶̶̶̶̶̶̶̶̶̶̶̶̶̶̶ Creator is still repugnant to him: he follo̶̶̶̶̶̶̶̶̶̶̶̶̶̶ was, we have seen, to "say as little as po̶̶̶̶̶̶̶̶̶̶̶̶̶̶̶̶̶̶̶̶̶̶̶̶̶̶ God the loving and careful Artist —Wordsworth's theory of art, unlike Coleridge's, was not a theory of making— and God the Sustainer are both familiar.

Again, in the 1805 *Prelude*, he speaks of men of great soul who, in their dealings "with all the objects of the universe,"

> for themselves create
> A like existence; and, whene'er it is
> Created for them, catch it by an instinct.
>   [1805 ed., XIII, 94–96]

In 1850, "all the objects" becomes "the whole compass," indicative of Wordsworth's loss of concentration upon particularity and the reciprocal principle; and the rest is much altered:

> for themselves create
> A like existence; and whene'er it dawns
> Created for them, catch it, or are caught

* [In *Letters*, 1811–20, ed. de Selincourt, p. 619—ED.]

> By its inevitable mastery,
> Like angels stopped upon the wing by sound
> Of harmony from Heaven's remotest spheres.
> [1850 ed., XIV, 94–99]

Clearly Wordsworth has come to dislike "instinct," with its natural and optimistic associations. In its place he introduces the equivocal "catch it, or are caught," and adds to this the angel simile. The simile is worth attention: it is more than a Miltonic flourish, just as the retreat from instinct is not mere cowardice or dishonesty. Wordsworth's movement from nature is also a movement towards art. There is an ever-increasing emphasis upon craftsmanship in his talk about poetry, and in his practice there is more of literary. Because of this, criticism that fails to use the criterion of Derivative with great tact may well go astray. Thus in the present case, the obvious Miltonism of the last line must not hide the sudden arrest of "angels stopped upon the wing," which is very effective and not quite Miltonic. And as for the general, angels work hard and successfully in Wordsworth's late poetry, speaking of heaven and earth as he requires them.

Angels live in heaven, but are sometimes seen by men. Thus they are persuaded by the beauty of spring on earth to "quit their mansions unsusceptible of change" [4] and walk abroad. Or a merciful errand may bring them here: Wordsworth tells how

> their own untroubled home
> They leave, and speed on nightly embassy
> To visit earthly chambers.[5]

They may have a purpose less specific than this comforting of sufferers. When attention seems wholly directed towards earth they sometimes remind us unexpectedly of the other order:

> In sunny glade,
> Or under leaves of thickest shade,
> Was such a stillness e'er diffused
> Since earth grew calm while angels mused? [6]

This extreme delicacy with firmness of suggestion is the angelic task. Their transcendentalism is often, as here, a matter of being convincingly apart; or, like the child, of coming from the courts of the holy city. And they have their natural counterparts, in Wordsworth's late poetry, in the heavenly bodies: in the moon, looking down upon the earth's "unsettled

---
[4] *Vernal Ode.*
[5] *The Cuckoo Clock.*
[6] *The Triad.*

atmosphere,"[7] in order to "shield from harm the humblest of the sleeping"; and the sun, "source inexhaustible of life and joy," worshipped once as "a blazing intellectual deity."[8] *The Excursion* opens with the prayer that the poem may shine "star-like," secure from "those mutations that extend their sway Throughout the nether sphere";[9] and it closes[10] with the analogy, too carefully developed, of the sun and the Deity. The invisible sun, shedding light on evening clouds, is called "this local transitory type Of thy paternal splendours." And when Wordsworth hears the cuckoo, his favourite among sky creatures,

> Wandering in solitude, and evermore
> Foretelling and proclaiming,[11]

he is now put in mind of

> the great Prophet, styled *the Voice of One
> Crying amid the wilderness.*

Everything in nature speaks of its Original to one who listens

> in the power, the faith,
> Of a baptized imagination.

Angels and shining things of earth serve Wordsworth's purpose in another way. Consider this glance at the world through a magnifying glass:

> Glasses he had, that little things display,
> The beetle panoplied in gems and gold,
> A mailèd angel on a battle-day;
> The mysteries that cups of flowers enfold. . . .[12]

Unnatural in the way of art in its jewelled proportion, the universe becomes a bright pageant that relates to God with a fineness too elusive for the wide-meshed vocabulary of symbol and analogy. Mastery of scale, in the shift from beetle to angelic wars, is another aspect of Wordsworth's

---

[7] *To the Moon.*
[8] *To the Clouds.*
[9] The very sharp contrast of Star-Poem and "nether sphere" only appears in later versions of the Preface. In his first draft Wordsworth merely expresses the hope

> that my song may live, and be
> Even as a light hung up in heaven to cheer
> The world in times to come.
> [In *Poetical Works*, vol. 5, 6 —ED.]

[10] Bk. IX, 590-633.
[11] *The Cuckoo at Laverna.*
[12] *Within our happy Castle* . . .

understanding of God the Artist; and later, in the great *Vernal Ode,* he exploits it to marvellous effect. He is resting his "tired lute," after a song of time and immortality, when there steals upon his ear

> the soft murmur of the vagrant Bee.
> —A slender sound! Yet hoary Time
> Doth to the *Soul* exalt it with the chime
> Of all his years;—a company
> Of ages coming, ages gone;
> (Nations from before them sweeping,
> Regions in destruction steeping,)
> But every awful sound in unison
> With that faint utterance, which tells
> Of treasure sucked from buds and bells,
> For the pure keeping of those waxen cells.

Then Wordsworth describes her pausing in flight, so that he can observe her parts:

> o'er this tempting flower
> Hovering, until the petals stay
> Her flight, and take its voice away!—
> Observe each wing!—a tiny van!
> The structure of her laden thigh,
> How fragile! yet of ancestry
> Mysteriously remote and high;
> High as the imperial front of man;
> The roseate bloom on woman's cheek;
> The soaring eagle's curvèd beak;
> The white plumes of the floating swan;
> Old as the tiger's paw. . . .

Scale is important for this reason, that by beating the bounds of creation, from the nature of time to the bee's humming and from her wing and thigh to tiger's paw, Wordsworth is able to suggest how God must see his own work. There is artistic love and justice in the handling of each element, none preferred before the rest since there is no small and no great within the work of art, but mutual support towards the end of coherence and beauty. Everything is intelligible in terms of everything else, as, by divine transposition, the temporal order in the voice of the bee; and the whole leans on the Artist's imaginative will. The idea of service directed to God's glory replaces the self-sustaining structure of the greater landscape: in terse little poems, not unlike those of Yeats's old age, Wordsworth sees the shadow of a daisy fulfil its nature by protecting

Wordsworth: The Baptized Imagination

a dew-drop from the sun,[13] or moon and planet together in the sky and wonders which is queen and which attendant.[14]

In natural things there is a new bright meaning: beak and plume and paw are the elements of a living heraldry, closely related to Wordsworth's jewelry and architecture, and adding to these the more urgent quality of ceremonious action. Only a poet grown old in wisdom would dare to use the conventions of "hoary time," "imperial front," "roseate bloom," because they exactly serve his purpose. The utterly conventional can thus approach the command of style proper to divinity.

Another aspect of heraldic nature is its anthropomorphism, mythical and heroic. Wordsworth at one time protested against the use of Classical mythology, as a kind of decadence. In a sonnet to a brook he said:

> If wish were mine some type of thee to view,
> Thee, and not thee thyself, I would not do
> Like Grecian Artists, give thee human cheeks,
> Channels for tears; no Naiad shouldst thou be. . . .[15]

The root of his objection is the offence that this sort of thing gives to his philosophy of inner and outer, the independence of each and the "ennobling interchange" between them. Nor in truth did he recant, for his late poetry is not in this sense anthropomorphic. Natural objects are not men in disguise; but there is a certain key, reached again through a kind of divine transposition, in which human inference may be drawn from all the music of the world. He speaks of trees that "tear The lingering remnant of their yellow hair," [16] of the eagle "shedding where he flew Loose fragments of wild wailing," [17] of waterfalls "white-robed" [18] priestlike, perhaps, as Keats's "moving waters." The only Roman among the English Romantics, Wordsworth still went to Greece for his mythology, and he made of it something strong and personal. Because things are seen in God's eye, the anthropomorphism of nature is curiously without human prejudice or condescension.

The same bee of the *Vernal Ode* is called

> a warrior bold,
> Radiant all over with unburnished gold,
> And armed with living spear for mortal fight;
> A cunning forager
> That spreads no waste, a social builder; one

---

[13] *To a Child, Written in her Album.*
[14] *The Crescent-moon.*
[15] *Brook! whose society . . .*
[16] *One who was suffering tumult . . .*
[17] *A dark plume fetch me . . .*
[18] *The Excursion*, Bk. III. 48.

In whom all busy offices unite
With all fine functions that afford delight.

In his *Georgics*, Vergil compares bees to men, and later, in *The Æneid*, men to bees: a coming full circle that has been related to his poetry's development.[19] Wordsworth is doing neither—or both. Warrior, forager, social builder are impartial titles, above and between the bee-world and the man-world, which have both an equal claim to them. And again the angelic brightness of description marks a divine authenticity, the impress of the Just Artist's hands on all his creatures. Art in this way becomes the heart of Wordsworth's late poetry, and figures like the humming-bee its agents. Through the bee's embracing of all functions, warlike, peaceful, utilitarian, ornamental, art achieves the controlled boundlessness proper to itself. If the bee-world can be described in terms intelligible to men, but without reducing bees to men in miniature, we will know better how God sees us, and what it is like to be concerned in heaven for happenings on earth. Art helps in this because of its power to lay paradox to rest: it is at once the hardest work and the purest play; it matters finally and finally it does not matter, since love which is richness of art is not quite love which is richness of life—yet it is still love, and godlike in the artist's simultaneous detachment and participation; so that heat and light are undiminished, and he can escape, though only in imagination, the precise human self-involvement that makes divine compassion unattainable.

The flowers of Wordsworth's poetry are no longer studied with literal passion, to discover what they are. Already, in the Immortality Ode, the "pansy at my feet" is completely formal, introduced with the barest of gestures to confirm Wordsworth's story of lost childhood, and interesting only for its relevance to the human predicament. Flowers, like the *Vernal Ode* bee, supply a transcendental correlative for the root situations of men. "The flowers themselves," with

> all their glistening,
> Call to the heart for inward listening—
> And though for bridal wreaths and tokens true
> Welcomed wisely; though a growth
> Which the careless shepherd sleeps on,
> As fitly spring from turf the mourner weeps on—
> And without wrong are cropped the marble tomb to strew.[20]

Again there is convention and ceremony, and the comprehension at remove peculiar to art.

In a very late poem, *Love Lies Bleeding*, the same elements are present,

---

[19] W. F. J. Knight, *Roman Vergil*, pp. 167, 170.
[20] *The Triad*.

and their organization is most subtle. Wordsworth's theme is the red flower that is always drooping, seems always to be dying, yet never dies, its "life passing not away":

> A flower how rich in sadness! Even thus stoops,
> (Sentient by Grecian sculpture's marvellous power),
> Thus leans, with hanging brow and body bent
> Earthward in uncomplaining languishment,
> The dying Gladiator. So, sad Flower!
> ('Tis Fancy guides me willing to be led,
> Though by a slender thread,)
> So drooped Adonis, bathed in sanguine dew
> Of his death-wound, when he from innocent air
> The gentlest breath of resignation drew;
> While Venus in a passion of despair
> Rent, weeping over him, her golden hair
> Spangled with drops of that celestial shower.
> She suffered, as Immortals sometimes do. . . .

The flower is compared with the sculptured figure that seems to be alive, and then with the mythical—the fighter and the lover who were both killed in sport. This is a large achievement in very small compass; ranging from flesh to stone and from stone to story, learning from each the same lesson which is also different because of their varying conditions. The passage has a great and almost anonymous distinction, like the blue of sky, and seems to resolve the inexplicable in its subject through some mystery of style. Wordsworth the unfanciful has reached an extreme of fancy which before and since has been the province of old imaginations.

This preoccupation with mere art is seen to be nothing limited. The starlit dome, in Yeats's *Byzantium,*

> disdains
> All that man is,
> All mere complexities,
> The fury and the mire of human veins.

Wordsworth also moves towards art, but not in order to oppose it to nature as Yeats does. His art is not in this way disdainful: there is no parallel to Yeats's rhetorical ascent towards his "artifice of eternity." Wordsworth placed the same human limits on art as on nature, but the difference between the two orders, as he experienced it, helped him in his poetry. *Love Lies Bleeding* has an added richness in its expression of suffering through art. All the figures suffer, in the modes of statuesque, literary and pictorial; until in the end suffering and immortality are brought together.

It was the fact of suffering that first set Wordsworth thinking about the necessity of "another and a better world": struck down by his brother's death, he suggested an answer which may easily prove small and rigid; a philosophy of pain, of life to be undergone but not assented to. That he escaped such an issue is due to his taking firm hold of the fact that God too must suffer. We have already studied *Hart-Leap Well* as an essay in the problem of pain, in which Wordsworth is undecided whether he is writing a landscape poem about an animal that dies where it was born, or asserting God's love for "unoffending creatures" like the hart. There is a third possibility, not hinted at in the poem, but clearly in Wordsworth's mind when he wrote some blank-verse lines a very short time before *Hart-Leap Well* itself. He says that a trance came over him when he stood at the well, thinking about the

> hunted beast, who there
> Had yielded up his breath, the awful trance,
> The vision of humanity, and of God
> The Mourner, God the Sufferer, when the heart
> Of his poor Creatures suffers wrongfully. . . .[21]

Hart-Leap Well was written too soon for Wordsworth to turn this experience to account. Later, in *Love Lies Bleeding* and in other poems, he is able to think of sadness as a kind of wealth, and suffering not without its divine likeness. And Wordsworth's Christianity also becomes rich, through acceptance of the consequences of the Incarnation. Eternal movement from heaven earthward, there manifested, justifies poetic effort; for although the poet must nourish his imagination at the "secondary founts" of time and space, he is still being "tutored for eternity."

In this there is a leaning on God, in His guarantee of the world for poets as for all men. Wordsworth accepts Bradley's dramatic conclusion that appearance *is* reality, but the conclusion rests in the life of the Trinity, as a matter of faith. In his early poetry the star is an important feature of the greater landscape: it helps the Pedlar, in his childhood, to reach thought-in-sense, and is one of the types of eternity. Now it serves a general transcendental purpose, and is of particular interest for its power "to testify of Love and Grace divine." The stars appear

> to mortal eye,
> Blended in absolute serenity,
> And free from semblance of decline;

and the certain mortality of stars does not gainsay this appearance:

> What if those bright fires
> Shine subject to decay,
> Sons haply of extinguished sires,

[21] [*Home at Grasmere,* MS variant, in *Poetical Works,* vol. 5, 319—Ed.]

> Themselves to lose their light, or pass away
> Like clouds before the wind,
> Be thanks poured out to Him whose hand bestows,
> Nightly, on human kind
> That vision of endurance and repose.

Often, as here in the *Vernal Ode,* reliance on the hand that sustains through mortal change and gratitude to the hand that bestows, are found together. In *The Primrose of the Rock,* Wordsworth thinks of the flower as a "link in Nature's chain," and traces this chain, link by link, to God. His late lyrical verse, Christian and conventional rather in the manner of eighteenth-century hymns, has been underestimated by those anxious to see this much and to see no more. Originality has many kinds: Wordsworth, like Burke, his counsellor in politics, can handle received ideas with authority deriving from a serene largeness of scale and vital control of emphasis. This primrose he sees, in its stem

> faithful to the root,
> That worketh out of view;
> And to the rock the root adheres
> In every fibre true.
>
> Close clings to earth the living rock,
> Though threatening still to fall;
> The earth is constant to her sphere;
> And God upholds them all:
> So blooms this lonely Plant, nor dreads
> Her annual funeral.

The immortality of succession becomes very dear to Wordsworth, as an earthly witness of eternal creative purpose. It also helps him in his personal struggle for humility and abatement of natural egotism: he is always trying to see himself a creature, to impress his finitude. In 1845 he instructed his printer to place a short passage of blank verse at the beginning of the volume, because, he said, "I mean it to serve as a sort of Preface." [22] This is not a good poem, but it catches this particular quality of his old age. He is once more watching the night sky, and the stars, some brilliant others dim, all owing their light to God. And he addresses himself thus:

> Then, to the measure of the light vouchsafed,
> Shine, Poet! in thy place, and be content.

His putting himself in his place has important consequences. Humility issues into thanks to God for all good things, and especially for the

[22] ["If thou indeed . . . ," in *Poetical Works,* vol. 1, pp. 1, 317—ED.]

beauty of nature. Again perfectly conventional, his attitude is still worth consideration. What he calls "the religion of gratitude" can be seen at work in his poetry: gratitude is at the centre of his religious life because, as he declares, "gratitude is the handmaid to hope, and hope the harbinger of faith." [23] It is as if he returned in different spirit to his first belief in the necessary connexion of poetry and pleasure. Pleasure that is coloured by gratitude to the giver is a sacrificial thing: the very taking joy becomes a handing back to God. As the motto of his Ecclesiastical Sonnets Wordsworth uses an adaptation of George Herbert's couplet:

> A verse may finde him, who a sermon flies
> And turn delight into a sacrifice:[24]

which makes the point entirely clear; and like other borrowings in thought and language, it shows how subtle is the question of originality.

Wordsworth's youth must not be set in judgment over his old age: nor, of course, must it be denied, as Wordsworth did when he pretended that he wrote the Preface to the *Lyrical Ballads* because "prevailed upon by Mr. Coleridge." [25] When he was a young man he felt impelled to attack the accepted canons of poetic orthodoxy. When he was old, he became orthodox himself. Both states deserve serious regard; yet there is general willingness to forgive his youth ignorant and dogmatic theorising and much bad poetry, while age is scarcely listened to. Wordsworth found, as an honest man must, that orthodoxy is no easier than its opposite; and he could not achieve it without a partial recantation. In particular, there is his changed attitude to the conventional in diction and imagery, which at his best he makes the controlled means of serving new ends. But this change is itself enough to deny his poetry a hearing: the eye lights on "hoary time" and "roseate bloom" in the *Vernal Ode,* and a great poem goes unread.

Convention is thus on the circumference and at the centre of Wordsworth's late poetry: convention that is a plain matter of style leads to convention less plain and already approached through God's artistic manner, through the heraldry of nature and through action determined by accustomed forms—still a matter of style, or concern with the How of things. The last of these, style in ceremony, takes him furthest in his Christian poetry: indeed it proves to be almost the whole truth, since the religion of gratitude makes the imagination everywhere ceremonious, intent to cast experience into a form acceptable to God.

Small wonder, then, that Wordsworth has a lot to say about the ritual of belief. He likes to compare the incense that "curls in clouds Around angelic Forms" depicted on cathedral roof with the "flower-incense" of the

---

[23] *Letters,* 1821–30 (ed. de Selincourt), p. 204.
[24] *The Church-porch.*
[25] *Letters,* 1831–40 (ed. de Selincourt), p. 910.

fields and "unwearied canticles" of birds and streams.[26] In a more exact sense he is fascinated by the externals of worship. *Processions* is a study of Pagan and Christian within these terms. He recounts how

> mid the sacred grove
> Fed in the Libyan waste by gushing wells,
> The priests and damsels of Ammonian Jove
> Provoked responses with shrill canticles;
> While, in a ship begirt with silver bells,
> They round his altar bore the hornèd God,
> Old Cham, the solar Deity, who dwells
> Aloft, yet in a tilting vessel rode,
> When universal sea the mountains overflowed.

He then turns to "Roman Pomps":

> The feast of Neptune—and the Cereal Games,
> With images, and crowns, and empty cars;
> The dancing Salii—on the shields of Mars
> Smiting with fury; and a deeper dread
> Scattered on all sides by the hideous jars
> Of Corybantian cymbals, while the head
> Of Cybele was seen, sublimely turreted.

And finally to "Christian pageantries": to

> The Cross, in calm procession, borne aloft
> Moved to the chant of sober litanies,

and his sight, one Sunday morning, of Swiss worshippers

> winding, between Alpine trees
> Spiry and dark, around their House of prayer.

This again is a small poem, but powerful in its dealing with ritual forms. Of all stylistic patterns, Wordsworth sees that of ritual as the most vital and comprehensive: within it he can blend sight and sound and movement in transcendental dedication. It is the favourite retreat of the baptized imagination; and while it serves perfectly the wish to touch all spiritual conditions, it can do so without the narrowness of judgment that seems unavoidable in any direct comparison of creeds. Thus in *Processions* the frenzy and compulsion of pagan rites are justly stated, but without prejudice to the poet's Christianity.

The finest achievement in this kind is the ode *On the Power of Sound*; and not in this kind only, for all the materials of his late poetry are here blended with supreme felicity. As physical eyesight failed, Wordsworth

[26] *Devotional Incitements*.

read few books, and he must have seen less as he walked abroad; but he still composed aloud, murmuring by the hour verses to himself. This too, I think, brought him to art in his old age, and a new love for the words themselves: unashamed delight in rhetorical utterance and much experimenting with the regular and the Pindaric ode, its fittest vehicles. Praise of sound, in the present poem, is also homage to poetry, as the thing that he was born to do.

Wordsworth approaches his subject, which is the divinity of sound, by way of the familiar road from nature to art. The voices of all natural things, streams and living creatures; echoes of voice

> From rocky steep and rock-bestudded meadows
> Flung back, and, in the sky's blue caves, reborn:

the voice that furthers action:

> the peasant's whistling breath that lightens
> His duteous toil of furrowing the green earth;

the voice that sustains patriot and martyr; the voice that renders the lunatic

> aghast, as at the world
> Of reason partially let in—

all lead him to the conclusion stated at the exact middle of the poem:

> Point not these mysteries to an Art
> Lodged above the starry pole . . . ?

In its second half the ode enquires more closely how sound can be art, or "tutored passion." Working with his favourite elements of story and ritual, Wordsworth achieves an astonishing result:

> The Gift to king Amphion
> That walled a city with its melody
> Was for belief no dream:—thy skill, Arion!
> Could humanize the creatures of the sea,
> Where men were monsters. A last grace he craves,
> Leave for one chant;—the dulcet sound
> Steals from the deck o'er willing waves,
> And listening dolphins gather round.
> Self-cast, as with a desperate course,
> 'Mid that strange audience, he bestrides
> A proud One docile as a managed horse;
> And singing, while the accordant hand
> Sweeps his harp, the Master rides;
> So shall he touch at length a friendly strand,

> And he, with his preserver, shine starbright
> In memory, through silent night.

The next stanza opens in heightened and frantic splendour:

> The pipe of Pan, to shepherds
> Couched in the shadow of Maenalian pines,
> Was passing sweet; the eyeballs of the leopards,
> That in high triumph drew the Lord of vines,
> How did they sparkle to the cymbal's clang!
> While Fauns and Satyrs beat the ground
> In cadence,—and Silenus swang
> This way and that, with wild-flowers crowned.

Myth, the kingship of story, a city walled with music; salvation in knowing what song to sing, and bright eternity reached through artistic action —the tale is of some great skill truly learnt, spiritual and gracious like the poetry itself, before it shifts to the terrible brilliance of the leopards' eyeballs and the beating on the ground.

Suddenly Wordsworth returns to the natural order, addressing those "who are longing to be rid Of fable," and bidding them

>   hear
> The little sprinkling of cold earth that fell
> Echoed from the coffin-lid.

He then asks why Nature cannot achieve the artistic modulation of her own voices, adding, as a premonition of the truth, this fine Pythagorean comment:

> By one pervading spirit
> Of tones and numbers all things are controlled,
> As sages taught, where faith was found to merit
> Initiation in that mystery old.
> The heavens, whose aspect makes our minds as still
> As they themselves appear to be,
> Innumerable voices fill
> With everlasting harmony;
> The towering headlands, crowned with mist,
> Their feet among the billows, know
> That Ocean is a mighty harmonist. . . .

The Greek answer has already been anticipated by

> What more changeful than the sea?
> But over his great tides
> Fidelity presides,

from another of the late odes.[27] It prepares Wordsworth for his own conclusion. There is a kind of artistry, a meaningful ordering, in nature; in the ebb and flow of air and wash of sea. He had said so long ago, in the poetry of solitude and relationship, building thereon a magnificent and single structure. Glory is not now vanished, nor the affirmative, enfolding optimism of creative purpose: rather, delight becomes a sacrifice, and all this sounding movement confessional of the religion of gratitude:

> All worlds, all natures, mood and measure keep
> For praise and ceaseless gratulation, poured
> Into the ear of God, their Lord!

And so to the final stanza, telling how sound was before the beginning, and will survive the end:

> A Voice to Light gave Being;
> To Time, and Man his earth-born chronicler;
> A Voice shall finish doubt and dim foreseeing,
> And sweep away life's visionary stir;
> The trumpet (we, intoxicate with pride,
> Arm at its blast for deadly wars)
> To archangelic lips applied,
> The grave shall open, quench the stars.

Not sound exactly, but a Voice, which is also, in the poem's final line, "the WORD that shall not pass away." He is using a Semitic and European highroad in this language of the Word, a convention that becomes commandingly personal in his apocalyptic vision of Thought Self-Voiced, of divine Action-in-Utterance perfecting the Christian mystery of life. What can be understood by the Word that was made flesh? For this essay the answer must rest in the energy and coherence of Wordsworth's transcendental symbolism.

I would not claim too much. There is no *Tempest* lying unregarded in this late work, or even such poetry as would reverse the universal judgment that the best is early. Even so, it has been grossly underestimated, too easily slipped into place to serve large theories of Romantic defeat. The final privacy of greatness in style has escaped notice. Wordsworth was not silenced by the music of Christianity, nor stifled by Victorian morals. He was profoundly changed. He writes now of stories and strange ritual acts, of "doubt and dim foreseeing," of the witness of faith and the spiritual eye: his waterfall-trumpeter is now the archangel.

---

[27] *The Triad.*

Chronology of Important Dates

1770	Born 7 April at Cockermouth, Cumberland.
1778	His mother, Ann Wordsworth, dies.
1779	Enters Hawkshead Grammar School, near Esthwaite Lake in the heart of the Lake Country. Boards at the cottage of Ann Tyson.
1783	His father, John Wordsworth, dies.
1787–91	At St. John's College, Cambridge University.
1790	Walking tour with a college friend, Robert Jones, in France, Switzerland, and Germany, one year after the fall of the Bastille.
1791	Tours North Wales with Robert Jones and climbs Mount Snowdon.
1791–92	Lives in France; becomes a fervent advocate of the French Revolution; has a love affair with Annette Vallon, who on December 15, 1792, bears his daughter, Anne-Caroline.
1793	Publishes *An Evening Walk* and *Descriptive Sketches*.
1795	A friend, Raisley Calvert, dies and leaves Wordsworth a legacy sufficient to allow him to live by his poetry.
1795–98	With his sister Dorothy settles at Racedown, Dorset, then at Alfoxden. Close association with Coleridge, living nearby at Nether Stowey, 1797–98.
1798	September: Publishes *Lyrical Ballads, with a Few Other Poems* with Coleridge; the "other poems" included "Tintern Abbey." The second edition, with Wordsworth's great "Preface," was published in 1800.
1798–99	Spends a cold and lonely winter with Dorothy at Goslar, Germany.
1799	Settles with Dorothy at Dove Cottage, Grasmere. Writes the first version of *The Prelude*, in two parts.
1802	Marries Mary Hutchinson.
1805	February 6: His brother, John Wordsworth, drowned in the wreck of his ship, the *Abergavenny*. May: *The Prelude*, in thirteen books, completed but left unpublished.

1807	Publishes *Poems in Two Volumes*, often said to mark the end of "the great decade" of his poetry.
1810–12	Estranged from Coleridge; their reconciliation fell short of the old intimacy.
1813–42	Distributor of stamps (i.e., tax collector) for Westmorland. May 1813: Moves to Rydal Mount, near Ambleside.
1814	Publishes *The Excursion*.
1835	Dorothy suffers a permanent mental collapse.
1843	Succeeds Robert Southey as poet laureate.
1850	April 23: Dies at Rydal Mount. July: *The Prelude*, in fourteen books, published posthumously.

Notes on the Editor and Contributors

M. H. ABRAMS, the editor of this volume, is Professor of English at Cornell. His writings on the romantic period include *The Mirror and the Lamp: Romantic Theory and the Critical Tradition* (1953) and *Natural Supernaturalism: Tradition and Revolution in Romantic Literature* (1971).

HAROLD BLOOM, Professor of English at Yale, has written, among other books, *Shelley's Mythmaking* (1959), *Blake's Apocalypse* (1963), and *The Visionary Company: A Reading of English Romantic Poetry* (1961).

A. C. BRADLEY, Professor of Poetry at Oxford and one of the most distinguished scholar-critics of his day, wrote *Shakespearean Tragedy* (1904) and *Oxford Lectures on Poetry* (1909).

CLEANTH BROOKS, one of the best known of the American "New Critics," is Professor of English at Yale. Among his books are *Modern Poetry and the Tradition* (1939), *The Well Wrought Urn* (1947), and *William Faulkner* (1963).

JOHN F. DANBY, Professor of English at the University College of North Wales, has published *The Simple Wordsworth: Studies in the Poems, 1797–1807* (1960) and *William Wordsworth: "The Prelude" and Other Poems* (1963).

PAUL DE MAN, after having taught at Harvard, Cornell, Johns Hopkins, and Zurich, is Professor of Comparative and French Literature at Yale. He has written a number of essays on romantic and postromantic European literature, as well as *Blindness and Insight: Essays in the Rhetoric of Contemporary Criticism* (1971).

DAVID RUSSELL FERRY, Professor of English at Wellesley College, is a poet and critic, and author of *The Limits of Mortality: An Essay on Wordsworth's Major Poems* (1959).

GEOFFREY H. HARTMAN is Professor of English and Comparative Literature at Yale. His books include *The Unmediated Vision* (1954), *Wordsworth's Poetry, 1787–1814* (1964), and *Beyond Formalism: Literary Essays, 1958–1970* (1970).

NEIL HERTZ, who teaches English literature at Cornell, has written various essays in criticism and is at work on a study of the Miltonic tradition through Wordsworth.

JOHN JONES, a Fellow of Merton College, Oxford, is author of a study of Wordsworth's poetry, *The Egotistical Sublime* (1954), of *On Aristotle and Greek Tragedy* (1962), and of *John Keats's Dream of Truth* (1969).

ROBERT D. MAYO is Professor of English at Northwestern University, a scholar in English fiction and periodical literature, and author of *The English Novel in the Magazines, 1740–1815* (1962).

STEPHEN MAXFIELD PARRISH, Professor of English at Cornell, is coauthor (with Hyder Rollins) of *Keats and the Bostonians* (1951) and author of *The Art of the Lyrical Ballads* (1972). He is also general editor of the Cornell Wordsworth Series of editions, from the manuscripts, of all Wordsworth's long poems.

DAVID PERKINS, Associate Professor of English at Harvard, has written *The Quest for Permanence: The Symbolism of Wordsworth Shelley and Keats* (1959) and *Wordsworth and the Poetry of Sincerity* (1964) and has edited the anthology *English Romantic Writers* (1967).

LIONEL TRILLING is one of the most distinguished of contemporary critics and essayists, University Professor at Columbia, whose critical writings include *Matthew Arnold* (1939), *The Liberal Imagination* (1950), *The Opposing Self* (1955), and *Beyond Culture: Essays on Learning and Literature* (1965).

ALFRED NORTH WHITEHEAD was the eminent mathematician, philosopher, and essayist who, with Bertrand Russell, wrote *Principia Mathematica* (1910–13), the foundation work of modern symbolic logic. His most widely read books, combining his philosophical ideas with excursions into intellectual history, are *Science and the Modern World* (1926) and *Adventures of Ideas* (1933).

JONATHAN WORDSWORTH, a descendant of the poet's brother Christopher, is a Fellow of Exeter College, Oxford, and a Trustee of the Wordsworth Library at Dove Cottage. He is the author of *The Music of Humanity: A Critical Study of Wordsworth's "Ruined Cottage"* (1969) and of various essays on Wordsworth.

Selected Bibliography

I. EDITIONS

The standard edition of the poems (exclusive of *The Prelude*) is *The Poetical Works*, edited by Ernest de Selincourt and Helen Darbishire (5 vols., Oxford, 1940–49). The same scholars have edited *The Prelude*, with the texts of 1805 and 1850 on facing pages (revised edition, Oxford, 1959); a new edition of these two versions of *The Prelude*, edited by J. C. Maxwell, is available in a Penguin paperback (1971). A convenient one-volume collection of all Wordsworth's poems, including *The Prelude* of 1850, was edited by Thomas Hutchinson for Oxford Standard Authors (revised by E. de Selincourt, London, 1950).

The Letters of William and Dorothy Wordsworth was edited by de Selincourt in six volumes, Oxford, 1935–39; a revised version, edited by C. L. Shaver, is in process, 1967– . A useful collection of the *Literary Criticism of William Wordsworth* was edited by Paul M. Zall (Lincoln, Neb., 1966).

II. BIOGRAPHY

Harper, George McLean. *William Wordsworth: His Life, Works, and Influence.* 2 vols., London, 1916; rev. 1929.

Margoliouth, H. M. *Wordsworth and Coleridge, 1795–1835.* London, 1953.

Moorman, Mary. *William Wordsworth.* 2 vols., Oxford, 1957, 1965.

III. CRITICAL STUDIES

James V. Logan, *Wordsworthian Criticism: A Guide and Bibliography* (Columbus, Ohio, 1961), combines a summary history of the critical treatments of Wordsworth with a bibliographical listing of critical books and essays, 1850–1944. For criticism since 1944, see Elton F. Henley and David H. Stamm, *Wordsworthian Criticism, 1945–1964* (New York, 1965), and the annual bibliography of "The Romantic Movement" in *English Literary History* (to 1949), *Philological Quarterly* (1950–1964), and *English Language Notes* (1965–).

Early critical writings on Wordsworth which have had enduring influence: S. T. Coleridge, *Biographia Literaria* (1817), especially Chapter XXII; William Hazlitt, in *Lectures on the English Poets* (1818) and in *The Spirit of the Age*

(1825); Matthew Arnold, "Wordsworth," *Essays in Criticism: Second Series* (London, 1888); Walter Raleigh, *Wordsworth* (London, 1903); A. C. Bradley, in *Oxford Lectures on Poetry* (London, 1909).

A. BOOK-LENGTH STUDIES OF THE POETRY

Bateson, F. W. *Wordsworth: A Reinterpretation.* London, 1954.
Danby, John F. *The Simple Wordsworth: Studies in the Poems, 1797–1807.* New York, 1960.
Darbishire, Helen. *The Poet Wordsworth.* Oxford, 1950.
Ferry, David. *The Limits of Mortality: An Essay on Wordsworth's Major Poems.* Middletown, Conn., 1959.
Hartman, Geoffrey H. *The Unmediated Vision.* New Haven, Conn., 1954.
———. *Wordsworth's Poetry, 1787–1814.* New Haven, Conn., 1964.
Jones, John. *The Egotistical Sublime: A History of Wordsworth's Imagination.* London, 1954.
Marsh, Florence. *Wordsworth's Imagery.* New Haven, Conn., 1952.
Miles, Josephine. *Wordsworth and the Vocabulary of Emotion.* Berkeley, 1942.
Murray, Roger N. *Wordsworth's Style: Figures and Themes in the "Lyrical Ballads" of 1800.* Lincoln, Neb., 1967.
Perkins, David. *The Quest for Permanence: The Symbolism of Wordsworth Shelley and Keats.* Cambridge, Mass., 1959.
———. *Wordsworth and the Poetry of Sincerity.* Cambridge, Mass., 1964.
Sperry, W. L. *Wordsworth's Anti-Climax.* Cambridge, Mass., 1933.
Woodring, Carl. *Wordsworth.* Boston, 1964.
Wordsworth, Jonathan. *The Music of Humanity: A Critical Study of Wordsworth's "Ruined Cottage."* London, 1969.

B. "THE PRELUDE"

Abrams, M. H. *Natural Supernaturalism: Tradition and Revolution in Romantic Literature.* New York, 1971. See especially chapters 1, 2, 5–7.
Gallie, W. B. "Is *The Prelude* a Philosophical Poem?" *Philosophy,* 22 (1947).
Havens, R. D. *The Mind of a Poet.* 2 vols. Baltimore, 1941. A detailed commentary on *The Prelude,* traditional in its views.
Lindenberger, Herbert. *On Wordsworth's "Prelude."* Princeton, 1963.
Wordsworth, Jonathan. "The Growth of a Poet's Mind." *Cornell Library Journal* (Spring 1970). Discusses the manuscript version of the two-part *Prelude* of 1799.

C. WORDSWORTH'S IDEAS AND THEIR SOURCES

Beach, Joseph Warren. *The Concept of Nature in Nineteenth-Century English Poetry.* New York, 1956.

Beatty, Arthur. *William Wordsworth: His Doctrine and Art in Their Historical Relations.* Madison, 1922; rev. 1927. Discloses, but overemphasizes, the influence of David Hartley's associationist psychology.

Durrant, Geoffrey. *Wordsworth and the Great System: A Study of Wordsworth's Poetic Universe.* Cambridge, England, 1970.

Stallknecht, Newton P. *Strange Seas of Thought: Studies in William Wordsworth's Philosophy of Man and Nature.* Bloomington, Ind., 1945; rev. 1958.

Willey, Basil. " 'Nature' in Wordsworth." In Willey, *The Eighteenth-Century Background.* London, 1950.

D. CRITICAL ESSAYS

Following is a highly selective list of essays not included in this anthology that indicates the diversity of subjects and views in recent criticism of Wordsworth's poems.

Abrams, M. H. "English Romanticism: The Spirit of the Age." In *Romanticism Reconsidered,* edited by Northrop Frye. New York, 1963. Reprinted in *Romanticism and Consciousness,* edited by Harold Bloom. New York, 1970.

———. "Wordsworth and Coleridge on Diction and Figures," *English Institute Essays* (1952).

Benziger, James. "Tintern Abbey Revisited." *PMLA,* 65 (1950).

Brooks, Cleanth. "Wordsworth and Human Suffering: Notes on Two Early Poems." In *From Sensibility to Romanticism,* edited by F. W. Hilles and Harold Bloom. New York, 1965.

Bush, Douglas. "Wordsworth: A Minority Report." In *Wordsworth Centenary Studies,* edited by G. T. Dunklin. Princeton, 1951. An attempt to show Wordsworth's limitations as a poet for the present age.

Davie, Donald. "Dionysus in *Lyrical Ballads.*" In *Wordsworth's Mind and Art,* edited by A. W. Thomson. London, 1969.

———. "Syntax in the Blank Verse of Wordsworth's *Prelude.*" *Articulate Energy* (1955).

de Man, Paul. "Symbolic Landscape in Wordsworth and Yeats." In *In Defense of Reading,* edited by R. A. Brower and Richard Poirier. Cambridge, Mass., 1962.

Empson, William. "Sense in *The Prelude.*" In Empson, *The Structure of Complex Words.* London, 1952.

Frost, Robert. "A Tribute to Wordsworth" (1950). *Cornell Library Journal* (Spring 1970).

Grob, Alan. "Wordsworth's 'Nutting.' " *Journal of English and Germanic Philology,* 51 (1962). Argues against the interpretation by Perkins (see Perkins's essay in this volume) and by Ferry, in *The Poetry of Mortality* (Middletown, Conn., 1959).

Hartman, Geoffrey. "Wordsworth, Inscriptions, and Romantic Nature Poetry." In *From Sensibility to Romanticism,* edited by F. W. Hilles and Harold Bloom. New York, 1965.

Huxley, Aldous. "Wordsworth in the Tropics." In Huxley, *Collected Essays*. New York, 1959.

Knight, G. Wilson. "The Wordsworthian Profundity." In Knight, *The Starlit Dome: Studies in the Poetry of Vision*. London, 1941.

Langbaum, Robert. "The Evolution of Soul in Wordsworth's Poetry." In Langbaum, *The Modern Spirit*. New York, 1970.

Leavis, F. R. "Wordsworth." In Leavis, *Revaluation: Tradition and Development in English Poetry*. London, 1936.

Pottle, Frederick A. "The Eye and the Object in the Poetry of Wordsworth." In *Wordsworth Centenary Studies*, edited by G. T. Dunklin. Princeton, 1951. Reprinted in *Romanticism and Consciousness*, edited by Harold Bloom. New York, 1970.

Trilling, Lionel. "The Immortality Ode." In Trilling, *The Liberal Imagination*. New York, 1942. Reprinted in *English Romantic Poets*, edited by M. H. Abrams. New York, 1960.

Williams, Charles. "Wordsworth." In Williams, *The English Poetic Mind*. Oxford, 1932. Reprinted in *English Romantic Poets*, edited by M. H. Abrams. New York, 1960.

Woolley, Mary Lynn. "Wordsworth's Symbolic Vale as It Functions in *The Prelude*." *Studies in Romanticism*, 7 (1968).

Wordsworth, Jonathan. "The Climbing of Snowdon." In *Bicentenary Wordsworth Studies in Memory of John Alban Finch*. Ithaca, N.Y., 1970. In opposition to the "apocalyptic" reading of this passage in *The Prelude* by David Ferry and Geoffrey Hartman.

———. "William Wordsworth 1770–1969." *Proceedings of the British Academy*, 60 (1969).

Index of Titles

This index lists the poems and prose-writings by Wordsworth that are discussed in the critical essays. Page-numbers in **boldface** indicate fairly extensive discussion; other references are printed in *italics*.

Affliction of Margaret, The, *17*, **82**
Alice Fell, or Poverty, **16**; *19*
Anecdote for Fathers, *15*
Animal Tranquillity and Decay, **58**
Borderers, The, *86*
Brook! whose society . . . , *195*
Brothers, The, *17*, *131*
Complaint of a Forsaken Indian Woman, The, *82*
Composed upon Westminster Bridge, September 3, 1802, **42–44**; *189*
Crescent-moon, The, *195*
Cuckoo at Laverna, The, *193*
Cuckoo-clock, The, *192*
Dark plume fetch me, A (The River Duddon, XVII), *195*
Devotional Incitements, **200–1**
Ecclesiastical Sonnets, *200*
Elegiac Stanzas . . . Peele Castle, **26**, *96*, *99*
Emigrant Mother, The, *82*
Essay, Supplementary to the Preface (1815), **1–2**; *3*, *157*
Excursion, The, **188–90**; *14*, *17*, *18*, *19*, *20*, *21*, *56*, *95*, *120*, *150*, *193*, *195*
Extempore Effusion upon . . . James Hogg, *18*
Gipsies, **36–38**; *40*
Goody Blake and Harry Gill, *15*, **69**
Hart-Leap Well, *198*

Home at Grasmere, **165–68**; *156*, *160*, *198*
I wandered lonely as a cloud, **40–42**; *15*
Idiot Boy, The, **85–94**; *5*, *15*, *57–58*, *82*
If thou indeed derive thy light from Heaven, *199*
Lines Written in Early Spring, *71*
Lines Written near Richmond, *71*
Love Lies Bleeding, **196–97**; *198*
Lucy Gray, or Solitude, **19–20**; *16*
Lyrical Ballads, **67–74**, **86–87**; *57*, *58*, *59*, *60*, *76–77*
Mad Mother, The, *82*
Michael, *17*, *101*, *123*, *131*
Night-Piece, A, **108–11**; *118*, *120*
Nutting, **29–30**
Ode, 1815, *13*
Ode: Intimations of Immortality, **170–87**, *191*; *5*, *58*, *81*, *98*, *103*, *129*, *132*, *152*, *154*, *196*
Old Cumberland Beggar, The, **103–6**, **126**; *10*, *58–59*, *99*
On the Power of Sound, **201–4**
One who was suffering tumult in his soul, *195*
Peter Bell, **81–82**; *31*, *86–87*
Poet's Epitaph, A, *18*
Preface to Lyrical Ballads, **1, 2**; *5*, *35*, *38*, *64*, *83*, *152*, *155*, *200*
Prelude, The, **23**, **28–34**, **55–56**, **60–62**,

140–41, 145–55, 156–69, 191–92; *1, 6, 7, 10, 19, 20, 57, 65, 81, 95, 101, 103, 110, 120, 132, 143–44, 189*
Primrose of the Rock, The, *199*
Processions, 201
Prospectus to The Recluse, 156–57, 168–69; *1, 10, 17, 159, 161*
Recluse, The, 156–69; *10, 95*
Resolution and Independence, *99, 103, 130–31*
Ruined Cottage, The, 120–22, 123–32; *5, 9, 107*
Ruth, *17*
Sailor's Mother, The, *15, 17, 82*
St. Paul's, *189*
Simon Lee, *89*
Slumber did my spirit seal, A, *31–32*
Solitary Reaper, The, *19, 25*
Stanzas Written in My Pocket-copy of Thomson's Castle of Indolence, *193*
There Was a Boy, *157*
Thorn, The, 75–84; *5, 15, 17, 87, 89, 93–94*
Tintern Abbey, Lines Composed . . . Above, 95–103; *10, 17, 57, 126, 184*
To a Child: Written in her Album, *195*
To a Skylark, *190*
To the Clouds, *193*
To the Moon, Composed by the Seaside, *193*
Triad, The, *192, 196, 204*
Vernal Ode, 194–96; *192, 198–99, 200*
Waggoner, The, *85*
We are Seven, *57, 69*
White Doe of Rylstone, The, *17*
Widow on Windermere Side, The, *190*
Yew-tree, Lines Left upon a Seat in a, *71*

Practical Suggestions for Teaching

Alice Miel, Editor

FROM THINKING TO BEHAVING

LOUISE BERMAN

Teachers College Press
Teachers College, Columbia University

Practical Suggestions for Teaching
edited by Alice Miel

From Thinking to Behaving

Practical Suggestions for Teaching

TITLES IN THIS SERIES

Teaching the Slow Learner
W. B. Featherstone

Science Experiences for Elementary Schools
Charles K. Arey

Individual Parent-Teacher Conferences
Katherine E. D'Evelyn

Building Children's Science Concepts
Mary Sheckles

Improving Children's Facility in Problem Solving
Alma Bingham

A Classroom Teacher's Guide to Physical Education
C. Eric Pearson

Observing and Recording the Behavior of Young Children
Dorothy H. Cohen and *Virginia Stern*

Helping Children in Oral Communication
Alberta Munkers

Helping Children Accept Themselves and Others
Helen L. Gillham

Independent Activities for Creative Learning
Helen Fisher Darrow and *R. Van Allen*

Phonics and the Teaching of Reading
Dolores Durkin

Reading Improvement in the Junior High School
Deborah Elkins

Learning through Movement
Betty Rowen

From Thinking to Behaving
Louise M. Berman

FROM THINKING
TO BEHAVING

LOUISE M. BERMAN
Associate Secretary
The Association for Curriculum
Research and Development, NEA

TEACHERS COLLEGE PRESS
*Teachers College,
Columbia University, New York*

© 1967 by Teachers College, Columbia University
Library of Congress Catalog Card Number: 67-19025

MANUFACTURED IN THE UNITED STATES OF AMERICA

EDITOR'S FOREWORD

This booklet had an unusual beginning. In 1960, Teachers College, Columbia University conducted a special seminar for a group of Iranian educators responsible for preparation of textbooks in their nation. The assistance of Louise Berman was sought for a presentation on the subject of "Teaching Devices Built into Textbooks."

In preparing for the group from Iran, Miss Berman did preliminary work on the notion that the development of a thinking person is a justifiable guiding aim of a textbook writer. Since that time, she has carried her investigation further, delving into studies of creativity and valuing. She has continued to explore ways teachers not only can make optimum use of assignments suggested in textbooks, but can help their students go beyond a class text in searching for and processing information.

The textbook continues to be a prime material of instruction the world over. If more teachers can learn to use it, along with other sources of information, as a means of developing thoughtful persons, the quality of education can be greatly increased. Teachers at all levels of education will find Dr. Berman's publication a source of challenge and assistance in improving the quality of the tasks they set for students.

ALICE MIEL

PREFACE

Many teachers want their students to become thoughtful persons. Such teachers usually see that the quality of their assignments can make a crucial difference in the ways their students take in, process, and use information. They realize that their assignments must not only be appealing and diversified but must also lead to significant learning. They are aware that the ultimate test of quality of assignments is the ability and inclination of students to set worthwhile tasks for themselves.

This little book deals with a variety of instructional devices. Teacher-initiated tasks, textbook assignments, and other commercially produced instructional materials are given major attention although the technicalities of programed learning are not treated. The problem of quality assignments bears much fuller treatment than is possible within these pages, but consideration of the ideas that follow may focus some fresh insights on the problem.

In dealing with the topic of ensuring high-quality tasks and assignments for the student, two basic assumptions are made. First, the teacher needs a frame of reference—some basic principles, perhaps, or a set of anticipated student behaviors—to guide the development of learning activities. Second, materials like textbooks, maligned in some quarters and praised in others, can, in most instances, be an aid in fostering the kinds of behavior that are crucial in today's world. Obviously, no one kind of instructional material can do the total job, but an evaluation of the study guides or assignments contained in the instructional material can help the teacher decide where he needs to exercise his own ingenuity and creativeness in designing tasks to promote learning.

Believing that it is useful for a teacher to state goals or objectives in behavioral terms, I have attempted in Chapter One to describe human actions around the focal point of the thoughtful person. These actions run the gamut from the familiar and the known to totally new constructs that necessitate highly imaginative and creative thinking. That an understanding of various thought processes can serve as a means to help man better develop his other uniquely human abilities is a central idea. To develop proficiency in thinking apart from such other human processes as decision-making, communicating, knowing, and loving means the enhancement of only one part of the person. To develop skill in thinking in the context of the total human personality means the enhancement of the whole person and not merely the development of the rational man. It is in this latter framework that this book was written.

Following the discussion of the thoughtful person in Chapter One, Chapter Two discusses the special assistance that the teacher, using textbooks and other instructional materials, can give children and youth in helping them achieve or further develop each of the stated behaviors. The focus is not on the total role of the textbook or other materials in the classroom but rather on the contribution of questions and other suggestions at the ends of chapters, of other prepackaged materials, and of teacher-planned tasks to a classroom program carefully designed to develop the thoughtful person. As teachers reflect on the behaviors described and the tasks suggested to promote them, they will note that some behaviors lend themselves rather well to development through experiences than can be found in certain textbooks, whereas others may require carefully designed teacher-initiated activities. In some instances, the limitation of a particular textbook device is noted; in others, the reader may need to be his own judge as to whether a textbook task or a teacher-planned assignment can best accomplish a stated purpose. It should be noted that "textbook," as used throughout this book, may refer to looseleaf materials and kits as well as to the traditional book.

It has not been easy to write Chapter Two. First, the book is addressed to teachers from the primary grades through the secondary grades, for the basic principles expressed seem appropriate for all grades. The reader will note that most of the illustrations in Chapter Two are at the reading level of children of third grade or above but may be adapted for younger children. Furthermore, an attempt is made to include a number of content fields in the illustrative material. However, the teacher may not find many illustrations in his particular field. Again, he may adapt the material.

After a representative application of the behavioral statements of Chapter One to tasks in Chapter Two, next steps are given in Chapter Three for the teacher who wishes to go beyond what has been suggested. First, the reader is invited to question, refine, and elaborate on many of the assumptions made in Chapter One. If such questioning and elaborating takes place, the book will serve a useful function, for basic to each teacher's success in establishing quality conditions for teaching and learning is his personal view of the behavior he wishes to develop. Obviously, this behavior can be too narrowly defined and can stifle the individual potential of the students whom the teacher serves; nonetheless, a teacher without a sense of direction is like a traveler without a map or guide.

Preface

Then the reader is urged to develop instructional tasks beyond those suggested in this volume. The writer by no means wishes to leave the impression that the textbook or other commercially produced materials should determine the tasks of instruction. Rather, the intent of this volume is to acknowledge that, since these materials are ordinarily used in some form in the classroom, the teacher should seek to use them as intelligently and wisely as possible with an awareness of what these tools can do. Such awareness may then lead the teacher to devise instructional tasks that far surpass in usefulness any found in current teaching materials.

Finally, the reader is invited to analyze instructional tasks. Consideration is given to questions that should be raised on the nature of assignments, to the nature of the total program, and to the ways in which students are made aware of the purposes of tasks they undertake.

In a more personal vein, I wish to acknowledge many sources of ideas and encouragement, especially those persons who stimulated me during my years in the classroom to develop my own philosophy of teaching and to select those modes and materials of instruction that would best carry out my purposes. I am also indebted to university students and professors who have raised questions relative to the *status quo* of the curriculum in light of what we can hypothesize and know about man's nature. Publishers, both in the United States and abroad, have provided many insights by inviting a dialogue about existing instructional materials.

Two graduate students were particularly helpful in the preparation of the manuscript. Mrs. Marta Arango Ziegenhagen of Colombia, South America, currently of Berkeley, California, stimulated interest in the initial stages of the writing through her concern about the process of reassessing and developing instructional materials in other countries. In the final stages, Miss Mary Lou Usery, doctoral intern, College of Education, Ohio State University, made many useful suggestions for the improvement of the manuscript and especially of the illustrative material.

Mrs. Glenys Unruh, Assistant to the Superintendent of Schools, University City, Missouri, and Chairman of the ASCD Commission on Current Curriculum Developments, made a number of valuable critical observations. To Prof. Alice Miel I am grateful for encouragement in the development of what seemed to be a potentially useful idea, for her precise suggestions and thought-provoking questions, and for her sustained help along the way.

How can the teacher provide suitable learning experiences to help students become increasingly thoughtful? The pages that follow invite a contemplation of the answer.

L. M. B.

Washington, D.C.
February 1967

CONTENTS

Editor's Foreword

Preface

I. The Thoughtful Person   1
    What is Thinking?, 3
    Qualities of the Thoughtful Person, 11

II. Activities in the Development of the Thoughtful Person   19
    Re-examining Content, 20
    Finding Additional Information, 29
    Encouraging Creative Thinking, 35
    Applying Learnings to Current and Local Happenings, 43
    Relating Thinking and Valuing, 48
    Relating Thinking to Decision-Making, 57
    Relating Thinking to Self-Other Understanding, 61

III. Getting Started   64
    Developing a Personal Construct of the Thoughtful Person, 64
    Thinking and Planning, 65
    Analyzing the Teaching Assignment, 67

ONE

THE THOUGHTFUL PERSON

Educators, especially teachers, who care about what happens to today's children and youth, are faced with a monumental task. To find ways of helping the young cope with a world changing at a dizzying speed calls for a most penetrating look at instructional objectives, methods, and materials. Using the procedures and textbooks that were prevalent when life was not so complex and hurried can spell disaster for those going through today's elementary and secondary schools.

Discerning teachers would like to prepare students to cope intelligently with the world of which they are a part. One of the best ways of fulfilling this desire is giving students tools for handling themselves wisely as persons. One such tool is the effective use of the thinking processes. In using the term "thinking processes," the author intends to include those resources related to thinking that enable a person to function fully and capably. These resources are inextricably linked to the totality of the person—his modes of decision-making, his feelings, and his values. Thus, our concern essentially is with man as a person who thinks, whose cognitive processes make of him a unique being.

How a school system, a teacher, a ministry, or a board of education views man partially determines the nature of the curriculum. Educators who do not conceive of man as possessing the capacity for the many skills described later in this chapter will develop a much more circumscribed curriculum than those instructional leaders who are concerned about enhancing man's diversity and his many truly human traits.

How a teacher, school board, or school system view the curriculum partially determines, therefore, the use of textbooks and other commercially produced materials. In certain countries, textbooks are emphasized to the degree that ministries of education assume the responsibility for planning, writing, and distributing these materials to teachers in their schools. The textbook or similar material is considered the medium through which are taught the major ideas the culture deems important. In other countries, commercial publishing houses operate on a competitive basis, seeking to develop instructional materials attractive in format, economical in price, and incorporating the best thinking in the field. Such is the practice in the United States.

Even as countries differ in the value that they ascribe to commercially produced instructional materials, so local school systems, individual schools, principals, and teachers differ. In some places, the commercial material may be the major determinant of the curriculum, whether or not it was intended to play a key role in the classroom. In other situations, perhaps relatively few in number, the commercially produced material is used in an incidental manner, often on a self-selection basis, by the student. No one material is considered so significant that it should be studied by large groups of students in an organized manner under the direct guidance of the teacher. This view places the textbook in the category of those instructional materials that are used to implement a curriculum developed on the basis of other criteria.

Instructional materials may also be co-instructors with the teacher. The materials are integral to and part of the teacher's planning and operation in the classroom. If a teacher is to use commercial materials in this other way, major common elements must be discernible between the nature of the commercial material and the teacher's ideas. The textbook, broadly conceived, must be used in such a way that it reinforces and amplifies many of the basic ideas of the teacher, providing learning opportunities that enhance the teacher's classroom performance. The commercially produced material becomes a co-teacher.

What are the implications if commercial instructional materials are considered co-teachers? First, the teacher must have determined his goals. Second, where possible, the teacher should have an opportunity to select materials that are in line with his intent. In many instances, they may be hard to obtain, and he may need to do much adjusting and adapting of the material. Third, the teacher needs to consider those goals that he can best attain by specially planned experiences and by the textbook. Questions, assignments, and opportunities for extension of thinking and choice-making are points at which the commercial material can often provide invaluable help to the teacher. At times, the teacher may feel that the material does not develop the insights he wishes children or youth to gain about a certain project. In such cases, he himself will need to design the appropriate kind of assignment to foster the desired learning. This book provides guidance for the teacher in analyzing tasks found in textbooks and other commercial materials and in developing more appropriate study aids, questions, and assignments where necessary.

Before the purposes of this book are stated more precisely, let us give some attention to the implications of focusing on man as a thinking person.

First of all, to focus rather heavily on one attribute of man may cause some distortion since the blending of the elements of his personality are central to man's uniqueness. However, thinking is seen as a means of helping man gain increasing control over himself as a being invested with power, although that power may often be stifled. The way in which persons use thought processes partially accounts for the fact that some persons live life very fully while others tap only the minimum of its potential.

Also one cannot consider the thought processes without a realization that man is governed by feelings, desires, attitudes, and values that to a large degree determine his behavior and choices. These attributes of man often not susceptible to easy verbal symbolization and logical description or interpretation. Despite their complexity, they must be given proper attention in attempting to explain peaks and valleys in man's productivity.

Although other institutions may assist in the enhancement of many of the critical areas of personality, perhaps no institution is better able to enhance thinking skills than is the school. A school program that helps students see the relationship of a given learning experience to the development of thinking processes can do much to leave with students enduring tools, enabling them to cope more intelligently with the vicissitudes of life. If a program focusing on the thought processes is to make its full impact, however, then those for whom the program is intended need to be aware of the purposes of the program as they relate to the tasks that they perform day by day. This understanding is crucial if transfer to everyday experiences is to occur.

In view of what has been said, the purposes of this book are as follows.

(1) To develop a view of the thinking person and to relate thinking to other components of man's personality.
(2) To indicate how teaching helps, suggestions, questions, or devices included in textbooks can be used to develop thought processes.
(3) To provide for teachers a statement about the thoughtful person that can be used in analyzing textbook helps, other commercial materials, and teacher-developed assignments.

The remainder of this chapter deals with two topics. First, attention is given to a description of the components of thinking. Second, the relationship of thinking to other facets of man's personality is briefly described.

What Is Thinking?

The intent of this volume is not to treat the highly fascinating, speculative, and involved topic of thinking with any degree of thoroughness. Such is not crucial to the purpose of the book. Although writers on thinking may have some points of disagreement, there appears to be enough agreement on general principles to suggest that certain modes of thinking can be described and that learning experiences can be designed to teach the various ways of thinking.[1]

---

[1] The reader interested in detailed analyses of thinking is referred to the selected bibliography.

Beyond this, research and testing must help us determine whether phrasing questions or designing tasks in certain ways accomplish their stated purposes.

Perhaps a few words should be said about how the term "thinking" is used in this book. Although thinking has been described with varying degrees of specificity and points of emphasis, one common element is evident in most definitions. *Thinking is a process.*[2] Hence, involved in thinking is a starting point and an end product. Between these points, some knowledge is lacking. According to Bartlett, "the process moves from the start to its finish with a kind of necessity."[3] David Russell says: "Thinking is a process rather than a fixed state. It involves a sequence of ideas moving from some beginning, through some sort of pattern of relationships, to some goal or conclusion."[4]

As we examine the meaning of thinking, we must consider whether thinking takes place in conscious "interconnected steps"[5] or whether the process takes place unconsciously without individual awareness of what is happening. Probably, thinking often takes place with the individual unaware of how the steps are moving him toward his goal and of how he goes about filling in the gaps in his knowing and learning. That knowledge of how thinking occurs will improve the quality of thinking is an assumption of this writer. At the present time, however, probably few persons—either children or adults—can describe what is happening when thinking occurs.

In this book, we are not primarily concerned with perceptions that often influence the character of thinking, nor are we basically concerned with memory, that is, how the products of thinking are stored. Obviously these factors must enter in, but our prime consideration is with the process of thought, or relating previously unconnected or unrelated elements. Consideration of the motives for thinking takes place somewhat later in the book, when thinking as it applies to the total person is considered. It will also be noted that the somewhat stabilized products of thinking—images, concepts, and memories—are not central to the theme of this book. Concern is basically with the *how* of thinking.

In describing the thinking process, three major categories may be used: (1) thinking that deals primarily with the known; (2) thinking that reaches beyond the known; and (3) thinking that judges, rates, or evaluates a product. Obviously, these categories are not mutually exclusive, but let us explore in greater detail those processes that might be included in each of the above three categories.

Dealing with the Known

Much thinking involves filling in gaps in a framework that has come into being either through common usage or through the acceptance of an authority.

---

[2] In this book "thinking skills" and "thought processes" are used interchangeably.
[3] Sir Frederick Bartlett, *Thinking: An Experimental and Social Study* (New York: Basic Books, Inc., 1958), p. 76.
[4] David H. Russell, *Children's Thinking* (Boston: Ginn and Co., 1956), p. 27.
[5] Bartlett, *op. cit.*, p. 75.

The Thoughtful Person

Thinking in such instances often consists in learning to utilize efficiently concepts that have been developed by another. Languages and number systems are good examples of fields having fairly well-defined and accepted concepts. Ideas central to the natural sciences or social sciences are also examples. In thinking about ideas that are already rather fully formulated but that necessitate the individual's bringing the knowledge together into some type of systematic pattern, certain kinds of skills are used. Among these skills are classifying, organizing, generalizing, synthesizing, defining, and summarizing. Each of these skills involves the associating or converging of symbols represented by words, pictures, or situations. The emphasis in this type of thinking is not the creation of something new, but rather the assimilating and organizing of material that is already available.

It might be said in passing that each of the thinking skills listed in the previous paragraph may be placed at some point in a continuum. Each mode of thinking may help us view existing knowledge more clearly or may lead to the development of new frameworks, revealing many gaps in the knowledge of the individual. For example, if an individual generalizes about material that he has read in the text and does not include in his generalizations ideas from his own experience that may amplify the point, he is working within the accepted framework of the author. If the individual amplifies the point in terms of an experience similar to that expressed in the text, he is still working within the framework of the author. If the individual's experience is, however, very different from the author's, a totally new structure or framework may be devised.

For the present, our concern is with the individual's ability to operate within commonly accepted frameworks or those developed by other persons, such as the author of a book. Later parts of the chapter deal with the ability to bring one's own experience to bear on the insights and organizational schemes of others in order to develop new frameworks.

Now let us consider briefly each of the modes of thought that unite a series of discrete elements into a commonly accepted framework or pattern.

Classifying is the arrangement of elements with common characteristics in categories. Classifying can be taught in any subject area to any school-aged child. The ability to engage in this mode of thinking is important if persons are to engage in learning economically, efficiently, and effectively. Without the art of classifying, each distinct impression, percept, or experience becomes an entity unto itself, and the relatedness of ideas is impossible.

The person who has facility in classifying can sort through many discrete bits of information or material objects and arrange them in such a way that at least one major common characteristic is evident in the various groupings.

Organizing is a tool related to classifying in that the notion of relationship is predominant. However, organizing involves the systematic relationship of each to each, whereas classifying does not necessarily involve systematized relations within categories.[6] Organizing is the attempt to develop an "organic structure" or a "coherent unity in which each part has a special system of function."[7] Organizing may be impersonal, as when one attempts to relate ideas from text material into a coherent whole, for example, in developing a broad outline for a chapter, then going back and filling in the details. An organizing scheme may become more personalized, as when one attempts to develop a new framework from a series of readings or experiences. When a person develops a way of organizing from a series of sources, his skill must be more encompassing, for then organizing involves finding a scheme from a multitude of ideas and resources.

Generalizing involves verbalizing "formulations of relationships among concepts—they appear as rules, laws, principles, or conclusions."[8] Possible processes involved in generalizing are given by Russell:

(1) perceptual accentuation, (2) assimilation with known figures, (3) deliberate voluntary analysis, such as isolation of a particular figure, (4) suggestion of a defining response, and (5) use of a hypothesis.[9]

Generalizing enables a person to be able to see similarities despite divergent qualities of experiences, objects, or ideas. Like classifying and organizing, generalizing is another process that helps prevent waste of thinking and learning. Unlike organizing, sequential ordering is not of central concern in generalizing.

A person is generalizing when, after a series of observations, he formulates a statement that includes common central elements in the observations. He is also generalizing when he is able to select from a series of similar but somewhat different statements that one best describing a given person, idea, or situation.

Defining involves the discovery of meaning. Important in the term is attention to precision and context. Defining involves the determination of the crucial, central, or essential qualities of the term. In a sense, defining is the establishment of limits within a context. Since dictionary definitions of words often do not denote the totality of meanings, defining often involves awareness of certain emotive connotations ascribed to some words.

A person is defining when he is becoming more familiar with dictionary definitions of words. He is defining when he is giving attention to words in context or taking into account the affective overtones of the word as well as the more literal meanings. He is also defining when he explicates personal meaning which may be derived from a variety of sources.

---

[6] The notion of systematic relations is included in the definition of "classify" in *Webster's Third New International Dictionary (Unabridged)* (Springfield, Mass.: G. and C. Merriam Co., 1961).
[7] *Ibid.*, p. 1590.
[8] Russell, *op. cit.*, p. 228.
[9] *Ibid.*, p. 230.

Summarizing involves the ability to recapitulate in a brief manner. If a person can summarize adequately, he should be expert in the other modes of thinking described in this section. Precise and correct summarizing presupposes the ability to classify with accuracy, to organize within an appropriate structure, to generalize with meaning, and to define with exactness. "Summarizing is the clear and concise expression of several ideas preserving the structure and the essential points of the material."[10]

A person is summarizing when he keeps records, such as a log, a notebook, or a diary, in which he records important and central ideas of a given type and places them in a logical order.

Synthesizing involves forming parts into a whole. The quality of an individual's synthesizing ability depends on the coherence of the totality. Synthesizing differs from organizing in that organizing involves the structure or framework that allows for the relatedness of parts. Synthesizing is a more subtle skill, in that the relationship of each to each is of greater significance than the framework that gives character to the total. The person may see a relationship to a piece within another framework, or he may see relationships between frameworks. Sometimes the broad outline may be only faintly visible when a person does a good job of synthesizing; a unity among parts is, however, visible.

Synthesizing also involves more creative thinking skills than some of the other thought processes listed in this section, since synthesizing often involves many elements from personal experience. If a person can propose a way to test hypotheses or if he can pull material together for a good extemporaneous speech, he is probably employing synthesizing skills. Synthesizing is thus placed near the next section of the chapter because of its close relationship to boundary-breaking, the imaginative use of knowledge to break down man-created walls and to build more useful constructs.[11]

Reaching beyond the Known

Generally speaking, children and youth are given learning opportunities that involve relating known parts into a consistent whole. Guilford has called the skills we have just discussed "convergent" thinking skills, especially when the thinking is directed toward *one* discussion of the correct answer.[12]

In his discussion of intellect, Guilford also discusses "divergent" thinking,

---

[10] Marta Arango, "Building Independence of Judgment through the Development of Critical Thinking: Implications for the Curriculum" (Master's project, University of Wisconsin—Milwaukee, 1963), p. 59.

[11] For a detailed discussion of synthesis, see Benjamin S. Bloom, (ed.), *Taxonomy of Educational Objectives: The Classification of Educational Goals. Handbook I: Cognitive Domain* (New York: David McKay Co., Inc., 1956), PP. 162–184.

[12] For a fuller consideration, see J. P. Guilford, "Creativity: Its Measurement and Development," in Sidney J. Parnes and Harold F. Harding, (eds.), *A Source Book for Creative Thinking* (New York: Charles Scribner's Sons, 1962), pp. 151–168.

or those thought processes that go beyond that which is already known. The possession of such skills is necessary if one is to become involved in the phenomenon of creative activity, the making of something new either to the individual or to society. Those interested in creative thinking are not in total agreement about the relationship of the degree of newness of the production to creativity. Some believe that a product must be new to the larger population; others believe that if the product is new to the creator, it can be characterized as creative. For purposes of this discussion, since our concern is with the thinking of children and youth, the widespread acceptance of the product as novel is of only minor importance.

Of more concern are the types of thought process that have been discussed in much current literature on the nature of creative thinking.[13] For our purposes, we will consider these types of creative thinking: fluency, flexibility, originality, and elaboration. Related to these are such qualities as sensitivity to problems, ability to see causes, ability to predict consequences, and ability to ask good questions. Each of these aspects of boundary-breaking is now briefly considered.

Fluency is a trait that has been described in terms of four categories: word fluency, ideational fluency, associational fluency, and expressional fluency. Guilford describes these four kinds of thinking as follows:

> It is the ability to think of words rapidly, each word satisfying the same requirements, such as containing a stated letter or syllable or containing two given letters.
>
> The factor of *ideational fluency* calls for tests involving the rapid listing of meaningful words in a specified category or the listing of ideas to meet meaningful requirements, for example, to list objects that are solid, white and edible. In another test the examinee names as many uses as he can for a common brick. In still another he writes as many titles as he can think of for a given short story. In any test of ideational fluency, speed is important and quality does not matter, the score being the total number of acceptable responses. Winston Churchill must have had this ability to a high degree. Clement Attlee is reported to have said about him recently that no matter what problem came up, Churchill always seemed to have about ten ideas. The trouble was, Attlee reported, he did not know which was the good one.
>
> *Associational fluency* is the ability to list words that bear some relation to a given word. The task is different from that in connection with ideational fluency, for in the latter the responses belong to a specified class. An example would be naming synonyms to the given word "dark." Other relations could be specified and would probably serve in a measure of associational fluency.
>
> *Expressional fluency* is the ability to put words into organized phrases and sentences. In one test, the examinee is told to make four-word sentences and

---

[13] E. Paul Torrance, of the University of Georgia, has done an extensive amount of writing and research in the development of creative thinking skills in children. See Selected Bibliography.

is given the same initial letters of the words to be used in all his responses. Given the initial letters w_____ c_____ e_____ n_____, one might write: "We can eat nuts," "Whence came Eve Newton," and so on. The test would work about as well without the four initial letters being given.[14]

For purposes of this book, the distinctions that Guilford makes concerning fluency are not central to the broader concept of the term. His ideas are included, however, for those who wish to pursue in greater detail the several meanings of fluency.

Flexibility is another characteristic of creative thinking discussed by Guilford.

> In the investigation of the hypothesis of flexibility of thinking we have found two different abilities. One of these we have designated as *spontaneous flexibility* and the other as *adaptive flexibility*. The reason for these particular qualifying adjectives, "spontaneous" and "adaptive," is that in the first case the thinker is flexible even when he has no need to be, whereas in the second case he would fail to solve a problem if he were not flexible.[15]

Originality involves thinking that has elements of the unusual—novelty, freshness, and cleverness. These qualities are usually related to some standard or, rather, the deviation from some standard. The high school youth, for example, may be attempting to perfect his skills in written communication. In his striving for a style of his own, he may try on the styles of Mark Twain or Ralph Waldo Emerson. Eventually, the youth may emerge with a unique style. Such is originality.

Ability to elaborate involves building up and changing an idea that may not necessarily be original. If one can elaborate well, he can embroider an idea so that it makes more sense and has increased meaning. The person who exhibits skill in elaboration may not necessarily have new or unusual ideas, but may be the group member who is able to develop someone else's idea to the degree that it has merit.

Sensitivity to problems is the awareness of problems or gaps. Seeing deficiencies or defects is often prerequisite to motivation for other types of creative thinking. Guilford has developed tests that measure this quality:

> One test calls for stating things that are wrong with common devices such as the telephone, the refrigerator, or the electric toaster. The other calls for stating things wrong with social institutions such as national elections, divorce laws, or tipping.[16]

The person who is sensitive to problems is quickly alert to the strengths and weaknesses of a situation. He is able to pinpoint those problems that merit attention and can discriminate between problems of major importance and those of lesser concern.

Seeing causes is necessary in looking at the total complexity of a situation.

[14] Guilford, *op. cit.*, pp. 157–58.
[15] *Loc. cit.*
[16] *Ibid.*, p. 157.

To be able to discern the central reason for an action is critical to creative thinking. Being sensitive to problems is an important skill, but possessing the ability to identify sources and roots of problems is even more important to imaginative thinking.

People who have this skill evidence it in a variety of ways. The young child may understand why the wheel does not stay on his bicycle. The teen-ager may notice not only that his friend is irritable but also that his father's being in the hospital is necessitating his friend's working many extra hours.

Predicting consequences involves seeing the potential outcomes or consequences of a contemplated action. This ability includes assessing the potential usefulness or value of a given action.

The person who anticipates and predicts consequences is adding a dimension of practicality to creativity. His prediction of consequences may cause him to reject a proposed solution to a problem or to look for alternative solutions rather than to accept the first idea that comes to mind.

Asking useful questions involves the power to determine the type of question that will evoke the appropriate knowledge or feeling tone to move a situation ahead. It is usually impossible to find answers until the right question is asked. A useful question may open up a relatively unpioneered field or one that had hitherto been unexplored; great persons such as Einstein, Wright, and Picasso have this type of question. A useful question may lead to the search for alternatives. A primary teacher might ask: "What are all the ways I can use to teach these children to read?" Another type of useful question is one asked in such a way that it clarifies; the central idea comes into focus, and the irrelevant falls away.

Judging, Rating, and Evaluating

Inherent in almost any situation in which thinking occurs are at least some elements of evaluative thinking.

> Evaluation is defined as the making of judgments about the value, for some purpose, of ideas, works, solutions, methods, materials, etc. It involves the use of criteria as well as standards for appraising the extent to which particulars are accurate, effective, economical, or satisfying. The judgments may be either quantitative or qualitative, and the criteria may be either those determined by the student or those which are given to him.[17]

Although many ways of classifying evaluative modes of thinking exist, in this discussion the following are briefly considered: comparing, analyzing, interpreting data, and criticizing. Let us briefly consider each of these modes. *Comparing* is the viewing of two or more objects, persons, or situations with the purpose of finding likenesses and differences. In making adequate comparisons, discrimination based on criteria applicable to the objects under consideration is important.

[17] Bloom, *op. cit.*, p. 185.

The Thoughtful Person

A person is making a comparison when he is examining two or more objects, ideas, or relationships in light of certain criteria. Similarities and differences may be noted among selections from literature, types of dances, or ways of attacking a mathematical problem.

Analyzing involves breaking a whole down into its parts in order to understand the distinct features of the whole. Bloom suggests that analysis may be a "prelude to evaluation."[18] Analysis enables the student

> to distinguish fact from hypothesis in a communication, to identify conclusions and supporting statements, to distinguish relevant from extraneous material, to note how one idea relates to another, to see what unstated assumptions are involved in what is said, to distinguish dominant from subordinate ideas or themes in poetry or music, to find evidence of the author's techniques and purposes....[19]

Although analysis takes place between comprehension and evaluation, it is being categorized with evaluative skills since this skill is constantly being called into play in the act of evaluation.

Interpreting data allows for the making of sound generalizations and the development of explanatory systems that permit the linkage of various sources of information about the same topic. Critical to the interpretation of data are the inferences made as data are handled. Implicit in inference is the passing of judgments. These inferences may be based on surmise or intuition, or they may imply the use of such more formal processes as deduction and conclusion. These latter processes imply judgment based on greater quality and quantity of knowledge than does surmising.

Criticizing is seeing the worth or worthlessness, the merits or demerits, of a course of action, a situation, or a product. Criticizing may imply positive or negative comments. These may be based on faulty observation or inadequate knowledge. At other times, criticizing may be prompted by accurate observation and complete knowledge. More sophisticated forms of criticism involve decisions based on the study of assumptions and hypotheses, the analysis of the logic of an argument, the weighing of supporting evidence, the detection of ambiguities and inconsistencies, the judging of the reliability of sources, or the detecting of statements that are either too vague or too specific.[20]

Qualities of the Thoughtful Person

Thus far, the various thought processes have been considered in their uniqueness and separateness. In actuality, however, thought is usually accompanied by such other human components as drives, feelings, attitudes, values, and be-

---

[18] *Ibid.,* p. 144.
[19] *Loc. cit.*
[20] For a full treatment of this subject, see Robert H. Ennis, "A Concept of Critical Thinking," *Harvard Educational Review,* 32 (Winter, 1962), 81-111.

liefs. Thought helps in the analysis and explanation of these more subtle components, thus permitting increased clarity in understanding the person.

Because the thoughtful person described earlier has more opportunity to be effective as a person than one who is not thoughtful, the school has a major obligation to help the person in this becoming. The school's obligation goes even further. In addition to helping the individual manage himself successfully as a person, the school has the additional task of stimulating him to be a contributing member of society. If one considers the qualities that are necessary for individual enhancement and social competence, a construct seems to emerge in which the following qualities are observable.

(1) The thoughtful person is an information-seeker.
(2) He evaluates information and learns to distinguish more worthwhile from less valuable sources.
(3) He engages in unusual and creative thinking.
(4) He applies the knowledge that he has acquired.
(5) He gives attention to the formulation of values.
(6) He becomes increasingly adept at making wise decisions.
(7) He uses his thinking skills to understand himself and others more fully.

Each of these statements is now examined for purposes of clarification and extension. Chapter Two then treats the above statements in terms of how teachers can enhance the seven attributes of the thoughtful person.

Information-Seeking

The truly thoughtful person has a real desire to know, to get the facts. One has only to watch and listen to the young child to understand the insatiable thirst for knowledge with which most children are endowed in their early years. That for some reason the desire to know is often dulled in later life is indeed unfortunate.

The successful information-seeker possesses a variety of skills. First, he is able to see the picture as a whole and to see amplifying and significant detail in proper perspective. The individual who first catches detail without understanding the intended design of the information source is likely to misinterpret and to give improper balance to key ideas.

Second, the thoughtful person seeks to clarify the whole. This may mean looking for new information. He may reach out to other resources, both human and material, in his search for understanding.

Third, he seeks to understand the several positions that are possible when an issue is at stake. Again, it may be appropriate to search a variety of sources.

Fourth, after looking for data related to the central ideas, the thoughtful person considers subordinate points. He studies detail carefully, attempting to pinpoint those items or arguments that are vital to increased clarity of the main idea. At all times, however, he is careful to keep detail in proper perspective.

Fifth, in addition to examining verbal statements in order to see the relationship to the whole, the thoughtful person studies illustrative material such as diagrams, charts, maps, and illustrations. He looks at these items to check accuracy and recency of information. He possesses skill in interpreting statistical data and is able to understand the language of numbers as well as of words. Charts, maps, illustrations, and the like are checked for their relevance to the whole.

Sixth, the thoughtful person defines terms. He seeks the most appropriate meaning for words or phrases that may have multiple meanings. He is sensitive to words or phrases that might have affective overtones, thus slanting the meaning of a given passage. As he reads, he notes those portions that lack clarity because of inappropriate selection of words.

Seventh, the thoughtful person differentiates between various kinds of statement. He can identify statements that are fact, those that are opinion, those that are inferences, those that are emotional declarations, and those that are judgments. In addition to identifying these various types of statement, he handles the statements in appropriate ways. He learns when an emotional appeal is appropriate to a situation, but he is an astute listener to such appeals in order to differentiate hasty inferences and hunches from reliable knowledge. He is wary of making a decision based on heated overstatements instead of cool facts.

Eighth, the thoughtful person has the ability to synthesize and summarize material. Synthesis involves putting elements together into a coherent whole. Oftentimes, the pattern is established by the nature of the material. Other times, the pattern may be something new, as when material is pulled together from a variety of sources. The thoughtful person is able to formulate generalizations that indicate accuracy of perception.

Evaluating Information

The thoughtful person evaluates information. Through the development of criteria for worthwhile material, he becomes a connoisseur of meaningful sources. He can distinguish between a specialist in a field, a capable eclectic, and a shoddy dilettante.

In his search for substantial and accurate information, the thoughtful person notices several things. First, he discovers overlapping and similarity of ideas. He detects those ideas in which agreement is generally to be found. Where a reliable source appears to disagree with material found in many other sources, the thoughtful person inquires into the causes for the disagreement.

Second, the thoughtful person evaluates sources. He seeks to determine the competence of authorities and seeks to understand the underlying assumptions of authors and the frames of reference from which they speak.

Third, he uses his own experience as well as that of others as a means for evaluating emerging principles and generalizations. He realizes that he is not competent to do this in all fields but that to some he may bring much personal knowledge, which, if rightly used, will aid in clarifying, extending, and evaluating a given idea. The thoughtful person realizes that circumstances, new findings, and increased probings cause knowledge to change; therefore, what appears to be appropriate knowledge today may be obsolete tomorrow.

Fourth, the thoughtful person recognizes, analyzes, and evaluates processes. He realizes that methods that may produce results in one field of study may not work in another. He delves into the process by which conclusions were formulated in order to evaluate their worth.

Fifth, the thoughtful person detects statements that are vague or that seem to indicate scant or faulty knowledge on the part of the author. Extremism and lack of clarity cause the thoughtful person to ponder the sources of such statements. He possesses an awareness of a hierarchy of sources, realizing that some sources of data have more validity than others. He realizes that rumor, for example, is less valuable than an eye-witness account.

Sixth, he holds conclusions, principles, or generalizations provisionally and modifies his views when necessary. As he evaluates sources and culls that information that is important for him, his conclusions and generalizations may change. In other words, his own frame of reference for evaluating sources has some openness and is subject to the influence of the material he reads.

Creative Thinking

The thoughtful person engages in unusual and original thinking that may be called creative thought. This differs from other types of thinking in that an element of newness is involved. Creative thinking involves seeking and breaking through the limitations of a situation when it warrants a new approach or unique solution. The thoughtful person prizes creative thinking, for he realizes that this quality, when put to useful purposes, leads to progress.

The thoughtful person has an unusual composite of qualities. Earlier, when dimensions of thinking were discussed, eight components of creative thinking were briefly analyzed. They were fluency, flexibility, originality, elaboration, sensitivity to problems, ability to see causes, ability to ask good questions, and ability to predict consequences. In addition to these qualities, the thoughtful person engages in activities that are related to his values.

First, the thoughtful person values toying with ideas. He likes to rearrange ideas, combine elements, and pull arrangements apart. He values seeing beyond the obvious to ways in which ideas can help man live a better and fuller life, even though his individual contribution may be small.

Second, the thoughtful person's values aid him in selecting those problems to which he should devote time and energy in seeking the solution. Sensitivity to problems without the quality of discrimination may result in inactivity or, in the face of an overwhelming number of problems seen, unfocused overactivity.

Third, once an individual has selected from a range of problems those to which he wishes to devote time and energy, he develops an interest in the process by which he pulls discrete elements together. In other words, the *process* of organizing rather than the finished organization is of interest to the thoughtful person. He explores many ways of arranging ideas, of designing categories, of making sense out of what may seem senseless to many. He is able to analyze and explain facts, theories, and impressions within the frameworks he develops. He is tolerant of situations that appear to be ambiguous, uncertain, or disorganized when the potential for a new order seems possible. He prizes the opportunity to create new syntheses when a group of seemingly discrete or unrelated elements demand to be set forth in a new framework.[21]

Fourth, the thoughtful person possesses a "spark," an inner drive, and goes beyond the expected in the expenditure of time, energy, and emotional involvement in the search for an answer to a problem important to him. At times, his search may simply be to *know* rather than to *solve*. Some persons speak of this intense search as commitment. Some attribute it to the need for individual fulfillment. In any case, the thoughtful person has a dedication to ideas that have personal merit and worth.

Applying Knowledge

The thoughtful person applies the knowledge that he has acquired. Although he enjoys learning for the sheer joy of knowing, he also realizes that through knowledge man has found and continues to find solutions to perplexing problems of life. The person who has learned to apply knowledge sees relevance of what has been learned to what is new. The person interested in applying knowledge has the following qualities.

First, the thoughtful person is interested in activities that have meaning for him. When purpose is evident to him, he brings his knowledge to bear in areas inviting penetrating thought.

Second, the thoughtful person is action-taking. He applies his knowledge to community problems, "community" being redefined as an increasingly larger world as the individual matures. He reaches out to the expanding world with sensitivity and awareness. He realizes that the application of his knowledge may help in the solution of vital problems.

Third, the thoughtful person applies knowledge and information to himself so that he becomes one with an idea. There is unity between the individual, specific knowledge, and the area to which he applies it. As a result of his encounter with knowledge and his use of it, constant change occurs in the individual. Because his knowledge is so much a part of him, to separate the idea from the person is difficult.

Fourth, in addition to applying knowledge in an intuitive and unplanned

---

[21] For further ideas about ordering or organizing, see Frank Barron, "The Psychology of Imagination," in Parnes and Harding, *op. cit.*, pp. 227–237.

way, the thoughtful person seeks to find ways to apply knowledge more fruitfully and precisely. He realizes that knowledge from one field does not necessarily apply to another field. For example, knowing the logic necessary to solve problems in geometry does not necessarily mean that the individual has acquired the logic necessary to detect half-truths in advertisements.

Valuing

The thoughtful person realizes that modes of thought and systems of values strongly influence each other. For example, the individual who holds a few values very firmly probably engages in different thought processes from the person who is constantly examining and rearranging his values. Again, the person probably thinks differently who has a degree of fluidity in his scheme of values but who also has certain values that he prizes and that are not easily changed. In other words, value systems vary in their degree of firmness or fluidity.

The teacher's concern is with helping an individual understand his value system and deal with it. The thoughtful person seemingly engages in several processes as he refines his values.

First, he clarifies the degree to which he holds his values. Raths says that, unless a value is preferred among alternatives, it is not a value.[22] Clarifying enables the person to examine what he firmly believes. How the individual clarifies his values varies. Some people have skill in self-analysis and are able to determine their own values through an internal mode of questioning. Others may need the help of another person or group.

Then, as a means of evaluating and changing his own scheme of valuing and establishing priorities, the thoughtful person becomes familiar with and seeks to understand the value systems of others. He is eager to inquire into the roots of other value systems and seeks for points of compatibility and incompatibility with his own values.

Finally, the thoughtful person seeks to include in his circle of acquaintance persons who differ in their ways of formulating values. By associating with those whose means of arriving at values differ, he provides himself the stimulus of a constant check and review of those ideas that he seems to value.

In brief, the thoughtful person is constantly examining and renewing the process by which he arrives at his values. He realizes that understanding not only his values but how he determines them enables him more easily to establish priorities among competing alternatives. Through the application of thought processes to valuing, the person can better come to grips with the determinants of much of his behavior.[23]

[22] James Raths, "A Strategy for Developing Values," *Educational Leadership*, 21 (May, 1964), 509–514.
[23] For a fuller description of valuing, see David R. Krathwohl, Benjamin S. Bloom, and Bertram B. Masia, *Taxonomy of Educational Objectives: The Classification of Educational Goals. Handbook II: Affective Domain* (New York: David McKay Company, Inc., 1964), pp. 139–175.

Decision-Making

In order to utilize concepts of thinking and valuing to their optimum, the thoughtful person has a certain understanding of the process of decision-making. First, he is aware of the steps involved in arriving at a decision. He realizes the means of engaging in the process that will prove most fruitful. For example, he learns that to examine alternatives gives a better basis for a choice than if only one course of action is contemplated.

Second, the thoughtful person realizes that to a large degree he is responsible for his behavior. Forces outside the individual may alter certain decisions somewhat, but most people do have a greater degree of freedom to make decisions than they commonly realize or make use of.

Third, in addition to making wise decisions for himself, he tries not to usurp the decision-making power of others. He may try to help others to make clearer, more forceful decisions, but he is careful not to make decisions that others can capably make.

Fourth, through increased knowledge and continuous evaluation of the decision-making process, he learns to make decisions more wisely and astutely. Where he sees that changes are necessary in the process, he makes them.

Ultimately he learns to utilize his thought processes in decision-making in such a way that the results are worthwhile for himself and those whom the decision affects.

Self-Other Understanding

Serious-minded persons are constantly searching for new insights about themselves in order to live richer, more intelligent, and useful lives. To discuss the many facets of the person's being is not necessary here. It is pertinent, however, to reinforce the theme that pervades the book—*an understanding of thought and skill in using a variety of thought processes is essential for increased self-understanding, productivity, satisfaction in daily living and improved relationships with others.*

If this premise is accepted, then the individual can begin to formulate a view of himself and his significance in the universe. He can synthesize the various factors that affect his life and see himself in relationship to what surrounds him. The diverse elements of life are placed in proper perspective, some being placed in the background in order to give priority to others. For example, in selecting a career, the thoughtful person is better able to take into account his dreams, vision, ambitions, motives, and points of expertise than his less thoughtful counterpart. Through such self-analysis, the thoughtful person has the data on which to base a wise career choice.

The thoughtful person also is able to establish more satisfying bonds with others since his introspection causes him to view himself in relationship with others in his world. He ponders the uniqueness of others and seeks to find ways of communicating so that both parties are mutually enhanced.

He understands the relationship of articulated language to thought and realizes that, despite the constant refinement of language skills, a person can never fully communicate with words what he thinks and feels. He seeks to find other modes of communication in addition to the spoken word. He also is aware of the misunderstandings that can result from inadequate or incorrect interpretations of the statements of others. Language is seen as a handy tool, but one that has limitations in that the totality of life cannot be expressed by it. Because of the inadequacy of spoken language, he becomes increasingly aware of telling nonverbal signs—gestures, facial expressions, posture, and grooming.

The thoughtful person values reflection or meditation, realizing that contemplation helps man to see the wholeness and relation of the parts in perspective. He believes that the person who fails to reflect on the activity and choices in his daily living may be sacrificing the better for the mediocre.

In the first part of this chapter, an analysis was made of ways in which persons think. Next, consideration was given to the meaning of the term "thoughtful person." A construct was developed in which the thoughtful person was described as being an information-seeker, creative thinker, applier of knowledge, formulator of values, and decision-maker. In addition, he was described as having the tools for increased understanding of self and others.

A consideration of man as a thoughtful being allows him to be examined from a perspective especially useful to teachers. The next chapter discusses specific help that can be given to children and youth to enable them to use their thought processes more fully.

TWO

ACTIVITIES IN THE DEVELOPMENT OF THE THOUGHTFUL PERSON

Today's teacher has the obligation to make available a wide range of learning possibilities to students. In an exceedingly complex age, no school system or teacher can afford programs in which students spend valuable time on inconsequential tasks. Tasks must be carefully designed to ensure personal meaning and reward for those undertaking them.

The construct of enhancing the thoughtful person suggests the necessity of a tremendous diversity of assignments. Some may be carefully selected from textbooks; some may be selected from commercially produced kits; others may be teacher-developed, initiated for a particular student or group of students. The construct of the thoughtful person suggests that learning activities should:

(1) Require a second look at the content of written materials, including textbooks, in order to help the reader gain a full understanding.
(2) Encourage the reader to go beyond the initial reading assignment to gather additional information.
(3) Stimulate unusual and creative thinking that often goes beyond the known.
(4) Suggest opportunities for the application of material.
(5) Serve as a means of relating the individual's value orientation to thinking.
(6) Stimulate wise decision-making and an understanding of the decision-making process.
(7) Enable the individual to move toward increased understanding of himself and others.

The remainder of the chapter deals with each of the above points. In addition to consideration of the reason for focusing upon these points, illustrative materials suited to various subjects and grade levels are included. It is hoped that the examples are such that teachers can easily apply them for the use of their own students.

Re-examining Content

When a student refers to printed sources he needs to look twice at the material for a full understanding of what the author is saying. If he is to have adequate information upon which to make value judgments or upon which to base creative thinking, then he should possess the ability to understand and recall facts from his reading. He should understand the whole, seeing the parts in relation to it. He should be able to define terms, to organize, to determine underlying assumptions, and to find any material that is extraneous to the logical outline.

A student should read with respect for the author's ideas and means of expression. Although he may not agree with the author's points, he should take care not to misinterpret him: when he elaborates or changes an idea of the author, he should do so knowingly. He may do this when seeking a new solution for an old problem.

Let us now consider the nature of activities that require a second look at content.

Checking Comprehension of the Whole

One of the first steps the student should take after reading a selection is to check his understanding of the whole. Such understanding involves going back and recalling the broad framework—the outline of major ideas that hold the selection together. In a day in which there is access to a wide variety of literature and in which selections read may be far too numerous to be digested, it is crucial to do an author justice by becoming familiar with his broad ideas without distorting them. Where necessary, the author's decisions as to *sequence* of ideas should be considered.

Students can be helped in a number of ways to check their comprehension of the whole. Questions at the beginning of a chapter can be worded to encourage the individual to look for certain key ideas as he reads, as in the following example.

> As you read the story, "Preparations for the Trip to San Francisco," list the four important tasks the Wing family accomplished before leaving Cincinnati.

Questions at the end of the story can encourage students to recall ideas that are basic to the story.

Developing the Thoughtful Person

Ability to see the whole can be ascertained by instructions in which students are asked to make up questions about the story which they have just read. The instructions such as those that follow should encourage students to write their questions in such a way that the central ideas must be included in the answer.

> Sometimes minor points distract readers from the general idea of a story. Write four questions that you can use with one of your classmates to help him determine whether or not he got the main ideas of the story.

Sometimes the flavor of the story can be captured in the questions. Consider the following questions found at the end of a story titled "The Airtight Case," the setting of which is a courtroom.

> What were the facts?
> What was the evidence?
> What was the testimony?
> What did Joe claim?
> What were the responsibilities of the lawyers?
> What new evidence was introduced?
> What did you witness?
> What is your judgment as a reader? [1]

Students can gain skill in understanding the whole through précis writing. In evaluating the précis, the teacher should help the student judge his ability to distinguish major from minor points.

Occasionally, a group of students may wish to write and dramatize a play in which accurate reporting rather than imaginative elaboration of events is stressed.

Comprehension of the whole may be checked by categorizing major points under the following headings: "Beginning of story," "Middle of story," and "End of story."

Since comprehension of the whole is prerequisite to other kinds of thinking, it is a skill that may need much attention. The teacher should present a variety of tasks in which students may practice it. Repetition of the same type of activity produces boredom in the students. Diversity of activity designed to develop the same skill may, on the other hand, result in increased competence in a particular skill.

Identifying Underlying Assumptions

As the student seeks to understand the whole, he should also become increasingly able to ascertain the assumptions underlying the author's point of

---

[1] Ullin W. Leavell and Alex M. Caughran, *Reading for Significance* (New York: American Book Company, 1959), pp. 298–310. Subquestions are included under each of the above questions in the original text.

view. Sometimes assumptions, values, or beliefs are clearly stated, but more often, they have to be inferred from the text. In the case of fiction, perhaps an exercise such as this one might be used.

> Most persons hold certain views or beliefs about people even though they may not always talk about them. What kinds of beliefs about people do you think Mr. Tewksbery held? Describe some of his actions that make you think your ideas are true.

In dealing with nonfiction, it is extremely important that students learn to identify underlying assumptions. With many diverse ideologies competing for their allegiance, they need to develop coherent, stable value systems. After reading two selections on communism, students might be given the following task.

> Describe the underlying ideas in the two selections about Communism. Which ideas do you think represent personal bias without much grounding in fact? Which underlying ideas seem to be authoritatively presented? Which of the two writers seems to express the soundest viewpoint?

Interpreting Graphic Detail

In addition to seeing the whole, students should develop increased skill in interpreting graphic material found in many textbooks—pictures, graphs, charts, maps, and tables.

Students in primary grades might begin to understand map-making through a task such as the following:

> You have just read about hiding places Joe found on the school grounds. Can you make a map of your schoolyard? First draw the school; then put on your map the walk leading to the school. Include on your map other things you want to remember about your playground. Now go back and put an X where you think are some good hiding places in your schoolyard.

Middle- and upper-grade students might make a map in more detail or deal with a larger area.

Many primary materials depend on pictures for telling a story. Students should learn to generalize from pictures and to see the relevance of the printed text to the pictorial material, as in the following exercise.

> Look closely at the picture on page 42 of your science book. Think up a title that describes the picture.

To read charts and graphs is another skill necessary in understanding certain types of material.

> Study the graph on page 22. What kinds of information does it give you? What points does the graph clarify for you that were not clear in the written material?

Of course, making models is a possible activity in either a teacher-planned or a textbook-designed activity.[2] Instructions might include the following.

After reading the part of your text on highway hazards, pretend you are a highway engineer responsible for developing exits from major four-lane roads. Develop a model out of cardboard and construction paper in which you make two different kinds of exits from a four-lane highway. When you have finished, check the text again to make sure you have interpreted the material correctly.

Defining Words and Building Vocabulary

Because words are tools with which we think, students should be helped to define and use words as accurately as possible. As they learn the power of the spoken and written word, they will learn the importance of precision in definition.

More is needed than asking students to define listed words or to match a word with a picture. Meanings of words out of context are often unclear. Questions such as the following sharpen definitions and better learning.

What is the meaning of the word *order* in this sentence?
A paper was distributed containing the *order* of service.

What is the meaning of *order* here?
The judge said, "I will not go on until there is *order* in the courtroom."

Can you think of other sentences that use *order* in different ways?

The use of contextual clues is among the ways that students can learn the meaning of words. Astute guessing can be improved by the following type of task.

Look at the words below within the context of the story. See if you can figure out the meaning.

comprehend	pandemonium
transitional	culinary
nebulous	charwoman
adjacent	

Students who become familiar with languages other than their own often are building vocabulary in their own language, since much similarity exists among some languages. Perhaps some features of the "general language" courses common in the schools some years ago might be revised to familiarize students with commonalities in vocabulary.

[2] For further ideas on model-making see George H. McCune and Neville Pearson, "Interpreting Material Presented in Graphic Form," in Helen Carpenter (ed.), *Skill Development in Social Studies.* Thirty-Third Yearbook of the National Council for the Social Studies, Washington, D.C.: National Education Association, 1963, p. 227.

Many books now being written in another language[3] with an accompanying translation can be used in cooperatively planned units, as follows.

After reading this story, which takes place in France, you may want to know a little of the language of the French people.

Another way of helping students understand the interrelatedness of words is through increased attention to root words, suffixes, prefixes, and the like.

As you can easily see, *signify* is built on the root *sign-*. *Signify* means to *show*. Can you think of other words with the root *sign?*

How many meanings of words can you work out using these prefixes?

 de .... down
 re .... again
 anti .... against
 pre .... before
 con .... with

Many of our words are derived from other languages. Latin and Greek have especially influenced the development of the English language. As you read your textbook begin to build a pool of "descendants." For example, how many words can you find from the Latin root *pell-* meaning *drive?* Consider repel, compel, propeller, etc. How many words can you find which have the Greek root *tele-* meaning *distant* or *far?*

In addition to knowing the literal meanings of words, students should realize that many words have subtle emotional meanings not usually found in the dictionary. A task such as the following may help teach the important skill of discerning the affective connotations of words.

Think of all the ways in which you can define *democracy, rights,* and *aristocrat.* Why isn't a dictionary definition always adequate in defining words?

Organizing the Facts

The skill of organizing usually receives much attention in elementary and secondary schools. Students are often told: "Outline pages _____ to _____ in your text." The teacher assumes, of course, that transfers will occur and that the student will thus learn to organize his own ideas and experiences.

Several procedures can be used in helping students learn to organize or classify material in the textbook.[4] Outlining is an obvious and probably rather

---

[3] A book of this type for children is Seslye Joslin (illust. Irene Haas), *There Is a Dragon in My Bed* (New York: Harcourt, Brace and World, 1961).
[4] The suggestions in this section are designed primarily to be used with textbooks. Students should also be taught how to organize material found outside the textbook. For further practical suggestions on the process of organizing, see Helen Fisher Darrow and R. Van Allen, *Independent Activities for Creative Learning,* Practical Suggestions for Teachers, No. 21 (New York: Teachers College Press, Columbia University, 1961), pp. 42–61.

Developing the Thoughtful Person

widely used activity in teaching the process of organizing. Many books at the elementary school level give tasks such as the following:

Ann did three things before going to Grandmother's house. Fill in number 2 with one of the things that she did.
1. Raked the lawn
2. ....
3. Went to the store

When Ann got to Grandmother's house she did three things. What is the third one?
1. Helped set the table
2. Made some cookies
3. ....

Students can gradually be left with increased responsibility for filling in the outline. In the intermediate and upper grades, the following directions might be appropriate.

Make a list of the important ideas in this story. Check whether you have listed the ideas in the order in which they occurred. Using the important ideas which have been arranged in the order in which they happened, go back and fill in important subpoints under each main idea.

Junior and senior high school students can be more sophisticated about outlining. They might approach a textbook selection with the following questions in mind.

Is there any one idea upon which the rest of the material is dependent for understanding?
Where should this idea be placed?
Are there some ideas that can be understood better after others have been explained?
What ideas or facts make more sense if they are arranged in a certain order in relationship to one another?
Are there some ideas or facts that make sense in whatever order they are placed in relation to the first and last idea?[5]

Learning to organize calls for knowledge of principles of classification. Old match boxes, cereal boxes, shoe boxes, and notebooks with dividers can be invitations to classify. Students might be given directions such as the following.

Get a shoe box or a file box of some type, some cards for the box, and some dividers. Classify material from your stories under these headings:

Words I Want to Learn
Poems I Like
Pictures of Storybook Characters
Unusual Descriptions of Persons

[5] Alice Eikenberry and Ruth Ellsworth, "Organizing and Evaluating Information," in Helen Carpenter, *op. cit.*, p. 79.

Arithmetic Facts I Know
Subtraction Facts I Need to Learn
Things I Want to Remember about My Friends
People I Know in My Community
Important News Events
The Most Useful Scientific Discoveries of the Past Year

Another way of helping persons learn to classify and organize is through questions that encourage grouping discrete items.

Now that you have read the story about Peter's farm, list each animal in the story under one of these questions:
Which animals can fly?
Which animals can swim?
Which animals can hop?

Although teachers need to be careful not to use this technique too frequently, the following procedure can teach an important skill. This modification of the questioning technique is the lotto game, with its many variants, common in the kindergarten and primary grades. Children have large cards with 9 to 12 pictures on each, headings such as "In the Pet Shop" or "On the Playground," and groupings of pictures. Children match the pictures on the larger cards with smaller cards.

At the primary level, children can develop skill in organizing by classifying pictures under given headings.

Look at pictures A-F below.
A. (Fire in a fireplace)
B. (Burning barn)
C. (Burning leaves)
D. (Steam engine)
E. (Burning forest)
F. (Campfire)
If the fire was helpful, put the letter of the picture under the heading "Helpful." If the fire was not helpful, put the letter of the picture under the heading "Not Helpful."

Pupils can also be helped to organize their thinking by beginning with contrasting categories. This provides an excellent starting point.

Fold a large sheet of paper in half. On the one side write, "Things That Grow above the Ground." On the other side write, "Things That Grow below the Ground." Make six pictures under each heading.[6]

Other headings might include "Ocean and Land Forms," "Fruits and Vegetables," "Heavy Things and Light Things," "Foods Then and Now."

Older students need to become aware of the more subtle contrasts possible

[6] Darrow and Van Allen, *op. cit.*, p. 53.

when the expressed differences appear to be only slight. For example, differences between socialism and communism are more subtle than differences between democracy and fascism.

Cartoons in local papers are often helpful to the student learning to compare more complex ideas. The contrasting of selected cartoons provides experience in the analysis of positions often presented in extreme forms.

Students might be asked to draw two cartoons representing different points of view, as follows.

> After reading about the War Between the States, pretend you are a newspaper cartoonist. Make two cartoons, one depicting the Northern point of view, the other the Southern.
>
> Show your understanding of the different points of view at the time of the Revolutionary War by drawing two cartoons, one representing the British viewpoint, the other the American.

Again, this type of activity might provide the stimulus for the study of contrasts.

> Select an Associated Press story. Secure a number of different newspapers carrying the story. Compare the headlines and the presentation and interpretation of the story.

After reading a selection in a social studies or a language arts book, students may be given these directions, designed to help differentiate fact from opinion[7]

> Make two columns on your paper. Label one "Fact" and the other "Opinion." From the three selections that you have just read, see if you can separate some of the major points into these two classifications.

Older students should have help in developing skill in content analysis, an important research tool for many of the tasks they may encounter in higher education. An assignment in literature might be made as follows.

> After reading the essay on India's population problems, write each of these headings at the top of a sheet of paper: (1) Reasons for the population problems, (2) Proposed solutions to the problems, (3) Persons who are trying to solve the problems. Now go back and write on each sheet the information from the essay which belongs in each of the categories. Check and discuss your paper with a classmate.

Identifying Extraneous Material

As students deal with textbook material, it is important that they learn to identify central ideas, supporting statements, and irrelevant or extraneous

---

[7] For further ideas about teaching controversial issues, see Leonard S. Kenworthy, *Guide to Social Studies Teaching in Secondary Schools* (Belmont, California: Wadsworth Publishing Co., Inc., 1962), pp. 238-241.

statements. Although an irrelevant idea may have merit in that it can spark a chain of thinking within the student, nonetheless students should be able to differentiate ideas that are a key to the understanding of a selection and those that have merit because of the individual interests of the reader. Perhaps a device such as the following might be used with primary children in connection with an appropriate story.

Below is a list of things you might need for a winter walk or for a summer swim. Make two columns on your paper. Label one "Winter Walk" and the other "Summer Swim." Now go through the list and put in each column the items important to your two headings. Some things might be listed in both columns and some in neither.

Bathing suit
Picnic lunch
Heavy coat
Warm hat
Light jacket or sweater
Bathing cap
Beach towel
Boots
An apple
Somebody to be with
A dog

Now discuss with one of your friends why you made the lists the way you did. Did you select only important things?

Older students may try a device such as the following.

After reading pages 96 through 100 in your book, mark statements A, B, and C with this code:
(+) every statement which is true and can be proved by the facts stated.
(0) every statement which might be true but cannot be supported by the facts stated.
(—) every statement which is false, as shown by the facts stated.[8]
_____ A. San Francisco is the sixth largest city in the United States.
_____ B. The weather is conducive to agriculture in the San Francisco area.
_____ C. San Francisco has one of the most mobile populations in the world.

Making Generalizations

Extremely important to the handling of the printed page is the ability to generalize. Proper attention to generalizing ensures the development of economizing skills. Persons who learn to have at their disposal the means to handle

---

[8] Code taken from a test for elementary school students: J. Wayne Wrightstone, *Critical Thinking in the Social Studies* (New York: Teachers College Press, Columbia University, 1938), Form A, p. 7.

material efficiently and economically can manage and make sense of material from an increasingly wide number of sources.

The student who is not yet skillful in generalizing might be asked to read a chapter in another book on a topic related to the one in the text and to find similarities between the two books. The more skillful student might have a task such as the following.

> Read a number of articles on the race to conquer space. Prepare a brief report on some of the major ideas you obtained from your readings.

Students can be helped to understand the process of generalizing by developing a sensitivity to the need for supporting evidence when a broad statement is made and the reasons for it are not clear. As a literary selection is reviewed, possibly the following assignment might be appropriate.

> In this story Mr. Claiborn described Janet as a pessimistic person. Do you agree? Find some statements in the story to support your position.

A task such as the following might be helpful occasionally.

> After reading the next selection, label two columns on your paper: (1) Main ideas and (2) Important supporting statements. Classify the ideas in the selection.

Summarizing

Certain assignments should help young people grasp the emphasis intended by the author. Instructions to students might include the following.

> After you have read this selection, go back, and in one sentence attempt to describe the main idea. Then list three important ideas that help to enlarge and clarify the main idea.

Young children not yet in control of a writing vocabulary adequate to carry out the above task might be asked to make a picture or series of pictures incorporating the major idea of a reading, science, or social studies selection. The young child might be provided the opportunity to dictate the main ideas he distilled from a selection to a tape recorder or to an older child, a parent, or the teacher.

Finding Additional Information

An individual should know whether he is comprehending what he is reading. However, comprehension is only prerequisite to other types of thinking. In this section our concern is with guides that take the individual beyond the textbook. Our immediate concern is evaluating and discriminating among sources. Later sections deal with other skills that may be developed as the individual goes beyond the text.

Finding Different Points of View

Individuals do not perceive in the same way and therefore may develop different viewpoints. This is an important learning. Examining another viwpoint in as unbiased a manner as possible and attempting to understand it does not necessarily mean accepting it. Such examination does mean, however, that one is open to knowing about it, at least at the intellectual level, other points of view. Perhaps a task like the one below will help encourage the findings of different points of view.

> Below is a list of books and articles related to the topic of this chapter. See whether you can locate some of them. Write an article for your classmates in which you point out some of the disagreements of the authors.
> The following type of task might stimulate the same kind of thinking. Which authors in this reading list on Germany seem to have a different point of view from the author of the text? Which point of view would you support? Why?

The young child who does not yet have an adequate writing vocabulary might be encouraged to draw a picture representing a viewpoint different from his own or that discussed in his textbook.

Children might be asked to review a current book, movie, or play. Personal reviews can then be compared with an adult review.

In addition, the student should turn to other media for finding additional information. Programed textbooks, films, posters, resource persons, periodicals, dioramas, radio, television, and informational games are but a few of the resources a student may use to understand points of view other than those discussed in class or presented in the text.

Since many schools are equipped with projectors, students may show appropriate eight- or sixteen-millimeter films or slides to a small group or a class. The teacher might supply a list of selected commercial and homemade films with an invitation to compare the ideas of the film with those of the text.

Teachers might also encourage the use of current magazines and periodicals to develop differing points of view.

> Write a play based upon some of the material found in this unit of your textbook. Search current magazines and newspapers for items related to your topic. Incorporate in the dialogue some of the differing points of view you may find on the topic.

Differentiating the Fully Treated from the Partially Treated

The balance given to various aspects of a topic in the school program determines to some extent whether a student can distinguish between the fully treated and the partially treated. Students should learn to tell when major issues related to a topic are developed and when such issues are left untouched.

For example, in the traditional units on "Community Helpers" common in primary programs, certain aspects of the topic of service agencies and helpers within the community are overly stressed. The services that the "helper" provides for the child are given pronounced attention. Other aspects are superficially treated or ignored. Because of the maturity level of the individuals for whom the work is planned, perhaps the imbalance can be justified; however, the child might begin to become aware that taxation is necessary to maintain service persons and that he will later learn more about the nature of taxation.[9] The following task might help make the above points.

> You have just finished studying community helpers. We have learned that these helpers are very important to you and your family. As you talk to other people or look at the newspapers, see if you can find who pays these helpers so that they can buy food and clothing and provide homes for their families.

With older children and youth, a teacher has the obligation, if a textbook only partially treats a given subject, to refer the student to sources that will round out his knowledge of that subject.

> In this chapter, the topic of civil rights was mentioned; however, the topic was not treated in detail. Try to locate material which points out the issues in the civil rights controversy. What new insights does your knowledge of the civil rights movement add to your understanding of the text?

Evaluating Underlying Assumptions

Although the point was made earlier that persons should receive help in learning to identify and evaluate underlying assumptions, the issue of the adequacy of underlying assumptions is redeveloped, because it is crucial to thinking and learning. When students are encouraged to go beyond the textbook or the assignment in their search for knowledge, they are apt to encounter many varied viewpoints. Those who would go beyond the textbook must do so with an open-minded but also critical attitude. Since it is possible to build a logical argument upon a faulty assumption, it is very important that individuals learn to test the validity of that which the author takes for granted. Checking the adequacy of assumptions is often difficult because assumptions are usually implicit.

In assignments which send the reader beyond the original text, these suggestions may be made to the learners.

> Identify the basic beliefs of the writer. Are they clearly stated? Why do you feel these are basic beliefs or assumptions? Are they adequate? After you feel

[9] For an excellent resource unit on the teaching of economics to elementary school children, see Lawrence Senesh, *Our Working World: Families at Work* (Chicago: Science Research Associates, 1964). Basic understandings integral to a full understanding of economics are taught in the early grades.

you have identified the basic beliefs, find another book by the same author. Do the same beliefs seem central in this book? If not, where do you find the differences?

A task appropriate for students both in elementary school and in secondary school might be the following.

Find as many stories (works of fiction) as you can about your state or your area of the country. What are some of the things that these authors say about your locale? Now read about your state or area in your social studies book. Which authors seem to agree with the opinions of the writer of the social studies text? Which writers seem to disagree? Where the writers are not in agreement, whose views do you value more? Why?

Evaluating Sources of Information

Another skill which should be encouraged by textbook devices and teacher-planned activities is the evaluation of sources of information. Early in their education, students should come to realize that sources are not infallible. They should develop guidelines "for the evaluation of authority represented by textbooks, speakers, personal interviews, eyewitness accounts, letters, autobiographies, public documents, personal diaries, local histories, minutes of meetings, and educational films."[10]

Among the questions that individuals should learn to ask are the following.
Who is the authority?
What is his background?
Is he speaking or writing on a subject on which he is a recognized authority?
What is the purpose of the material?
When and under what circumstances was the information recorded? Were primary sources used? If a primary source was used, was the information from memory or was it a direct account of what happened?
Is there corroboration of the facts from other sources?
Is the authority objective in the treatment of the material?
Is the material pertinent?[11]

Perhaps students will find it difficult to answer some of these questions. They may obtain help by writing to the publisher. Some questions can be answered only by secondary students, since younger students may not yet be able to handle the sources needed to gather the appropriate information. Nonetheless, students of all ages should begin to develop an awareness of the need to be well-grounded in a field before sharing one's wisdom with the wider population.

Students should also be given tasks that encourage them to check publication dates. Where possible, they might check the time lapse between the actual

---

[10] Eikenberry and Ellsworth, *op. cit.*, p. 89.
[11] *Loc. cit.*

writing and the date of publication. Such information assists in the evaluation of sources. Primary-grade students might have a task such as the following.

> After reading some of the facts about a dairy farm in your social studies book, choose a story book about a dairy farm from the list below. Compare the information from the story book with the facts in your social studies text. Are there any parts of the story from the fiction book which make you think the author lived on a farm? Do you think the author knew about an older farm or a modern farm? Why?

Activities such as the following, which might be developed in conjunction with literature, should encourage students to evaluate sources.

> Check on the credentials of the writer whose work you have just read. Look for information about him in *Who's Who,* encyclopedias, periodicals, or books. In some communities it may be possible to interview persons who have known the author. What kinds of evaluative statements are made about him by others? How well prepared do you think he was to write this selection? How does he rank among the writers within the same field?

In some communities, children may not have ready access to information that will enable them to evaluate sources. In such cases, perhaps an arrangement can be made with the nearest library or university to provide services and resources for students.

Detecting Vague, Ambiguous Statements

Detecting vague, ambiguous statements is really a part of evaluating sources. Along with noting passages that are ambiguous, students should be helped to differentiate between an author's lack of knowledge and lack of good communication skills.

Dealing with the ambiguous passages of a work requires some knowledge of the subject on the part of the reader. For this reason, students should ordinarily read more than one selection about a given topic. As students become increasingly able to detect glittering generalities and ambiguities, they will become better able to ascertain that which has merit and worth.

To gain skill in detecting lack of clarity a device such as the following is appropriate.

> Reread the passage you have just read. Which statements are vague or confused? What are some possible interpretations that might be made of these statements?

As students become able to spot ambiguities on the printed page, they should be better able to detect such statements as they hear them. To listen for distortions and ambiguities is very essential in a day of pervasive mass media. Often it is implied that an idea is true of all individuals within a group when in actuality the statement may apply to only a few. The following is an invitation to look for such statements.

Can you find any parts of this chapter in which the author says something as though the idea applies to all people, but when you stop to think about it you realize the idea applies to only a few? Where would you look to check an idea when you suspect the author is guilty of distortion?

Distinguishing the Degree of the Affective

Sometimes writers appeal to the emotions in order to get a selected response from the reader. At other times, the writer strives for objectivity in order to let the reader make his own judgments on the basis of his own emotional responses. Magazines and books differ very greatly in their reliance upon the affective to make an impact. Some newswriting may only attempt to state facts; other writing may move the reader to judgment through the appeal to the emotions. Students need to be aware of the stance of the writer when reading a selection. Is the writer attempting to report, or is the writer attempting to move the reader to a predetermined conclusion?

Consider Hayakawa's suggestion for becoming familiar with affective words and passages. Below are Hayakawa's directions and two selections to which to apply the instructions.[12]

> A useful practice, even for an experienced reader, is to take short passages of prose and verse—especially passages he has long been familiar with—and to find out by careful analysis (a) what the author is trying to communicate; (b) what affective elements help him to convey his meaning; (c) what elements, if any, obscure his communication; and (d) how successful, on the whole, the author is in conveying his ideas and feelings to the reader. The following passages may serve as material for this kind of analysis:
>
> "It was a crisp and spicy morning in early October. The lilacs and laburnums, lit with the glory fires of autumn, hung burning and flashing in the upper air, a fairy bridge provided by kind Nature for the wingless wild things that have their home in the tree tops and would visit together; the larch and the pomegranate flung their purple and yellow flames in brilliant broad splashes along the slanting sweep of the woodland; the sensuous fragrance of innumerable deciduous flowers rose upon the swooning atmosphere; far in the empty sky a solitary oesophagus slept upon motionless wing; everywhere brooded stillness, serenity, and the peace of God."
>
> —Samuel L. Clemens

[12] For a further discussion, see "The Language of Affective Communication," Chapter Eight *in* S. I. Hayakawa, *Language in Thought and Action* (New York: Harcourt, Brace, and World, 1949).

"A poem should be equal to:
Not true
For all the history of grief
An empty doorway and a maple leaf
For love
The leaning grasses and two lights above
   the sea—
A poem should not mean
But be."

—Archibald MacLeish [13]

Encouraging Creative Thinking

The skills needed for creative production are diverse and many, and it is not likely that all persons can develop creative thinking skills equally well. All persons, however, can probably improve to some degree certain of the ways of thinking often characteristic of imaginative individuals.

Among the creative thinking skills to which the school can give attention are perceiving richly, developing new or unusual ideas, seeing relationships, understanding the process of organizing, being sensitive to and aware of problems, redefining uses of common objects, being fluent in the expression of ideas, developing a sense of commitment, and personalizing the creative process. Each of these is treated separately.

Perceiving Richly

The ability to perceive correctly, fully, and without distortion strongly influences how a person thinks, feels, and acts. Perceiving is integrally related to what we already know. Some rely so heavily upon their past experiences that they allow little of the new to enter; others have learned to value, even look for, the new in their day-by-day experiences. The more an individual allows his ways of perceiving to be broad and open, the greater the number of perceptions the individual has out of which to create.

Perhaps an activity such as the following calls attention to some of the fundamentals of perceiving.

> Go to the nearest street corner. Take a paper and pencil with you. Spend the first five minutes recording everything you hear. Listen hard. Perhaps you will hear sounds you have not heard before.
>
> Spend the second five minutes recording everything you see. Look carefully in order to see the unfamiliar as well as the familiar.
>
> Compare lists when you return to the classroom. What were some of the

---

[13] Permission was granted by the Houghton Mifflin Company to reprint a portion of "Ars Poetica" from *Poems 1924-1933* by Archibald MacLeish.

common sights and sounds heard or observed by most students? What sights or sounds were heard or observed by only one or two?

Persons tend to perceive objective phenomena in different ways. A means of helping students understand that the same human behavior can be perceived in different ways is through an activity such as the following.

> With some of your classmates observe for ten minutes a three- or four-year-old child at play. Write down everything you see. Compare your observations with those of your classmates. How do you account for the similarities and differences in your observations?

Developing New, Original, or Unusual Ideas

The creative person is one whose uniqueness is characterized by the ability to be original and to invent new or unusual ideas. Sometimes, creativity may involve uncommon use of a familiar object or situation or stating something that appears to be common in an uncommon way. Or, it may involve finding a methodology that is unusual or particularly appropriate to a given task. This ability to produce original ideas can be stimulated by planned attention to the production of unusualness. For example, the following assignment, an adaptation of which might be found in a reading book at any level, directs attention to unusual procedures.

> Instead of presenting a book report, try to "sell" a book to the rest of the class. Use any selling techniques you know of to arouse the interest of the class in reading the book.[14]

Another way to encourage originality is to give students the plot of a story and ask them to suggest a title. The plot may be written by the teacher or the students, or one may be summarized from parts of a collection of stories. Students should be encouraged to give as clever a title as possible.

Teachers should be aware that when used frequently, a technique that may at first appear fresh and unusual loses its power to excite children. It is important, therefore, that a wide range of techniques be used.

Seeing Relationships

Another characteristic of creative thinking is having the ability to see relationships between elements that might not ordinarily seem to be related. Sequential tasks such as the following will help students see far-reaching relationships.

> This is an exercise that has you look for the relationship between things. Here is an example of what you will do:

---

[14] A book having many practical suggestions for encouraging creative thinking skills is Louis J. Rubin, (ed.), *Nurturing Classroom Creativity* (Ventura County Secondary Schools, 1960), p. 38.

Light is related to *dark* in the same way that *day* is related to (a) noon, (b) midnight, (c) morning, or (d) night.
The correct answer, of course, is night (d). So you should underline *night*.
Work each of the problems below in the same manner as the example above. Think carefully about the connections between the items.
1. An author is related to his *book* in the same way that a painter is related to his (a) brush, (b) paint, (c) painting, or (d) easel.
2. Comedy is related to *tragedy* as laughing is to (a) shouting, (b) chortling, (c) sobbing, or (d) snickering.

Why don't you see if you can make up an exercise like the one above? Try to think of unusual relationships, if you can. The space below is to be used for working out your ideas.[15]

An exercise suggested as a follow-up of the one above is to select two or three of the relationships and to write a story about them.
Another activity designed to help students see relationships follows.

Here are some adjectives:
grim, gritty, intrinsic, intrepid, gloomy, glossy, innocent, innocuous, acid, acrimonious, crisp, cryptic, bright, brash, dreary, dreadful, curt, cursory, wary, weary.[16]

The rest of the directions indicate that the adjectives should be paired off but that words with the same beginning sound should not be put together unless it can be shown that the words have other commonalities. The relationships between words are then shown with words and pictures. Seeing deeper meanings, subtleties, and relationships among words is possible in this kind of task.

Understanding the Process of Organizing

Earlier in the chapter, attention was given to ordering the ideas of another person without distortion and within a meaningful pattern. This section emphasizes the relationship between the process of patterning and the creative process. The creative person is able to put complex, far-reaching, and often seemingly unrelated ideas into a scheme that has freshness, meaning, and often beauty. The process of patterning is seemingly so crucial to creativity that intense study of this area alone may enable us to better understand the creative process.

In addition to possessing an awareness of pattern, the creative person needs to develop an appreciation of the worth of ideas that appear to be discrete and do not lend themselves at the moment to a design. Indeed, premature patterning if often a deterrent to truly creative thinking. Therefore, activities for students should include invitations to record fascinating or new ideas, ideas that

[15] R. E. Myers and E. Paul Torrance, *Invitations to Speaking and Writing Creatively* (Minneapolis: The Perceptive Publishing Co., 1962), p. 7.
[16] *Ibid.*, p. 13.

warrant further thought at a later time. Examples of invitations to record ideas include the following.

> Scattered Impressions
> Scintillating Words
> Things I Like to Do
> Suggestions for a Moment of Leisure
> When I Have Time I'll...
> Titles for a Story
> For Further Exploration[17]

Students might also be encouraged to collect unusual titles of books, plays, movies, or television programs. At a later time they might try outlining a plot suggested by the title.

As students begin to value the worth of ideas, they may then move into activities leading to a rather penetrating study of the process of patterning. Activities that encourage the understanding of principles of patterning might include some of those listed below. This skill can be related to any subject at any grade level, although obviously organizing is a developmental process and the effective learning of a new facet of it is often contingent upon the learning of prerequisite but related skills. Consider these tasks, which might cause students to reflect on the human quality of patterning or organizing.

> How many different ways do you think the main events in this story could have been arranged? How would the outcomes have differed under each of the ways that you have organized the main points?
>
> List ten things you did today in the order in which they happened. Now go back and rearrange the items in any way you please. How might your day have been different if the events had occurred in the second order?

If learning opportunities sponsored by the school can help persons learn the intricacies of patterning, then the individual possesses a better chance for shaping into meaningful wholes the many experiences he encounters during a lifetime.

Developing Sensitivity to Problems

Unless an individual is aware of a problem, he may not engage in the creative process for constructive purposes. Sensitivity to problems and awareness of the relative significance of a problem are two skills that the creatively constructive person often possesses.

Learning tasks can do much to help young people become aware of the problems within a given field. Activities that require an individual to find

---

[17] Louise M. Berman, *Creativity in Education: A Guide to a Television Series* (The University of Wisconsin—Milwaukee, in cooperation with the Milwaukee Public Schools, 1963), p. 45. For more complete development, see pp. 42–50, "Order-Disorder: Ingredients of the Creative Process."

the key problem within a passage or to think of problems a storybook character might have encountered in certain situations are two examples of ways in which students may be helped to become sensitive to problems.

At the primary level, a language arts lesson might concern the following situation.

> Take parts and act out this situation: "John and Jim learned how to play checkers this week. They have played the game every day after coming home from school. John's brother, Bob, who usually plays with the boys has been ill all week but is feeling much better today. When the boys arrive at John's home, eager to play checkers, Bob is waiting for them, anxious to do something exciting." Go beyond this point in dramatizing the scene. When you are through, discuss how each boy felt about the situation.

Population mobility is a major consideration, not only in our society, but in many societies around the world. Selections in books dealing with travel lend themselves to assignments concerning the problems of mobility.

> As you read the story of George Stowell, what problems do you think he encountered as he arranged for his move from New York to Rangoon?

Another example of an activity that develops sensitivity to problems is the following.

> The recent trouble Jim encountered with his father probably indicates that Jim is having other problems at home. Using the material from your story and your own intuition, try to identify other difficulties Jim may be having.

Of course, persons need to be cautioned as they learn to become sensitive to problems not to read too much into a situation. Like other skills, if carried to extremes, sensitivity to problems may be stressed to the point that an important way of thinking loses its effectiveness.

Redefining Uses for Common Objects

Redefining uses for common objects may be considered part of original thinking. Because of its potential usefulness, however, we have chosen to look at it separately. As new uses are found for the commonplace, the usual takes on unusual dimensions. Such objects as nails, doors, combs, boxes, and cans can be put to extraordinary uses in the hands of the creative person. Consider an exercise such as the one below.

> Find as many solutions as you can to this problem
> You are going on a picnic with your family to an isolated spot along a river. The river bank is covered with large rocks; there are small trees and a sandy beach for swimming. After working up an appetite you discover you have forgotten the frying pan in which you were going to fry the steak and potatoes. You have no other cooking utensils except forks, knives, and paper plates.

You have the means of making a fire. How will you cook the steak and potatoes? Can you think of a way to fry the steak without a pan or other ordinary conventional cooking equipment?[18]

Elaborating an Idea

It has been said that there are no new ideas in the world: we merely restate and embroider the old. Whether or not one accepts this statement, old ideas certainly often lend themselves to expansion—to further development or enhancement.

One way of giving practice in elaborating is to give the student a paper with some scattered and irregular lines on it and to ask him to make a drawing utilizing the lines on his paper.[19]

Older children might be asked to elaborate on the idea of a classmate or on ideas found in their reading.

Developing Fluency

Another skill important to productive thinking is fluency with ideas—ability to express many ideas in rapid succession without immediate consideration of the worth of each idea. Alex Osborn and his colleagues at the University of Buffalo have done much to make people aware of the necessity for fluency.[20] Osborn's technique of "brainstorming" has become rather well known because of its effectiveness in helping people loosen up so that ideas can begin to flow. The four simple rules of brainstorming are:

> Rule out judgment.
> Welcome free-wheeling.
> Try to get quantity.
> Combine and improve the ideas of others in order to get new ideas.
> An activity of the type below encourages fluency in students.
> With a group of your classmates brainstorm to answer the question: How can the United States make the youth more aware of their responsibility toward participating in government? Remember that quantity of ideas is wanted. Do not yet evaluate your ideas. Judging the worth of the ideas will take place later.

Another way of inducing fluency is to ask an individual to name all the possible uses of an object.

> In the story you have just read, Michael discovered an old sea chest in the basement. Think of all the ways Michael can use the chest.

---

[18] Rubin, *loc. cit.*
[19] See E. Paul Torrance, *Guiding Creative Talent* (Englewood Cliffs, New Jersey: Prentice-Hall, Inc., 1962), pp. 47, 52, 215, and 219 for an expansion of the concept of elaboration.
[20] Osborn is noted for his writings, courses, and institutes on creative problem-solving. See his *Applied Imagination* (New York: Charles Scribner's Sons, 1957).

A peculiar characteristic of fluency is that it is not always possible to plan for the moment when ideas are going to begin to flow. Fluency often comes during moments of relaxation, when one is doing something out of the ordinary, or when one is engaging in a new project after immersion in a subject. The mind often continues subconsciously to stay with a subject even though it may appear to be occupied with other things. Students should learn to record those insights and unexpected thoughts that come in unguarded moments for consideration at a more propitious time.

Developing Commitment

A characteristic of a creative individual is that he tends to possess inner drives that send him beyond the expected in the expenditures of time, energy, and involvement in the search for a solution to a problem important to him. The release of tension that follows involvement is one reward of commitment. Problems may be very broad in scope. They may be as diverse as getting an idea onto canvas, putting a somewhat obscure thought into words, forming a group that works together harmoniously, or solving a baffling mathematical problem. Often a person will commit himself to the exploration of a problem over a period of many years.

One way of helping students become aware of the nature of commitment is through tasks that cause them to consider the nature of the commitment of persons who have made major creative contributions. For example, as students read the theories of famous persons in their textbooks, they might be asked to complete an assignment such as the following.

> See if you can find some evidence that describes how Edison (Einstein, the Wright brothers, Beethoven, etc.) went about his work. What did you identify as some of his major values? Search for material that indicates the degree of commitment that Edison seemed to have in order to bring his product into being.

Certain devices may be personalized so that students can begin to identify areas in which they are willing to put in extra time and energy to find solutions to problems. Consider this task.

> You will have two mornings to work on some projects that are of interest to you. During one of the mornings you should select a topic from the unit on machines to pursue in more detail. During the second morning, select a topic from the unit on human beings. Narrow your topic down so that you can complete the major portion of the work in the allotted time.
>
> After you have completed the topic from each unit, fill out the form given below for each project. Compare the information on these two sheets. Have you learned anything about yourself?

Of course, a task such as the one just described would need to be modified for various classes. Opportunity should also be provided for students to become

COMMITMENT TO YOUR TASK

Each question may be answered by checking the appropriate part of the line below it.

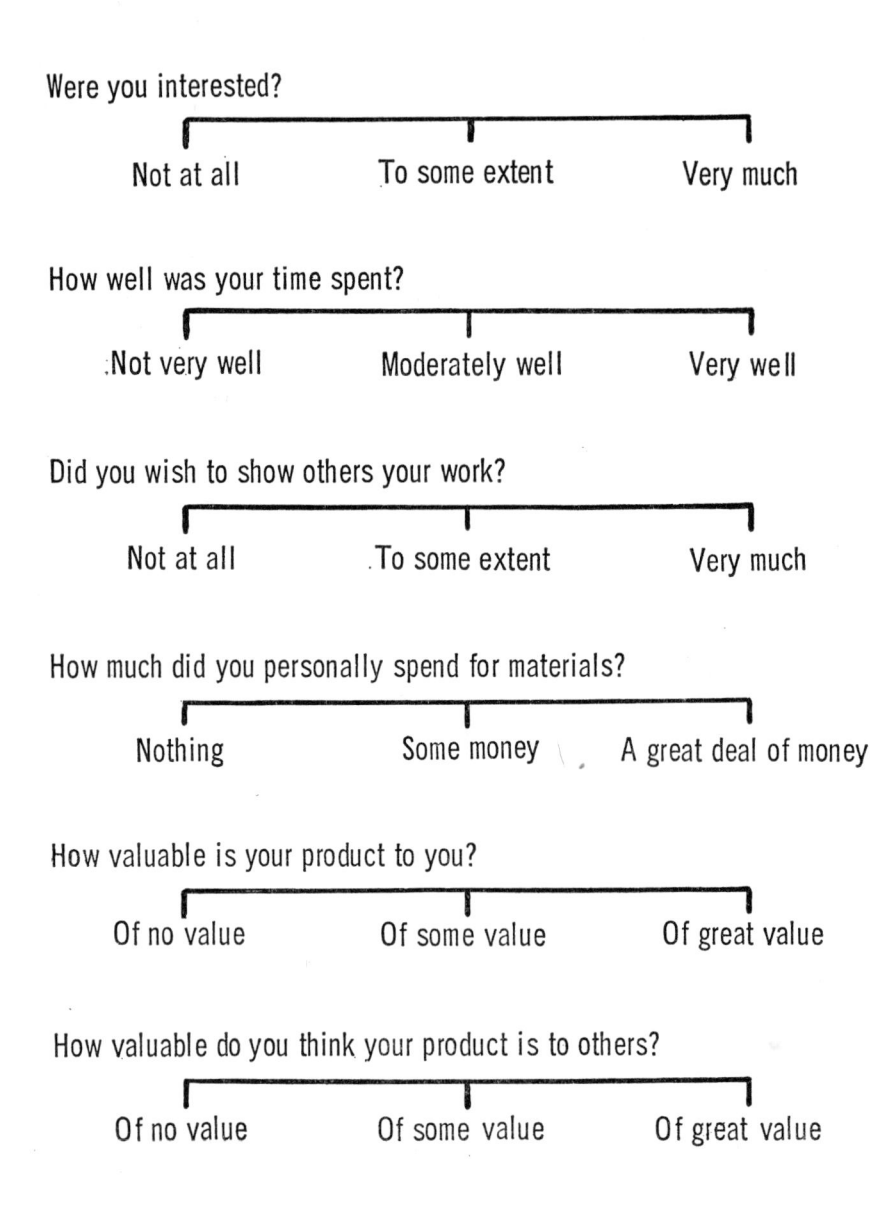

Were you interested?

| Not at all | To some extent | Very much |

How well was your time spent?

| Not very well | Moderately well | Very well |

Did you wish to show others your work?

| Not at all | To some extent | Very much |

How much did you personally spend for materials?

| Nothing | Some money | A great deal of money |

How valuable is your product to you?

| Of no value | Of some value | Of great value |

How valuable do you think your product is to others?

| Of no value | Of some value | Of great value |

involved in projects that may take weeks or months. The purpose is to help individuals begin to ascertain the things to which they think they are committed and evaluate their own involvement.

Personalizing the Creative Process

Related to the previous item is the notion of personalizing the creative process. Research in creative thinking indicates that such thinking often does not take place in any type of logically patterned sequence. From the moment that one identifies a problem until a solution emerges, the procedures used may differ considerably depending upon the nature of the person. Each individual needs to understand the outer circumstances and internal conditions that seem to cause him to be the most productive. Consider this type of task.

> Write down your feelings about what makes you like to create something on your very own. Use these questions to help stimulate your thinking.
> What do *you* like to create?
> What sets the mood for you to begin work on it?
> Under what conditions do you like to work?
> Is there any particular time of day you like to work on your ideas?
> Do your surroundings make a difference?
> What equipment do you like to have beside you when you start working?
> Do you like to work alone or with others?
> Does the idea just pop into your mind, or do you have to look for something to do? [21]

Other questions that might give insight into how the individual goes about his work when creating include:

> Do you tend to finish something once you have started it?
> Do you start one project at a time, or more than one?
> Are you easily distracted from your work?
> How do you feel when your mother calls you for dinner, or your friends want you to join them when you are engrossed in an idea?
> When you have finished what you have set out to do how do you feel if your friends do not like your product?

Applying Learnings to Current and Local Happenings

If the use of a textbook and other classroom material is to serve a purpose beyond the mere acquisition of knowledge, then instructional tasks should encourage the application of material to current and local happenings. The need for improving a local situation or updating knowledge acquired and recorded a few years ago is ever with us. Tasks planned by the teacher or included

---

[21] Rubin, *op. cit.*, p. 46.

in the textbook, therefore, should provide experience in bringing assigned written materials up to date, localizing the material or relating it to environmental conditions, personalizing the material, and developing new plans for further action.[22]

Updating Written Materials

Being able to update materials is very important, for much of what happens is outdated before it is recorded on the printed page. Children and youth should learn to analyze what they are reading in terms of current happenings, in addition to what the writer is actually saying. They should learn to apply what they read to those things for which they are responsible.

In addition to knowing how to bring materials up to date, students should also see the need of such activity and should *desire* to do so. This is an idea of much consequence in a society where all can and should have a voice.

What is said below of the college student might be said of the high school student and even of the elementary school pupil.

> Too many of our brilliant students coming out of college today tend to be merely commentators, observers, and critics of society. We seem to have an oversupply of detached observers, young people who are skilled cocktail party conversationalists and brilliant analysts of other people's activity and behavior. We have a great undersupply of young people who can and will take responsibility—"doers," innovators, and risk takers. So many young men and women from first rate colleges reveal an unwillingness to be fully committed. They seem reluctant to participate actively in the world in which we are living.[23]

In helping students bring material up to date the task is twofold: (1) A sense of commitment must be developed that incorporates a sense of responsibility and a caring for the times in which the student lives. (2) Materials related to the present scene must be available in order for students to be able to evaluate their texts. The first point, touched upon earlier, enters into discussion later in the book. The second point is treated briefly here.

Teachers who wish students to bring textbook knowledge up to date should encourage the use of current periodicals, newspapers, new films, and interviews with persons involved in the area of study. Attention should be given to comparing textbook material with current happenings. At other times, a synthesis of new ideas with what is in the text might be an appropriate assignment.

> Write a play based upon some of the material found in this unit of your textbook. Search current magazines and newspapers for items related to the topic that might make the treatment of your subject more pertinent to today's world.

---

[22] Obviously the social, physical, and natural sciences are most appropriate for this treatment.
[23] Vernon R. Alden, "What Kind of Excellence?," *Saturday Review,* 47 (July 18, 1964), 52.

Occasionally, a class or a small group may decide to write a chapter dealing with the interval between the date of publication and the present. The task might be assigned as follows.

> Although authors revise their books every few years, nonetheless new things have happened since this science book was published. Select one chapter that especially interested your group. Assign the topics treated in the chapter to members of the group. Have them gather new information since the book was published. Then write a new chapter which could be used as a follow-up to the one in your book.

Localizing Materials

Those who engage in the learning activities planned by the school should be able to use these experiences to (1) better themselves as persons and (2) better the community of which they are a part. Our concern now is with the latter point.

If schools are to have an influence upon the community that sponsors them, then teachers should provide the stimulus for students to apply the material being studied to local situations. Obviously the local situations vary greatly. Although currently some attempt is being made on the part of publishers to write materials appropriate for different populations, it is more often true that the same learning materials are used in economically depressed areas where hundreds of families are crowded into small, inadequate living quarters as in wealthy suburban areas where children and youth have no shortage of those things that money can buy. Whether or not the content is localized, the tasks which accompany the text material can be adapted to the setting of each individual school. That persons be reponsible and interested in the wider community cannot be left to chance. Such attitudes must be taught.

In several grades, both at the secondary and elementary level, usually some aspect of government is taught. This might be a helpful suggestion to students.

> List all the services that your community provides its citizens. Then make a chart for a bulletin board showing how local and state governments cooperate to provide the services on your list.

This type of activity might also be helpful.

> Collect all the newspaper stories about the activities of the governor (or other state official) for one week. Then take a piece of paper and make the following headings.
> Activities that will affect me directly
> Activities that will affect the adults of the community directly
> Activities that will have no direct bearing on the immediate community
> Activities about which I can do something
> Classify the articles under the headings. Some articles may fit under more than one heading.

Census reports provide a valuable resource for teachers desiring to help children and youth see the larger world in relationship to the local community and may be used as follows.

Take a sheet of paper and make three columns. In the left hand column list these items: level of schooling, per capita income, number of books in libraries, number of churches, and any other items that might be of interest to you. Head the middle column with *United States* and the right one with the name of your town or city. Using the latest census reports, fill in these columns with information about your country, about your community.

Field trips have often been used as a means of helping children familiarize themselves with the community. Follow-up is extremely important. Activities should be designed that will enhance thinking skills and community spirit as well as refresh in the student's mind the things heard, seen, or felt. Teachers should bear in mind that children may need time to reflect on the meaning of the trip; therefore, not all follow-up activities should be scheduled immediately afterwards. Suitable activities are suggested below.

Make a chart with the title, "Getting Ready for Trips." In the right hand column list these items: reason for trip, tasks to be done, how money is collected, how leaders are selected, and any other important items. Make four vertical columns and keep a record of several trips so that plans can be compared.

Make a chart with the title, "After Trips." In the right hand column list these items: questions I wish I had asked, books I've found related to the trip, new ideas from the trip, and any other important items. Make four vertical columns so that reactions to several trips can be compared.

Write a story. Focus on two or three strong feelings about things you experienced on the trip. Why do you think these impressions stand out so strongly? Include in your story a discussion of any future action you intend as a result of the trip.

Make a cut-paper picture. This picture should be a representation of the most unusual feature of the trip for you. Write a paragraph describing the reason for your choice.

Make a map of the trip. Make drawings on the map to show the places that made the greatest impression on you. Write a few paragraphs explaining why you chose to show these places.[24]

In localizing material, activities using resource persons from the community often prove very helpful.

Invite a representative from the telephone company to discuss current innovations in the telephone and latest developments in telephone communication in your city or town. Compare latest developments in telephone communication in your town with situations discussed in your text.

[24] For further suggestions see Darrow and Van Allen, *op. cit.,* p. 59.

In summary, here are some suggestions by Kenworthy for worthwhile use of the community.

Field trips—to factories, businesses, labor unions, political party headquarters, churches, museums, etc.
Studies of the history of the community.
Interviews and polls on various topics.
Studies of the community—its history, its people, social processes, occupations, health and welfare, transportation and communication, etc.
Resource personnel in the classroom or school.
First-hand experiences in government in watching the courts, town council, clinics, hospitals, etc.
Providing resources for classwork—books, records, pictures, government reports, budgets, etc.
Social service projects—the community fund drive, Y's, social service centers, etc.
Exposing pupils to new types of experiences—such as concerts, plays and other cultural activities.
Work experiences, as a means of trying out what the pupils think they want to do after graduation from high school or college.
Understanding the relation of community problems to national and world problems.
Experiences in working with adults.[25]

Personalizing Materials

If knowledge is to make a difference to the individual and to his world, personalizing is a process to be encouraged. When an individual personalizes, he may rearrange old ideas and concepts, incorporating the new so that a different structure emerges. This process is similar to developing new frameworks or patterns mentioned earlier. The person may become immersed in the material, causing a sense of commitment often eventuating in action. Or he may compare his personalized view with that of others, thus learning that varied perceptions of the same phenomenon can help him clarify, strengthen, or change his viewpoint. Personalizing is the source of relatedness to knowledge, as opposed to detachment.

Consider the following exercise.

> After reading the story about America in 2000, jot down ideas that are meaningful or important to you. Describe how these ideas compare with your ideas. Compare your list of important ideas with ones prepared by some of your classmates. At what point were your lists different? How do you account for the differences?

---

[25] Kenworthy, *op. cit.*, p. 167.

Developing New Plans for Further Action

One of the purposes of schooling is to encourage action-taking when appropriate. Part of the task of the school is to provide the setting in which persons develop attitudes of wanting change and planning for action that will affect both themselves and others.

Perhaps the young child can see simply what he can do to make his own back yard neater. The slightly older child can focus his plans upon the improvement of a bigger area. The high school youth can begin to make plans for including in his thinking and caring, persons further away, as in exchange programs. With an increasing number of high schools throughout the world sponsoring exchange programs, high schoolers are given the opportunity to understand more directly the impact of other cultures. As they begin to explore diverse ways of living and thinking, they can begin to think in terms of acting as well as knowing.

Textbooks and teachers together can encourage students to consider:

Something I wish to do as a result of a news event.
Something different I wish to do for my family.
Something to do for someone I don't know.
Something I can do to improve my home.
Something to do for someone I need to understand better.

Relating Thinking and Valuing

The remainder of this chapter was challenging for this writer: it was undertaken, however, because the ways in which a person thinks are so critical to valuing, decision-making, and the general understanding of one's self.

The reader will recall that in Chapter One, three basic types of thinking were discussed—thinking that deals primarily with the known, thinking that goes beyond the known, and thinking that is evaluative or judgmental. The extent to which an individual consciously and judiciously uses these skills in various situations partially determines his moral and ethical decisions.

Valuing is the process of establishing priorities among competing alternatives. Valuing usually implies a set of principles, examples of which are respecting the rights of another person, cherishing honesty, seeking for diversity of opinion, etc. These principles are prized and often discussed, but the application may vary depending upon the situation. For example, even though a person may prize both individual uniqueness and individual responsibility, he may on occasion find himself in a setting in which only one of these values can receive priority. The individual who tends to think primarily in terms of dealing with the known, without reaching out to do some occasional boundary-breaking, may view valuing as a static process with one set of behaviors which he uses in all situations. On the other hand, for the person who excels in creative thinking, valuing is a dynamic and exceedingly absorbing process.

In the area of valuing, textbooks and other materials can help, but the teacher must set the stage. The example of a teacher who is constantly using his own thought processes to better understand his patterns of valuing is most important. The ability to perceive the internal frames of reference of students in at least a limited way is critical in teaching valuing and its relation to thinking.

The following learning opportunities are discussed in this section: opportunities to understand and clarify the values that influence one's thinking; opportunities to defend important values; opportunities to compare and understand other value systems; opportunities to change, modify, or develop new values.

Understanding the Values that Influence Thinking

If persons are to use their rational powers for some significant purpose, then attention should be given to understanding the values which shape thinking. Clarifying values is prerequisite to intelligently modifying or changing them.

Questions for discussion. If an individual knows the right questions to ask, he has made a good start toward understanding the interplay between processes of thinking and valuing. Teachers can help children see more clearly those things they value or prize by asking questions. Louis Raths has developed a technique whereby students begin to become aware of their values.

We can repeat back to children in exactly their own words what they have said, and ask: "It this what you mean?" When children *hear* what they have said, they often restate it with modifications which seem more clearly to express what they want to say.

We can say back to the children *in our* words what we interpret as their meaning, and ask if this represents their point of view. Sometimes we quite consciously distort what they have said and ask if this is what they mean.

On other occasions, we ask children for definitions of a term they have used. We ask them to give examples or illustrations of the point they are trying to make. Our assumption is that as children try to make things more clear to us, they must first make them more clear to themselves, and this is the process of clarifying. We cannot do this, of course, unless children have an opportunity to say or to write about matters of concern to them, and we cannot carry the process forward unless we *listen* to what they are saying.

Sometimes we help the student to clarify by asking him to tell more about what he has said. We say, sometimes, that we don't see where it leads, what the consequences will be. We sometimes ask what is good about the particular interest or attitude or purpose or activity. On occasion we ask if he believes that everyone should accept his idea and why. At other times we raise questions about possible assumptions he is making. We could ask him to tell us how he happened to get involved with the idea or project or belief.[26]

Much clarifying of values must be done on an individual or small-group basis, with the teacher asking the pertinent questions. Writing open-ended themes in which students are asked to discuss some of their values in a given area is another way to help students clarify their values and to see how thinking has influenced their values.

Textbooks and teacher-made assignments related to the text can do much to clarify values through asking the student to indicate ways in which his values have been made clearer after reading a selection or studying about a situation or a person.

Assignments such as the following assist in value clarification.

> The story you have just read is a searching one, for Jim's values came strongly into play in the decisions that he made. If you were in a similar situation, list the values that might influence your actions. See if you can define your meaning of the word *value*.

Understanding through dramatization. The use of simple drama or role-playing is sometimes a means of helping persons understand the values that may unconsciously be influencing thinking. Direct participation in some type of drama enables one to "feel" a part. This "feeling" usually involves more than verbalization.

The following invitation to dramatize in order to get at basic beliefs may be found in the book *When Men Are Free*.[27]

> Discuss books or stories you have read that illustrate some of the beliefs concerning the free individual. Divide into committees and dramatize episodes in the stories. If some of the committees prefer, they may write their own stories.

Understanding through illustration. Oftentimes schools have been accused of moralizing without making general principles relevant to everyday living. Students often hear platitudes that make sense in the abstract, but that may not have much meaning in terms of specific behavior. It is necessary, therefore, that schools ask students to bring such general statements down to an operational level.

Give examples of situations in which young people sometimes find themselves

---

[26] Louis Raths, "Sociological Knowledge and Needed Curriculum Research," in James B. Macdonald, (ed.), *Research Frontiers in the Study of Children's Learning* (Milwaukee: University of Wisconsin—Milwaukee, in cooperation with the Edward A. Uhrig Foundation, 1960), pp. 27, 28.

[27] The Citizenship Education Project, *When Men Are Free* (Boston: Houghton Mifflin Co., 1955), p. 45. This book is an excellent source for those looking for unusual devices for the social studies program. The teacher may want to substitute "value" for "belief" in the example quoted.

when they feel they "shouldn't go along with the gang," but find it very hard not to.[28]

This can also be done through the use of skits. Through playing out certain problems and possible answers to them, individuals can come to understand better their own behavior.

> Divide into committees to write and present a series of skits showing the various social responsibilities of the citizen in our democracy.[29]

Children might be asked later to describe the thought processes by which they arrived at a solution.

Understanding through reflection. In the haste to cover material, students oftentimes are not provided the opportunity to think about the values that have meaning for them. Sometimes the assumption is made that real learning is taking place if the student is engaged in the active process of reading or writing, of "doing something." Probably the most penetrating learning takes place during periods of meditation or reflection or when an individual may be engaged in an unrelated activity. Students need time to incorporate their new learnings into previously developed constructs or frameworks. Such incorporation cannot easily take place when teachers rapidly introduce new material without providing the opportunities for reflective thinking such as the following.

> Record scattered impressions you have as a result of your readings of the past few days. Do not do anything with these ideas until you have had a chance to reflect upon them. In what ways have you been helped through this process to understand your own values better?
>
> Record ideas from this selection which are confusing in terms of your values. What procedures will you take in the clarification of your values?

Defending Values

Perhaps the concept of whether a person is willing to defend his values is inherent in the definition of *value*. Whether or not one considers defense an integral part of valuing or something that happens after a value has been identified and clarified is not central to this discussion. The point is that however a value is defined, the opportunity to defend it helps an individual identify the degree to which he holds it and the priority that he gives to it.

One way of providing opportunities for the defense of key values is for the individual to list a group of values commonly held by various individuals or societies. He is then asked to select the values that have special meaning for him. Further directions might ask him to make a list of circumstances in which he would not be sure about the priority of his values.

[28] *Ibid.,* p. 59.
[29] *Loc. cit.*

Among the statements which might be discussed by students are the following.

It is better to allow the guilty to go free than to punish the innocent.
Do unto others as you would have them do unto you.
Whatever the circumstances, a person should always be honest.
Love is the highest principle of life.

As persons are taught to defend values, they may be asked to select a value and defend it in a meaningful way to others.

Select a value important to you. Choose any means that seems appropriate to defend your value to others. Analyze your procedure to see that your thinking about your value is clear and concise.

Understanding Other Value Systems

Although persons should be helped to clarify and defend their value systems, a degree of openness should be encouraged in value formation that will enable the person to look honestly at the values held by others.

With young children invitations to understand others better may have to start with a consideration of things that are easily observable about others, such as the color of the hair or of the eyes. A task such as the following may be suggested for the elementary school aged child who is beginning to become aware of likenesses and differences in others.

Over a period of time, compare yourself with two members of your class. Make a chart to show the likenesses and differences that you find. Begin by describing the color of the hair, eyes, and skin. As you come to know each person, describe what he likes to do most, what he likes to do least, what his parents like about him, the kinds of food he likes, what he feels is his most difficult problem, what he likes in people, what he dislikes in people.

Older students might learn to understand and compare value systems through assignments such as the following.

Compare two such persons as Albert Schweitzer and Harry S. Truman or Kennedy and Nehru. From their writings try to determine the values these persons seemed to hold. What likenesses and differences do you find between the values of the persons you are comparing?

Compare two such groups as the John Birch Society and the Americans for Democratic Action or the Ku Klux Klan and the Congress of Racial Equality. What are the values held in common? How do the two groups differ in values?

Occupational values. From an early age children are made aware that persons earn a living in different ways. Such knowledge causes them to wonder about what they "want to be when they grow up." High school students, through planned counseling and guidance programs, often begin to explore different types of occupations with the intent of making a vocational choice.

Developing the Thoughtful Person

By understanding the modes of thinking and values characteristic of an occupation, a person is in a better position to make an occupational choice.

As a part of a unit either in the elementary or in the secondary school, occupations might be examined from various perspectives. Students might be asked to explore reasons why individuals tend to select a given occupation. Further exploration might be made of the advantages, disadvantages, and satisfactions of selected occupations. The modes of thought necessary to the occupation should be considered along with the basic values. Within the primary grades, commonly taught units on community helpers are appropriate places to consider the professions beyond the service that is rendered to individual persons.[30] Courses in the secondary school should give planned attention to the meaning of the various skills students are acquiring for possible use in the occupational world.

The reasons are threefold: (1) New technological developments are causing major changes in the world of work. Hence, students need information about the most recent kinds of occupations, rather than ones common twenty years ago. (2) Many children are not oriented to academic achievement. Relating current studies to possible occupations may help the potential dropout see the relevance of his current work for what he might be doing in the near future. (3) A student's values and ways of thinking should be given careful consideration in helping students ascertain the type of work most appropriate for them.

It is suggested that students at the secondary level have assignments of this nature.

In the story you just read, Mr. Katz was an insurance claims adjuster. See what you can find out about the work that he does. What kinds of qualities do you think are important to be successful in this type of job? Is this work that you would be interested in? Describe your own characteristics including your manner of thinking and the things that you value. How do your personal qualities compare with those you listed which you think are necessary for the job?

Values of different generations. It goes without saying that differences in values are often caused by the varied perspectives of different generations. Unfortunately, many children do not want to profit by the mistakes of parents, nor are their parents often able to stand off in a detached manner and examine their own values. Teachers and classroom materials can help children and youth deal with this conflict of values. A task such as the one following might help young people bring the problem into focus.

Do you think part of Mr. William's failure was the infliction of his values on his son? Should parents have a vital part to play in the shaping of the values

---

[30] See Lawrence Senesh, *op. cit.,* for further ideas about occupations.

of their children? If you feel that parents should have a major part in the shaping of their children's values, do you have any suggestions for settling disagreements that often exist between parents and children?

Values assumed by authors. Whenever possible, students should be encouraged to compare their values with those found in the materials that they are reading. Some material may deal rather explicitly with values, as do many social studies materials. Selections from literature often lend themselves to examining and comparing the values of characters.

> In this story Mr. Hunt spent a large portion of his time each week writing his book. His son, Scott, saw his father only a few hours each week. When Scott became angry because his father did not have the time to take him to the fair, his father said that his writing was very important. When he finished it he would take Scott on a long trip.
>
> What do you think of Mr. Hunt's use of his time? Was Scott justified in becoming angry with his father? How do you feel about persons who seem to spend disproportionate amounts of time on one thing? What happens to the husband or wife of an individual deeply engrossed in a project? Would you be willing to spend a large portion of your time writing a book? How do you feel you should spend your time?

Changing Values or Developing New Values

No deep, pervasive change in behavior comes easily, nor does meaningful change usually come about through verbalisms or single experiences. The teacher who desires to establish a setting in which students can examine, change, or modify values needs to provide opportunities for students to have a wide range of experiences, with the opportunity to reflect about their meaning. Below is a range of suggested activities in which students might engage. The activities are grouped under the headings of procedures offering the opportunity to be alone, to go into the community, to work with others, and to do things for others. Obviously the way in which teachers encourage students to relate these activities to their values will to a large degree determine the degree of value change within each student. In other words, activity alone does not create value-oriented, thinking persons. Activity must be coupled with invitations to reflect about the meaning of activity.

Being alone. The opportunity for solitary activity can help the individual develop new insights or re-evaluate the old if the activity invites a reflective or exploratory mental set. Examples of such activities follow.

> Keep a diary for a week in which you give special attention to your feelings.
> Test different arrangements of your room.
> Jot down puzzling questions that come up in conversation.
> Jot down strange ideas about a place you see every day.

Developing the Thoughtful Person

Record words that you find in your readings that have special meaning for you.

Write a story in which the main character has a problem in which he must think about some conflicting values.

Sit down (or walk around) and think about a trip to a place you have never been.

Skim books related to a subject outside your studies that interests you.

Read with abandon some subliterary work—a western, a cookbook, a serial in the daily paper.

Reflect on a topic a few days, then write down your reactions.

Keep a file of newspaper clippings that reflect basic values of various people.

Write a fictitious newspaper article about a brave act.

Set up a research study in which you compare two different ways to work with a younger child.

Paint anything you would like.

Using the flannelboard, make some unusual designs.

Make a notebook titled, "I'd Like to Know More about...."

Write a short play.

Make a tape recording of a talk about something that interests you.

Going into the community. Work in the community provides the opportunity to learn through local human and material resources. Contact with persons whose value orientations differ may cause reflection, and possibly change of values.

Attend a public hearing.

Conduct a survey in which you try to find out what persons in the community think the major problems of young people are.

Prepare a questionnaire and poll the people in your community about what the school should do to help young people spend their leisure time wisely.

Form a committee of young people and some adults to meet and decide what citizens can do about air and water pollution.

Select members of your group to visit the office of public health, a welfare agency, or some other public agency.

Go to the travel bureau to obtain help in planning an imaginary trip to a part of the world different from yours.

Visit the place of employment of a member of the family or a friend and try to decide the advantages and disadvantages of the jobs you observe.

Form a group to adopt and exchange letters with a foster child in another part of the world.

Plan and take a field trip to a vocational training center.

Evaluate the worth of a visit to the neighborhood club.

Working with others. To provide opportunity for enhanced thinking through the sharing of ideas, and to provide opportunity for contact with other value systems, the teacher should suggest activities that can be carried through with another individual or a group.

Conduct a debate about a community issue.

Plan to invite an expert in urban renewal or the county agricultural agent to visit your class.

With some friends, make a large poster for your bulletin board.

Form a committee to make a collection of official forms taxpayers must fill out.

Arrange a panel discussion with students from a neighboring school.

With an interested group, keep a scrapbook of newspaper articles and clippings. Study your ways of working together.

Make a chart of the school fund drive with a friend. Discuss how you worked together.

Listen to a record and discuss what you hear with a classmate.

Make an eight millimeter film with a committee.

With a younger child reconstruct a story by making a diorama.

Brainstorm with others about a persistent school problem. Analyze what speeds up or slows down brainstorming.

Try to "sell" a book that you like to someone with interests different from yours.

Form a committee to consult your congressman for information.

Get a group of your classmates to write your congressman, stating their positions on foreign policy.

Your group may like to role-play a scene suggested by a television program.

With a group, plan a mural about an imaginative work of literature. Later describe the contributions of some of the group members.

Evaluate the process your group used in arriving at some decision.

Doing things for others. Planning and carrying through a project designed for others helps individuals relate thinking to altruistic purposes.

Write to a pen pal in another school in the community.

Make a crossword puzzle for a friend.

Invite some of the younger children to see a puppet play.

Assist some of the younger children in your school with committee work.

Invite the parents to school to discuss the after-school program.

With a group of your classmates, consider how to improve intergroup relations in your community.

Plan a **service** like reading to a homebound person or getting a child with language handicaps to practice talking with you.

In carrying through any of the procedures listed above, students should be encouraged to put into words the thought processes that accompanied their activity. Constant invitations to be active and productive and then to reflect upon the process encourages an awareness of the importance of thinking in all aspects of life.

Relating Thinking to Decision-Making

Decision-making occurs at the point where past experience and future hopes meet in the moment of *now*—a transitional moment in which new directions become evident. In this moment, the past is left behind and the new emerges. How a person makes the break between the past and the future is partially determined by how he thinks. Some persons make decisions that cause life to be lived on a dull, mediocre level. Such persons may not have used their thought processes as fully as possible, and hence critical possibilities have been ignored. Other persons make decisions in such a way that life for themselves and others has freshness and vitality. In these cases, various conscious or subconscious thought processes have probably enabled the person to see alternatives that might not have been considered had he been less thoughtful.

We do not mean to imply that a direct relationship exists between the quality of decisions and the quality of thinking. Too many other factors enter the picture. We are saying, though, that the individual who has learned to think in a variety of ways has a tendency to make better decisions than his less thoughtful counterpart.

Attention to the following areas will help students make decisions more ably and thoughtfully: understanding the nature of the decision-making process, accepting the consequences of a decision, reacting to the decision of others, and bringing about change in the decision-making process. Each of these topics is worthy of more adequate treatment than is given in the next few pages. The topic is opened up, however, so that the reader will see its importance to thinking and perhaps pursue it in more detail at a later time.

Understanding the Decision-Making Process

Books on management and business administration have long given attention to the process of making decisions; however, school personnel have paid little direct attention to the teaching of this important process. Teachers, after identifying the areas in which it is appropriate for students to make decisions, should, through various methods, help the student become familiar with the process. Among the concepts in which students should be given help in understanding are

> Identifying the nature of the situation necessitating a decision.
> Considering as many alternative choices as possible.
> Weighing the possible outcomes if a decision is made in a given way.

Selecting among the alternative ways of making the decision.

Evaluating the outcome of the decision.

Analyzing the procedures used in making the decision, in order to modify or deliberately utilize the procedures of the process at a future time.

Young children might be asked to identify the areas in which they feel they are qualified to make a choice and then to analyze how they choose among alternative ways of making a decision. For example, this follow-up activity might be used for a story in a reader.

Suppose you had a chance to go either to your grandmother's farm or to the fair with your father. Which would you choose? Why? What was going on in your mind as you made the decision?

Or, children might be given a task such as the following.

You have received some money for your birthday, and you can do with it as you please.

List all the ways you can think of to spend your money. Then list what would happen if you were to spend your money in each of these ways. Decide the best way to spend your money. Is your decision a good one? Why? Go back, and see if you can figure out why you made the decision. Did you learn anything that will help you in making future decisions?

As students learn to handle the decision-making process wisely, they may learn to react to their own decisions and others' on several bases: (1) They will see the meaning of a decision in terms of the kind of thinking they do. (2) They will also be able to see the meaning of a decision in terms of others' viewpoints. (3) Increased experience in decision-making may cause appropriate change in the process.

Accepting the Consequences of a Decision

As students learn to handle the decision-making process wisely, perhaps they will learn to accept the consequences of a decision even if the consequences, at times, may not be the most desirable. Oftentimes persons narrow down the range of areas in which they wish to make decisions to such a degree that they are not living a full and varied life. Fear of making mistakes and of the ensuing consequences are often back of the indecisiveness of many persons. Although one would certainly not encourage decision-making in areas in which a person has no knowledge, many persons need to be helped to enlarge the boundaries within which they are willing to assume the responsibility of taking action and to live with the consequences.

An assignment such as the following might be appropriate to help the elementary-school child become aware of responsibility and the consequences that ensue.

You have just read the story of Peter and the many responsibilities he had, even

Developing the Thoughtful Person

though he was a young boy. Perhaps you often are asked to assume certain kinds of responsibilities. Underline things for which you would be willing to assume responsibility.

Caring for younger brother or sister
Preparing breakfast
Helping a new child in school
Introducing a visitor to the class if you know the visitor, and the teacher is out of the room
Going ahead with the next pages in your textbook if you have finished your assignment and have nothing else to do
Helping a hurt child on the playground
Reporting to the principal a dangerous corner on your way to school
Writing to your town or city government about some action that needs to be taken in your town

Select one of the underlined items and write a paragraph telling why you would assume the responsibility. What would you do if you could not carry out the task well?

At the secondary level, a similar type of check list might be devised. Directions could be different, however.

Use this code to check the items listed below:
A. Could assume this responsibility regularly now
B. Would like to assume this responsibility but am not prepared
C. Do not know how to assume this responsibility and am not eager to learn

———Report to the student council on a way to help new students become acquainted with the high school.

———Take a position on a minority decision and see that your position is heard among persons concerned.

———Take care of your younger brothers and sisters for an extended period of time in an emergency situation.

———Solicit votes in your high school for a person who is in the minority, but who stands for a platform in which you believe.

———Work with a parent group interested in establishing some common understanding of appropriate social activities among young people, when you know the decisions this group makes may not be in accord with the desires of many of your friends

Students at the high school level should be given the opportunity to discuss in detail their feelings and frustrations when they become involved in making rather important decisions and the consequences cause uncomfortable repercussions. Only as this process is seen as a normal part of growing up will persons continue to be active participants in difficult decision-making situations. Learning to accept the consequences of a decision cannot be left to chance. This aspect of decision-making must be taught.

Reacting to the Decisions of Others

One way of better understanding the decision-making process is to react to the decisions of others. Current-event topics, selections from literature, passages from history, and excerpts from scientific reports can be used as sources. Students should consider the possible consequences of alternative decisions. They might be asked to analyze problems from various perspectives.

> Consider these topics. Make two columns on your paper. In the first column, make a statement about each topic from the perspective of a North American. In the second column make a statement from the perspective of a Colombian or a person from another Latin American country in which you are interested.
> The population explosion
> The increased amount of leisure time
> Problems of urbanization
> Differences between generations

Hopefully, as individuals get in the habit of becoming aware of the values and attitudes that underlie decision-making, they will understand more fully the rationale of decisions that are made from a perspective different from their own. Understanding does not mean acceptance, but understanding does give a better base for appropriate action. Analysis of the thinking accompanying a decision helps reinforce the necessity of understanding the thought process.

Bringing about Changes in the Decision-Making Process

As students learn to understand more clearly the decision-making process, they should come to see their own weaknesses and strengths in making decisions in all types of situations. Teachers should be sensitive to times when it is appropriate to verbalize aspects of the process. Of course, verbalization may be meaningless until persons have had much experience in decision-making and relating this process to modes of thought.[31]

To show increased sophistication in the decision-making process, teachers and students should also keep records of growth in this skill. Students might jot down evidence of increased ease in finding different alternatives, of weighing consequences, and of taking in the totality of the situation. To analyze the decision-making process at the beginning is not easy, but as teachers and students gain increased command of its elements, they are better able to make wise decisions and to know how the decisions came about.

---

[31] Teachers or textbook publishers wishing further ideas on decision-making should see Joseph D. Cooper, *The Art of Decision Making* (Garden City: Doubleday and Co., Inc., 1961). The ideas from such a book need to be adapted, however, to the appropriate grade or subject.

Relating Thinking to Self-Other Understanding

Thinking in itself may or may not serve a useful end. The development of thinking skills can cause persons to live a richer, fuller, and more satisfying life; on the other hand, thinking may leave a person coldly analytical without the means or the desire to use the skills for a worthwhile purpose. It has been mentioned that the focus of this book is not upon the perfecting of the rational man but rather upon the development of the thoughtful person. The thoughtful person possesses many other characteristics besides rationality, but the person is able to handle and analyze these other components of personality through the use of the various thinking skills. Thinking is an ongoing process inextricably related to those aspects of being such as feelings and understanding of self and others. The thoughtful person engages in reflection or meditation so that the parts can be seen in relation to the whole. In brief, our concern is that the person move toward increased understanding of himself and others.

Relating Thinking to Feeling

Students should be helped to understand that thought and feeling are closely bound together, that the two are very difficult to separate, and that different types of thinking evoke different ways of feeling.

Feelings when an individual is dealing with the known are usually different from feelings that are generated when a person is dealing with the unknown, that is, when he is striving to find new information. Sometimes rather unpleasant emotional states accompany the search for new ideas and new ways of organizing the old. That satisfaction and pleasure may accompany dealing with the known, while anxiety and frustration may often accompany creative thinking, should be taught.

To get students to analyze the relation of thinking to feeling, a task such as the following might be adapted.

> Thomas Edison is given much credit for the invention of the electric light bulb. What do you think he had in mind that caused him to become interested in such a task? How do you think he felt the day before it was invented? An hour before it was invented? A few minutes after it was invented?
>
> Students may be asked to analyze their own feelings relative to tasks involving different kinds of thinking.
>
> How do you feel while writing an essay in English, as contrasted with doing a set of column arithmetic examples or some problems involving square roots?

A follow-up of this assignment might suggest that the student and a friend compare feelings about similar tasks.

Some fields lend themselves better to relating thinking to feeling than others. Mathematics, for many, is a field in which much attention is given to logical thinking, but often inadequate attention is given to student's feelings about the subject. A "Preferences Inventory" might be helpful in ascertaining the feelings of an individual toward mathematics, including items such as the following.

> Sometimes I get so upset about my mathematics assignments that I don't even get the problems right that I thought I understood. Check one.
> ———Strongly agree
> ———Agree
> ———Mildly agree
> ———Mildly disagree
> ———Disagree
> ———Strongly disagree
> Describe the reasons for checking the item you did.[32]

If a teacher suspects that the development of a variety of thinking skills in a particular subject is being impeded by lack of feeling for the subject, perhaps an essay which focuses upon feelings might help. Possible titles are given below.

> How Should the School Teach Mathematics?
> Mathematics Homework
> Why Mathematics Is (Isn't) My Favorite Subject
> I Wish This Class Would ...

Obviously, a teacher might substitute another subject for mathematics.

Seeking Unity in Experience

Unfortunately, we are living in a society where many persons have forgotten the meaning of the terms "loafing," "relaxing," or "reflecting." Earlier, the point was made that creative thinking involves time for incubation of ideas and for their maturing and reorganization. Time for reflection, then, is necessary for the forming of new and meaningful wholes.

Attention to the whole through periods of planned contemplation may cause less discreteness and more wholeness in human experience, less alienation and more involvement, less separateness and more worthwhile togetherness, less Bohemianism and more creative productivity. As persons organize and sort out their perceptions, life can become more satisfying both to themselves and others. The development of an individual framework, structure, or point of view (or whatever term is used) enables the individual to make decisions more wisely because he has a way of viewing the universe of which he is a part. It goes without saying that flexibility is needed to modify the existing frame-

---

[32] See the "Ideas and Preferences Inventory" of the *National Longitudinal Study of Mathematical Abilities* (Stanford University, 1962) for many items designed to ascertain feelings toward mathematics.

Developing the Thoughtful Person 63

work in order to assure a way of living adequate for the present. Invitations to find unity in experience, such as the following, may help students to evaluate their concepts and the means by which their concepts were formulated.

> Take a half-hour and just let your thoughts ramble. Jot down any new ideas or insights you get during this period.

Perhaps too much is demanded if the school is held responsible for integration of personality in addition to the development of skills. We are not suggesting that providing opportunities for unifying experience is the responsibility *only* of the school; but as a key agent of the culture, the school, along with other agencies, cannot ignore this function.

In this chapter, activities that encourage the individual to become a thoughtful person have been discussed, with emphasis on experiences that (1) encourage the individual to understand what the author is saying, (2) encourage the individual to search beyond the known, (3) stimulate creative thinking, (4) provide opportunity for the application of material, (5) serve as a means of relating thinking to decision making, and (6) relate thinking to understanding of self and others.

THREE

GETTING STARTED

Man is such a complex creature that the attempt to describe and predict his behavior presents problems not easily solved. As educators, we find that to tell whether a given activity promotes a desired end is usually difficult—and at times impossible. Yet, struggle we must to plan learning opportunities for the enhancement of the individual, if society is to maintain any degree of orderliness and commonality and if individual differences are to be prized.

The thesis of the preceding pages has been that the school is in a unique position to plan these opportunities: to design tasks which will enable a student to think with greater efficiency and to relate his thinking skills to related human functions of feeling, decision making, and valuing. The thinking skills seemingly are an appropriate starting point for curriculum development in this country or any other. The materials used and individual assignments made may differ according to the background of the learners, but the aims of the curricula and some of the basic activities may be quite similar.

If teachers are interested in creating opportunities for learnings related to this behavior, what can be done? It is suggested that teachers may use the ideas of this book in order to analyze their own teaching in three ways: First, teachers may refine statements about the thinking person to describe behaviors they wish to foster in their own classrooms. Second, teachers can develop further tasks, aids, and questions appropriate to the grade or subject being taught. Third, teachers can learn to analyze teaching assignments.

Developing a Personal Construct of the Thoughtful Person

Some readers may find in the definition of the thoughtful person a reflection of their own thoughts, organized in a systematic fashion, and may find this statement closely enough related to their own best judgments about desired behaviors in children and youth that they may accept the basic assumptions. In such cases, the analysis may stand somewhat as it has been presented. Other persons may find points of agreement and disagreement as they study the definition of the thoughtful person and will want to make a statement incorporating their own ideas with those they accept from the construct described earlier.

In either case, once a teacher has formulated the behaviors that he believes should be developed in the teaching-learning situation, a next step might be making checklists of these behaviors, which may take many forms. Some teachers may prefer to focus for a time on a few behaviors; other teachers may prefer to make longer checklists. Through the use of a list of this type, the teacher can check over a period of a month or semester the relative attention being given to each behavior and can plan for systematic development of the skills of the thoughtful person, on either an individual or a group basis.

The value of a checklist of skills that students can mark themselves should be emphasized. This helps students see the relationship between a task and the skill it is intended to improve. Obviously, a list for young students would differ in the degree of detail from a list designed for older students. Perhaps including a few thinking skills at a time, changing the list rather frequently to keep interest high, would be wise.

Thinking and Planning

Once a teacher has developed a statement about behaviors that he wishes to foster, the statement serves no truly useful function unless the behaviors are related to tasks and assignments for the students. These tasks may be ones selected from the textbook, or they may be teacher-designed. As teachers attempt to develop tasks related to behavioral goals, they might engage in planning that takes into account content, methodology, and thinking processes —"three-dimensional" planning. Teachers might also consider some of the current research taking place in the academic disciplines. Many of these projects take into consideration a wider range of student behaviors than previously thought important. A consideration of the relative emphasis given to the variety of thinking skills in these projects might prove helpful in planning.

Becoming Involved in Three-Dimensional Planning

Teachers differ in their habits of planning for teaching. From the amount of detail included in plans, to the emphases that teachers make, written and more informal plans vary. Despite the fact, however, that teachers do show individual differences when planning is involved, nonetheless one similarity ordinarily does exist. Teachers tend to plan in two dimensions only: subject matter and methodology.

A third dimension often given unconscious consideration by some teachers, but which should be given planned attention by all, is that of *process*.

One of the major values in giving planned attention to process is that students are then provided tools to gain additional knowledge after present knowledge no longer is valid. Giving attention to some of the dimensions of the thoughtful person discussed in the earlier pages helps students not only to acquire the heritage of the past but also to be part of making the heritage of the future. The student has access to modes of thinking and knowing which enable him to be a continuing learner.

In planning for a third dimension in teaching, then, the teacher can do three things. First, he can spell out what is to be taught, whether the subject is social studies, mathematics, one of the sciences, the language arts, or any other curricular area. The major concepts, generalizations, or questions with appropriate supporting detail can be listed.

Second, he can describe the methodology to be employed in dealing with the content—whether it be independent study, lecture, discussion, special projects, reports, a textbook or library assignment, and so forth.

Third, the teacher can indicate the processes which seem feasible to develop within the lesson. Using thinking as a base, the emphasis might be the pulling of discrete elements into a unified whole, as in actions of classifying, organizing, synthesizing, and generalizing; or the type of mental activity involving creative thinking, such as elaborating, showing originality or sensitivity to problems. The emphasis might be on those mental processes that involve evaluating or rating, such as criticizing, interpreting data, and analyzing.

Thinking as a process might be treated also in relation to the total person, as it is in the latter part of the first chapter. The third dimension would then involve teaching such processes as information seeking, the application of knowledge, and value formulation as it relates to thinking.

A New Look at the Academic Disciplines

As a result of the rapid accumulation of knowledge within each of the scholarly disciplines, academicians and educators have banded together to redesign the content and methods of school subjects. Analyzing the structure of the various disciplines in order to see how they can be reconstructed for school programs includes several steps:

First, the language of the discipline is scrutinized. The basic vocabulary of the field is analyzed to determine the key words that will help the reader unlock meanings in the field, whether he reads a daily newspaper or a scholarly journal. The assumption is that through an awareness of important terms, the student can continue to understand the discipline even at the end of formal study.

Second, the basic questions are enumerated and refined. It is felt that by understanding the basic concerns and points of inquiry within a discipline, better understanding of the boundaries and the critical issues of the discipline can be determined. Learning the questions basic to the various domains of knowledge enables the student more easily to identify sources or solutions to ever-recurring questions.

Third, the important teachniques, modes of inquiry, and methodologies in each field are systematized. The student learns to add to his knowledge of the subject through utilization of the most fruitful ways of searching within the field. He learns to think and act like a scholar within the various academic fields.[1]

The current emphasis upon the academic disciplines within school programs has implications for teachers interested in stimulating different modes of thinking. Indiscriminate use of new programs can mean a heavy emphasis on the development of certain skills to the neglect of others. Carefully planned programs, however, can mean new and exciting opportunities for students to enhance their thought processes while acquiring new knowledge.

The degree to which students may be usefully involved in learning opportunities of this sort varies with their age and background. Perhaps all students should have chances to see how the scholar derives knowledge. At the present time, however, some teachers may be emphasizing this approach to knowing to the detriment of other human functions. Children need to know how to consider, analyze, and use previously formulated knowledge—a process that involves thinking skills different from those involved in the making of knowledge. The reality-oriented person enjoys both formulating knowledge and utilizing the formulations of others. The school should provide opportunities to do both.

Analyzing the Teaching Assignment

Teachers interested in developing the thoughtful person may want to give systematic attention to analyzing the assignments made available to students. The teacher wishing to consider whether his assignments are enhancing the principles described earlier may wish to look at:

1. The nature of assignments.
2. The nature of the total program.
3. The plan for ensuring student awareness of the purposes of assignments.

---

[1] For further discussion of the use of the academic disciplines in the school program see Jerome S. Bruner, *The Process of Education* (Cambridge: Harvard University Press, 1960); Stanley Elam, (ed.), *Education and the Structure of Knowledge* (Chicago: Rand McNally and Co., 1964); Arthur W. Foshay, "A Modest Proposal for the Improvement of Education," in *What Are the Sources of the Curriculum? A Symposium* (Washington, D.C.: The Association for Supervision and Curriculum Development, NEA, 1962), pp. 1–13; Philip H. Phenix, *Realms of Meaning* (New York: McGraw-Hill, Inc., 1964); Glenys G. Unruh, (ed.), *New Curriculum Developments* (Washington, D.C.: The Association for Supervision and Curriculum Development, NEA, 1965).

The Nature of the Individual Assignment

As teachers plan their day-by-day activities, they may select certain tasks from textbooks or other commercial materials or exercise individual initiative in the designing of others. Whatever the source of the assignment, it should be analyzed in terms of criteria such as those given below. Two such criteria might include the relationship of the assignment to one of the behaviors of the thoughtful person and the suitability of the assignment for the interests of a particular student or group of students. Others are the following:

1. Does the assignment help develop a specific skill directly or only tangentially?
2. Are enough varied tasks available that enhance the same skill so that students can get sustained practice in learning a skill through different types of assignments?
3. Does the assignment provide for stimulating out-of-text tasks when the student is asked to go beyond the textbook?
4. Do the tasks a specific student undergoes provide for individual and group endeavor?
5. If assignments are selected from the textbook, do students have some choice, or do all students work on the same task?
6. Are assignments differentiated in their level of difficulty, or are all assignments equally hard or easy?
7. If a textbook-designed task is used, has the writer let the student in on the purpose of the task, or is this information included only in the teacher's manual, if it is included at all?
8. Are the tasks characterized by thought-provoking qualities, or are they apt to be met by inertia on the part of students?
9. Do the tasks invite personalizing of the material?
10. Is attention given to the modes of thought characteristic of the academic discipline to which assignment is related?

Analysis of the Nature of the Total Program

In addition to planning for specific day-by-day programs of students, teachers have the responsibility of ensuring balance in the total curriculum. This balance requires a look at the total planned program for a particular class. In addition, an all-school look at the program can help teachers determine the subject or grade level where attention to certain processes in the construct are more appropriate than others. Obviously such planning can only be rough, for the teaching of a concept does not necessarily ensure its learning. Therefore, whether or not total school involvement in planning is emphasized, teachers will need to consider each student's growth in acquiring processes of the thoughtful person.

Getting Started

Specific questions that teachers in a school may wish to address to themselves include:

1. Over a period of time, do all concepts central to the development of the thoughtful person receive planned attention?
2. Are the various school subjects studied with the intent of ascertaining which skills can be most appropriately taught in each subject?
3. Is provision made for the continuation of assignments related to the development of a skill until a skill is learned? Are opportunities made for increasing sophistication in the skill as the student moves through the grades?
4. Among the criteria used in the selection of new textbooks and other instructional materials, is attention given to points found in the construct of the thoughtful person?
5. Are modes of evaluating students' progress in achieving concepts described earlier planned on a school-wide as well as on an individual-teacher basis?

The Student's Own Perception of These Objectives

Unless a person understands the reason for undertaking a specific task, the task may not accomplish that for which it was intended. Very often teachers plan purposeful assignments but fail to plan for students' sharing in the knowledge of the purpose. In planning opportunities for students to become aware of the purposes of assignments, teachers might want to consider these questions:

1. Are procedures established to ascertain whether students are aware of the reasons for a given task?
2. Are specific plans designed to help students clarify their purposes and to see them in relationship to the tasks which they perform?
3. Are plans laid for recording informal student-student and teacher-student conversations indicating that students see a relationship between an assignment and its purpose?
4. Are students encouraged to make checklists and other evaluative instruments on which they can check progress in achieving skill in selected processes?

Teaching with emphasis on processes of the thoughtful person requires careful and constant analysis. At times, analysis may mean developing a simple checklist and searching for evidence. At other times, analysis may mean the most perceptive and critical observation and interpretation that teachers can possibly bring to bear upon the reactions of students to their assignments.

How can the teacher who wishes to help students become increasingly thoughtful provide suitable learning experiences? This question was raised in the first pages of this book. It has been only partially answered. A more complete and satisfying answer depends upon several factors:

The vision and insight of wise teachers willing to go beyond the call of duty in selecting and preparing assignments designed to help students develop more fully their peculiarly human processes.

The boldness of educational publishers willing to delete from materials tasks which encourage student inertia and to substitute tasks which invite student excitement.

The thrust and imagination of administrators and curriculum developers willing to encourage selected teachers to experiment with new ways of making school learning more related to basic human functions.

The insistence of all educators that today's schools must produce a citizenry with the inner resources that will enable them to handle problems which cannot even be predicted today.

Dare those involved in the education of children do less than provide experiences which will help them function more adequately? The lowly teaching assignment needs reconsideration by educators concerning its potential in realizing major goals.

SELECTED BIBLIOGRAPHY

Arango, Marta. "Building Independence of Judgment through the Development of Critical Thinking: Implications for the Curriculum." Unpublished M.S. project, University of Wisconsin—Milwaukee, 1963.

Aschner, Mary Jane McCue. "Thinking and Meaning" in *Language and Meaning*. James B. Macdonald and Robert K. Leeper (eds.). Washington, D.C.: The Association for Supervision and Curriculum Development, NEA, 1966.

Barron, Frank. "The Psychology of Imagination" in *A Source Book for Creative Thinking*, Sidney J. Parnes and Harold F. Harding (eds.). New York: Charles Scribner's Sons, 1962.

Bartlett, Sir Frederick. *Thinking: An Experimental and Social Study*. New York: Basic Books, Inc., 1958.

Berman, Louise M. *Creativity in Education: A Guide to a Television Series*. Milwaukee: The University of Wisconsin—Milwaukee in cooperation with the Milwaukee Public Schools, 1963.

Bloom, Benjamin S. (ed.). *Taxonomy of Educational Objectives: The Classification of Educational Goals. Handbook I: Cognitive Domain*. New York: David McKay Company, Inc., 1956.

Bruner, Jerome S. "Man: A Course of Study," in *ESI Quarterly Report* (Summer-Fall). Watertown, Mass.: Educational Services, Inc., 1965.

──────. *On Knowing: Essays for the Left Hand*. Cambridge: Harvard University Press, 1962.

──────. *The Process of Education*. Cambridge: Harvard University Press, 1960.

──────; Goodnow, Jacqueline J. and Austin, George A. *A Study of Thinking*. New York: John Wiley and Sons, Inc., 1956.

Carin, Arthur and Sund, Robert B. *Discovery Teaching in Science*. Columbus: Charles E. Merrill Books, Inc., 1966.

Carpenter, Helen (ed.). *Skill Development in Social Studies*. Thirty-Third Yearbook of the National Council for the Social Studies. Washington, D.C.: National Education Association, 1963.

Citizenship Education Project, The. *When Men Are Free*. Boston: Houghton Mifflin Company, 1955.

Cooper, Joseph D. *The Art of Decision Making.* Garden City: Doubleday and Co., Inc., 1961.
Darrow, Helen Fisher and Van Allen, R. *Independent Activities for Creative Learning.* New York: Teachers College Press, Columbia University, 1961.
Elam, Stanley (ed.). *Education and the Structure of Knowledge.* Chicago: Rand McNally and Co., 1964.
Ennis, Robert H. "A Concept of Critical Thinking," *Harvard Educational Review,* 32 (Winter, 1962), 81-111.
Foshay, Arthur W. "A Modest Proposal for the Improvement of Education," in *What Are the Sources of the Curriculum? A Symposium.* Washington, D.C.: The Association for Supervision and Curriculum Development, NEA, 1962.
Getzels, Jacob W. and Jackson, Philip W. *Creativity and Intelligence: Explorations with Gifted Students.* New York: Charles Scribner's Sons, 1962.
Guilford, J. P. "Creativity: Its Measurement and Development" in *A Source Book for Creative Thinking,* Sidney J. Parnes and Harold F. Harding (eds.). New York: Charles Scribner's Sons, 1962.
————. "The Three Faces of Intellect" *American Psychologist,* 14: (September, 1959), 469-479.
Harper, Robert J. C., et. al. *The Cognitive Process: Readings.* Englewood Cliffs, New Jersey: Prentice-Hall, Inc., 1964.
Hayakawa, S. I. *Language in Thought and Action.* New York: Harcourt, Brace and World, 1949.
Hollister, William G. "Preparing the Minds of the Future: Enhancing Ego Processes Through Curriculum Development" in *Curriculum Change: Direction and Process,* Robert R. Leeper (ed.). Washington, D.C.: The Association for Supervision and Curriculum Development, NEA, 1966.
Hullfish, H. Gordon and Smith, Philip G. *Reflective Thinking: The Method of Education.* New York: Dodd, Mead, and Co., 1961.
Kenworthy, Leonard S. *Guide to Social Studies Teaching in Secondary Schools.* Belmont, California: Wadsworth Publishing Co., Inc., 1962.
Kneller, George F. *Logic and Language of Education.* New York: John Wiley and Sons, Inc., 1966.
Krathwohl, David R.; Bloom, Benjamin S. and Masia, Bertram B. *Taxonomy of Educational Objectives: The Classification of Educational Goals. Handbook II: Affective Domain.* New York: David McKay Company, Inc., 1964.
Loretan, Joseph O. and Umans, Shelley. *Teaching the Disadvantaged: New Curriculum Approaches.* New York: Teachers College Press, Columbia University, 1966.
Massialas, Byron G. and Cox, C. Benjamin. *Inquiry in Social Studies.* New York: McGraw-Hill, Inc., 1966.
Miel, Alice. *Creativity in Teaching: Invitations and Instances.* Belmont, California: Wadsworth Publishing Company, 1961.
Myers, R. E. and Torrance, E. Paul. *Invitations to Thinking and Doing.* Minneapolis: Perceptive Publishing Company, 1961.
Nietz, John A. *The Evolution of American Secondary School Textbooks.* Rutland, Vermont: Charles E. Tuttle Co., 1966.

Selected Bibliography

Osborn, Alex. *Applied Imagination.* New York: Charles Scribner's Sons, 1957.

Parnes, Sidney J. and Harding, Harold F. (eds.). *A Source Book for Creative Thinking.* New York: Charles Scribner's Sons, 1962.

Patterson, Franklin K. *Man and Politics: Curriculum Models for Junior High School Social Studies.* Occasional Paper No. 4. Cambridge, Mass.: Educational Services, Inc., 1965.

Phenix, Philip. *Education and the Common Good: A Moral Philosophy of the Curriculum.* New York: Harper and Brothers, 1961.

_____. *Realms of Meaning.* New York: McGraw-Hill, Inc., 1964.

Raths, James. " A Strategy for Developing Values," *Educational Leadership,* 21 (May, 1964), 509-514.

Raths, Louis. "Sociological Knowledge and Needed Curriculum Research" in *Research Frontiers in the Study of Children's Learning,* James B. Macdonald (ed.). Milwaukee: University of Wisconsin—Milwaukee in cooperation with the Edward A. Uhrig Foundation, 1960.

Rubin, Louis J. (ed.). *Nurturing Classroom Creativity.* Ventura County Secondary Schools, 1960.

Russell, David H. *Children's Thinking.* Boston: Ginn and Company, 1956.

Sanders, Norris M. *Classroom Questions: What Kinds?* New York: Harper and Row, Publishers, 1966.

Senesh, Lawrence. *Our Working World: Families at Work.* Chicago: Science Research Associates, 1964.

Taba, Hilda; Levine, Samuel and Elzey, Freeman F. *Thinking in Elementary School Children.* Cooperative Research Project No. 1574, San Francisco State College, 1964.

Torrance, E. Paul. *Guiding Creative Talent.* Englewood Cliffs, New Jersey: Prentice-Hall, Inc., 1962.

Unruh, Glenys (ed.). *New Curriculum Developments.* Washington, D.C.: The Association for Supervision and Curriculum Development, NEA, 1965.

Vygotsky, Lev Semenovich. *Thought and Language.* Cambridge, Mass.: Massachusetts Institute of Technology, 1962.

Whitehead, Alfred North. *Modes of Thought.* New York: The Macmillan Co., 1938.

$1.60

EDUCATION

Other Practical Suggestions for Teaching . . .

Reading Improvement in the Junior High School
*Deborah Elkins, with the assistance of
Thelma Hickerson and George Krieger*

This report traces the effective steps taken by three teachers to help groups of junior high school pupils seriously below grade in reading ability make a new start. Their efforts involved pupil participation in projects of intrinsic interest and educational value.

1963 76 pages Paper, $1.25

Pupil Progress in the Elementary School
Willard S. Elsbree

Professor Elsbree evaluates methods of measuring pupil progress and describes the experience educators have had. Principles and techniques in marking, grouping, promotion, and reporting to parents are reviewed in detail. The value of a procedure is judged by its effect on the whole personality of the child.

1943 86 pages Paper, $1.25

Independent Activities for Creative Learning
Helen F. Darrow, R. Van Allen

A useful guide for teachers in helping children learn how to continue learning through the rest of their lives and in encouraging children to approach their work and learning more creatively.

1961 112 pages Paper, $1.25

Teachers College Press
Teachers College, Columbia University
New York, New York 10027